A COSMOS I[

ARCHAEOLOGY OF RELIGION
A Book Series from AltaMira Press

SERIES EDITOR
David S. Whitley

Few topics have been more neglected by archaeologists than religion, yet few subjects have been more central to human social and cultural life. In part, this neglect has resulted from a longstanding division in Western thought between science and religion; in part from archaeological beliefs concerning what can and cannot be readily interpreted about the past. But new models of science, increasing concern with symbolism and belief, improved interpretive models and theories, and a growing reconciliation between humanistic and scientific approaches now contribute toward making the archaeology of religion a viable and vibrant area of research. This series will publish syntheses, theoretical statements, edited collections, and reports of primary research in this growing area. Authors interested in contributing to this series should contact AltaMira Press.

VOLUMES IN THE SERIES:

Volume 1. J. David Lewis-Williams, *A Cosmos in Stone: Interpreting Religion and Society through Rock Art*

Volume 2. James L. Pearson, *Shamanism and the Ancient Mind: A Cognitive Approach to Archaeology*

A COSMOS IN STONE

Interpreting Religion and Society through Rock Art

J. DAVID LEWIS-WILLIAMS

PRESS

A Division of
ROWMAN & LITTLEFIELD PUBLISHERS, INC.
Walnut Creek • *Lanham* • *New York* • *Oxford*

ALTAMIRA PRESS
A Division of Rowman & Littlefield Publishers, Inc.
1630 North Main Street, #367
Walnut Creek, CA 94596
www.altamirapress.com

Rowman & Littlefield Publishers, Inc.
4720 Boston Way
Lanham, MD 20706

12 Hid's Copse Road
Cumnor Hill, Oxford OX2 9JJ, England

British Library Cataloguing in Publication Information Available

Library of Congress Cataloging-in-Publication Data

Lewis-Williams, J. David.
    A cosmos in stone : interpreting religion and society through rock art / J. David Lewis-
Williams.
        p. cm.—(Archaeology of religion)
    Includes bibliographical references and index.
    ISBN 0-7591-0195-7 (alk. paper)—ISBN 0-7591-0196-5 (pbk. : alk. paper)
        1. Archaeology and religion.   2. Rock paintings.   3. Prehistoric peoples—Religion.
    I. Title.   II. Series.
    BL65.A72 L49   2002
    291'.042—dc21   2001045870

Printed in the United States of America

♾ ™ The paper used in this publication meets the minimum requirements of American National
Standard for Information Sciences—Permanence of Paper for Printed Library Materials, ANSI/
NISO Z39.48–1992.

Contents

Foreword

RCHAEOLOGY IS A DISCIPLINE characterized by tensions, if not polar oppositions. It is, for example, a practice conducted in the present that aims to know the past. One result stemming from this paradox is the disquieting fact that our work is problematized by the need to eliminate implicit presentist biases in order to understand prehistory in its own terms. Depending upon one's theoretical perspective, archaeology is either one of the humanities or one of the sciences. Many academic departments are still divided into groups of professors with inflexible commitments to one of these two major branches of modern Western scholarship, with no thought of accommodation to the other. And archaeology typically uses what is inarguably the most mundane of evidence—the discarded rubbish of our forebears—in the hopes of explaining some of the most profound problems of human existence: How did we come to be the way that we are?

The most long-lived opposition in our Western intellectual tradition, one which archaeology has shared, began during the Enlightenment. This was a divide initially between then-newly emerging science and its rationalist thought versus religious belief and its perceived irrational or superstitious bases. More recently, with religion now rarely given any consideration at all in many academic disciplines (beyond quick dismissal), a perceived opposition between science and art has inserted itself into this same place. (Science apparently is viewed by many as needing a definitional foil; something that can be readily pointed to as everything that science *is not*.) The outcome of these intellectual oppositions is straightforward: Since religion and art are thought the opposite of science, they are likewise not thought appropriate subjects for scientific study.

Yet given the universality of religion and art and their centrality to social life, it is clear that they constitute key cognitive and behavioral attributes of the human career. With this fact in mind it is obvious that no treatment of prehistory (or even parts of it)—regardless of whether promoted as scientific explanation or humanistic description—can be complete with these two elements fully excluded.

Traditional scientists may not "like" religion or art, but any effort to explain the human condition at any point in time that ignores these phenomena constrains itself from the outset to only partial success, which is also to say to a starting goal of partial failure.

Given the tensions inherent to archaeology and our disciplinary efforts to struggle through them, it is perhaps appropriate that archaeology has recently made great headway in bridging and then understanding this particular set of oppositions. No one has made a greater contribution to this effort than J. David Lewis-Williams, Emeritus Professor of Cognitive Archaeology at the University of the Witwatersrand in Johannesburg, South Africa. David's research is well known for its importance to rock art studies, per se. British anthropologist Robert Layton (2000, 171), for example, cites David's work on the San (or Bushman) paintings of the Drakensberg Mountains as responsible for transforming rock art research from a largely descriptive, empiricist exercise into a theoretically informed effort to explain the past. As subsequent events have shown, this transformation has been worldwide in effect, with his research providing a model for archaeologists in Europe, Australia, and especially North America.

Yet to focus on David's research and its significance solely or primarily in terms of rock art studies is to miss the real importance of it. For while rock art has served as one of David's most important data sets, and even though his work has partly revealed the intellectual coherency and complexity of this prehistoric art, the focus of his work has concerned equally the larger cognitive world of the past and its relevance to understanding prehistoric social life in its largest sense. Along the way, this has also required David to solve certain key methodological problems, not the least of which was finding a means for accessing the minds of Paleolithic artists who lived tens of thousands of years prior to any written records. American archaeologist Timothy Earle (1994, ii) has specifically noted David's neuropsychological research on this problem as providing archaeologists with a middle-range theory of the mind.

The story of David's contributions is told in the following pages of this volume. As a compilation of his most important published papers, this charts David's intellectual quest, ostensibly first to understand the painted rock art made by the San (or Bushmen) in the Drakensberg Mountains of South Africa, and then to interpret the Paleolithic cave art of France and Spain, with the many ancillary issues that these initial concerns engendered. His introduction and commentary, written for this compilation, provide a context for and intellectual biography of the development of his ideas over the last three decades.

As the perceptive reader will see, this is a book that is *concerned with* rock art but, as much as anything, it *is about* archaeological method and especially theory.

Inasmuch as David's theoretical discussions are in each case firmly grounded in empirical data and analysis, it is a strong counterpoint to arguments that recent theorizing is largely an armchair activity for those who can't be bothered with fieldwork.

Much more importantly, David's contributions reflect his efforts to bridge the deepest oppositions in our Western intellectual tradition: those between science, on the one hand, and religion and art on the other. His contributions thus represent not simply a landmark in the development of Western archaeology, but also a needed break from four hundred years of divisive academic research and discourse.

David S. Whitley

Acknowledgments

ORTY YEARS OF RESEARCH, always a communal activity, breed a very long list of people whose input demands to be acknowledged. Were it not for them, each in his or her own way, little could have been accomplished. They include John Argyle, Jean Auel, Norbert Aujoulat, Paul Bahn, Bill Barnes, Robert and Eric Bégouën, Megan Biesele, Geoff Blundell, Carolyn Boyd, David Burt, Colin Campbell, William Challis, Chris Chippindale, Jean Clottes, Meg Conkey, Janette Deacon, Brigette Delluc, Paul den Hoed, Marcia-Anne Dobres, Thomas Dowson, Mike Evers, Bruce Fordyce, the late Jean Gaussen, Paul Gebers, the late John Goodwin, Robert Gordon, Mathias Guenther, Yanik Le Guillou, the late André Leroi-Gourhan, the late Paulo Graziosi, Simon Hall, David Hammond-Tooke, Jamie Hampson, Knut Helskog, Richard Hift, Ian Hodder, Hilton Holding, Anne Holliday, Jeremy Hollmann, Tom Huffman, George Hughes, Ray Inskeep, Richard Katz, Zac Kingdon, Terrence Kohler, Rodion Kraus, Neil Lee, Richard Lee, Larry Loendorf, Michel Lorblanchet, Jannie Loubser, Tim Maggs, Tony Manhire, Alexander Marshack, Lorna Marshall, Elizabeth Marshall Thomas, John Marshall, Rory McLean, Ian McClure, Siyakha Mguni, Fabrizio Mori, Jaques Omnès, Sven Ouzman, the late Harald Pager, John Parkington, David Pearce, John Pfeiffer, Aleth Plenier, Colin Richards, Jean-Philippe Rigaud, John Robinson, Yoan Rueau, Alan Rycroft, Dominique Sacchi, Georges Simonnet, Benjamin Smith, Keith Stannard, Judith Stevenson, Tim Stranack, Mike Taylor, Taole Tesele, Tony Traill, Denis and Agueda Vialou, Patricia Vinnicombe, Tom Volman, Denise Voorvelt, Luc Wahl, Jeremy Wallace, Randall White, Ed Wilmsen, Lyn Wadley, Gavin Whitelaw, David and Tamy Whitley, Bert Woodhouse, Royden Yates, and many others, including landowners who provided hospitality and access to sites on their property, and those Ju'/uan San people who, with Megan Biesele as interpreter, gave all they knew so that their way of life and beliefs would become better known: Kan//a, !Kun/obe, Kaishe, T!nay, /Xwa, and ≠Oma !Oma.

I am also indebted to Tina and Jeremy Hollmann and David Pearce for proofreading, collecting illustrations, and making the index. Successive librarians at the Jagger Library, University of Cape Town, permitted access to and publication of the Bleek and Lloyd texts. Research has been funded by the University of the Witwatersrand, Human Sciences Research Council, National Research Foundation, and Anglo American.

Credits

Portions of these chapters were previously published. Citations for original publication follow.

Chapter 2: Lewis-Williams, J. D. 1972. The syntax and function of the Giant's Castle rock paintings. *South African Archaeological Bulletin* 27: 49–65.

Chapter 2: Lewis-Williams, J. D. 1974. Superpositioning in a sample of rock-paintings from the Barkly East district. *South African Archaeological Bulletin* 29: 93–103.

Chapter 3: Lewis-Williams, J. D. 1980. Ethnography and iconography: Aspects of southern San thought and art. *Man*, 15: 467–82.

Chapter 4: Lewis-Williams, J. D. 1997. The Mantis, the Eland and the Meerkats: Conflict and mediation in a nineteenth-century San myth. In *Culture and the commonplace: Anthropological essays in honor of David Hammond-Tooke*, edited by P. McAllister, 195–216. Johannesburg: Witwatersrand University Press. *African Studies* (special issue) 56 (2).

Chapter 5: Lewis-Williams, J. D., and T. A. Dowson. 1990. Through the veil: San rock paintings and the rock face. *South African Archaeological Bulletin* 45: 5–16.

Chapter 6: Lewis-Williams, J. D. 1987. A dream of eland: An unexplored component of San shamanism and rock art. *World Archaeology* 19 (2): 165–77.

Chapter 7: Lewis-Williams, J. D. 1995. Seeing and construing: The making and "meaning" of a southern African rock art motif. *Cambridge Archaeological Journal* 5 (1): 3–23.

Chapter 8: Lewis-Williams, J. D. 1991. Upper Palaeolithic art in the 1990s: A southern African perspective. *South African Journal of Science* 87: 422–29.

Chapter 9: Lewis-Williams, J. D. 1997. Harnessing the brain: Vision and shamanism in Upper Palaeolithic western Europe. In *Beyond art: Pleistocene image and symbol*, edited by M. W. Conkey, O. Soffer, and D. Stratmann, 321–42. Berkeley: University of California Press.

Chapter 10: Lewis-Williams, J. D. 1997. Agency, art and altered consciousness: A motif in French (Quercy) Upper Palaeolithic parietal art. *Antiquity* 71: 810–30.

Chapter 11: Lewis-Williams, J. D. 1995. Modelling the production and consumption of rock art. *South African Archaeological Bulletin* 50: 143–54.

Introduction

Yet all experience is an arch wherethro'
Gleams that untravell'd world, whose margin fades
For ever and for ever when I move.

—ALFRED, LORD TENNYSON

THIS COLLECTION OF PAPERS on rock art charts a personal journey. It is not a history of southern African and west European rock art research, though much is said about historical contexts and their influence on research. Nor does it try to give a full account of the work of other researchers; if it were a general history it would, in this regard at least, be incomplete. Rather, I deal with a series of issues that I faced over the years, how those problems became more complex as time went by, and how the resolution of one led to the uncovering of another.

Southern Africa, where my journey began, is a vast storehouse of rock art. There are, literally, thousands upon thousands of sites scattered throughout the subcontinent. I have been concerned with only one category of this art—rock paintings, or pictographs. My interest in rock paintings, largely a result of where I have lived in South Africa, should not obscure the importance of another kind of rock art—rock engravings, or petroglyphs. Engravings are found, principally, on the open, low hilltops of the central plateau; apart from a few notable exceptions, they are not found in rock shelters. By contrast, paintings occur, again principally though not exclusively, in the shallow rock shelters of the escarpment of the plateau and its associated mountain ranges—the Cederberg in the Western Cape Province, the Cape Fold Mountains to the south, the Malutis in the eastern interior, and the great basalt-capped Drakensberg range that forms the eastern edge of the plateau.

Most of this art, both paintings and engravings, was made by San, or Bushman, hunter-gatherers, and it is with their rock paintings that this book begins. There are, however, other rock arts in the subcontinent. Some images were apparently made by Khoekhoen cattle and sheep herders; still another, very distinctive, rock art was produced by black, Bantu-language-speaking agriculturalists. This art, known as "Late White," is found extensively in the northern parts of South Africa and in other countries farther to the north. Notwithstanding the interest of southern African pastoralist and agriculturalist rock art, I believe it is fair to say that, although many parts of the world can claim to be rich in rock art, few, if any, have art not only of the richness but also of the variety, animation, astounding draftsmanship, and multitude of tiny but highly significant details that characterize southern African San rock paintings.

To this cornucopia of data must be added a voluminous ethnographic record that extends back into the nineteenth century and that contains, albeit in cryptic form, the answers to many questions about the art, who made it, and why. The trick of southern African rock art research is, very largely, knowing how to mesh the painted data with the ethnography. San ethnography and the images are like two interlocking cog wheels: Turn one and the other moves proportionately. Research can start with either of the wheels. But whichever researchers choose, the other will respond if the two are appropriately meshed. Perhaps one could take the metaphor further and add that the dual lubricant that facilitates the smooth turning of the wheels is theory and methodology. Researchers need to find theory appropriate to the questions they are asking and to the kinds of data available. Then they must struggle to make their method—or mode of argument—explicit; too often rock art publications are vague about the structure of argument being developed. As subsequent chapters repeatedly show, it is explicit theory and methodology and, most important, the tightness of fit between San beliefs and the rock art images that makes an explanation of what the images may have meant to their makers and original viewers persuasive.

This meshing of images with ethnography has turned out to be the principal research tool since the 1970s; as subsequent chapters show, other approaches to the problems posed by the images were essayed before researchers turned to what is today so obvious a source of enlightenment. San ethnography is a bulwark against strange, exotic explanations; it precludes the flights of Western fantasy that characterized the work of some of the early writers. As researchers moved deeper and deeper in their understanding of San beliefs and cosmology, they penetrated into more and more complex problems. They found an entirely "foreign" worldview, a set of tropes, rituals, and experiences with which they had no option but to grapple if they wanted to explain anything at all about the art. Further problems seemed to be nested inside solved problems in an infinite regression.

Speaking of Russian foreign policy shortly before World War II, Winston Churchill declared it to be "a riddle wrapped in a mystery inside an enigma." Southern African rock art research has been rather like that. Churchill went on to say that the key to the riddle–mystery–enigma of Russian policy was "Russian national interest." Without pushing the analogy too far, one can say that the key to southern African rock art lies within the art itself and the beliefs of the people who made it, not in other arts or other belief systems. As soon as a description or explanation of San images begins to sound like Western art history, we should become uneasy. Granted, some analogies with Western art illuminate and help to bring home points about San rock art, but San art is constructed on different structural, or compositional, principles and, moreover, deals in foreign ways with social issues. San rock art is not a replica of Western "art" in its production, composition, consumption, and multiple functions.

Neither is the cave art of Franco-Cantabria, the final destination of this book. Indeed, a pivotal point on my journey was when I began to think that what we had learned about San rock art may be of use in understanding the paintings and engravings in the deep Upper Paleolithic caves of western Europe that I first visited in 1972. That extension could not, I hasten to add, be achieved by straightforward, naive analogy, an approach that had skewed southern African research for so long when researchers were writing about "sympathetic magic." On the contrary, we needed to explore some universals of human neurology that had become evident through the southern African work. These universals underlined the need to distance "rock art" of the kinds found in southern Africa and western Europe from "art," certainly from the sort of "Art" that we find in the Louvre or the Metropolitan Museum of Art in New York City.

That handy monosyllable, with or without an uppercase initial, has misled many a researcher. It is, I believe, wrong to think that the principles—or essence—of what we today understand by "art" were all present, even if in inchoate form, in the Upper Paleolithic images of France and Spain. Entertaining such reservations, writers (e.g., Conkey 1991) have explored the ways in which the word *art* carries cultural baggage and tacit assumptions foreign to the indigenous arts it is used to designate. This work may elicit a negative response from those who see "art" as a universal language and "aesthetics" as cross-cultural. That is a debate I wish to avoid. All I can say is that my continuing use of *art* does not imply universal aesthetics, specialization, commodification, and so forth, all the things that one associates with Western art galleries. *Some* San images may have *some* features in common with some Western art, but those features must be clearly demonstrated, not simply assumed.

To appreciate how my interest in rock art research moved from enigma to mystery to riddle and from southern Africa to western Europe, I begin by sketching in brief outline some of the assumptions that informed work in the first half of the twentieth century. Here was a complicated web of personal relations and imported explanations—chiefly, arguments by simple analogy. Chapter 2 goes on to deal with the first attempt to break out of what had, by the beginning of the second half of the century, become a stifling matrix of ideas and people. It was a struggle to bring science into rock art research. Unexpectedly, this aim led to another source of enlightenment—San ethnography. In chapter 3, I illustrate some of the ways in which close reading of San texts, with attention being paid to actual San words (often in the now-extinct /Xam language) and their connotations, broke through an initial barrier to understanding. Once through that barrier, new vistas opened up. San narratives could now be approached from within and not as if they were Aesop's fables or fairy stories. Chapter 4 takes one San myth and shows, step by step, word by word, that the issues with which it deals have much in common with the issues that chapter 3 showed are treated by the rock art.

All this ethnographic work began to point more and more clearly, and contrary to my initial expectations, to a central, probably overwhelming, tripartite theme in San rock art: the tiered San cosmology, the mystical potency that permeates it, and the ritual specialists who transcend it. Chapter 5 shows how knowledge of the essence and manner of San cosmological transcendence contributes to a deeper understanding of numerous images and motifs and the ways that they interact with the rock on which they were painted. San rock art is three-dimensional; it does not, as is usually assumed, comprise simple, two-dimensional images on a plane support.

Chapter 6 goes on to explore a component of San religion that had and still has, strangely, received little attention—dreams. As ethnography continued to work in harmony with iconography, it became apparent that the artists had dealt with this component, but by way of animal behavior that was opaque to city-dwelling Western viewers of the imagery. By this time, a new line of enquiry had begun to make itself felt in southern African rock art research: Neuropsychology had much to say about dreams and the altered states of consciousness that San ritual specialists enter in order to traverse their tiered cosmos. Chapter 7 therefore considers one visual experience of altered states and how San painters construed it and came to terms with it.

All this southern African work was, for me, preparatory to moving on to the dark, yet brilliantly embellished, caverns of western Europe with their Upper Paleolithic paintings and engravings. But hunches have to be given substance. I therefore drew on what I saw as the success of neuropsychological enquiry in southern Africa to build a bridge to those remote, subterranean images. Chapter 8 outlines the structure of the bridge that I propose.

Thereafter, this book follows up some of the avenues to which neuropsychology gave initial, but by no means complete, access. Chapter 9 offers a broad overview of my arguments concerning the cognitive and social provenance of Upper Paleolithic art and also provides a specific study of two caves and the distribution of imagery in them, while chapter 10 wrestles with the social implications of image making in the Upper Paleolithic. It illustrates some of those implications by means of a detailed investigation of an intriguing motif—the so-called wounded men of Cougnac and Pech Merle.

In the final chapter, I come full circle and deal with both Upper Paleolithic and southern African rock art. I essay a tentative model of the "chain" of social circumstances of which the actual making of an image was but one link. Setting rock arts in their wider social and political contexts is the ultimate goal of research. For it is only when we have accomplished that contextualization that we shall be able to see the coordination of iconography and community and how real people used rock images to construct their own realities and histories.

Historical Setting

Man is a history-making creature who can neither repeat his past nor leave it behind.

—W. H. AUDEN

THE YEAR 1950 is a neat and convenient one to name as a turning point in the history of southern African rock art research, for it was about then, during the decade following the end of World War II, that a technological innovation triggered a new approach to the rupestral images of the subcontinent. Although not designed explicitly for use by rock art researchers, this new technology, coming as it did at that particular point in social and scientific history, eventually triggered far-reaching theoretical and methodological developments that were certainly not foreseen at the time. Science is seldom the neatly planned, step-by-step incremental acquisition of knowledge, or facts, that empiricists envisage. Empiricists believe that science consists in the collection of objective facts and the induction of explanations, or laws, from them. They see science as a steady, perhaps inexorable, advance in knowledge. But the development of science is quirky rather than linear. In southern Africa, at any rate, an unexpected route from an apparently peripheral invention to the complex theoretical debates of today is a central theme of this book.

To understand the chain of events that started in the 1950s we need to backtrack in time and consider the state of research in the decades that preceded and included World War II. The images with which we are concerned, were, we now know, made by the San (or Bushmen), and it was colonial constructions of their supposed depravity, simplicity, backwardness, and incorrigibility that constituted the intellectual and social matrix of research during the first half of the twentieth century—and, as we shall see, to a lesser extent the first decades of the second half. Working in such negative but unfortunately formative circumstances, three forceful personalities, who knew each other well, controlled the production of knowledge about the art prior to 1950 and established a baseline of assumptions that came to be considered self-evident. Along with technological and theoretical developments we need to take into account a tangled skein of personal relations that influenced the course of research history. Interaction between the intellectual milieu of the time and dominating personalities with powerful political connections and personal agendas generated notable possibilities but also a stifling ethos.

Perhaps the most significant personality was the Abbé Henri Breuil, the famous French prehistorian whose name was inseparable from the Upper Paleolithic cave art of western Europe. Since the first years of the twentieth century Breuil had been the arbiter of received opinion about the reasons why Upper Paleolithic people braved the dark depths of the French and Spanish caves to make pictures in what were not only capacious chambers but often small, hidden niches. He declared that "sympathetic magic" was what drove them to such otherwise inexplicable behavior. They made the images in the expectation that they would thereby achieve success in the hunt and that the species of animals they depicted would multiply and thus guarantee the bounty of nature on which their communities depended. These notions derived principally from early reports emanating from Australia and influentially crystallized by Solomon Reinach (1903) in his article *L'art et la Magie: À Propos des Peintures et des Gravures de l'Age du Renne*. As we shall see, even richer ethnographic records and rock art images were lying dormant in, respectively, notebooks and rock shelters in South Africa; had they, rather than the Australian material, been tapped, the course of Upper Paleolithic rock art research may well have been very different: Sympathetic magic may not have become the accepted explanation for West European cave art.

Hand in hand with sympathetic magic, according to Breuil, went an innate drive to produce Great Art (Breuil was prodigal with uppercase initial letters). This was a subject on which he waxed effusive. In 1952, toward the end of his life, he summed up his insights in a monumental book, *Four Hundred Centuries of Cave Art*. In the Franco-Cantabrian Upper Paleolithic caves, he wrote:

> For the first time, Men dreamed of great Art. . . . [They found in art] the silken ladder, apparently useless, enabling Man, through the dreams of his spirit, to endure life and develop that moral force by which he plunges into the immense contemplation of the Invisible, dominating the Cosmos. (Breuil 1979, 11)

Sheer nonsense, of course. Not for the last time, purple prose cast its obscuring, prolix miasma. Still, obfuscation aside, it should be noted that, for Breuil, no contradictions were to be found in the dual notions of sympathetic magic and a conception of "high Art":

> It has often been discussed whether Quaternary Art was the fruit of the Artist's spontaneous reaction to Beauty, "Art for Art's sake" as the saying runs, or if these creations were not due to a practical aim, the multiplication of game, to assure its capture, or, in the case of Animals of prey, their destruction. Indeed these aims are not opposed and do not exclude each other, being merely complementary. (Breuil 1979, 23)

The comfortable complementarity of magic and "Art" is an important point in the trajectory of this book because Breuil brought the idea with him when he visited South Africa, and it became entrenched in the thinking of numerous South African researchers.

Breuil first went to South Africa in 1929 to participate in a joint meeting of the South African Association for the Advancement of Science and its British sister organization. While in South Africa, he examined the ethnographic collections in the Anthropology Department in the University of the Witwatersrand, Johannesburg. There he found a color copy of the central figure in a complex painted panel in a rock shelter in the Brandberg, a stark, rocky, arid massif in what is today Namibia. The site had been discovered by a German geologist, Reinhardt Maack, when he was traversing the Brandberg in 1917. Having exhausted his water supply, Maack began to descend the mountain, but, overtaken by nightfall, he was forced to bivouac in a rock shelter. The next morning he awoke to find a series of ancient paintings on the rock wall behind him. Greatly struck by their detail and interest, he made a rough sketch of the central figure before continuing his downward scramble through the jagged rocks. Later he made a full-color copy, the one that the Abbé saw in Johannesburg.

Breuil was intrigued, but he did not have an opportunity to travel to the remote Brandberg. He returned to Europe dissatisfied. Some years later, when France was occupied by Nazi forces during World War II, the Abbé fled to Lisbon, where he briefly taught prehistory before moving on, at the request of General J. C. Smuts, the South African premier, to Johannesburg. There, once more at the University of the Witwatersrand, he found monochrome photographs of the same Brandberg paintings. His enthusiasm to see the actual paintings, especially the striding central figure with its curious, elaborate body decorations, was reignited. He at once wrote to General Smuts: "I send you the portrait of a charming young girl, who has been waiting for us on a rock in the Brandberg range for perhaps three thousand years; do you think it well to keep her waiting much longer?"

The astute Abbé was playing on Smuts's declared interest in South Africa's prehistory; perhaps his use of "us" was an attempt to persuade the premier to accompany him to the Brandberg and, of course, foot the bill. He also knew that Smuts, like many others at that time, considered the "Bushmen" "mentally stunted" and a "desert animal" and he would welcome the discovery of any evidence of European influence in the art. But Breuil was again disappointed: Wartime austerity did not permit frivolous expeditions to remote parts.

Eventually, in 1947, when Breuil was again in South Africa, he managed to reach the Brandberg. Later, when he was writing a book about his adventures, he built up the drama of his approach to the painting of what he took to be a "charming young girl." His romanticizing of the (comparatively mild) privations to be endured in reaching southern African rock art sites set a trend that other researchers were to follow. He wrote:

> As we approached the place, the impression it conveyed of a great fallen acropolis or palace was intensified; between the granite slabs and boulders there are flat sand-covered surfaces like squares or courts between dwellings. At noon on the day of our arrival in the ravine, we climbed a natural stairway and passed two boulders. We then found ourselves confronting the painting which had been haunting me for eighteen years and which we had come so far to see.

"Acropolis," "squares or courts," "a natural stairway," "dwellings"—the Abbé's vocabulary conjures up a picture of a ruined Minoan or Greek city, despite the fact that the place is a perfectly natural, unexceptional (at least for that area) mountain valley. Already the San are being relegated off stage, and exotic influences are being foregrounded. So it was that the Abbé and his assistant, Mary Boyle, declared that the figure that had "haunted [him] for eighteen years" was that of a lissom young woman of Minoan or Cretan origin, a mysterious, ancient visitor to the southernmost parts of Africa. Breuil felt himself to be standing in the presence of Great Art.

Not surprisingly, "she" features prominently in a purple and somewhat sensual passage at the beginning of Breuil's *Four Hundred Centuries of Cave Art*:

> Eternally she walks there, young, beautiful and supple, almost aerian in poise. In ancient times, all her own people also walked to contemplate her adored image and all went on walking for centuries, not only Men, but Oryxes, Springbuck, Ostriches, Giraffes, Elephants and Rhinoceros swayed by her magic. . . . One day she drew me from the sombre gloom of our European caverns, and the great Jan Smuts sent me towards her,

in the fierce sunshine of Damaraland. Across deserts, we walked towards her. I and my friends and guides, captivated by her incomparable grace. (Breuil 1979, 9)

For Breuil, it was not necessary to argue such fanciful interpretations; he felt that his years of experience and his authority were sufficient to establish his point. Although he copied the image and those surrounding it, his magisterial disposition seems to have prevented him from examining it closely. Had he been a bit more careful, he would have seen that the figure has a penis. Moreover, the penis is "infibulated," that is, it has a short line drawn at right angles across it, and, to make the questions that this overlooked detail raises even more interesting, the line is fringed with small white dots. These dots suggest that the infibulation is associated with another feature of San rock art that is found in other parts of South Africa and to which we return in a subsequent chapter: a sinuous, bifurcating red line, similarly fringed with white dots, that sometimes links images in various ways. Breuil's "charming young girl" is certainly male and has no features to distinguish it from other elaborately detailed San rock art images.

Today the political and racial implications of Breuil's interpretation of Maack's discovery are crudely obvious. The "White Lady of the Brandberg," as the figure became famously known, is still, in some quarters, a symbol of white influence and domination. Soon other images said to depict exotic visitors were being discovered all over South Africa. Not content with the Mediterranean, some writers believed they could identify Chinese travelers as well.

Along with supposed Great Art and exotic influences, the Abbé brought his other interpretative angle to bear. Even as he believed the Franco-Cantabrian cave art to have been associated with sympathetic magic, so he declared the southern African rock shelter images to have been involved in magical rites. He does not seem to have shared the low opinion that many of the colonists had of the Bushmen, but the idea of sympathetic magic marched in step with the notion of the San as simple, childlike people with a "primitive mentality" embracing beliefs that civilized Westerners had long ago abandoned.

Similar notions permeated the thinking of the second pre-1950 influential figure in southern African rock art research. Walter Battiss, one of the most celebrated South African artists, frequently acknowledged the influence of the subcontinent's rock art on his own work. Battiss met Breuil when he was first in South Africa and became one of the Frenchman's protégés. When Battiss brought his work together in his final and beautifully designed book, *The Artists of the Rocks*, he asked his mentor to write a foreword. In it, Breuil commented that rock art

research "needs Youth, with a long stretch of Time before one and a body hard-
ened to fatigue, rock-climbing and riding."

> It is my hope, my dear Mr Battiss, that you will bring to this great
> work, all these qualities, some of which you eminently possess, and that
> real Archives will be assembled in a South African Institution forming
> a catalogue from which an easy comparative study can be made from
> conscientious and complete copies and photographs of these thousands
> of rock panels, scattered leaves of a vast chapter of the human history
> of this country, stretching from one ocean to another. I see you starting
> forth on this great voyage in the Past—I shall follow the first stages
> with deep interest, I cannot promise myself, at my age, to see the dis-
> tant goal. (Battiss 1948, 8)

Like Breuil, Battiss was given to flights of flowery prose liberally punctuated
with upper-case letters: "The extremist Delectation would be to steal the soul of
a Chinese sage and thus metamorphosed contemplate the delicacies and braveries
of prehistoric art in a high mountain rock-shelter—to contemplate long until the
art spoke without being questioned twice" (Battiss 1948, 67). But he nevertheless
tried to adapt the Frenchman's views in what he believed to be a more serious
way, though today we may not agree with him. How to "dive into this maelstrom
of opinions" and emerge with "sober ways of approaching prehistoric art" was a
question with which Battiss struggled. His way out of the dilemma derived from
his position as an artist rather than from any rational, logical procedure. First, he
said it is necessary

> to ignore all theories and to look at the originals of prehistoric art as
> one would look at paintings in an art gallery, that is, to look at them
> so that the *eye* enjoys them for their calligraphy, their colour, their com-
> position, their form and structure. That is pure aesthetic enjoyment.
> . . . It is far better to have no pet theories seeking confirmation, for the
> happy research worker is he who learns from the paintings what really
> is, rather than he who tries to teach the paintings to be what he wants
> them to be. Some men go to the sites to prove their fantastic theories,
> other, more humble and honest, go to learn what they can. (Battiss
> 1948, 22)

This passage is illuminating in a number of ways: It reveals Battiss's essentially
subjective and Western approach to the art and, at the same time, his desire to be
objective, to put aside all preconceived ideas. The tension between these two

rather ill-formulated positions contains the seeds of the rock art work that was done in the period immediately after 1950: Researchers of that time tried various ways to attain objectivity but at the same time believed that the art spoke directly to them and that the meanings of the images were self-evident—the more "objective" a researcher became, the more "self-evident" would the meanings of the images be, or so they believed. "Objective" and "self-evident" were the twin jaws of a methodological trap.

The foundation for Battiss's work was his belief that southern African rock art, both engravings and paintings, can be divided into three periods. In this he was influenced by the then-current view that the European Stone Age could be divided into three major periods: Paleolithic, Mesolithic, and Neolithic. Similarly, he believed that southern Africa's Stone Age could be divided into three periods, Early, Middle, and Late. In arriving at this conclusion, Battiss was guided by Clarence van Riet Lowe who accompanied him to the richly painted Drakensberg. Van Riet Lowe, together with the Cape Town but Cambridge-trained academic, A. J. H. Goodwin, had published a pioneering and highly influential study that first proposed the three-period southern African lithic sequence. Tripartite histories seem to have been de rigueur at that time.

Battiss's three-age model for the rock art stylistic sequence led him into an error that may have derived from the pervasive view that the Bushmen were simple and primitive. He declared, rather than argued, that the first period, the one he believed was characterized by beautiful polychrome depictions of eland, was "pre-Bushman." The artists of this period were "unidentified"; all that could be said was that they "were a settled people who were in South Africa for thousands of years. They were probably not Bushmen" (Battiss 1948, 98). It was they who "discovered foreshortening and with their fine sense of colour produced the famous shaded polychromes—thus their art too has no equal in the primitive world. There is a chance that the unidentified painters may have been Bushmen but of a kind very different from the last Bushmen" (Battiss 1948, 99). The mandatory Middle Period was for Battiss complex and obscure. But matters became clearer in the third period. The images of this time were "true Bushman" paintings and constituted "a silhouette art of descriptive scenes" (Battiss 1948, 99). These scenes differed from the Early Period art not only stylistically but also intellectually: "The earlier art . . . was an art of reverence, while the art of the little Bushmen was one of illustration" (Battiss 1948, 96).

Underlying these ideas, none of which, it should be noted, stood up to further research, is the notion that the "little Bushmen" were primitive and naive and consequently incapable of Great Art. The popular Western stereotype of the San hunter-gatherers as the archetypal "other," primitive yet romanticized, had been so widely disseminated that no one questioned it. Even when considering his final period, the one that he believed had indeed been produced by the Bushmen, Battiss did not bother to turn to any records of San beliefs, myths, and rituals. All the published work of the Bleek family, the foundation of many of the chapters that follow, seems not to have been of much interest to him: The really Great Art was pre-Bushman, and the final period comprised merely illustrative pictures of primitive daily life. In a rare citation of Dorothea Bleek, Wilhelm Bleek's daughter, Battiss disagreed with her view that the San had made rock engravings as recently as the second half of the nineteenth century. In the 1870s, /Xam San people from the former Cape Colony had told her father that their parents had made rock engravings, but this information did not impress Battiss.

Who, then, made the paintings? Breuil had attributed the sophisticated southern African images to travelers from Europe; Battiss declared the early artists to be "unidentified," but he still could not bring himself to imagine the "little Bushmen" as capable of producing sophisticated, shaded, foreshortened images and experiencing what he termed "reverence."

In the late 1950s and the 1960s, Battiss's work raised the ire of some researchers, including me. The long shadow that it cast seemed to obstruct any hope of progress. But today, four decades on, we can see a sadness in Battiss's work. He genuinely tried to free himself from the influences that molded his thinking, but he found it impossible to break loose. He remained a product of his time and the authoritarian personalities who influenced his early years. Still, inspired by the undeniable beauty of San rock art, he did a great deal to raise public perceptions of it, and he must be given his due on that account. Unfortunately, his estimate of the artistic and intellectual capabilities of "the little Bushmen" is still current among some sections of the southern African population. The end of the road has not yet been reached.

Among Battiss's more practical endeavors was the removal of paintings from rock shelters. Assisted by a stone mason, he cut out images that attracted his artistic sensibility and that he believed to be threatened by erosion or vandalism. Unfortunately, he often destroyed adjacent images in the process. Today, some of the panels that Battiss removed are, together with other treasures, such as Maack's copy of the "White Lady of the Brandberg," in the Rock Art Research Institute at the University of the Witwatersrand; others are in MuseumAfrica, also in Johannesburg. Despite the manner of their removal, these painted stones are among the nation's greatest treasures (Lewis-Williams et al. 2000).

Battiss was encouraged in his removal of rock paintings by Clarence ("Peter") van Riet Lowe, the third pre-1950 figure to whom I shall refer. Van Riet Lowe was a personal friend of General Jan Smuts, the South African premier and international statesman, and was also close to the Abbé Breuil. Van Riet Lowe had gotten to know Smuts on a long sea voyage from Southampton to Cape Town. By training a civil engineer, van Riet Lowe soon became well known as an amateur prehistorian. Indeed, he accompanied the Abbé Breuil and other eminent archaeologists on a tour of sites in the eastern Free State. Later, it was he who helped to persuade Smuts to invite Breuil to South Africa to join the South African Archaeological Survey, a government-funded institution that was located at the University of the Witwatersrand. Through his connections with Smuts, van Riet Lowe was appointed first director of the Survey and granted the title "Professor."

Apart from his support of Breuil and Battiss, van Riet Lowe is known for a massive undertaking that is still valued today. He compiled a list of all known rock art sites in South Africa. This monumental survey was based on the work of members of the Archaeological Survey, including Breuil, and associates, such as Battiss. Van Riet Lowe also circulated questionnaires to magistrates and other people likely to be in a position to supply information. The list, organized by provinces and magisterial districts, gives farm and area names; often there is more than one site on a farm, though this is not evident from the list. When the list was first published in 1941 (Van Riet Lowe 1941) 1,766 localities were noted; by 1952 (Van Riet Lowe 1952) the total had risen to 1,938. Today, approximately 15,000 sites are listed. Perhaps as many still await discovery.

Although van Riet Lowe followed the trends of his day in attempting to discern periods and regions of southern African rock art, he did not slavishly accept everything that the Abbé said. In a L'Anthropologie article published in 1950 he challenged a number of points that Breuil had made in a 1949 article in the same journal. In particular he questioned the extreme age that the Abbé had ascribed to large paintings of eland and also his interpretation of the irksome "White Lady of the Brandberg." Overall, van Riet Lowe's work was an attempt to bring order to the knowledge of South Africa's rock art, to establish a platform for systematic research. Apart from this effort, he followed in the footsteps of Breuil and Battiss as far as the significance of the art is concerned. Sympathetic magic and "art for the sake of art" remained the twin pillars of interpretation.

By the end of the 1940s it was already evident that rock art research was lagging behind "mainstream" archaeology, that is, archaeology that entailed excavation, typology, categorization, and seriation. Stone Age archaeology had established definitions of artifact types and had, despite the paucity of professional excavations of stratified rock shelter deposits, formulated the three-age sequence that, in broad outline, is still valid today. By contrast, rock art research was entangled in racial stereotypes of the San, methodological confusions, and explanations for the production of the art so debilitating that they effectively prevented any advance of knowledge.

1950

World War II brought many technological innovations, one of which was to effect far-reaching changes in rock art research: Comparatively cheap color film became generally available. Suddenly, a new hobby was born. In South Africa the absence of television allowed the amateur slide show to become a significant feature of social life. Many families owned a slide projector, and guests were treated to screenings of comprehensive holiday snaps. More adventurous photographers collected shots of birds, wildlife, or scenery. Moreover, the meetings of ornithological, zoological, geological, archaeological, and other kinds of learned societies tended to be built around slide presentations. The amateur photographer's hour had come. The slide show became a vehicle for education and entertainment, as well as for fame and influence.

Those interested in rock art soon saw the possibilities of color photography. In addition to his own artistic re-creations of San images, Battiss had used one or two color photographs in *The Artists of the Rocks*, but the great majority of his photographs were monochrome. At once, researchers saw that the advent of cheap color film made a new degree of accuracy and objectivity possible: At last the true color and the quality of both the paintings and the rock surface could be captured. But perhaps it was the other way round. The availability of color film and the popularity of slide shows could be said to have created rock art researchers. Either way, they were genuine enthusiasts who scoured the country for photogenic paintings and engravings and amassed huge collections of slides that are today extraordinarily valuable research resources; many of the paintings captured on film at that time no longer exist, having been destroyed by natural processes and vandalism.

At this time, too, the great influential figures of the pre-1950 era were passing. Van Riet Lowe retired from the directorship of the Archaeological Survey in 1954 and died in 1956 at the comparatively early age of sixty-two. The Abbé devoted his last years to publishing a series of volumes of his copies, especially those made in present-day Namibia, and died at the age of eighty-four in 1961. An obituary in the *South African Archaeological Bulletin* described him as having been "the world's greatest living authority" on rock art (Clarke 1962). Battiss produced no major or influential publication on rock art after his 1948 book; he died in 1982 at the age of seventy-six, a revered father figure, but not an active researcher. An empty stage awaited younger people.

In addition to technological advances, the end of World War II brought demographic changes. South Africa became an attractive destination for emigrants from Europe. The affluence of the white population contrasted with the hardships of life in war-ravaged European cities. Among those who came to South Africa were a number of people who were to have a major impact on rock art research. It seems that, at that time at any rate, people living in Europe had a greater interest in history and archaeology than South Africans; those born and brought up in South Africa knew very little about the continent's archaeology and generally thought that little of interest happened before the colonial period. The names of the more enquiring immigrants from Europe recur in the following chapters. A new web of human relationships, diverse expertise, and, it should be added, rivalries was woven. Some of the newcomers revered the old establishment and entrenched their views; others were critical of what they saw as outdated, haphazard, and inaccurate research, but they remained a silent minority until the whole discipline of archaeology began to change as new theory and methodology were adopted in the 1960s.

Among the new immigrants was Alex Willcox, who soon found that the Abbé's mantle fitted him admirably. Some researchers became "experts," but Willcox was an "authority." He was the first of a number of avocationists who turned rock art research into a burgeoning field. Willcox was by profession a quantity surveyor and had developed an interest in archaeology before he emigrated from the United Kingdom. Neil Lee and Bert Woodhouse, also emigrants from the United Kingdom, were, respectively, a businessman and an accountant. Jalmar and Ione Rudner—he a town planner, she a museum technician—came from Scandinavia. Harald Pager, a designer and commercial artist from Austria, introduced a new technique for recording rock art; his colored, life-size, black-and-white photographs of the Ndedema Gorge rock art are of outstanding interest and competence (Pager 1971).

There were local workers as well. In the Western Cape Province, Townley Johnson, a Cape Town newspaper cartoonist, and his friends Hyme Rabinowitz and Percy Sieff developed a technique of tinted photographs that combined real rock surfaces with traced images (Johnson, Rabinowitz, and Sieff 1959). Patricia Vinnicombe, who grew up on a southern Drakensberg farm with rock art sites, was trained as an occupational therapist. Her marriage to Cambridge archaeologist Patrick Carter later enabled her to work full-time on rock art. There were others, but it was principally Willcox, Lee, and Woodhouse who made color photography the principal tool in rock art research. Willcox's pioneering photographic survey, *Rock Paintings of the Drakensberg*, was published in 1956 and was reprinted in 1960. Soon a series of photographic books by Lee and Woodhouse began to appear. The 1950s and 1960s were primarily the era of the amateur, and interest in rock art reached unprecedented levels. Armed with van Riet Lowe's list of site locations, they scoured the land, delighting, as did the Abbé and Battiss, in the thrill of conquering rugged and forbidding terrain. Their efforts extended van Riet Lowe's list of sites considerably.

Photography was, however, a two-edged sword. Certainly, the glowing color reproductions of the period revealed the beauty and detail of the painted images as never before. It was as if the art was being seen anew. As soon as the photographic books began to appear, it was clear that the copies that Breuil, Battiss, and others had made were not fair reflections of the art. Especially, close-up photographic techniques, developed by Lee and Woodhouse (1964; Woodhouse 1979), revealed tiny details that had escaped earlier workers. The art was seen to be a set of cameos, miniature miracles of draftsmanship, shading, and fascinating, if frequently enigmatic, detail.

The downside was that photography contrived an illusion of objectivity. The popular misapprehension that the camera does not lie led researchers into a cul-de-sac. The nature of the illusion was, however, not immediately apparent. Photography in a San painted rock shelter poses problems, not just of light availability, exposure times, and the difficulty of setting up a tripod on an uneven, rocky floor. Mastering these practical techniques of photography tended to obscure conceptual problems that, unnoticed, inhibited understanding of the meanings of the paintings, paradoxically, simultaneously as the same photographs were revealing their richness.

San images are often densely spread over surfaces many meters long; it is not uncommon to find a couple of hundred images crowded together and superimposed on one another in a single shelter. Further, the images are generally very small, some measuring only a few centimeters. A photograph taken from a distance so as to include the whole sweep of a panel renders the individual images indistinct, if not invisible. One must also remember that the images in a given panel are not uniformly preserved: Some may be very clear, but others are so faint as to require long examination to discern them. When photographers move up close to such a jumble of images they naturally enough concentrate on well-preserved paintings that can fill their rectangular frames and produce stunning color slides. Faced with the apparent confusion of densely painted panels, photographers asked: What goes with what? Perhaps unthinkingly, their answer was: What makes a good picture. When these photographs were published, they gave the impression that the art was a collection of individual images or small groups of images; the overall panel was fragmented, and indistinct images and details of images failed to register. Each published photograph appeared on the page as a framed "picture" of an animal, a person, or comparatively small "composition."

In short, the photographs continued to present San "works of art" in the tradition of Battiss.

In theory, it should be possible to construct a large mosaic of close-up photographs, but such a procedure poses practical problems. A mosaic would have to be no less than half the size of the painted panel if the details of the images are to register. Even then, images on the rock face that are so faint as to be virtually invisible without long study are completely invisible in photographs. Finally, rock faces are seldom plane surfaces: They comprise facets set at varying angles. Not surprisingly, the ultimate goal of a publishable photographic mosaic that shows all the details and all the faint images was never realized. To get around these problems, Harald Pager developed a novel technique in the 1960s. He photographed painted rock faces in black and white, enlarged the photographs to life size, and then, using oil paints, colored in all the images he could see, not just in the photographs, but as a result of long study in the rock shelters themselves. But this was an isolated, if monumental, task that neither he nor anyone else essayed again. Most researchers were obliged to remain with photographs of isolated images and small groups of images.

From these "framed," selected extracts it was a short step to "realistic" interpretations. Battiss's view that "the art of the little Bushmen was one of illustration" seemed to be confirmed by the portraits of exquisitely shaded eland and rhebuck, elaborately "decorated" human figures, and so forth. The art was taken to be a record of daily San life, on a par, indeed, with photography itself: Each published, rectangular photograph was taken to be a candid-camera shot of a particular activity in San life. Each "framed" book illustration seemed to invite its own interpretation, and the overall interrelated complexity of the art was lost. Needless to say, this view led to some strange, even bizarre, interpretations, but they need not detain us now. More significantly, Battiss's assumption that the art was "one of illustration" of daily life guided the selection of photographs for publication. Researchers consulted early colonial travelers' reports on San communities and then sought paintings of the activities about which they had read—hunting, tracking, food gathering, dancing, recreation, types of equipment and clothing, and so forth.

Still, there remained images that defied even the most ingenious literal interpreter, and most researchers were content to ascribe these paintings, in decidedly vague terms, to myths or rituals. Because it was generally believed that San myths and religion had been lost forever, these puzzling images remained, and were entertainingly presented as, insoluble mysteries. There was thus a tension between researchers' beliefs about literal, "pure" art and what might be called enigmatic religious or mythical images, though these were believed to be an insignificant minority and not of central importance. As with so many ethnographies from around the world, books about San rock art started with daily subsistence activities and human–environment relationships before, finally, touching briefly on religion and myth. Structurally, the books thus paralleled the (erroneous) view of small-scale societies as concerned principally with an unremitting search for sustenance; religion was merely a quaint appendage. It did not occur to researchers who followed this line of thought that, at any rate in rock art, religion may have been the central concern.

It would, however, be wrong to deny the great value of the work that was done by the rock art photographers. True, their photographic skills diverted their attention from interpretative problems, and their publications served to entrench Battiss's "illustrative" view of the art that denied deeper meanings and symbolic associations. Nevertheless, their publications remain a monument to their devotion, and researchers today constantly turn to them. The photographers established a database on which theoretical and methodological developments stirring in mainstream archaeology could build.

While rock art studies were in their heyday and books of photographs were appearing regularly, professional archaeology was undergoing profound changes that would challenge the sort of work and results that avocationists were equipped to produce. This clash between professionals and amateurs was felt first in Stone Age archaeology and somewhat later in rock art research. Unfortunately, with fault perhaps on both sides, a lot of bitterness resulted. Amateurs were angry because they were no longer considered capable of excavating caves. If they were fortunate, they were demoted to sorters of the material that the professionals meticulously excavated; if they were unlucky in their personal contacts, they were excluded altogether.

It was at this time of general distress that matters were made worse by the introduction of new techniques for gathering, sorting, and handling data. Exciting though they were at the time, they have since fallen into disuse. Nevertheless, their legacy should not be underestimated.

Man Must Measure 2

The essence of science: ask an impertinent question, and you are on the way to a pertinent answer.

—JACOB BRONOWSKI

THE CHANGES IN MAINSTREAM archaeology that marginalized amateur researchers came from what is today known as the New Archaeology, or processual archaeology. In the 1960s and early 1970s, there was a new emphasis on explicit theory and methodology, though the novelty of this emphasis is sometimes exaggerated. For New Archaeologists, description of the past was inadequate and tendentious. Researchers should rather concentrate on the *processes* that brought about change in social formations and technology.

Systems theory seemed to offer a framework within which to discuss change. Past cultures were not simply ragbags of traits; rather, the different parts of a culture were systemically related to one another. In this regard, the New Archaeology was similar to the structural-functionalism of British social anthropology, which we shall shortly consider, but it went further: Cultural systems were said to be in important ways comparable to systems in the physical world.

Essentially, the New Archaeology was an anthropology of the past. In America archaeology and anthropology are, of course, taught in the same department, and archaeologists in the 1960s consequently learned much about culture and the lifeways of "primitive" communities.

But it was a "scientific" anthropology. The philosophy of science and exactly what constituted scientific method became central archaeological debating points. Researchers realized that artifacts from the past do not simply "speak" to those who study them. Stone artifacts and, for that matter, rock paintings do not tell us anything about what the past was like, how people lived, what they believed. Items of all kinds that survive from the past have to be explained, interpreted, understood. That process of understanding has to be more than guesswork; it has to have some explicit logic to support its conclusions. In response to these demands, the hypothetico-deductive scientific method and multiple hypothesis testing became cornerstones of the New Archaeology. These methods require researchers to make bold hypotheses, deduce potentially testable observations from them, and then to verify or reject these observations. This procedure was frequently advocated in situations in which multiple hypotheses could be so tested. Rival hypotheses could then be compared with one another according to established criteria, such as the number and diversity of data that they explained (for an account of the problems inherent in such methods, see Chalmers 1978). Struggling for greater precision and more explicit logic, researchers at the same time explored quantitative techniques; graphs, histograms, and complex numerical tables became the outward signs of inward change.

In South Africa, Revil Mason, van Riet Lowe's successor as director of the Archaeological Survey (though by this time the Archaeological Research Unit and no longer government funded, Smuts having been defeated in the fateful 1948 election), was one of the most innovative researchers. His paper "The Transvaal Middle Stone Age and Statistical Analysis" (Mason 1957) was an early move in the direction of more scientific methods. Mason brought his work to a climax with the publication of his book *The Prehistory of the Transvaal* (1962), with its eminently sane chapter on rock art. His presidential address to the South African Archaeological Society, delivered in 1967, was entitled "Prehistory as a Science of Change—New Research in the South African Interior." His emphasis was on science, precision, and, in the tradition of the New Archaeology, the processes that caused change, not on mere descriptions of what took place. Sadly, subsequent researchers often overlook pioneering work like Mason's.

Other archaeologists followed suit, and it was not long before members of the public began to complain that the *South African Archaeological Bulletin*, a journal originally intended for both professional and general readers, was no longer intelligible to them. Only one field remained accessible to people without professional archaeological training—rock art, an interest that most professionals ignored because the data seemed intractable. Beside such erudite, abstruse, and statistically informed articles as Mason's, rock art research publications seemed small beer.

Soon there was evidence for a rift in the ranks of rock art researchers themselves. Some were happy to continue on the periphery of professionalism and to exploit the contact that they were able to maintain with the estranged public. For them, the images were pictures from and of the past, and each one was worth a thousand words: The paintings indisputably *showed* us what the past was like. Other researchers realized that things were not that simple: In David Clark's famous phrase, they suffered a "loss of innocence." The simple, though undeniably real, joy of tracking down sites, taking stunning photographs, and understanding the art as a straightforward record of the past had now to be tempered with science; they would have to devise new ways of studying rock art. These workers yearned to join the professional fold, but it all seemed a bit too much for them. How could rock art research possibly emulate the abstruse work of mainstream archaeologists? There seemed to be no way of getting a scientific grip on rock art data.

Then, in 1967, new possibilities for rock art research opened, thanks to Patricia Vinnicombe and Tim Maggs. In that year, Vinnicombe published two key articles. The first (Vinnicombe 1967b) was a detailed account of the quantitative system that she was using to analyze the rock art of a restricted area in the southern Drakensberg; the second gave preliminary results of her survey (Vinnicombe 1967a). In introducing her system, she acknowledged assistance given by various scientists, including physicists, statisticians, zoologists, and archaeologists.

For each and every image in her selected area she noted the following:

I.   Subject (human, animal, miscellaneous)
II.   Sex
III.   Size
IV.   Style (monochrome, bichrome, polychrome, or shaded polychrome)
V.   Color
VI.   Paint (stain, film, powdery)
VII.   Execution (fine, medium, thick)
VIII.   Condition (good, fair, poor)
IX.   Elevation (facing left or right, head turned, etc.)
X.   Action (body and leg positions as determined by templates; standing, walking, running, false action; squatting, sitting, kneeling)
XI.   Proportion
XII.   Weapons and equipment
XIII.   Composition (scattered, processions, superimposed friezes)
XIV.   Scene description (hunting, fighting, domestic activities, dancing or acrobatics, ceremonial, ritual, and mythical scenes)
XV.   Superposition
XVI.   Human head types (five)
XVII.   Human hairstyles (six)
XVIII. Human dress (six)
XIX.   Human decorations, physical details, physical details of animals (horns, tusks, eyes, mouth, etc.)
XX.   Physical details (e.g., steatopygia, fingers, toes, hooves)

Vinnicombe used punch cards to sort these data. When one recalls that her final sample comprised 8,478 individual images (Vinnicombe 1976, 362), one gains some idea of the daunting physical labor involved in such an undertaking, conducted, it should be emphasized, not in the comfort of a laboratory but in remote mountainous terrain.

In identifying the need for so detailed a quantitative approach, Vinnicombe put her finger on the tension between rock art research, as it was then practiced, and mainstream archaeology:

> If . . . the study of rock-art is to make a meaningful contribution to the field of archaeology where quantitative techniques and statistical methods are becoming increasingly important, an analytical approach is essential. . . . The greatest value, however, will lie not so much in correlating information from a circumscribed area such as that covered by the present survey, but in comparing one area with another on an objective basis. Valid statistical similarities could suggest cultural homogeneity, while differences might indicate separate clan areas. A distribution map based on a large enough sample from a wide enough area may reflect the ecological zones formerly occupied by specific animals or peoples, and could reveal possible migration routes or areas of contact. . . . Even more pertinent, however, will be the final marshalling of relevant data, when a beginning can be made on reconstructing the behaviour of the people responsible for the paintings. . . . Without this understanding, the full significance of rock-art will for ever remain obscure. (Vinnicombe 1967b, 141)

This passage contains the fundamental elements of the work that it triggered: quantification, statistical testing, ecological factors, objectivity, and regional comparisons designed to establish migration routes and cultural boundaries. Vinnicombe emphasized in her *South African Archaeological Bulletin* article that rock art could be used to tell us about the issues that were at that time interesting mainstream archaeologists. In accordance with the current notions of ecology, these archaeologists saw culture as an extrasomatic mechanism for adapting to the environment. They were especially interested in the ways in which people migrated seasonally to exploit their environments, evidence for which could be found in stratified rock shelter deposits. But if the ultimate goals of regional comparisons and understandings of human movement across ecological zones were to be achieved, more samples would have to be collated, even if "it is a laborious and time-consuming task" (Vinnicombe 1967b, 141). What is striking here is that, at that time, Vinnicombe and others who were to follow her were using rock art principally to inform on other aspects of human behavior, such as seasonal migrations, not first and foremost to tell us more about rock art itself, the meanings of the images, and the reasons why the San made them. Those interests, marginal to the thinking of mainstream archaeologists, though hinted at, were kept under wraps, or at least in the background, for the time being. The important thing was to be accepted by mainstream archaeologists.

In the meantime, the quantitative approach to rock art followed in the footsteps of Miles Burkitt, the Cambridge archaeologist who toured South Africa in 1927 in the company of Goodwin and van Riet Lowe and who swiftly published his book *South Africa's Past in Stone and Paint* (1928). He wrote, "All four methods of investigation that have been employed in studying the [stone] industries can be used in the study of the art, and, as before, stratigraphy and typology are the most important" (111). In rock art research, stratigraphy became superimposition, and typology became style. Rock art research should, in his view, be methodologically related to mainstream archaeology. Now, in the 1960s, methods were once more being transferred from mainstream archaeology to rock art research. And, for the time being, researchers were leaving the vexed problems of meaning alone, as did Burkitt, who wrote, "As regards the motives which prompted the execution of the paintings or engravings, little can be said" (Burkitt 1928, 156).

Vinnicombe's desire for further quantitative samples was immediately fulfilled. Working independently in the Western Cape Province, Tim Maggs, a trained archaeologist, had already followed the methods of the New Archaeology and completed a quantitative analysis that he published in a 1967 issue of, significantly, the *South African Journal of Science*. The system of recording that he used was far simpler than Vinnicombe's; he concentrated on subject matter and omitted nearly all the details that Vinnicombe sought to capture. One of Maggs's conclusions was prophetic of much research that was to follow. The marked numerical emphasis on large herbivores, especially eland, the largest African antelope, suggested that the painters were not simply painting their environment or what they were eating: "Apart from ecological factors . . . [the large number of eland paintings] might also be influenced by the eland having some particular importance of a religious nature" (Maggs 1967, 102). Independently, Vinnicombe (1967a, 284), in her preliminary report of the same year, argued cogently that the high percentage of eland paintings indicated "the important part this animal played in both the economy and religious beliefs of the painters." Similar ideas had previously been tentatively and fleetingly expressed by Werner (1908, 61) and Battiss (Battiss et al. 1958, 61); the large percentage of eland paintings is, after all, evident upon inspection, but now there was hard numerical evidence for this emphasis. At last, rock art research had something substantial to say, something more than subjective description and speculation—it had hard facts.

Indeed, in 1967 quantification seemed to offer an escape from the cul-de-sac in which so much of rock art was trapped. As soon as I had read proofs of Vinnicombe's forthcoming description of her inventorial system I set about a study in the Giant's Castle area of the KwaZulu-Natal Drakensberg. The proofs had been shown to me by Ray Inskeep, editor of the *South African Archaeological Bulletin* and Goodwin's successor at the University of Cape Town. A mainstream archaeologist of distinction, he was engagingly and infectiously enthusiastic about the possibilities of Vinnicombe's recording system.

So it was that I began five or six years of intensive fieldwork in a restricted area in the Drakensberg. Laboriously, I and my collaborators examined each image and noted its characteristics. But, once we had left unstructured photographic research behind and become more quantitative, what could all the statistics teach us? Without recourse to other kinds of data, what could we infer from our statistics about meaning? To what extent were our quantitative analyses skewed by the criteria for categorization that came out of earlier, if now suppressed, views of the art? Vinnicombe's "Scene description" category, for instance, required that a recorder decide if the group of images in question depicted hunting, fighting, domestic activities, dancing, acrobatics, ceremonial, ritual, or mythical scenes. The emphasis of these categories on quotidian activities derived from the old belief that San rock art was a record of daily life with a yet-to-be-determined slice of "mythical" elements. It became clear that, behind the notion of objective recording, there was a vitiating flaw: Every time a scene was recorded, the recorder had to interpret it. Is this a "dance"? If so, could it be said to be "mythical" or "ritual"? The system of recording thus depended on a priori interpretations and the notion that one could determine what a scene depicted by simply looking at it. Interpretation was molding the statistics, not deriving from them.

In practical terms, then, it was clear that the categories that Vinnicombe had established were, as, to be fair, she herself recognized, putting the images into preconceived packages, and any interpretations that we essayed were contingent upon the integrity of those packages. Whatever explanations of the art had to say about meaning would have to be said in the language of the categories.

Then, too, it was evident that poor preservation of so many images was skewing the statistics to some degree. In almost every rock shelter, there are images that are so faint that one cannot determine their nature. They had to be omitted from the inventory. But did they matter? Could one assume that the processes of weathering had been random and had thus not affected one's overall numerical results? But, if weathering was a function of the passage of time, then it was not random: Images from earlier periods, which may well have been different in form and content from those of recent times, were being selectively and inexorably eliminated.

Was this kind of quantification much different, at least in one respect, from the older photographic approach? Did the record cards, one for each image, not fragment complex panels even more seriously than close-up photographs? Was the supposed but, in reality, highly deceptive objectivity of photographs being carried over, perhaps even more seriously, into the imposed, a priori categories of quantification? These were some of the issues that bothered me. They became evident, not just in contemplative moods, but much more acutely in the field, when I was standing in front of painted panels; again and again impossible decisions had to be made. Subjectivity and old, questionable ideas about the meaning and function of the art that quantification was intended to eliminate were still an integral part of the conceptual foundation of our work.

My first rock art publication, apart from a copy that appeared on the cover of a *South African Archaeological Bulletin*, was on rock engravings near the small town Tarkastad in the Eastern Cape Province. It was published in 1962, five years before Vinnicombe and Maggs published their quantitative studies. My model was Goodwin's 1936 study of the Vosburg engravings, a sensible account that eschewed the lavish prose and vague notions of his contemporaries. Even at the time of its publication, however, seeing my 1962 article in print was a profoundly dispiriting experience: All too plainly, it consisted of no more than superficial, qualitative description.

The reason for my discontent lay in my educational background. As an undergraduate in the early 1950s at the University of Cape Town, I had taken a course in social anthropology, during which Goodwin's lectures had awakened in me a special interest in the San and South African archaeology. Perhaps more to the point, we had enjoyed a visit by one of the great social anthropological luminaries of the time, A. R. Radcliffe-Brown, who had been head of Social Anthropology at the University of Cape Town some years earlier. His influential collection of essays, *Structure and Function in Primitive Society* was published in 1952, my first year as an undergraduate.

Another of our lecturers was Monica Wilson, who had been a student of Bronislaw Malinowski, the pioneer of participant observation, fieldwork that entails living among a community for a year or more, learning the local language, and studying every detail of the people's life and culture. Malinowski's ideas on myth and ritual among the Trobriand Islanders were, for us students, fascinating.

So too was E. E. Evans-Pritchard's book on the Nuer. It had been published in 1940; his *Nuer Religion* appeared in 1956. No doubt about it, we were brought up as committed structural-functionalists. We believed that the structure of society could be divided into four major institutions: kinship, economy, politics, and religion. These institutions were said to be compatible and to interact with one another, and it was this functioning interaction that sustained society. The tasks of a social anthropologist were to discern these institutions in the flux of daily life, to describe them, and to show how they were interdependent.

The problems inherent in structural-functionalism were not apparent to us at the time. As it was generally practiced, structural-functionalism was synchronic, that is, it focused on the functioning of a society at one time, not as it changed through time. Emphasis on this sort of functioning and the equilibrium it was said to sustain suggested that change tended to come from outside of society, perhaps as a result of environmental changes. Structural-functionalism thus diverted attention from internally generated change. It also focused on groups and society as a whole, not on the role of individuals and their influence on a community. Overall, cooperation and harmony, not conflict, were the structural-functionalists' watchwords. Recognition of these and other limitations was to come later—and eventually to impact on rock art research. Still, what I had learned about structural-functionalism propelled me to the threshold of dissatisfaction: My Tarkastad article lacked the kind of insights that the great names in anthropology were achieving. What, I wondered, would Malinowski, Radcliffe-Brown, or Evans-Pritchard have said about those images on the rocks near Tarkastad? Because participant observation in an extinct community is impossible, I could see no way forward.

Then, at last, it seemed that quantification was something we could actually *do*. It was a way of grappling with the elusive data of rock art, despite any misgivings one may have entertained about doubtful objectivity. In some ways, camping in remote painted rock shelters as we meticulously noted down multiple features of each image recalled the kind of participant observation that Malinowski had advocated and that he, Wilson, Evans-Pritchard, and others had so spectacularly practiced. But, no matter how long we stayed in a rock shelter—hours, days, or weeks—we were no closer to understanding the meanings of the images or why the San had placed them there.

Always at the back of my mind was a niggling question: When all the fieldwork had been done, when all the data had been collated, when all the histograms had been prepared, how was I to move from those numbers to the kind of insights that my course in social anthropology had shown me were waiting to be uncovered? Whilst quantification seemed to hold some promise, there was a great gulf between the numbers that we were so laboriously collecting in the rock shelters and any sort of meaning of the kind that the structural-functionalists had produced. To be sure, eland paintings were numerous, but what did *the eland* mean to the San? Could eland have possibly had any significances comparable to those that cattle held for the Nuer? Evans-Pritchard (1940, 16) had written: "*Cherchez la vache* is the best advice that can be given to those who desire to understand Nuer behaviour." Should San rock art researchers focus their attention on the eland?

To answer such questions I explored various avenues in my first post-Tarkastad article; it came a full decade after that unsatisfactory essay. First, I presented my quantitative results as an objective inventory from which I could make inferences. After I had analyzed multiple characteristics of 1,335 images in 20 sites in the Giant's Castle area of the Drakensberg, it appeared that little purpose would be served by persevering with the approach in the chosen area. Comparison of my results with those of George Hughes, later chief executive officer of the KwaZulu-Natal Conservation Service, who recorded 4,056 in an adjacent area, showed that little more could be learned by increasing the total number of paintings: Totals went up but percentages remained the same. Following Vinnicombe's call for regional comparisons, I used histograms to compare my results with those of Maggs (1967; Western Cape Province), Pager (1971; Ndedema Gorge, Drakensberg), Smits (1971; Lesotho), and Rudner (1971; thirty painted stones from the southern Cape coast). The differences between the regions did not appear significant; certainly, I was unable to make any inferences from the data.

I entitled the article "The Syntax and Function of the Giant's Castle Rock Paintings" (Lewis-Williams 1972b). The title betrays not only Radcliffe-Brown's structural-functionalist influence but also one of my major university subjects, English. Neither Vinnicombe nor Maggs had considered the problems of syntax, or grammar; they remained with "comparative vocabularies." Perhaps the vital clues lay not so much in individual images but rather in the ways that those images were linked to each other to make statements, or "sentences," about relationships between people, between people and nature, or between people and a supernatural realm. Under the rubric of "syntax" I struggled thus:

> The significance of any representation is in its context. This is unfortunately destroyed by a system of recording that places each representation on a separate card. Although such a system provides information about the vocabulary of the art, it divorces related elements. Furthermore, the information concerning the vocabulary is limited by the method to the denotation of the representations: the full semantic

range cannot be explored if the representation is not studied in context. . . . To understand the full semantic import of a word it must be seen in its context. As with words, verbal symbols, the graphic symbols of primitive art are manipulated in various ways and in different syntactic structures to make statements and to express relationships. In language this happens on the simplest level when words are arranged to form a sentence according to rules which both speaker and listener accept. More complexly, the verbal symbols can be arranged and manipulated in myths in which their symbolic meaning is more important than their denotation. In primitive art the symbols are arranged in graphic compositions of varying complexity. (Lewis-Williams 1972b, 53–54)

I went on to distinguish three types of syntactic structures: scenic relationships, superpositioning, and juxtapositioning. I return to superposition later in this chapter. For the present, I look at the notion of juxtapositioning, paintings placed next to each other but in no apparent scenic, or narrative, way. This is the sort of interimage relationship that I imagined may underlie those complex, densely painted panels but that is masked when each image is recorded and analyzed separately. To explain what was happening in such groupings, I turned to the work of Marshall McLuhan, a writer much cited at the time.

The technique of juxtapositioning graphic symbols has a parallel in western society. McLuhan (1967) has cited the Berkshire stocking advertisement as an example. In this well-known advertisement the lady wearing the stockings is depicted with a rearing stallion in the background. There is no logical connection between the two, but the symbolic quality of the stallion is strong and the mind makes the necessary inference instantaneously and non-rationally. Another use of the technique is in the highly successful "tiger in your tank" campaign. The non-logical picture of the tiger's tail hanging out of a car's petrol tank is memorable and says a great deal about the qualities of the petrol. . . . McLuhan has shown how clusters of images are comprehended by the subconscious simultaneously. When the symbol is separated from a sequential unit, it becomes poly-allusive. Untrammeled by any limiting logical sequence, the symbol can operate on its full semantic range. (Lewis-Williams 1972b, 59–60)

Looking back at this passage after thirty years, I think that it has ideas that are still useful in understanding juxtapositioning in San rock art: There are many instances where painters placed images next to one another but not in any scenic relationship. But the last two sentences of the passage contain an error that, I now believe, led me astray for a long time. I return to it in a subsequent chapter. Now, I move on to the section of the 1972 article that was entitled "Intention and function."

Here, I briefly discussed the explanations that the Abbé Breuil and Walter Battiss had advanced—sympathetic magic and art for art's sake. Citing the results of archaeological excavations of Later Stone Age deposits, I pointed out that "the pictorial bestiary was not related to the diet of the Bushmen, small antelope, dassies [rock rabbits], tortoises etc. accounting for the bulk of their meat" (Lewis-Williams 1972b, 61). Maggs had come to the same conclusion. As for art for art's sake, I argued: "Other facts learned from a detailed study of a limited area that militate against acceptance of an aesthetic explanation are the highly restricted subject-matter of the art and the linking of representations by super-positioning" (Lewis-Williams 1972b, 61). Both these observations suggested a symbolic function, as Vinnicombe (1971) had pointed out. Thereafter my argument was a mixture of functionalism and, especially, Lévi-Straussian structuralism, a theoretical paradigm that had appeared some years after I had left the university.

Drawing on linguistics, Lévi-Strauss proposed that the human mind thought in binary oppositions, such as light : dark, good : evil, up : down. One element was meaningless without its opposite. If such thinking was intrinsic to the functioning of the human brain, then it was universal. In other words, the thinking and, by extension, the myths of small-scale societies were, first, no different from those of Westerners and, second, analyzable in terms of binary oppositions. In France, André Leroi-Gourhan (1968a) took up these structuralist notions in his study of west European Upper Paleolithic art; at the time, he seemed to be producing encouraging results. Could something similar be achieved in South Africa?

Citing Claude Lévi-Strauss's *Structural Anthropology* (1968) and his essay "The Story of Asdiwal" (1967), I analyzed a panel, indeed a whole site, that comprises only four images: a faded eland, a large standing figure with quiver and bow, a seated figure with a baby on its back and a weighted digging stick, and a walking figure apparently wearing a hairy kaross.

> The graphic compositions [of San art] make, as do the myths, statements and resolve oppositions on various levels (Lévi-Strauss 1967): sociological, techno-economic, metaphysical, and, possibly, geographical. Statements made on these levels were superimposed upon one another to produce a complex reaction in the prehistoric viewer who did not, of course, attempt to distinguish them.

To deal with the last-mentioned first, it is very diffidently suggested that part of the significance of the eland may have been geographical. It seems highly probable that the prehistoric Bushmen of the Natal Drakensberg moved seasonally with the antelope, even if such movements may not have been as extensive as those envisaged by Carter (1970). . . . [If seasonal movements between higher and lower altitudes] did in fact take place, the eland symbol may have been, in addition to its operation on other levels of meaning, connected with the geographical rhythm of the people and the attendant changes in social structure, type of habitat, etc.

The sociological import of the panel under discussion is clearer. The dichotomies within the unity of the human group are shown: adults and children, men and women, hunters and gatherers. As the myths proclaim, these divisions must be subordinated to the solidarity of the group if society is to continue. This is just what the painted group does. The division of labor between the sexes is also validated by the panel: the man is shown with his equipment, while the digging-stick lies next to the woman. Children, too, are shown as the concern of the women.

On the techno-economic level statements are made sanctioning food sources and the approved means of obtaining an adequate supply. . . . The juxtaposed eland is probably, on one of its levels, a symbol of food, but its exact position in this regard is not yet clear.

The eland is, however, undoubtedly far more than a symbol of food supply. Its juxtaposition with the human group makes statements on the metaphysical level concerning man's position in and difference from nature as well as bringing into play the association of the quality and emotive value of the symbol. . . .

The composition doubtless gave pleasure to the viewer, but it is inadequate to say this and to go no further. Whether such pleasure could be termed "aesthetic" is open to question. Like the mythology the panel presents a world composed of antitheses: men : women; adults : children; men : animals; culture : nature. (Lewis-Williams 1972b, 64)

So again I had a mixture of functionalism and the binary oppositions of structuralism. But again there was a barrier to understanding; one could go so far and no further. Having, with hard work and luck, isolated binary oppositions and, perhaps, the elements of myths that Lévi-Strauss called "mythemes," what did they *mean?* Was it enough to follow Lévi-Strauss and assert that they dealt with contradictions and binary oppositions in San society? In what sense did the painting of binary oppositions help to resolve, or mediate, contradictions? In any event, what were these binary oppositions?

At this point, I thought longingly of Malinowski's participant fieldwork. Being there would surely have helped to answer at least some of the worrying questions. But the people who made San rock art had all died, and mainstream archaeologists constantly impressed on those who studied rock art that their absence was a seriously restricting, possibly entirely vitiating, factor in any research program that hoped to deal with meaning. It would be better, they advised, to stay with numerically expressed regional variations. Still, *pace* these pessimistic mentors, I hoped that San ethnography would, in some small measure, compensate for the impossibility of participant observation. I had explored Isaac Schapera's (1930) compilation of early reports, *The Khoisan Peoples of Southern Africa*, and Bleek and Lloyd's (1911) *Specimens of Bushman Folklore*, but I had not been able to make much of them. The myths seemed impenetrable, despite Lévi-Strauss's guidance and my search for mythemes. I therefore likened what quantitative analysis had achieved to the identification of the rhyme scheme of a Petrarchan sonnet: The rhyme scheme does not bring the student nearer to the meaning of the poem, though it underpins and clinches meaning.

Although some of these thoughts took me further along the road to meaning than the Tarkastad article of a decade before, I still had not gone as far as I had hoped to go. My concluding sentences expressed not only my frustration but also what I knew was the route out of my dilemma, even though I did not know how to negotiate it:

> Whilst further detailed work on the paintings may reveal more about the symbolic entities and the patterns according to which they are manipulated in this particular field, the significance of eland, kaross-clad figures and so on will remain obscure; the study must move from syntactics to semantics. The only possibility of clarifying the themes which most deeply moved the mind of the prehistoric Bushmen lies in the, albeit fragmentary, mythology. (Lewis-Williams 1972b, 64)

The final sentence contains an intentional echo of a statement by Wilhelm Bleek, with whose nineteenth-century San folklore research many of the following chapters are concerned. But, in 1972, that folklore remained, for me, stubbornly obscure. So, moving from Giant's Castle to another area, I persevered with quantitative analysis. I still held out some hope, however evanescent, of making meaningful comparisons between regions. My second area was the Barkly East district of the Eastern Cape Province, a region astonishingly rich in well-preserved imagery. Here, I recorded 2,361 images in detail in 38 rock shelters situated on, or on tributaries of, the Kraai and Bell Rivers, the Bell being itself a major tributary of the Kraai. The task took about three years.

While engaged with the Giant's Castle fieldwork, a realization had been borne in me, and this idea informed much of my Barkly East work. Almost by chance, it seemed, I had stumbled on a pattern that could, just possibly, lead me through the miasma of statistics to some sort of grasp of meaning. In the Giant's Castle area I had found that, in superpositions, "the initial element had a very strong influence over the choice of the second element. . . . [Superpositioning was] used to link representations in a special way" (Lewis-Williams 1972b, 58). To demonstrate this proposition I resorted to simple finite state grammar, as described by Noam Chomsky (1957). Now, working day after day in the Barkly East rock shelters, this form of syntax seemed more and more important as a means of getting at the meaning of the art. Some unexpected patterns came to light.

Before describing them, I need to distinguish between *superpositioning* and *overlapping*. I regarded cases in which only a small portion of a painting impinged on another as overlapping and did not record them. In order to qualify for recording as superpositioning, the upper painting had to be executed directly on top of the lower. I adopted this course because it seemed that overlapping could result from chance more easily than could superpositioning as I defined it. I then reviewed what earlier writers had concluded about the superimposition of one painted image on another. I wrote in the third person in the (mistaken) hope that the article would sound "scientific."

Superpositioning in a Sample of Rock-Paintings from the Barkly East District

Views on superpositioning

Stow (1905, 27–28) was the first writer to comment on superpositioning in the South African rock paintings. He was of the opinion that the painting of the second representation constituted a defacement of the first, and that such over-painting would not be attempted as long as a recollection of the first artist was preserved. Then, forced by the limited rock surface of the shelter, "some aspirant after artistic fame . . . unceremoniously painted over the efforts of those who preceded him."

In perpetuating these ideas Battiss (1939, 28) distinguished three kinds of superpositioning: "The first type consists of a casual painting of an animal over a faded painting. The second type appears as sheer vandalism. Crude figures are superimposed above clear, beautiful work. The third type is intentional and done to represent perspective." Later Goodwin (Rosenthal and Goodwin 1953, 22)

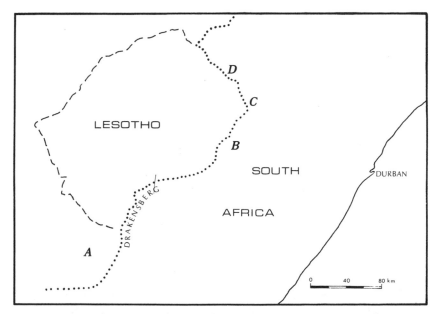

Figure 2.1.   Map showing areas mentioned in text: (A) Barkly East; (B) Underberg (Vinni-combe 1976); (C) Giant's Castle (Lewis-Williams 1972b); (D) Ndedema Gorge (Pager 1971).

expressed similar views: "The scarcity of a smooth and sheltered 'canvas' on which to paint led these artists to ignore the older faded paintings they found, and to paint over them in bright colours."

Brentjes (1969, 8), who believes that the paintings were a means to success in the hunt, claims that there is no relationship between superimposed paintings: "The later additions bear no relationship to the earlier ones, which is proof that these rock galleries were not thought of as 'exhibitions' and that once the game was killed they had no further significance."

There are three important assumptions in these widely held views:

1. That the later paintings constituted a defacement of the earlier and that no relationship was intended
2. That the later paintings were generally executed on top of faded older work
3. That superpositioning is a result of limited rock surface suitable for painting

These assumptions are now examined in the light of the data recorded in the Barkly East district.

The Barkly East superimpositions

Themes in Superpositioning

Figure 2.2 shows the situation with regard to sixty-nine cases of two-element superimpositions. In this part of the analysis the thematic pattern is examined, that is, a case of an eland superimposed on three human figures has been regarded as one case of "eland on human figure." The total numbers of figures involved in superpositioning are discussed later. Figure 2.2 reveals a distinct preference for two combinations (eland on eland; eland on human figure) and a lesser preference for another (rhebuck on human figure). The avoidances are also noteworthy. Eland are painted on eland twenty-five times, but only once does rhebuck appear on eland. No human figures are recorded as having been painted on eland, but two were noted in the Giant's Castle sample. The initial element clearly exercised an influence on the choice of the terminal element.

Figure 2.3 compares the initial and terminal themes in the Barkly East sample with those from Giant's Castle. There is a remarkable uniformity. As in the Giant's Castle area, there is a strong tendency to paint animals on human beings rather than human beings on animals.

UPPER THEMES

LOWER THEMES	Eland	Rhebuck	Indet. ant.	Hartebeest	Feline	Cattle	Human figs.	Antelope-man	Flying buck	Myth. animal	
Eland	25	1			1		1				28
Rhebuck	1										1
Indet. ant.	1	2				1			1		5
Hartebeest	1										1
Feline							1				1
Cattle											0
Human figs.	20	6		1			2	1			30
Antelope-man	2										2
Flying buck											0
Myth. animal	1										1
	51	9	0	1	1	1	4	1	1	0	69

Figure 2.2.   Positions of themes in sixty-nine cases of two-element superpositioning; for example, "eland on eland" occurs twenty-five times; the "rhebuck on human figure(s)" occurs six times.

Eland: Identifiable representations of *Taurotragus oryx*.

Rhebuck: Identifiable representations of *Pelea capreolas* (Vaal rhebuck), *Redunca fulvorufula* (Mountain rhebuck), and similar species of small antelope.

Hartebeest: Identifiable representations of *Alcelaphus caama*.

Indeterminate antelope: All antelope that is impossible to identify.

Feline: Leopards, lions.

Cattle: Domestic cattle.

Human: All representations of human beings.

Antelope-man: Pager's (1971) definition is as follows: "A human being whose legs and arms end in hooves. Most antelope men also have antelope heads but this feature is not considered sufficient for identification" (231). The present study includes in this category figures whose legs and/or arms end in hooves.

Flying buck: Theriomorphic figure, often lacking legs, with trailing streamers. See Lee and Woodhouse 1964, 1968, 1970, and Pager 1971, 231.

Mythological animal: Theriomorphic figure clearly intended to represent a fantastic creature.

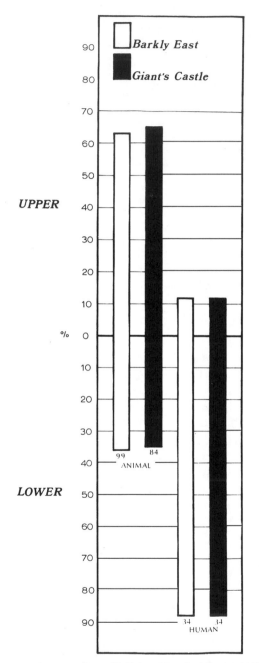

Figure 2.3.   Diagrammatic comparison of initial and terminal themes in the Barkly East and Giant's Castle samples of two-element superpositioning.

Total Numbers of Representations in Superpositioning

Attention is now given to the total numbers of the various categories of representations involved in superpositioning. Table 2.1 sets out this information. The three categories that contain sufficient examples to warrant close attention are eland, rhebuck, and human figures.

Of the 586 eland in the total sample 20.6 percent were involved in superpositioning; this is in excess of what would be expected if superpositioning were random (9.19 percent). Conversely rhebuck (5.0 percent of total 240) and human figures (4.6 percent of total 1,253) tended to be avoided by the painters when composing cases of superpositioning. A chi-square test showed that the observed results differ significantly from expectation in these three cases ($chi^2 = 116.71, p < 0.001$).

The observed number of rhebuck in superpositioning (12) is less than the expected number (22.049). It appears that the painters were less inclined to employ representations of this antelope, although it should be remembered that six cases of its being superimposed on human figures were recorded. Ninety percent of the rhebuck are in the upper layers of two-element superpositioning (figure 2.4).

There are too few hartebeest, felines, and mythical creatures to make analysis reliable. Cattle appear in superpositioning only once (2.5 percent). Baboons (five in total sample) and horses (seven in total sample), which are probably both more recent subjects, are not used in superimpositions. Higher percentages of hartebeest than rhebuck are noted in both the Barkly East sample (10.0 percent) and the Giant's Castle sample (83.5 percent), but again the small numbers involved make assessment difficult.

Table 2.1.   Total numbers of representations involved in superpositioning in the Barkly East sample

Category	No. in 38 sites	No. in superp.	% in superp.
Eland	586	121	20.6
Rhebuck	240	12	5.0
Hartebeest	20	2	10.0
Indeterminate antelope	96	8	8.3
Feline	10	2	20.0
Cattle	40	1	2.5
Human figures	1,253	58	4.6
Flying buck and mythological animals	24	2	8.3
Antelope-man	19	3	15.8
All other representations	73	0	0.0
	2,361	209	8.8

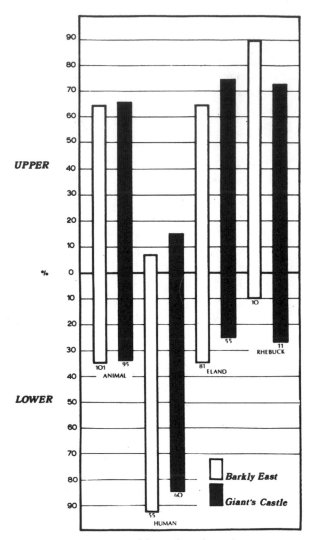

Figure 2.4.   Diagrammatic comparison of the total numbers of representations in upper and lower levels in the Barkly East and Giant's Castle samples of two-element superpositioning.

In the total sample there are nineteen antelope-men; of these three are in superpositioning (15.8 percent). Although this is a comparatively high percentage, the small number of representations involved advocates caution in interpretation.

Only 4.6 percent of the total number of human figures (1,253) are used in superpositioning (observed frequency 58; expected 115.113). In spite of this, two-element combinations incorporating human figures are second in number only to those composed exclusively of eland. As is shown later, it seems that a certain type of human figure was favored in superpositioning.

There are noteworthy points of similarity between the Barkly East and Giant's Castle samples (figure 2.4). In both there is a high percentage of eland involved in superpositioning: Barkly East 20.6 percent; Giant's Castle 35.0 percent. The position of rhebuck is virtually the same: Barkly East 5.0 percent; Giant's Castle 4.8 percent. A low percentage of human figures is reflected in both samples: Barkly East 4.6 percent; Giant's Castle 8.5 percent. These similarities suggest a close link between the painters of these regions. This is supported by the historical evidence (Vinnicombe 1976; Wright 1971).

Three-Element Superpositioning

Fourteen cases of three-element superpositioning were recorded. Eleven of these are composed entirely of eland. One was noted as "eland on indeterminate antelope on indeterminate antelope." In another the upper two elements were eland and the lower was two human figures with white faces. The only three-element superimposition to involve rhebuck was composed as follows: rhebuck on eland on rhebuck.

One complicated case not included in the preceding comprised four warthogs, one human figure, and one indeterminate antelope on eland on eland.

The three-element superimpositions thus appear to be a development of the two-element superimpositions according to the same principles.

Eland in Superpositioning

The most common animal in superpositioning is eland, accounting for 83 percent of the animals in superpositioning. Sixty-five percent of the eland in two-element superpositioning are in the upper level (figure 2.4).

Of the 586 eland in the Barkly East sample 92.5 percent are painted in more than one color, whereas only 71.6 percent of the rhebuck are so treated. The animal on the depiction of which the painters expended most care is also the one most frequently used in superpositioning. If aesthetic excellence were the sole aim of the painters, it would be difficult to account for this fact; they would surely have selected a rock surface free from the distracting effects of other paintings.

An analysis of the twenty-five cases of "eland on eland" shows that in twenty instances (80 percent) both the upper and the lower eland face in the same direction and in only five cases (20 percent) do they face in opposite directions. This suggests an intentional relationship between the initial and terminal elements. Of the twenty instances in which both face the same way, sixteen pairs (80 percent) face right and four pairs face left. In 84 percent of these "eland on eland" compositions the upper element faces right.

When the eland are superimposed on human figures a different situation obtains (figure 2.5). Of the twenty recorded cases both eland and underlying figures face the same way in twelve instances (60 percent). Eight of these twelve compositions face left and four face right. It appears that, when paired with human figures, more eland face left than when paired with other eland (chi^2 = 5.988, p < 0.02). This point will be taken up again in the consideration of the human figures.

The "haphazard blobs," usually bright orange, that Vinnicombe (1976) reports as being often superimposed on eland have not yet been found in the Barkly East area.

Human Figures in Superpositioning

Of the 209 representations involved in superpositioning fifty-eight (28 percent) are of human beings. Of the total sample of 1,253 human figures those involved in superpositioning account for 4.6 percent. The human figures usually form the initial element (93 percent) in cases of two-element superpositioning (figure 2.4).

An analysis of head types reveals a tendency to involve figures with white faces. This head type has been recorded as "hooked head" and "hooked head with white face" (Vinnicombe 1967, 140), but it now appears that the significant feature is the white face rather than the shape of the "hook." This type will hereafter be referred to as "white face." Figure 2.6 compares the head types of figures in superpositioning with the distribution of head types in the total sample. The round and indeterminately shaped heads diminish from 35.27 percent in the total sample to 3.44 percent in superpositioning. The figures with white faces increase from 18.19 percent to 44.82 percent. A chi-square test showed that the distribution of this type is not comparable with the ratio of the total sample (chi^2 = 44.696, p < 0.01). The concave type of head is also more prominent in superpositioning: 25.86 percent as against 16.12 percent in the total sample. The similar behavior of these two head types in superpositioning suggests that they may have some significance in common. This analysis of head types helps to explain an apparent anomaly. Although only 4.6 percent of human figures are involved in superpositioning, they feature prominently as a thematic element. The "eland on human figure" pairing (twenty cases) is second only to the "eland on eland" composition (twenty-five cases). The anomaly is explained by noting that the group

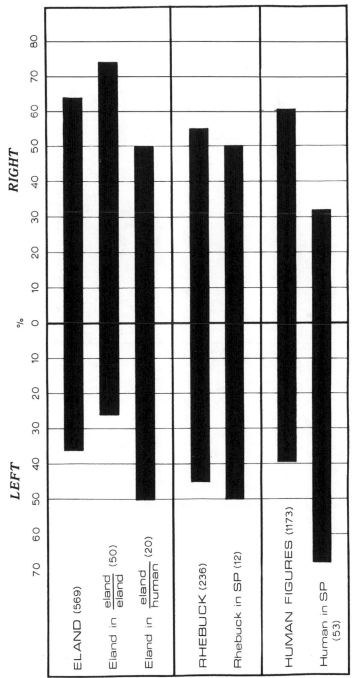

Figure 2.5.   Elevation of representations.

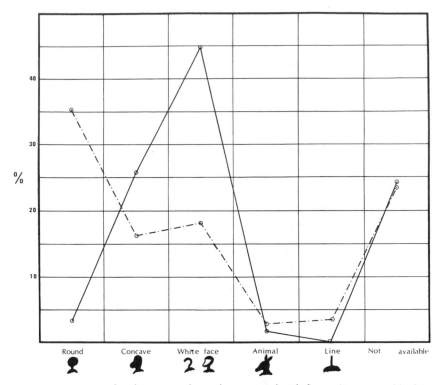

Figure 2.6.   Human head types: total sample compared with figures in superpositioning.
Solid line: figures in superpositioning; broken line: total sample from Barkly East.

"Human Figures" is heterogeneous: It comprises fundamentally different classes
of human figures as basic categories and so renders them comparable with the
other categories shown in table 2.2.

The association, but not specifically in superpositioning, of white-faced figures with eland has been noted by Vinnicombe (1976). She points out that the
white face "would seem scarcely utilitarian, and in some detailed groups their
bodies too are decorated with paint as though for a special ceremony rather than a
routine activity." The present study of superpositioning has supplied quantitative
evidence for this association. Of the twenty-six white-faced figures in superpositioning, twenty are under eland, three under a single rhebuck, and two under other
human figures. Half of them carry hunting equipment of one sort or another.

An analysis of human figures in lateral elevation shows that in the total sample
60.35 percent face right (figure 2.5). Of the figures in superpositioning only 32
percent face right. A chi-square test shows this shift to the left to be significant

Table 2.2.   Human head types involved in superpositioning in the Barkly East sample

Head type	No. in sample	No. in superp.	% in superp.
Round etc.	442	2	0.45%
Concave	202	15	7.42%
White face	228	26	11.40%
Animal	36	1	2.77%
Line	45	0	0.00%
Not available	300	14	4.66%
	1,253	58	4.62%

(chi^2 = 17.72, p < 0.001). As indicated in the discussion of eland, the tendency of the human figures in superpositioning to face left seems to be transferred to the eland which are superimposed on the human figures. The painters thus tended to use in superpositioning figures facing left. The significance of elevation and head type points to a complex symbolism in the paintings which will be discussed elsewhere.

There seems to be justification for treating a case of "eland on three men" as one case of "eland on human figure" in that the men are in all instances in a clear group. Frequently, the group extends beyond the limits of the superimposed eland, that is, the eland does not impinge upon all members of the group. These cases should probably be regarded as "eland on social group," rather than "eland on three individual human beings." The statement being made is a social one: An aspect of the symbolism of the eland is being related to social groups of specific kinds.

This and the foregoing analyses show that the first assumption noted previously, that there is no intended relationship between superimposed paintings, is no longer tenable.

Relative Preservation

In order to test the belief that it was the custom to paint only on top of older and more faded paintings a three-point scale was employed to indicate the degree of preservation. The number 1 was allocated to the upper painting in all cases. If there was no discernible differences between this and the lower painting, the latter was also allocated 1. If the lower painting was noticeably more faded, it was allocated 2, and, if it was considerably more faded, it was allocated 3. The scale is thus relative only to the individual cases of superpositioning. There did not appear to be any easy objective way of assessing the degree of preservation so that it could be applied uniformly to all the paintings. For the particular purpose in hand the present scheme proved satisfactory.

The analysis of two-element superimpositions showed that in 78 percent of the cases there was no discernible difference between the upper and lower representations. A difference of one point was noted in 15 percent of the cases and a difference of two points in only 7 percent. Thirteen cases of three-element superpositioning reflect the same pattern (in one instance the data are not available). In eight cases it was not possible to discern any appreciable difference between the top and lowest representations; in two cases a difference of one point was noted, and in three cases a difference of two points.

These data reflect a situation quite the reverse of what would be expected if the artists had painted over only the faded work of long-forgotten predecessors. Assumption two is thus shown to be untenable.

Availability of Rock Surface

The assumption that the painters were forced by a scarcity of suitable "canvas" to paint over older work is easily refuted by simple observation of the shelters. Sometimes quite large shelters contain only a few paintings and yet some of these are superimposed. Densely painted panels are frequently adjacent to apparently suitable rock surface that has not been used. One shelter, for example, contains only eight paintings and yet half of these are involved in superpositioning. Table 2.3 shows the percentage of paintings involved in superpositioning in twelve selected sites; in none of these is all the available rock surface used.

This position is confirmed by Pager (1971, 327): "One cannot really ascribe this tendency to paint upon other figures to a lack of available wall space. In nearly all the painted rock shelters at least some areas of the rock faces have remained untouched." (See also Vinnicombe, 1976). Assumption three is not supported by the evidence.

A similar situation obtains in the paleolithic caverns of western Europe. Ucko and Rosenfeld (1967) report: "Many natural rock panels and large stretches of apparently suitable rock surfaces were left plain whereas, elsewhere, representations are so closely crowded that they overlap into a virtually indecipherable maze of lines only a few centimetres away from blank spaces" (114).

A variation of this assumption has been proposed by some writers (e.g., Pager 1971, 327) who have suggested that the first painting may have provided a more suitable surface on which to paint, that is, it acted as a primer. Even though blank spaces existed, the areas already used may have been considered more suitable

Table 2.3. Percentage of paintings involved in superpositioning in twelve sites

Site	Total number of paintings	Percentage in superpositioning
A	247	4.5%
B	232	12.5%
C	171	3.5%
D	168	25.3%
E	108	1.9%
F	100	0.0%
G	98	16.3%
H	54	0.0%
I	42	11.9%
J	27	7.4%
K	14	14.3%
L	8	50.0%
38 sites	1,269	8.8%

simply for technical reasons. This could be argued in the case of some of the "eland on eland" compositions in which the upper painting often closely coincides with the lower, but not in cases of "eland on human being" in which, although the eland is painted directly on top of the human figure, only a small portion of its total area is actually over the painted area of the human figure. Furthermore, this explanation does not account for the marked preferences to which this paper draws attention. If there were any truth in the primer theory, numbers of smaller, possibly human figures, would be expected on top of the larger areas of the underlying eland, but this is not the case. Of the twenty-eight instances in which eland constitute the initial element, twenty-five are superimposed by further eland. Vinnicombe's Phase 4 paintings, which are characterized by a more marked emphasis on the human figures, tend to be painted away from the complex panels rather than on them.

Conversely, no evidence has been found to suggest that the painters made any attempt to erase or obliterate the earlier works. This, too, suggests that the relationship between the two or more levels of painting was intended to be perceived by the viewers.

Chronology

Superpositioning has been generally interpreted as the result of later painters' disregard for the work of their predecessors. Together with the subjective analysis of style it has been used as a means for determining periods in the development of the art.

Breuil (1930), working in four shelters in the eastern Orange Free State, believed it was possible to distinguish two main periods comprising seventeen phases. Phases one to eight form the first period of entirely naturalistic paintings largely concerned with hunting; the second period, phases nine to seventeen, reflects a "degenerate" art, less naturalistic and associated with pastoralism. Bleek (1932c, 78), after an examination of eighty-eight shelters, found it impossible to concur with the Abbé; her work did "not bear out the idea of a sequence of colours, each being used by a different generation." But she enigmatically adds: "To me there does not seem to be evidence of any change greater than would be natural in an art practised through centuries."

Willcox (1956), working in the Drakensberg, concluded that it was impossible to establish a clear, constant series of phases, but found "nothing inconsistent with the sequence having followed the order one would expect, that is monochromes first, then the bichromes, unshaded polychromes, and shaded polychromes in that order; but it is clear that the monochromes, especially the little red human figures, continued to be painted through all stages of the development of the art" (61).

In the Ndedema Gorge, Pager (1971) found that "the painting techniques evolved from flat application to the shaded style and later retrogressed to the flat paint application. Colour schemes started with red and white and during later periods additional pigments such as black and yellow were added to the palette" (353). He also found that the later periods were characterized by a greater variety of subject matter and more complex scenes.

In the Underberg area, Vinnicombe (1976) analyzed quantitatively seventy-seven shelters containing superimposed paintings. She found attempts to recognize phases of development disappointing: "There was little correlation between subject matter, style and size, but some consistency emerged in the colour application of the paints." She was, nevertheless, able to recognize four phases:

Phase 1. Vinnicombe believes it would be unwise to deduce that these earliest paintings were monochromes because of the poor state of preservation and the fugitive nature of the colors. She shows there was a predominance of animals in the subject matter.

Phase 2. These paintings "include clearer representations of humans and animals in various shades of red, sometimes with additional details in white, and specific compositions are recognizable."

Phase 3. Shaded polychromes make their appearance in this phase, although the monochromes continue. Several levels of superimposition occur within this shaded polychrome period. Vinnicombe comments: "In many instances the superimpositions are apparently intentional and contemporaneous. . . . It is possible that the high percentage of superimpositions in Phase 3 reflects a period of intensified ritual activity."

Phase 4. "During the fourth and final phase shaded polychromes diminish although they persist, and many newly introduced subjects such as guns, brimmed hats, and horses appear. There is a greater use of black, yellow ochre, and bright vermilion or orange at the expense of the more traditional dark reds." She notes greater variety in the subject matter and composition in this phase; there is also a more marked emphasis on human figures. "The sample studied reveals an increasing emphasis on the human figure at the expense of animal representations."

It would be unwise to use the Barkly East data, which were recorded with another end in view, to construct a chronology. Nevertheless, the relevance of Vinnicombe's results to the matter in hand is important.

Most of Vinnicombe's findings are borne out by the Barkly East sample. The bright vermilions and orange colors appear exclusively in the upper layers of the superimpositions. The greatest concentration of superimpositions appears to be in the shaded polychrome phase. At least 61 percent of the cases of three-element superpositioning are composed entirely of shaded polychrome paintings. In 27 percent of the sixty-nine cases of two-element superpositioning both representations are shaded, and in a further 30 percent the upper element is shaded. In only 10 percent of the two-element superimpositions is the upper element monochrome.

Vinnicombe's finding that with the passage of time there was an increasing emphasis on human figures is relevant to the present study. If superpositioning were a random phenomenon, more human figures would thus be expected in the upper layers than in the lower. This is not the case. Only 7 percent of the human figures involved in two-element superpositioning, as defined in this paper, are in the upper layers (figure 2.4). This important point tends to confirm the conclusion reached in this paper that the pattern in superimposed paintings is not simply the result of changing conventions over a long period, but the deliberate choice of the painters.

Comparisons with the Ndedema Superimpositions

Much of the foregoing is not directly comparable with Pager's Ndedema sample owing to the different criteria employed in defining superpositioning. However, in order to render the Barkly East sample more comparable with Pager's rating, the following exercise was undertaken. The entire sample of two- and three-element superimpositions was reworked according to Pager's technique. The underlying cases of each category were then deducted from the overlying cases and the lowest category (human—49) brought to zero, according to Pager's method. The scale of ratings in table 2.4 was thus obtained.

Table 2.4.   The rating of rock paintings in the Ndedema Gorge and the Barkly East area

Barkly East		Ndedema Gorge	
Eland	95	Eland	220
Rhebuck	60	Mythical	130
Flying buck	50	Bees	125
Mythical animal	50	Indet. quadrupeds	86
Cattle	50	Rhebuck	82
Hartebeest	49	Indet. antelope	39
Feline	49	Other	30
Indet. antelope	43	Human figures	0
Antelope-man	46		
Human figures	0		

Eland and human figures are respectively top and lowest in both samples. The main difference lies in the high position occupied by the mythical creatures in the Ndedema sample. These are shown in the Barkly East sample according to the three subdivisions, flying buck, mythical animal, and antelope-man. If these subdivisions are combined and so rendered comparable with Pager's omnibus category of mythical creatures, they would receive a rating of 45 and so occupy a position third from the lower end of the list. It is not clear whether this is a result of Pager's method of recording overlappings as well as superimpositions as understood in this paper, or whether it is a real divergence. It must be borne in mind that very few examples are being considered. In the Barkly East sample there are only five mythical creatures in superpositioning, 2.4 percent of the total number of paintings in superpositioning. Pager's sample includes thirty mythical creatures, also 2.4 percent of his total sample of paintings in superimpositions. The category bees, which is rated third in Pager's list, comprises only eleven examples in superpositioning. In view of the limited number of examples in these categories caution should be exercised in interpretation.

A difficulty with this method of rating is that human figures, the lowest rating in both samples, are in fact the second most numerous after eland, accounting for 28 percent of the representations involved in superpositioning in the Barkly East sample. In Pager's sample there are more than twice as many human figures in superpositioning as eland. Although the prominence of human figures is apparent in his figure 2.2, Pager considers these absolute numbers "only a preliminary . . . before derived quantities are . . . introduced." It seems that the method obscures the importance of the human figures; the analyses of head types and elevation given previously indicate that their presence is highly significant. The combination "eland on human figure," the most common after "eland on eland" in the Barkly East sample, is an important one and should receive due consideration in an interpretation of superpositioning.

Discussion

The three assumptions noted previously have been shown to be no longer tenable. It must be concluded that the practice of superimposing one painting upon another was deliberate and that such superimpositions were governed by a set of rules that favored certain combinations and avoided others. This conclusion is incompatible with the generally held view that the paintings were executed solely for artistic reasons, that they are *art pour l'art*. An alternative explanation must be found.

Leroi-Gourhan (1968a) in his analysis of the paleolithic paintings of western Europe concluded that superpositioning was a means of pairing themes: "There are isolated cases where a later figure is actually superimposed over a considerably earlier figure, but there are many more cases where the artist himself deliberately superimposed one figure over another" (107). Ucko and Rosenfeld (1967), who entertain some reservations regarding Leroi-Gourhan's work, have suggested among other possibilities that the superimposed panels may have been "the visible expression of the energies of the particular group who 'owned' or 'used' the cave" (173–74). They also accept as proved that association was sometimes indicated in the paleolithic paintings by superpositioning (228). These views have merit in that they recognize the painters' use of animals to make symbolic statements.

Pager (1975b) quotes Trezise's (1971) observation on the Australian aborigines who believe that new representations gain magical power from the older ones on which they are superimposed. He draws a parallel between the Australian practice and the situation in South Africa, concluding that the paintings in superimpositions "were accessories to magico-religious practices" reflecting a belief "basically similar to that . . . of the Australian rock painters."

A more perceptive view of magic may be required. Magic is essentially a symbolic language, although it is frequently thought of as instrumental by those who practice it. It is a way of acting out and so saying something that is considered important, and, because the magic is so effective in saying what it does, it is thought of as being instrumental. The person performing the magical ritual may well say that he believes that his actions will bring about the state of affairs he desires. A rain dance may be thought of as causing rain to fall, but primarily it is a statement in symbolic terms of the high value placed on rain and an expression of the actor's attitude to rain. This is certainly so in the !Kung Bushman rain dance. Marshall (1962) states emphatically, "The Rain Dance is not danced as a specific rain-making ceremony" (249). One of Bleek's informants claimed that the rain medicine men seized and broke "the rain's ribs" when the wind blew from the north, the direction from which rain could be expected to come (Bleek 1932b, 327; Bleek 1933, 387; Vinnicombe 1976). Accusations of cunning will be made only by those who see the medicine man's activity exclusively in instrumental terms. The medicine man was not merely trying to impress gullible people with his powers; the fact that Bleek's informant (and presumably many others) was aware of the medicine man's technique confirms this. He was expressing the high value placed on rain.

The rain dance is one of a series of medicine dances or songs possessed by various !Kung bands; others are Sun, Giraffe, Eland, Honey, Buffalo, Mamba, Gemsbok, and Spider. Marshall (1962) comments: "The dances named for animals do not produce magic to control these animals in hunting or to prevent snake-bite, for example. The dances are named for these things because the things are vital, life-and-death things and they are strong, as the curing medicine in the music is strong." The "curing" ritual is performed on everyone, whether they are sick or not: The "strength" of these things is important to the whole group present at the dance (see also Lee 1968.). All the things for which the songs or dances are named have what Radcliffe-Brown (1952) calls high ritual value and "are either themselves objects of important common interests linking together the persons of a community or are symbolically representative of such objects" (151). The use of these symbols in the medicine dance is to make social statements and in this way to maintain and reinforce the social equilibrium; the "strength" of the symbols consists in the degree to which they make statements concerning social values. Ritual values are mostly social values: "When two or more persons have a common interest in the same object and are aware of their community of interest a social relation is established. They form, whether for a moment or for a long period, an association, and the object may be said to have social value" (Radcliffe-Brown 1952, 140). The placing of a painting on top of another may, in these terms, be regarded not merely as instrumental or vaguely "beneficial," but as a means of making a value statement. This point is further discussed later.

Levine (1957) has attempted to use the Australian aboriginal ethnographic material to provide "trial interpretations" of Paleolithic art. He suggests that "the profusely superimposed drawings are the traces of a restitution ritual. When an animal was killed, his essence was restored to nature by ritual rendering of his image at a sacred spot" (960) (see also Vinnicombe 1976). This interesting notion is also better seen in expressive rather than instrumental terms. In the South African context it would not explain the pairing of themes in the "eland on human figure" composition. The painting is executed not simply because it is believed that the act of painting or the finished product will secure the fecundity of the species concerned. The artist is making a value statement about the animal and its social and economic significance.

The syntactical rules governing superpositioning in the Barkly East sample of rock paintings that the present paper has described are only part of a larger and more complex system. This system will be discussed more fully in semiological terms in another paper. For the present, a few observations will be made on super-positioning as a mode of syntax.

The Western viewer has usually asked questions about Bushman paintings such as: What were they painted for? The answers have generally been, on the one hand, simply to delight the eye, or, on the other, to secure by magical means either success in the hunt or the fertility of the animals depicted. (These views are discussed in detail elsewhere: Lewis-Williams 1974; Vinnicombe 1972a). It would be better to eschew the instrumental bias to the question and ask: What do the paintings *say?* To move in the direction of answering this question the art must be seen, not as an isolated phenomenon, but as related to social structure, economy, mythology, religion—indeed all aspects of culture. The paintings can-not be examined in isolation any more than, say, religion. Other social institutions may be seen as saying something about social relationships and relationships between humans and nature. The paintings do the same (Lewis-Williams 1972a).

It is now suggested that the function of superpositioning was to emphasize a portion of the semantic spectrum of the representations involved, as do the other forms of syntax. Turner (1967), discussing the multivocality of symbols, observes: "Such symbols possess many senses, but contextually it may be necessary to stress one or a few of them only" (51). Superpositioning was one of the ways in which the artist stressed or isolated one of the senses of the symbols he was employing.

Of the 209 representations involved in superpositioning in the Barkly East sample, nearly 58 percent are of eland, while human beings, the next most numer-ous category, account for approximately 28 percent. Both categories have a wide semantic range. A few remarks on the eland must now suffice. The animal gener-ates three signs: a linguistic, a ritual, and an iconographic. The linguistic signifier is the animal itself as it is used in ritual; and the iconographic signifier is the representation of the antelope on the wall of a rock shelter. In semiological termi-nology the signifiers together with their signifieds (the mental concepts) consti-tute the signs (Barthes 1967).

The linguistic signifier, the Bushman word for eland, appears in acoustic con-texts. Of particular interest is its position in mythology (see Vinnicombe 1972c, 1976; Lewis-Williams 1972a) where it signifies the "eland concept," or rather part of the "eland concept" according to its relationship with the other elements in the myth. The ritual signifier is an individual member of the species. Here, too, the context determines the particular emphasis. The antelope may, for instance, be ritually hunted as a prelude to eligibility for marriage (Marshall 1959, 351) or dismembered and shared by a band, a situation in which it signifies social relationships (Marshall 1961, 238; Fourie 1928, 101; Lévi-Strauss 1966, 103–4). In these contexts, acoustic and ritual, the signifier is being manipulated to make statements, to *say* things about what the people consider to be important, rather than to *do* things or cause other things to happen. The expressive element is more important than the instrumental.

Similarly, the iconographic signifier, the painting of an eland, is manipulated in various contexts and articulated with other signifiers to make statements about important issues. The context determines the emphasized area of what is surely a very rich semantic spectrum. Superpositioning, as this chapter has tried to show by means of quantitative analysis, is not haphazard but one of the ways in which the painter isolated for particular emphasis certain areas of meaning in the "eland concept" and the concepts signified by other representations.

Superpositioning is one of the modes of syntax that establish relationships between representations and so contribute to the coherence of what it is proposed be termed reticular panels (Lewis-Williams 1972b, 61). Scenic groupings, juxtapositioning (Lewis-Williams 1972b, 59–61), and superpositioning are three forms of syntax that possibly contribute different shades of meaning to parts of densely painted reticular panels that may have evolved over a long period and make complex statements: The panel presents a network of interrelated significances.

Conclusion

Quantitative evidence from three areas bordering the Drakensberg has shown that superpositioning is not random but intentional. This conclusion has far-reaching implications: The paintings can no longer be regarded simply as a splendid efflorescence of *art pour l'art*. The painters in the Barkly East area, along with those in the Giant's Castle area and the Ndedema Gorge, took cognizance of the paintings on which they chose to execute another: Certain categories were favored as initial elements and the lower painting exercised a limiting influence on the range of subjects from which the second could be selected. The rock paintings of these regions constitute a complex signifying system concerned largely with social relationships.

Note

Extracts from "Superpositioning in a Sample of Rock-Paintings from the Barkly East District," *South African Archaeological Bulletin* 29 (1974): 93–103. Also from "The syntax and function of the Giant's Castle rock painting," *South African Archaeological Bulletin* 27 (1971): 49–65.

Retrospect

All in all, the Barkly East study showed that San rock art was a "signifying system" with a structure and rules of its own. Today, this may seem a pretty mild claim, but at the time it stirred up controversy. Willcox (1978a), still committed to the view of the art as *art pour l'art*, took issue with the statistics that I had presented, although I had been guided by Dr B. Faulds of the University of Natal, my own statistical expertise being negligible. With further professional statistical advice, I responded to Willcox (Lewis-Williams, Butler-Adam, and Sutcliffe 1979). He remained unconvinced. As it turned out, this was merely a preliminary skirmish. Far more serious debates were sparked by my attempts to go beyond the conclusion that the art was a signifying system and to try to say something about *what* the images signified for the people who made and originally looked at them. The "message" was the mystery inside the enigma.

Today, I would not advocate quantitative techniques in rock art research unless important questions can be formulated in such a way that they can be answered numerically. Before we begin the extremely arduous task of counting, we need to know what our categories mean and we need to know that an answer above, say, 60 percent will mean one thing and exclude another. Blind numerical recording undertaken in the hope that questions will present themselves once all the results have been collated is, quite simply, an enormous waste of time and energy.

Harald Pager saved a good deal of energy by compiling his numerical results from his copies, not from the paintings themselves, though, of course, making the copies in the first place was a monumental task. His book *Ndedema* (Pager 1971) contains an eighty-page inventory that gives numerical descriptions of 3,909 individual rock paintings. As far as I am aware, no one has used this compilation to answer any questions that Pager himself did not pose. This is a cautionary tale for those who hope to gather "objective" numerical data in the hope that others will be able to use them.

In the event, it was not quantitative work of this kind that led most researchers to reject art-for-the-sake-of-art and sympathetic magic but rather the persuasiveness of an alternative explanation that was founded not on numerical generalities of "the art" but on details of the images. Confronting the form and content of specific images, rather than a quantified summary of San rock art, entailed leaving numerical work behind and tackling San ethnography more vigorously. This change of direction was, arguably, the most significant innovation in the history of San rock art research.

Ethnography and Iconography 3

Against the theoretician, the observer should always have the last word, and against the observer, the native.

—CLAUDE LÉVI-STRAUSS

URING THE 1970s, I was much absorbed by the potential of San ethnography to supply the "message" of the painted images. My attempts at structural analyses of San myths in the manner of Lévi-Strauss were fruitless. Some other approach seemed to be required—but what?

I now see two experiences as crucial in determining the path that I took. The first was the uncanny experience of paging through the numinous notebooks that Wilhelm Bleek and Lucy Lloyd had compiled in the 1870s; the other was time spent in the northern Kalahari Desert with Megan Biesele, the American anthropologist and friend of the Ju/'hoansi (!Kung) San. Together, these two experiences uncovered an unexpected pattern in San belief and ritual that was to impact in a major way my thought and that was to mesh the twin cogwheels of ethnography and rock art images.

The story of the Bleek family is now well known and need not be rehearsed here in detail (Lewis-Williams 2000). The German philologist Wilhelm Heinrich Immanuel Bleek and his sister-in-law Lucy Lloyd worked in the 1870s in Cape Town with /Xam San people who came from the central parts of what was then the British Cape of Good Hope Colony. Using a phonetic script that Bleek developed, they took down by dictation twelve thousand pages of myths, accounts of rituals, personal histories, and much about daily life (e.g., Bleek and Lloyd 1911; Bleek 1924; Lewis-Williams 2000). In those verbatim texts, the voices of long-dead /Xam San people speak to us. The informants who gave all this information to Bleek and Lloyd were not themselves rock artists, but they were familiar with the practice of making both rock engravings and paintings. They also had much to say about the eland, that most frequently painted antelope, and the spirit world.

Overcautiously, I believed then that researchers should concentrate on this nineteenth-century resource because it was contemporary with the making of the last images. The new material that was coming to light as a result of the Marshall family expeditions to the northern Kalahari was, I believed, too remote in time and space to be relevant to the Drakensberg images I was studying. Then, in the early 1970s, I happened to meet Megan Biesele in Cambridge, England, and we exchanged information. We were both surprised to find that what I had been reading in the Bleek notebooks of the 1870s was remarkably similar to what was still believed and practiced in the northern Kalahari. At once, we resolved to go together to the Ju/'hoansi. Thus began an endeavor that showed that, whatever regional differences there may be between San linguistic groups, major beliefs and central rituals were virtually identical among the nineteenth-century /Xam and the twentieth-century Ju/'hoansi. The pan-San cognitive system about which McCall (1970) had written was demonstrable. To begin with, Biesele and I collaborated on a comparison of boys' first-kill eland rituals as told to us by the Ju/'hoansi and as recorded in the Bleek and Lloyd Collection (Lewis-Williams and Biesele 1978). From there I went on to comparisons of girls' puberty rituals, marriage observances, and healing practices conducted during the communal trance dance. It was in these sets of rituals and their associated beliefs, all, as numerous ethnographers had shown, central to San life and thought, that I felt the message of the art would be found. I formulated that message in a Ph.D. thesis (1977c) that, apart from a few cosmetic changes, was published intact as *Believing and Seeing: Symbolic Meanings in Southern San Rock Paintings* (Lewis-Williams 1981a).

In writing that book, I found that the key to the records of San myths and rituals lay not, as I had originally supposed, in some form of structural analysis, though they do indeed follow discernible narrative, or syntagmatic, structures (Hewitt 1986), but in significant San words and tropes, in San cosmology, and in the activities of those who transcend that cosmology, the so-called medicine people. It is at this detailed level, not at a broader structural level, that the cogwheels of ethnography and art mesh so convincingly. Explanations of San rock art are convincing in their specifics, not their generalities.

At that time, too, I was using the phrase *medicine man* to denote those San ritual specialists (though not full-time specialists) who, by entering a state of trance, transcended the tiers of their cosmos. Today, the phrase has clear disadvantages, not least of which is its sexist connotations—there were certainly female San ritual specialists who performed the same functions as the men, and I mentioned them specifically. I now think that *shaman* is a more appropriate word because it avoids the sexist and other connotations of *medicine man* and points to the world-wide occurrence of comparable specialists (for a full discussion of this problem of nomenclature, see Lewis-Williams 1992; see also Guenther 1999). In the extract that forms the bulk of this chapter, I have left *medicine man* unaltered.

The Bleek Collection is not, however, the only access we have to the beliefs and rituals of the nineteenth-century San rock painters. A remarkable article was published in 1874 in the *Cape Monthly Magazine*. In it were contributions from a young Maluti San man and from one of Bleek and Lloyd's /Xam informants. The way in which such comments should be studied is illustrated in an article published in 1980. Close lexical analysis rather than broad structuralist work yielded up significant insights.

Ethnography and Iconography: Aspects of Southern San Thought and Art

The 1874 article contained, in addition to a number of myths and tales, independent comments by two San informants on four sets of paintings (figure 3.1) copied by J. M. Orpen in what is now Lesotho. The first informant came from the area of the paintings and showed Orpen some of the sites. The other was one of the /Xam San who lived in the Cape Colony 600 km to the west: He was shown Orpen's copies by Wilhelm H. I. Bleek, the German linguist at that time living in Cape Town and studying the /Xam language. Many subsequent writers (e.g., Stow 1905, 123; Rudner and Rudner 1970, 207; Fock 1971, 94) have concluded that neither of these informants was privy to the possibly arcane concepts which seem to lie behind much of the art. Those concepts were, I argue, encoded in certain key metaphors not understood by the recorders: The nineteenth-

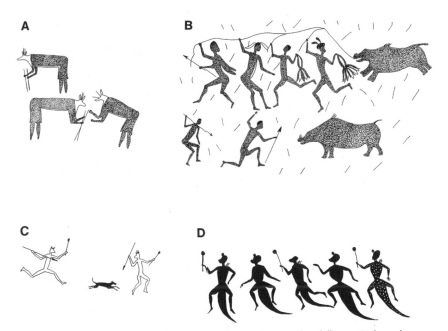

Figure 3.1.   Orpen's copies of the paintings; his captions read as follows: (A) from the cave of Medikane in the Maluti; (B) from the cave Mangolong in the Maluti; (C) from cave at source of Kraai River, District Wodehouse; (D) from the upper cave at Mangolong in the Maluti.

century record has consequently seemed an ethnographic galimatias irrelevant to an understanding of an equally obscure iconography.

One writer who recognized the extraordinary value of the seemingly confused interpretations recorded by Orpen and Bleek was Vinnicombe (1976); she wisely advocated close scrutiny: "Because Qing is the only Bushman ever questioned about rock paintings in the area . . . it is important to follow up as fully as possible every clue he left" (314). It is to that task of ethnographic detection I now attend. Those unique comments on the art are valuable for two reasons: First, they point to certain conceptual links between the extinct southern groups and the better known contemporary San of the Kalahari (Marshall 1976; Lee and deVore 1976; Tobias 1978), who speak a different language and do not paint; and, even more important, they provide evidence that at least some of the rock paintings were not, as Arbousset (1846) believed, merely "innocent playthings" (252), but, as W. H. I. Bleek (1874) concluded, "an attempt, however imperfect, at a truly artistic conception of the ideas which most deeply moved the Bushman mind, and filled it with religious feelings" (13). By elucidating the informants' interpretations of the paintings I try to show that Bleek was essentially right in his belief that the art was concerned with "religious" concepts; but the connection between those religious ideas and the art lay in a San ritual which neither Bleek nor Orpen fully understood.

The Informants and the Comments

The "Qing" mentioned by Vinnicombe was Orpen's informant who, at the time Orpen employed him as a guide, was a young hunter attached to Nqashe, a son of Morosi, the Sotho chief. Before meeting Orpen, Qing had "never seen a white man but in fighting" (Orpen 1874, 2). Nevertheless, he overcame his initial reticence and not only gave Orpen a valuable collection of tales, but actually guided him to some of the rock paintings. Indeed, it was by enquiring about the paintings that Orpen started his work with Qing. Interviews were conducted by means of interpreters; the language Qing knew best besides his own was "that of the 'Baputi,' a hybrid dialect between Basoto and Amazizi" (1874, 3). Orpen's reference to "different translators" may, however, imply more than one stage of translation: It is possible that San concepts were translated first into Baputi, then into Xhosa, and finally into English. In any event, it does not seem as if Qing was speaking San to a San interpreter.[1]

The Bleek collection is generally more satisfactory because we have not merely English paraphrases, but the original verbatim /Xam text with a literal translation. The /Xam informant to whom W. H. I. Bleek showed the Orpen copies was Diä!kwain, who lived with the Bleek family from December 1873 to March 1874 and then again from June 1874 to March 1876. Diä!kwain's ability to speak a little Dutch and his other name, David Haesar, show that, unlike Qing, he had some contact with white settlers; indeed, one of his narratives suggests that he and his wife had lived for a while with a Dutch farmer (D. F. Bleek 1932, 328), but this appears to have been only a brief sojourn, for most of his contributions to the Bleek collection describe the "nomadic" life of the /Xam bands. Diä!kwain commented more than once on Orpen's copies of the paintings (W. H. I. Bleek 1875, 18). W. H. I. Bleek first showed them to him on June 21, 1874 (B. XXVII. 2540–2608; D. F. Bleek 1933a, b, 375–76), before he had received (and possibly been influenced by) Qing's interpretations. Bleek died in 1875, but Lucy Lloyd, his sister-in-law and collaborator, showed Diä!kwain them again in 1876 and he offered further explanatory remarks.

The copies of the paintings shown to Diä!kwain were Orpen's originals, now preserved in the South African Library, Cape Town. Figure 3.1, on which I have lettered the four sets of paintings, is a black-and-white reduction of the original colored version. The painting which elicited most comment from both infor-mants was the one from Mangolong or, as it is now known, Sehonghong (B); it has subsequently been reproduced many times (e.g., van Reenen 1920, 31; Frobe-nius 1931, fig. 4; Willcox 1963, fig. 9; Brentjes 1969, fig. 6). Most subsequent reproductions omit the important short strokes, as did Orpen's own publisher in 1874.[2] I begin with the comments on this painting because they point to rituals, concepts, and metaphors that must be understood before the remarks on the even more curious antelope-headed figures (figure 3.1A and C) can be clarified.

Orpen (1874) recorded Qing's comments thus:

> That *animal* which the men are catching is a *snake* (!). They are holding out charms to it, and catching it with a long reim. They are all under water, and those strokes are things growing under water. They are peo-ple spoilt by the—dance, because their noses bleed. Cagn gave us the song of this dance, and told us to dance it, and people would die from it, and he would give charms to raise them again. (10, emphasis in original)

Bleek's paraphrased version of Diä!kwain's response is as follows:

> The paintings from the cave Mangolong represent rainmaking. We see here a water thing, or water cow, which, in the lower part, is discovered by a Bushman, behind whom a Bushwoman stands. This Bushman then beckons to others to come and help him. They then charm the animal, and attach a rope to its nose—and in the upper part of the picture it

is shown as led by the Bushmen, who desire to lead it over as large a tract of country as they can, in order that the rain should extend as far as possible,—their superstition being that wherever this animal goes, rain will fall. The strokes indicate rain. Of the Bushmen who drag the water cow, two are men (sorcerers), of whom the chief one is nearest to the animal. In their hands are boxes made of tortoise (!khu) shell (containing charmed boochoo) from which strings, perhaps ornamented with beads, are dangling down. These are said to be of Kafir manufacture. The two men are preceded by two Bushwomen, of whom one wears a cap on her head. (12)

The fundamental point of agreement is that both informants thought the Sehonghong painting had some connection with rain or water. Vinnicombe (1976, 336) explains the apparent contradiction between the two interpretations by remarking that the "Bushman language has but one word for both water and rain" and that Qing probably meant "in the rain" rather than "under water." This was true of the /Xam language, but we cannot be sure that the same was true in the Malutis, because the Bleek collection contains evidence which suggests that there were some linguistic differences between the two areas (D. F. Bleek 1927, 56). Certainly, the !Kung and other San groups use different words for water and rain (Biesele, personal communication). In any case, Orpen says that the interviews were conducted in Baputi, not in a San language. A more likely explanation is that Qing was referring to an initial apprehension of the rain-animal under the surface of the water, while Diä!kwain saw the scene as representing a later stage when the captured creature was being led across the veld in a successfully induced rainstorm. This reading accommodates Qing's explicit remark that the "strokes are things growing under the water."

An apparently more serious disagreement concerns the identity of the animal that the men appear to be leading. Qing said that it was a snake—at which point Orpen understandably adds a parenthetical exclamation mark. More reasonably, Diä!kwain identified it as a "water thing or water cow." Various creatures such as snakes, tortoises, fish, swallows, and frogs were said to be the personified Rain's "things" (L.V. 6. 4385 rev.; D. F. Bleek, 1933a and b, 301); the "water cow" was also one. The identification of the creature as a snake might therefore have arisen through some confusion over the multiple translation and explanation of a phrase such as "the Rain's thing." On the other hand, the interpreter may well have been substituting his own Sotho or Xhosa belief about a large serpent dwelling in rivers.[3]

There was no disagreement concerning the actions being performed by the men. Qing said the men were catching the animal with a long *reim* (thong) and to accomplish this they were holding out "charms" to it. Similarly, Diä!kwain said they were "charming" the animal and attaching a rope to its nose. In his later account, given after Bleek's death, he added that the thing being held by the first man from the right is like the thing smelled by medicine men "when they are practising sorcery" (D. F. Bleek 1935, 14). Such items, said Diä!kwain, were tortoise shells containing *buchu* (aromatic herbs), thought to pacify the "angry" rain. Both informants, then, agreed that the animal was being "charmed" so that a rope could be attached to it. The /Xam informant went on to explain how it was subsequently led over a wide tract of country to cause the rain to fall; Qing did not say what they did with the creature once it had been apprehended.

Diä!kwain identified two of the four men leading the rain-animal as "sorcerers" and "water's medicine men" (D. F. Bleek 1933a and b, 376–77). The /Xam recognized four overlapping categories of medicine men: There were the curers known as *!gi:ten* (sing. *!gi.xa*), the medicine men who "possessed" and had control of game (⊙*pwaiten-ka !gi:ten*), those who used their powers to cause harm (//*xi:ka !gi:ten*), and those who performed the rain-making rituals (*!khwa-ka !gi:ten*). The Bleek collection contains a good deal about the *!khwa-ka !gi:ten* and Diä!kwain identified these people in a painting from the Western Cape Province (Lewis-Williams 1977a).

Qing, in his more enigmatic explanation of the men leading the rain-animal said, "They are people spoilt by the ____ dance, because their noses bleed." This curious statement requires careful consideration because it contains the key to understanding much of the art.

Orpen says he did not record the San name for the dance, but he gives the Sotho for it as "Moqoma," a word Arbousset (1846, 247) translates as "the dance of *blood*." The epistaxis (nasal bleeding) to which Qig referred and which gave the dance its Sotho name is frequently depicted in the paintings. He went on to describe such a "dance of blood":

> Cagn gave us the song of this dance, and told us to dance it, and people would die from it, and he would give them charms to raise them again. It is a circular dance of men and women, following each other, and it is danced all night. Some fall down; some become as if mad and sick; blood runs from the noses of others whose charms are weak, and they eat charm medicine, in which there is burnt snake powder. When a man is sick this dance is danced round him, and the dancers put both hands under their arm-pits, and press their hands on him, and when he coughs the initiated put out their hands and receive what has injured him—secret things (Orpen 1874, 10).

This account distinguishes two types of curing dance. Qing first described the *general* curing dance during which, it is very probable, all present were "cured" of ills both known and unknown as evil was exorcised from the entire band. The *special* curing dance, on the other hand, was directed toward a specific person known to be physically ill.

/Xam ethnography contains descriptions of similar ecstatic dances,[4] but the /Xam also used nasal blood in special curing rituals which, it seems, did not include dancing. Such curings involved sniffing out of the patient's body what was believed to be harming him, a practice known as *sū* (which Lloyd, perhaps following Campbell [1815, 316], translates as "snoring"). After the medicine man had sniffed out the evil, he sneezed out the "harm's things" which were said to resemble arrows, little sticks,[5] or various animals: As he did this he suffered a nasal hemorrhage and rubbed his blood on the patient in the belief that its smell would keep evil things away (D. F. Bleek 1935, 20, 34). Descriptions of /Xam "snoring" do not mention the use of sweat from the armpits, but they did use sweat in other ritual contexts in which it seems to have been thought to have restorative properties (D. F. Bleek 1936, 149; see also W. H. I. Bleek and Lloyd 1911, 27; D. F. Bleek 1924, 49).

While the /Xam medicine man was curing, he experienced a rising sensation, trembled, sweated, bled from the nose, and sometimes behaved quite violently. This pattern of /Xam curing behavior together with Qing's description of the Maluti dance suggests very strongly that the southern medicine men practiced a type of trance performance essentially similar to that experienced by contemporary !Kung (Marshall 1969; R. B. Lee 1967; 1968; and Katz 1976b). The !Kung medicine man gradually works himself up into a state of trembling and sweating. When he approaches trance, he feels a rising sensation which he ascribes to the "boiling" of his medicine (*n/om*); as he enters deep trance, he falls to the ground, sometimes executing a somersault. Then, in a more controlled trance, he takes sweat from his armpits and rubs it on those whom he is curing. The numerous similarities between !Kung trance performance and the activities of the southern medicine men suggest that Qing's identification of the figures leading the rain-animal as men who participated in the "dance of blood" means that the rain-making rituals were performed by medicine men who practiced trance performance.

This far-reaching conclusion is further confirmed by a metaphor common to the !Kung, the /Xam, and the Maluti San. Qing said that "Cagn," the chief figure of both the Maluti and the /Xam mythology, had given them the song of the dance and had told them that "people would die from it, and that he would give charms to raise them again." I believe that "die" does not here refer to physical death: It is a metaphor for entrance into the altered state of consciousness of trance—as it still is among the !Kung (R. B. Lee 1968, 40; see also Lewis 1971, 58). The same metaphor was used by the /Xam: Diä!kwain, in his second response to Orpen's copy, said quite explicitly that people "die" "of sorcery" and that they are then given substances (probably *buchu*) to smell—no doubt the "charms to raise them again" of which Qing spoke. In an account not given in response to Orpen's copies, Diä!kwain again referred to the catching of rain-animals and spoke of a medicine man's heart making a sound like rain, and, "dying," leaving him and going into a waterhole where the water is "alive" (L.V. 19. 5506–5530; D. F. Bleek 1935, 32); he added that "this is the water from which sorcerers are wont to fetch water-bulls." If "dying" again refers to entrance into trance, then possibly the ritual of "leading out" the rain-animal was, like the curing, accomplished while the medicine men were in such a trance.

Diä!kwain's statement that the medicine man enters a waterhole when he "dies" also should be interpreted metaphorically. This is particularly suggested by a !Kung medicine man who explained that he learned to become a curer while under water, and that, when in trance, he "fought the water for a long, long time" (Biesele 1980). It seems that being under water is recognized as analogous to the experience of trance: the struggle, gasping for breath, sounds in the ears, a sense of weightlessness, inhibited movement, affected vision, and final loss of consciousness. This view explains Diä!kwain's otherwise incredible description of the man entering the waterhole and the subsequent capture of the rain-animal. The medicine man "died" (entered trance) and was then immersed in the "water" (trance experience) in which the apprehension of the imaginary rain-animal was accomplished.[6]

Other aspects of San trance experience are better understood as altered vision. In some cases such "visions" seem to have no relation at all to reality: !Kung medicine men told Marshall (1965, 270; 1962, 241) that they had "seen" the lesser God, //Gauwa, as "a gray mist" or a grotesque manikin covered with yellow hair; others claim that when in trance they "see" the animals after whom their *n/om* (supernatural potency) is named standing in the darkness beyond the campfire. A man who, for instance, has eland *n/om* believes he attracts eland to the place of the dance and that he is able to "see" them; similarly, a medicine woman who has elephant *n/om* speaks of leaving the dance, going to an elephant, and being cradled in its tusks (Biesele, pers. comm.). Other "visions" seem to be alterations of real objects: A !Kung medicine man told Lee (1967) that when he was in a trance he saw "all the people like very small birds, the whole place will be spinning around." Katz (1976b, 86) believes that such men have "richer fantasies" and are more "inner directed" than those who do not regularly experience trance. This heightened sensitivity may account also for the "waking hallucinations" that medicine men sometimes experience and in which the great god may appear to give them *n/om* (Marshall 1965, 271).

Persuasive evidence that the "leading out" was at least sometimes an hallucination of this kind comes from a rock painting now preserved in the Natal Museum, Pietermaritzburg (Vinnicombe 1976, fig. 240). It depicts a scene very similar to the one copied by Orpen: A number of men hold out "charms" to a rain-animal and lead it by a rope attached to its nose, but in this painting some of the men are clearly bleeding from the nose. The painting recalls a statement by another of Bleek's informants that a /Xam medicine man with control of clouds and lightning "sneezed" and suffered epistaxis while he was exercising his powers (W. H. I. Bleek and Lloyd 1911, 115). Both the art and the ethnography, then, confirm the view that the rainmaking rituals described by Qing and Diä!kwain might, at least on some occasions, have been the hallucinations of trance and not an actual ritual performed with a real animal of whatever species.

Certainly Lloyd seems to have suspected that she was not hearing about "real" events. One of the /Xam words meaning "to lead out" a rain-animal was ≠xamma. At first she translated this as "work magic" (B. XXVII. 2545) and "conjure" (B. XXVII. 2546), but in another published version D. F. Bleek has given this word as "fetch" (D. F. Bleek 1933a and b, 376, 381), perhaps because of a variety of other more prosaic contexts. Lloyd translated another word, //kai, as "by magic lead out" (L.V. 13.4990), but in a different account of rainmaking she gave the same word simply as "called forth" (D. F. Bleek 1936, 134–35); the *A Bushman Dictionary*, however, retains the magical connotations (D. F. Bleek 1956, 550). Lloyd and D. F. Bleek were evidently unsure about the nature of the rainmaking rituals. A highly significant note by W. H. I. Bleek shows that he, at any rate, did not think the "leading out" was a "literal" account, but that "the sense is apparently the reverse" (B. XXVII. 2540 rev.). It was essentially this impression that led him to declare that the paintings "are evidently either of a mythological character, or illustrative of Bushman customs and superstitions" (W. H. I. Bleek 1874, 12), but he did not know that one of those "Bushman customs" was trance performance.

The metaphors and beliefs which I have so far described suggest that the southern informants' reports of "death" journeys beneath the water, and the capture of a fantastic rain-animal should all be seen as accounts of trance experience rather than other events. At least some of the paintings of rain-animals therefore probably record hallucinations of rain medicine men in trance. This thesis also helps to clarify remarks on the paintings of men with antelope heads (figure 3.1A and C),[7] a widespread feature of the southern San iconography that has been thought to depict masked hunters (How 1962, 20, 43) or spirits of the dead (Pager 1975c, 62; Woodhouse 1974, 17). I now turn to the informants' comments on these paintings.

Qing's response to the therianthropes was characteristically anfractuous: "They were men who had died and now lived in rivers, and were *spoilt at the same time as the elands* and by the dances of which you have seen paintings" (Orpen 1874, 2, his emphasis). The complexity of this statement suggests that it combines responses to persistent questioning on a topic which Orpen did not understand; indeed, he admits to having made his "fragmentary" material "consecutive" (Orpen 1874, 3). Vinnicombe (1976, 316), not unreasonably, takes the first part of the sentence to mean that the therianthropes depict medicine men "who, in the form of therianthropic figures, lived under water when they died." There is, moreover, support for this reading in the /Xam ethnography which shows that medicine men were sometimes addressed after their death (D. F. Bleek 1933a and b, 304–5; 1935, 35–37), and also that the /Xam believed in "water maidens" (Leeuwenberg 1970; Lewis-Williams 1977a); but, if Qing's remark is considered together with other statements by him, a different reading is suggested. Not knowing anything about trance, Orpen could well have mistaken the related metaphors of "death" and "under water" for separate and literal explanations; so the "under water" experience of trance became "lived in rivers" after death.

Qing went on, probably in a further explanatory response, to say that the antelope-headed figures had been "spoilt . . . by the dances." This same puzzling phrase he used to describe the medicine men in the rain-animal scene, adding that they were "spoilt" "because their noses bleed." Stow (1905) takes this to mean "ruined . . . by too frequent indulgence in these somewhat licentious performances" (120). "Spoilt" is used a number of times by Orpen and, although it sometimes appears to have connotations of harm (Vinnicombe 1976, 233, 320), there is a more plausible explanation in this particular context. The !Kung use one word, *kxwia*, to mean both "spoil" and "to enter deep trance" (Biesele, personal communication). It seems, therefore, that "spoil," like "death" and "under water," is another trance metaphor common to both southern and northern groups. The sentence can, then, be understood as a series of synonymous metaphors; Orpen, believing Qing's translated replies to be literal and different in meaning, made them "consecutive" and so fabricated the complex and misleading conflation I have tried to unravel. The sentence is a threefold metaphorical statement: The therianthropes do not depict mythical, subaquatic people on whom no further information was obtained, but medicine men who have "died" or been "spoilt" in trance (they were "*spoilt* . . . by the dances") and whose experience is analogous to being under water.

In further remarks on the therianthropic paintings (probably C rather than A because he names only two men), Qing again insisted that they lived "under water," naming the men as Haqwé and Canaté. If these names refer to mythical personages, as has been generally supposed, it is strange that they do not feature in any of the tales; Orpen would surely have asked Qing for such tales to add to the collection that forms the bulk of his paper. Moreover, only two names would not account for the groups featuring larger numbers of therianthropes—as does the Medikane painting (figure 3.1A). If we accept that the therianthropes depict medicine men, it is possible that the two names refer, not to members of a class of mythical people, but to two specific medicine men known personally to him and who he believed were depicted among the therianthropes.

In any event, he said that these men with rhebok's heads "tame" elands and snakes. I suggest that "tame" is yet another confused translation of a San concept and that Qing meant "controlled" or "possessed." Although we have no further information on this point from the Maluti San, we know that the /Xam thought certain medicine men "possessed" (/ki) specific animals. This notion also incorporated ideas of control because a medicine man who, for instance, "possessed" springbok could control their movements. There is further evidence in the Bleek collection that a man could "possess" more than one creature. It is therefore likely that Qing was identifying the paintings as two medicine men who "possessed" (rather than "tamed") eland and snakes and who, in the "death" of trance, were changed by their own and their companions' trance vision into therianthropes with characteristics of one of their "possessed" creatures. As with the !Kung, the "possession" of an animal probably designated that animal as the medicine man's source of mystical power, which boiled up in him as he entered trance.

Qing's observation on a relationship between the therianthropes and eland and snakes explains many otherwise obscure paintings. One (figure 3.2) portrays four men dancing in the frequently depicted bending forward posture (see also figure 3.1A), while other figures clap. To the left is a therianthrope with a very distinct eland head and horns; it also has hooves and bleeds from the nose. It is very possibly a medicine man in trance and fused with the animal he possesses, in this case eland. Also bleeding from the nose, but more profusely, is an antelope-headed serpent which protrudes from a natural step in the rock face. I suggest that this curious depiction is also a medicine man in trance, in this instance one who "possessed" both snakes and eland and therefore displays characteristics of both these creatures with trance blood. A close relationship between eland and men is even more remarkably suggested by a painting near Giant's Castle (figure 3.3). A single man dances in front of a similarly "dancing" eland; the head of the

Figure 3.2.   Dance group: Burley II, Barkly East, Cape Province.

man tapers off into a long white streamer comparable with the depiction of the eland's horns.

These and many other paintings which associate eland with trance performance imply that this antelope played a prominent role in the activities of the Maluti medicine men, perhaps even more than it does today among the !Kung (Lewis-Williams 1981a). The eland is, indeed, the most prominent component of the rock art: It was painted more frequently than any other animal and more care was lavished on its depiction (Maggs 1967; Pager 1971; Vinnicombe 1976; Lewis-Williams 1972, 1974). It was also believed to possess exceptional supernatural potency (D. F. Bleek 1932a and b, 237) and to be Cagn's (/Kaggen in Bleek's orthography) favorite creature (D. F. Bleek 1924, 10–12). So, when Qing said that the antelope-headed figures had been "*spoilt at the same time as the elands* and by the dances," he probably meant that the medicine men in trance exploited the eland's power as they danced and that this relationship is a feature of the art.[8]

Qing's interpretation of the therianthropes as medicine men was unequivocally and clearly confirmed by Diä!kwain. Referring to both the Medikane and Kraai River paintings (figure 3.1A and C), he said that the antelope-headed figures depicted "sorcerers," yet suggested that the therianthropic features were not the result of trance vision, as I believe Qing thought, but rather that the men were literally "wearing gemsbok horns" (W. H. I. Bleek 1874, 13). This apparent difference of opinion requires some clarification.

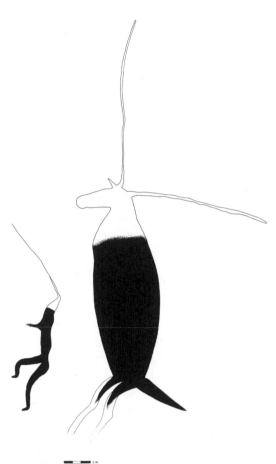

Figure 3.3.   Dancing man and eland: Upper Ncibidwane, Giant's Castle, Natal.

Although the notion of "possession" is frequently found in the /Xam ethnography, there is no mention of therianthropes as such. There is, however, a clear statement that a medicine man named !Gvrriten-dé, who "possessed" springbok, wore a cap made of a springbok scalp and sewn so that the ears stood up (D. F. Bleek 1936, 144). A springbok medicine woman, Tãnõ!khauken, believed that springbok would follow her when she was wearing such a cap (D. F. Bleek 1935, 46). Caps with antelope ears are frequently depicted in the art; Vinnicombe's (1976, fig. 239) accurate copy of the Sehonghong group (figure 3.1B) shows that three of the men are probably wearing such caps. In addition to caps with ears Diä!kwain also spoke of people performing a gemsbok medicine dance while wearing caps with the horns of small gemsbok (Stow 1930, pls. 13 and 14; L.V. 10.4754 rev.). It seems that, for both the /Xam and the Maluti San, these caps with antelope ears or horns were often symbols of the intimate relationship between a medicine man and his "possessed" creature, a relationship which the Maluti medicine men further perceived through trance vision in the fusion of man and animal and then depicted in the form of theriantropes. I do not say that the /Xam did not experience hallucinations similar to those of the Maluti San, but simply that they tended to express the concept of "possession" more concretely. On the other hand, I do not believe the more literal (and simpler) interpretation applies to the Maluti painted therianthropes, because many of the paintings show distinct antelope hooves as well as heads, and still others show the process of "tranceformation" in a more advanced stage: Some of these figures are half-man and half-animal and could not possibly depict disguised human beings.[9]

There is clearer disagreement between the informants' responses to the paintings from the upper cave at Mangolong (figure 3.1D). Diälkwain seems to have believed these tailed figures to be part of the Sehonghong rainmaking scene and said they depict Bantu-speaking people assisting in the ritual. I suggest that Daïkwain, confused by the juxtaposition of the Sehonghong and Mangolong paintings in Orpen's copy, was speculating and drawing on his knowledge of San performing rainmaking rites for Bantu speakers (Report 1883; Stanford 1910, 439; Callaway 1969, 10).

Qing, possibly because he had seen the originals in the rock shelters, did not think these tailed men were part of the rainmaking scene; he classed them with the antelope-headed figures who "live under water" and who "tame elands and snakes." According to my reading, he was, therefore, saying that the tailed figures were also medicine men. Support for this view comes from the few surviving Batwa San of Lake Chrissie, a southern group who came originally from the Malutis. A Batwa man wishing to become a medicine man plunged into a deep pool and seized a large snake "as big as a python." After he had killed and skinned the snake, he performed a public dance with the skin. During the dance, to which any Batwa had a right to come, the neck of the skin was tied to his head, while the rest formed a weird train behind him (Potgieter 1955, 30).

We cannot be sure if the capture of the large snake was an actual occurrence; it might have been another trance experience. Either way, the underwater capture of the snake recalls very strongly the "taming" of "snakes and elands" that Qing mentioned, and, indeed, the capture of the rain-animal itself and Qing's apparent identification of it as a snake. It seems possible, then, that these tailed figures are not Bantu-speaking assistants as Diälkwain assumed, but medicine men who "possessed" snakes and had associations with water very much like the /Xam and Batwa medicine men. Nevertheless, whether Diä!kwain or Qing was right, the tailed figures do not form a significant part of San iconography; I know of only one similar painting (Smits 1973, 33). Therianthropes, on the other hand, are a common and widely distributed feature of the art about which the informants could more reasonably be supposed to know.

Conclusion

Apart from the nugatory disagreement about the tailed men, the overall unanimity between the informants' responses to all the paintings shown to them was that they depicted the rituals of medicine men and the experience of trance perform-ance. This unanimity suggests very strongly that the comments are reliable; despite Diä!kwain's ignorance of the original paintings and the unsatisfactory way in which Qing's views were recorded, both independently communicated to their respective interlocutors some of the concepts which inform the art. What may at first glance seem to be confused ethnographic nonsense "of little value except to indicate caution in our own interpretations" (Rudner and Rudner 1970, 207) is, in fact, comprehensible in the light of the San concepts I have described. Once the key metaphors in which those concepts were expressed are understood, much that is puzzling in both the ethnography and the iconography is clarified: Many of the paintings are vivid depictions of ecstatic religious experience. In the Kala-hari the !Kung listen respectfully and with interest to the medicine men who are keen to communicate their trance experiences; each account is received as a revela-tion of what is really going on in the other world (Biesele, personal communica-tion). For the southern San the art was probably part of this revelation and was executed either by the medicine men themselves or by painters to whom they described their experiences. Indeed, Dornan (1917) was told of a man who was both a painter and "a great rain doctor" (49). There is, however, no evidence that the art played any role in the rainmaking rituals (Lewis-Williams 1997b).

It seems, then, that, despite linguistic differences (Westphal 1971; Jenkins and Tobias 1977; Trail 1978) and wide separation in time and space, southern San and modern !Kung beliefs about trance were remarkably similar. Other simi-larities in belief and ritual can also be cited: They concern girls' puberty rituals (Lewis-Williams 1981), first-kill rituals (Lewis-Williams and Biesele 1978), as well as beliefs about n/om and n!ow (Vinnicombe 1972b: 199–201). Biesele (1975, I: 5) has also shown that the linguistic divisions of present-day Kalahari San should not be thought of as impervious barriers. McCall (1970) was right when, at the end of his discussion of the relationship between hunting and mating, he suggested that certain concepts are "pan-Bushman or nearly so" (18). Certainly, there is growing evidence that the nineteenth-century southern San shared many concepts with the modern Kalahari San, and it is therefore probably legitimate to use the northern material to explicate the southern in certain clearly defined areas. That limited, if voluminous, southern San ethnography cannot now be extended in any other way: The people whose beliefs and customs it records are no more.

A second and even more important kind of relationship—between ethnography and iconography—has also been established. As I have tried to show in this article, one can illumine the other to give an understanding of the complexity and subtlety of southern San thought and its expression in the rock art. The ethnography and the iconography are interrelated expressions of a single belief system (Lewis-Williams 1981a). Taken together these two sources can provide a cognitive dimension to the final stages of the southern African Later Stone Age in a way hitherto thought impossible.

The mutually confirmatory comments given by Qing and Diä!kwain show that many of the paintings evoked an experience linking humans with the invisible and mystical world. Unlike the ephemeral dance, which afforded humans access to the beyond, the paintings remained constantly on view to affirm the reality of the otherworld and to proclaim the ultimate values of San society.

Notes

I thank Megan Biesele, David Hammond-Tooke, Tom Huffman, Patrick Pearson, John Pfeiffer, and Tom Volman for kindly commenting on an early draft of this article; the director of the South African Public Library for permission to reproduce the Orpen copies; the librarian, Jagger Library, University of Cape Town, for permission to quote from the Bleek collection; and Arlene Guslandi and Wendy Cullinan for typing successive drafts of this paper.

1. By modern anthropological standards the manner in which the Maluti material was collected is unsatisfactory and may have contributed to Orpen's belief that the tales were "fragmentary"—a condition which he also ascribes (probably erroneously) to Qing's being a young man and therefore knowing the stories imperfectly.

2. A modern and more accurate tracing has been published by Vinnicombe 1976, 37; also in Smits 1973, 32.

3. Schmidt (1979, 216) argues, on diffusionist grounds, that the serpent is the older of the two beliefs.

4. Borcherds 1861, 115; D. F. Bleek 1935, II; see also Barrow 1801, I: 283–84.

5. A belief held by the Kalahari !Kung (Marshall, personal communication).

6. Some informants on the other hand (but not contradictorily) seem to have thought of the "underwater" experience more as out-of-body travel while in trance. The /Xam believed that when a man entered trance his spirit left his body and traveled freely even under water;

they called such supernatural journeys /xāu. Very similar beliefs about trance journeys are still held by the !Kung (Biesele 1975, II: 151–74).

7. Also Frobenius 1931, II: 22; How 1962, 24; Woodhouse 1968, 38; D. N. Lee and Woodhouse 1970, 112. Cf. Smits 1973, fig. 4.

8. The second most frequently and carefully painted antelope is the rhebok, and it is significant that Qing spoke of "men and rhebok heads." Indeed, many of the painted therianthropes do have rhebok rather than eland heads: In the paintings shown to Qing, one group (figure 3.1A) appears to have eland heads, while the heads of the men in the other group (figure 3.1C), though more difficult to identify, may well be rhebok. But it is also true that Orpen may have influenced Qing's remarks with a leading question because he "commenced by asking him what the pictures of men with rhebok heads meant." Nevertheless, it seems that the multitudinous paintings of both eland and rhebok are probably symbols of (among many other things) the medicine man's access to the potency which lies at the heart of his religious experience.

9. Willcox 1960, fig. 34; Lewis-Williams 1972b, fig. 9; see also Pager 1975a.

From "Ethnography and Iconography: Aspects of Southern San Thought and Art," *Man* (N.S.) 15: 467–482.

Retrospect

In 1980 (and more acutely today), I realized that far more can be said about the texts that this article analyzes, but the interpretations given remain valid, as far as they go. The statements provided by Qing and paraphrased by Orpen bring together three key elements in southern San thought: (1) the shamanistic dance; (2) eland, that potency-filled and most frequently painted antelope; and (3) paintings of "nonreal" antelope-headed (and often hooved) therianthropic figures. Further, transformations of shamans into partial or entire animals took place by means of the process that Qing called "spoiling," as Kalahari San communities still call it. This process was set in motion by "the dances of which you have seen paintings"—that is, by the healing, medicine, or trance dance. It is important to remember that the "spoiling" was done by the dances, not by physical death, as some writers have thought.

This nexus of San notions (eland, dance, rock paintings) should not have come as a surprise to researchers: The twentieth-century ethnographers had shown, and in the twenty-first century ethnographers continue to show, beyond reasonable doubt that these notions and, especially, the ritual dance are overwhelmingly important in San life and thought.

Still, in 1980, when this article was published, I did not appreciate the centrality of the tripartite conceptual nexus. I believed that the southern San rock art of the Drakensberg dealt, perhaps equally, with girls' puberty rituals, boys' first-kill rites, marriage observances, and, to be sure, the nexus (Lewis-Williams 1981a). Then it began to dawn on me that I had no difficulty in finding paintings to illustrate the nexus, but I could find none that pointed unequivocally to the three rites of passage. True, I had *one* painting that seemed to depict the eland bull dance performed at a girl's puberty (Lewis-Williams 1981a, fig. 10), but subsequent discoveries of comparable paintings have led me to believe that it too depicts a curing dance. I was allowing preconceived theoretical notions about the polysemy of images and the apparent diversity of San rock art itself to guide my thinking. Close contact with the art did not confirm my theory and hypotheses.

As a result of this sobering experience, I came to accept a notion of "focused polysemy" that I derived from Victor Turner's work among the Ndembu of Zambia (e.g., Turner 1967). The eland is demonstrably a polysemic symbol for the San in that it refers to girls' puberty rituals (they perform the eland bull dance), boys' first-kill rituals (they try to kill an eland and use parts of it in subsequent rituals), marriage rites (a bride is anointed with eland fat), and the healing dance (eland potency is greatly desired). But it does not follow that all these ritual contexts are equally represented in the art. *The art is itself a specific context in which the eland appears.* Following Turner, I argue that the context of an image of an eland (the rock face, the paint used to make it, adjacent images; see subsequent chapters) focuses on a particular segment of the antelope's semantic spectrum, that is, on its potency and transformative power in the context of the dance and other shamanistic circumstances. The other associations of the polysemic eland symbol are present as a penumbra and radiate much of the power and resonance of a painted image, but they are peripheral to the central focus of shamanistic transcendence that the context provides. San rock art images of eland are thus polysemic, but in a focused way.

Mystery Wrapped in Myth 4

Science must begin with myths, and with the criticism of myths.

—KARL POPPER

We all of us, grave or light, get our thoughts entangled in metaphors and act fatally on the strength of them.

—GEORGE ELIOT, *MIDDLEMARCH*

RYING TO GRAPPLE with the actual San words and tropes used by informants in their recounting of beliefs led to an approach to the larger and potentially confusing context of mythology. Writers on southern African rock art had long referred to myth and suspected that the meanings of many images would eventually be found in myths. Some believed that paintings illustrated myths rather in the way that pictures illustrate a child's storybook, but they could find no convincing matches between specific tales and paintings. To be sure, there are many paintings of eland and also myths dealing with the creation of the first eland, but are they in anyway related? And, if so, how?

Despite this sort of problem, mythology is an obvious source to which to turn when confronted with the problem of hidden beliefs. Even if no direct link between particular myths and the art can be found, it cannot but be beneficial to glean from the myths all we can about San belief and cosmology in general. Perhaps, as it did indeed turn out to be the case, the issues with which some, by no means all, myths dealt were also evident in the art, though not by what Battiss called "illustration." As we shall see, fundamental metaphors and cosmological beliefs feature in both myths and paintings, though neither mode of expression is directly posited on, or derived from, the other. This, it seems to me, is a key point.

As I have already indicated, my own assault on San mythology was, at least initially, fruitless. My principal sources were two books of material selected from the Bleek and Lloyd Collection (for more on this collection see Deacon and Dowson 1996; Schmidt 1973, 1989; Lewis-Williams 2000). In 1911, Lucy Lloyd published *Specimens of Bushman Folklore* (Bleek and Lloyd 1911), a substantial and erudite book that included a number of tales and other texts together with the original /Xam language phonetic transcriptions. Just over a decade later, Dorothea Bleek published *The Mantis and His Friends* (1924), a slim volume in which she gathered English translations of a number of tales that feature the Mantis— /Kaggen, the trickster-deity of the /Xam. Her title to /Kaggen's picaresque adventures suggests a book for children rather than a serious attempt to understand profound, life-supporting myths. In her introduction, she betrayed her low estimate of the tales: "The Bushman . . . remains all his life a child, averse to work, fond of play, of painting, singing, dancing, dressing up and acting, above all things fond of hearing and telling stories" (Bleek 1924, unnumbered page). Despite Dorothea's view, *The Mantis and His Friends* and *Specimens of Bushman Folklore* do indeed hold the answers to many of the larger questions about San rock art, though what we seek to know is by no means on the surface of the tales. We need to go beyond the English translations to the actual /Xam words as Bleek and Lloyd took them down in their notebooks.

By the 1950s and early 1960s, Malinowski and many others having published insightful accounts of mythology, it was evident that there must be more to the tales of /Kaggen than Dorothea Bleek had suspected, though rock art researchers, largely unfamiliar with advances in social anthropology and folklore studies, remained convinced that the "simplicity" of the tales was paralleled by the "simplicity" of the paintings as an art of illustration. It was, nevertheless, evident that there are, by and large, two ways to get behind the apparent simplicity to what lay beneath the surface of the seemingly trivial tales. Malinowski had influentially seen myth as a "charter," an authoritative statement from the past that validated present-day social and political relations. Could the /Xam myths be seen in this light? I, at any rate, found it hard to come up with any interpretation that was not blatantly trivial and naively functionalist. Perhaps, I wondered, the tales may have validated relationships within the nuclear family and thus constituted a conservative force within /Xam society. Not very convincing. This sort of functionalist view does not allow for the malleability of myth: Each performance of a myth is a personal intervention that is tailored to a specific set of circumstances and to personal and group interests.

Then, in the 1960s, Lévi-Strauss, a name that had been unknown to the social anthropology undergraduates of the early 1950s, came to dominate the study of mythology with a specific notion of structure. Prior to his work, *structure* meant narrative, or the linear structure of a myth, a series of episodes that narrators selected and combined to construct a performance. Vladimir Propp's *Morphology of the Folktale* (1968), which adopted this view, had been published in Russian in 1928 but had remained inaccessible to Western readers. When Propp's book first became available in English in 1958, his ideas seemed to make some sense of the /Xam tales: There did seem to be a repeated narrative structure, at least in the tales about /Kaggen. The stories start in /Kaggen's camp and then move out onto the hunting ground, where /Kaggen becomes embroiled in a fracas of some sort. Then after a "magical" episode, /Kaggen returns to his camp (cf. Hewitt 1986). Looking at the /Xam tales in this way was interesting but still not particularly illuminating, especially as far as the art was concerned.

Against this background of narrative, or syntagmatic, structure Claude Lévi-Strauss propounded his notion of "deep structure," or paradigmatic structure. He argued that the surface narrative was of little significance. Researchers should rather seek deep structure, a set of binary oppositions that dealt with contradictions inherent in the society in which the myth lived. This was a much more taxing task than the one that Propp proposed: The narrative structure was empirical, and analyses of it could be replicated by different researchers; paradigmatic studies, on the other hand, were more intuitively discerned and not necessarily replicable.

To cut a long story short, I could never generate much confidence in the deep structures that I thought I could detect in the /Kaggen tales. In the end, it seemed to me better to abandon that approach and pursue the line that I had taken with the statement that Qing had given Orpen (chapter 3); that is, to worry at the /Xam words and tropes preserved in the Bleek and Lloyd Collection. First, I tackled "A Visit to the Lion's House" (Bleek 1924, 15–18; Lewis-Williams 1996), and then "The Mantis, the Eland and the Meerkats" (Lewis-Williams 1997a). Both analyses were many years in the making and clearly influenced by both Propp and Lévi-Strauss, though more recent social theory concerning agency (the influence of individual actors in the practice of daily life) governs the outcomes of the studies. More importantly, the analyses took up the point that I made in the final sentence of my 1972 article on superpositioning in the Giant's Castle rock paintings: "The only possibility of clarifying the themes which most deeply moved the mind of the prehistoric Bushmen lies in the, albeit fragmentary, mythology" (Lewis-Williams 1972b, 64). The reference to Wilhelm Bleek that is built into this sentence turned out to be prophetic. I now turn to the second of the two studies.

The Mantis, the Eland, and the Meerkats

[The principal episodes of the /Kaggen myths] include the Mantis's creation of the Eland from a shoe, the death of the Eland, the Mantis's fight with the Meerkats (suricates: small furry mammals), and the Mantis's creation of the moon. What we may call auxiliary episodes include the Mantis's nurturing of the Eland on honey, the Mantis's piercing of the Eland's gall, and the Mantis's seizure of the Meerkats' belongings. Hewitt (1986, 216) has shown which of these episodes were used by each of Bleek and Lloyd's informants. Only one of the episodes, the fight with the Meerkats, appears in each of the recorded performances of the tale that describes how the Mantis created the Eland. Early in the twentieth century, the fight with the Meerkats was also recorded by Currlé (1913).

The Bleek and Lloyd manuscripts do not make it clear whether each of the narrations that they recorded was seen by its narrator as a complete performance. The myths were told under what were, for the San, highly unusual circumstances—painstaking dictation in a suburban garden. Some episodes may have been specifically requested by Bleek or Lloyd; the omission of certain episodes may therefore be no more than a function of the way in which the narratives were recorded rather than any conceptual unity that the narrators may have entertained. It seems misleading to refer to each of the narratives as a "version." Nevertheless, differences between the performances show that, even if Bleek and Lloyd influenced the direction of the tales, the narrators felt free to combine, eliminate, and, especially, elaborate the episodes and auxiliary episodes as they wished (Hewitt 1986). For a full analysis, it is tempting to conflate all the available performances and so be in a position to demonstrate the relationships between such recurring symbols as honey, water, shoes, and gall.

My interest here, however, is more restricted, and I consider only the performance that Lloyd recorded in September 1871 but did not translate until October 1896. The narrative was given by one of the Bleek family's most prolific informants, //Kabbo, a man who, according to Lloyd, "much enjoyed the thought that the Bushman stories would become known by means of books" (Bleek and Lloyd 1911, x). Elsewhere (Lewis-Williams 1996), I have argued that //Kabbo was a !gi:xa, a /Xam word that has been translated as "medicine man" (Bleek 1933b), "sorcerer" (Bleek 1935), and I believe legitimately, as "shaman" (Lewis-Williams 1992). As we shall see, his status as a shaman gives his narratives a special interest and helps to explain certain aspects of his performance. Very similar kinds of shamanism were practiced by most of the San groups that have been studied, such as the !Kung (Lee 1968, 1993; Marshall 1962,

1969; Biesele 1978, 1993; Katz 1982), the Nharo (Guenther 1975, 1975–76, 1986), the G/wi (Silberbauer 1963), the !Kō (Heinz 1975), and, of course, the /Xam (Bleek 1933b, 1935, 1936). Where necessary, I cite some of these other San groups' shamanic beliefs and practices to supplement the Bleek family's record of the /Xam. Demonstrable parallels between various beliefs and rituals (not only in shamanism) of many San groups justify my recourse to this material (cf. Lewis-Williams and Biesele 1978; Lewis-Williams 1981a, 1992).

The narrative with which I deal was published, in part only, as a component of what Dorothea Bleek, Wilhelm Bleek's daughter, called a "First Version" of "The Mantis Makes an Eland" (Bleek 1924, 2–5). In fact, this "First Version" is not a version at all; it is her own compilation of parts of performances given by //Kabbo (two performances) and another informant, Diä!kwain (one performance). //Kabbo's complete narrative is summarized here for the first time from Lloyd's manuscript pages L.II.4.489–493 and 504–514. I entitle it as follows:

The Mantis, the Eland, and the Meerkats

The Mantis stole /Kwammang-a's shoe and put it into a waterhole. When /Kwammang-a missed his shoe, he asked his wife, the Porcupine (the Mantis's adopted daughter), about it. She replied that she knew nothing about the matter.

Then, at the waterhole, the Mantis made an Eland out of the shoe and fed the animal on honey that he should have taken home to his family. /Kwammang-a was angry when he missed his shoe, and he told his son, the young Ichneumon,[1] to spy on the Mantis to see what he was doing with the honey.

The next day, the Ichneumon accompanied the Mantis, and, whilst pretending to sleep beneath a kaross, he saw him call the Eland out of the waterhole. When the Eland came up to the Mantis, he wetted the animal's hair and smoothed it with honey. When the Ichneumon saw this, he jumped up and cried out, "This is the creature who is eating the honey! The Eland is drinking the honey!" The Eland went back into the reeds, and the Mantis and the Ichneumon returned home.

The Ichneumon told /Kwammang-a what he had seen and said that /Kwammang-a should collect honey and take it to the waterhole. Then, if he moistened the honey and called, he would see the Eland.

He did so, calling out what the Ichneumon had told him to call: "/Kwammang-a's shoe heel!" The Eland jumped out of the reeds and trotted up to /Kwammang-a. As it drank the water and the honey, he shot it. It sprang back and ran off to die.

Later, the Mantis went to the waterhole and found that his Eland was no longer in the reeds; he wept. He saw blood on the ground. He returned home.

Meanwhile, /Kwammang-a went to Ki-ya-koe and the Meerkats, and together they tracked and found the dead Eland. /Kwammang-a took his arrow out of the carcass and returned home.

While the Meerkats were cutting up the Eland, the Mantis came and pierced open the Eland's gall, thus angering the Meerkats. The Meerkats then fought him and threw him on the Eland's horns. The Mantis fled.

At home the Mantis lay down because his head ached. He trembled, and the tree on which the Meerkats had placed the Eland's meat and their clothes came out of the ground, flew through the sky and came down near the Mantis's head, thus making a shelter for him.

The Meerkats returned to their home naked, and the women asked them why they had brought home neither eland meat nor their quivers.

This myth is so rich in significances that it is doubtful if a full exposition of its meanings could be achieved; I certainly do not claim that what follows is the only possible interpretation of the myth (cf. Schmidt 1996, 105–8). As we shall see, it communicates simultaneously on a number of different levels; its complexity is especially apparent if it is considered along with the other performances of the same and related episodes. Here, however, I concentrate on one of the social dilemmas that the myth addresses. I argue that the negotiation of social relations between affines and a specific conflict resolution mechanism lie at the heart of the myth. This mechanism was brought into play to deal with internal social stress in the years of contact with Bantu-speaking agropastoralists and, later, white settlers, with the stresses that increasingly characterized the final years of the southern San communities. To provide an understanding of the functioning of this mechanism, I first outline, very briefly, the cosmological stage on which many southern San myths were played out and also the kinship relations within the Mantis's family.

Cosmology

An analysis of the Bleek and Lloyd Collection suggests that southern San cosmology was not rigidly conceived by every member of the community, let alone expounded. What follows is therefore one researcher's formulation inferred from a reading of the texts; it is essentially an heuristic device.

In broad terms, it seems that the /Xam conceived of a two-component universe that, I argue, was informed by shamanic concepts and experiences. San shamanism was not some sort of floating, virtually independent superstructure (Lewis-Williams 1982); rather, it lay at the heart of the San worldview and permeated many areas of life (Lee 1968; Marshall 1969; Katz 1982; Biesele 1978, 1980, 1993). As a result, many (possibly all) San myths are unintelligible without an understanding of how shamanic beliefs and experiences articulated with San cosmology. Certainly, that is true of "The Mantis, the Eland, and the Meerkats."

The /Xam cosmos comprised the realm of material, daily life and an "adjacent," immanent, spiritual realm that included a region below the earth and another situated in the sky. I deal with each realm in turn.

The realm of /Xam material life comprised three conceptual areas: //nein, !kau:xu, and !khwa. Bleek and Lloyd translated these words, respectively, as "home" (sometimes "hut" or "house"), "hunting-ground" and "water." Because //nein is frequently used to mean a collection of dwellings, I prefer to use "camp." "Hunting-ground" has a distinctly male gender bias, even though the women's important food gathering also took place there. Bleek and Lloyd's choice of the English word may have been a result of their informants' being principally men. On the other hand, "hunting-ground" may be a legitimate translation of the word (at any rate as used by men) that reflects the /Xam gendering of space. In which case, !kau:xu may have been contrasted in some contexts with //nein because, in the narratives, the women often remain in the camp while the men go out on to the !kau:xu. Despite the word's gender bias, I retain Bleek and Lloyd's "hunting-ground." The third element, !khwa, I give as "waterhole" because this word more adequately denotes the nature of water sources in the semiarid Northern Cape Province than simply "water."

The camp, located a mile or so from the waterhole, was the focus of /Xam social activity, and its associations were essentially of order and cooperation. It was here, by and large, that shamanic curing dances took place. By contrast, the hunting-ground was the place of wild animals and unknown people. Its quintessential animal was the "angry" lion. Its associations were of danger and unpredictability. This binary opposition of (positive) camp and (negative) hunting-ground was mediated by the waterhole, where both people and animals met by chance or by design (see, for example, Heinz 1966). Relationships here with animals could be either beneficial, in the case of antelope which could be shot, or dangerous, in the case of carnivores which could attack people. Carnivores, antelope, and people were all dependent upon waterholes in the semiarid veld.

Notions of regions below and above the plane of material life were closely associated with shamanic experiences and were less well defined. Taken together, they seem to have comprised a spiritual realm that was immanent rather than separated spatially from the daily world. Nevertheless, distinctions can be made.

The region below was associated principally with the dead, and the region above with god, shamans, and the spirits—though spirits can also be "by you," even if you do not realize it (Bleek and Lloyd MS L.II.27.2463 rev.). Ascent to a realm in the sky and descent through a hole in the ground are common shamanic experiences worldwide. The division between the level of material life and the two spiritual realms was, like the division between the camp and the hunting-ground, mediated by water, which both falls from above and wells up from below (Lewis-Williams 1996, fig. 1). The /Xam had only one word for water and rain, !khwa. In numerous myths !khwa has transformative and regenerative powers. For example, in one narrative an ostrich feather placed in a waterhole grows into a full ostrich (Bleek and Lloyd 1911, 136–45). In other, better-watered, parts of southern Africa the walls of rock shelters seem to have played a similar mediatory role between the material world and the spiritual realm (Lewis-Williams and Dowson 1990).

Even as waterholes and rock shelters mediated the two-component cosmos, so too did /Xam shamans. The spiritual journeys that they undertook between realms, accomplished in an altered state of consciousness, often started in a waterhole or in a rock shelter (Lewis-Williams 1981a; Lewis-Williams and Dowson 1989a, 1990). From these points of breakthrough, the shamans could travel underground (cf. Biesele 1980, 54–62) or through the sky (Lewis-Williams 1996). One of the shamans' tasks on these journeys was to make rain, and this also involved transcending the realms: They left the material realm and entered a waterhole where they captured an hallucinatory creature known as !khwa-ka xoro, animal of the rain. They then led this rain-animal through the sky to the place where they wished the rain to fall, often the top of a mountain. There they killed it, its blood and milk falling as precipitation (Bleek 1933a and b; Lewis-Williams 1981a, 103–16).

The /Xam cosmos that I have now briefly outlined was the home of the Mantis and his family, as well as the place where ordinary San people lived. Indeed, for the most part, the Mantis and his relatives behave as normal San people, hunting, visiting, and so forth. In exceptional circumstances, such as those in numerous myths, including the one I have summarized, the Mantis, unlike any other member of his family, is seen to have the ability to transcend the realms.

The Mantis's Family

I now consider only those members of the family who are germane to an understanding of "The Mantis, the Eland, and the Meerkats" (figure 4.1). As we shall see, the Mantis's kinship relations paralleled certain aspects of the /Xam cosmos and were, moreover, underpinned by complex symbolism that is directly relevant to "The Mantis, the Eland, and the Meerkats." I deal first with the Mantis's family and then with his affines.

"/Kaggen" has long been translated, somewhat misleadingly, as "the Mantis." The praying mantis insect, *Mantis religiosa*, is in fact only one of his numerous avatars: He could also change into a snake, an eland, a louse, an eagle, and a hartebeest (Lewis-Williams 1981a, 117–26). Although other transformations take place in the /Xam tales, /Kaggen's highly protean aspect is not shared by any other /Xam mythical people; he alone frequently transcends categories of creature as well as realms of the cosmos. He is able to accomplish this by means of his shamanic powers; indeed, the Mantis was the original shaman. The Mantis's wife was /Huntu!katt!katten, the Dassie (rock rabbit, or hyrax), and their adopted daughter was !Xo, the Porcupine.

The factor that unites this seemingly disparate nuclear family is important, though not immediately apparent. The Mantis, the Dassie, and the Porcupine are all associated in various ways with fat and honey. First, dassies and porcupines are both creatures known for the large amount of fat that they possess. Second, the dassie is an animal that lives in the rocky cliffs, which are associated with bees and honey (Bleek 1924, 47); indeed, among the !Kung the wife of the principal deity, though not said to be a dassie (there are few cliffs and, consequently, few dassies in the Kalahari), is known as "Mother of the Bees" (Thomas 1969, 145). The Mantis himself, being a hunter, is the provider of both fat and, as the myth I am analyzing confirms, honey.

In San thought, honey and fat are associated with one another in that they are both anomalous foods. They are the only two foods that people both eat and drink (Biesele 1978). In the myth that I am discussing, the Eland is, significantly, said to eat and drink honey. Honey and fat are both greatly desired as food, but they are also closely associated with a supernatural potency that the /Xam called

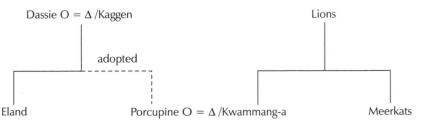

Figure 4.1.   Members of /Kaggen's family as they feature in "The Mantis, the Eland, and the Meerkats."

!gi, //ke:n, and /ko:ode (Lewis-Williams 1981a). The !Kung believe that a fat eland has more potency than a lean animal; the potency resides largely in its fat. They also have a medicine song called "Honey" (Marshall 1969, 367). Marshall (1962) has likened this potency (the !Kung call it n/om) to electricity: In intense concentrations or out of control, it is dangerous, even lethal; harnessed, it can be used for the good of all people. It is this potency that shamans harness to go on journeys between the realms and to cure people of sickness, both known and unknown, physical and social (Lee 1968; Marshall 1962, 1969). Importantly, this potency is associated, through fat and honey, with the Mantis's family.

Another member of the family, one who draws together some of the themes I have outlined, is the Eland. Although the Eland does not live in the camp with the rest of the Mantis's family, this animal may, in some respects, be considered his child. In a performance of the "Creation of the Eland," /Han≠kass'o, //Kabbo's son-in-law, repeatedly spoke of the Mantis as the Eland's "father" (Bleek 1924, 6). The Eland is indeed the Mantis's special creation: Although it never assumes a fully human role, as do the other members of the family, the Mantis loves it dearly and weeps when it is killed (Bleek 1924, 3, 8). Diä!kwain, another of Bleek and Lloyd's informants, explained, "The Mantis does not love us if we kill an Eland" (Bleek 1924, 12). Further, the Mantis sat between the Eland's horns and sprang various ruses to facilitate its escape from the hunters.

A San man from what is now Lesotho explained more about this special relationship between the Mantis and the Eland. In his version of the creation of the Eland, the Mantis's wife, here called Coti, gives birth to an Eland calf; the Mantis "folds it in his arms" and leaves it to grow in a secluded kloof (Orpen 1874, 3–4). When Orpen (1874, 3) asked the man where the Mantis was, he replied, "We don't know, but the Elands do. Have you not hunted and heard his cry, when the Elands suddenly start and run to his call? Where he is, Elands are in droves like cattle." This was no doubt the same cry that, in the /Xam myths, the Mantis used to call the Eland out of the reeds.

In addition to being the Mantis's favorite creature, the Eland has a physical characteristic that links it to other members of the Mantis's family. Like porcupines and dassies, it is an animal that has a large quantity of fat; San people talk a great deal about the extraordinary amount of fat that can be obtained from an eland, especially a bull eland (Lewis-Williams 1981a). The large quantity of fat on a bull is, moreover, the factor that makes it an anomalous creature. In the 1970s, San people explained that in antelope species the female has more fat than the male; in the eland, this contrast is uniquely reversed, the male having more fat than the female (Lewis-Williams 1981a, 72). In some sense, the eland is androgynous (Dowson 1988). It thus mediates categories, as do the shamans who draw potency from it. Moreover, the eland was, in /Xam thought, associated with honey. //Kabbo told Lloyd that the kudu eats honey, and its scent is therefore like that of the eland (Bleek and Lloyd MS L.II.3.466). The eland thus smells of honey. Although they do not mention honey specifically, some early writers noted the distinctive aroma of the eland; they commented on the strong, sweet perfume that arises as an eland is skinned, and the sweet, aromatic smell that it leaves in the grass where it has been lying (Bryden 1899, 422, 427; Shortridge 1934, 613).

The importance of this animal in /Xam thought is summed up in an explicit statement that Lloyd obtained from Diä!kwain: "The Hartebeest and the Eland are things of the Mantis; therefore they have magic power" (Bleek 1924, 10). This "magic power" is the potency that shamans harness, and it is this power that links the Mantis and the Eland so closely. In /Xam thought, the Eland was at the center of a nexus of interrelated significances.

We now come to the other group of actors, the Mantis's affines. The Mantis's adopted daughter, the Porcupine, was married to /Kwammang-a who came from a family that comprised carnivores—Lions in the older generation and Meerkats in the younger. /Kwammang-a's origin explains why his and the Porcupine's son was the Ichneumon, a small, furry carnivore. The unity of the Mantis's affines is thus easier to discover than the unity of his own family: The affines are all carnivores, or "pawed creatures," a phrase the !Kung also use to denote strange and potentially dangerous people (Biesele 1978). Significantly, /Kwammang-a is the only member of the Mantis's family who does not have an animal identity. It is as if his origin as a carnivore—a dangerous stranger—is being suppressed, a point to which I return later.

In summary, the Mantis's family comprises honey-fat creatures; his affines are all carnivores. The Mantis's family is associated with the camp, the location that embodies concepts of harmony and cooperation. By contrast, the Mantis's affines are associated with the hunting-ground, which embodies concepts of danger, strangeness, and conflict. The two groups are linked by the marriage between the Mantis's daughter, the Porcupine, and /Kwammang-a, whose carnivore origins are concealed by the suppression of his animal identity.

These preliminary remarks about the realms of the /Xam cosmos and the Mantis's family enable us to discern certain themes in "The Mantis, the Eland, and the Meerkats." For convenience of analysis, I divide the narrative into two major sections: the creation of the Eland and the fight with the Meerkats. The principal theme that I emphasize, tension between affines, has already been hinted at by the anomalous status of /Kwammang-a as a carnivore who married into the Mantis's family.

The Creation of the Eland

This part of the myth starts in the camp, moves to the waterhole, and then back to the camp.

The very birth of the Eland sprang from tension between affines: The Mantis stole /Kwammang-a's shoe. Understandably, /Kwammang-a was angry when he discovered that his shoe was missing. The shoe itself has various significances. One is that San are able to recognize people from their bare footprints in the sand. This ability is seen in another myth in which the young Ichneumon recognizes individual members of his father's family when they visit the Lion's house: "This is my brothers' spoor. One brother's spoor is here, the other brother's spoor is there. My grandfather's spoor is here, my other grandfather's spoor is there" (Bleek 1924, 15). By wearing a shoe made of antelope hide, /Kwammang-a was able to alter his footprints, thus masking his identity as a pawed creature and concealing his anomalous position in /Kaggen's family. When the Mantis stole his shoe, his true spoor (and thus identity) was revealed. The concealment afforded by shoes may account for the nineteenth-century San practice of placing their weapons and their shoes on the ground when approaching people whom they were visiting; bare feet expose the truth (Chapman 1868, 2:23).

The Mantis's theft of the shoe points to a fundamental contradiction in San society: how to live and share resources with one's affines, people with whom one is, at least in some measure, in competition. Linked to this dilemma was the problem of residence. Should a newly married couple live with the bride's or the groom's family? Among the San, the couple usually goes to the bride's camp, where the groom performs bride-service until a couple of children have been born. They then return to the groom's camp. Many narratives in the Bleek and Lloyd Collection deal with the tensions created by bride-service, as do the !Kung narratives that Biesele (1993) collected. In "The Mantis, the Eland, and the Meerkats," /Kwammang-a was performing bride-service for the Mantis, having married his daughter, and this accounts for his residence in the Mantis's camp.

In the next part of the narrative, the Mantis takes /Kwammang-a's shoe from the camp to the waterhole, the mediatory element and locus of transformation in the San cosmos. At this point, it is important to note another aspect of the significance of the shoe. It would have been made from antelope hide; further, some sources suggest that it was probably made from eland hide (Spaarman 1789, 156; Bleek and Lloyd MS L.II.3.454; Steyn 1971, 291). Out of the shoe, the Mantis fashions a creature that will itself be anomalous, or mediatory, and that will have more supernatural potency than any other creature. The eland will become the shamans' power-animal par excellence (Lewis-Williams 1981a, 75–102).

According to the /Xam, there was potency in an eland's heart. Diä!kwain said, "When they have cut it [an eland] to pieces and cut out the heart, then he [the man who shot the animal; probably a boy in his first-kill ritual; Lewis-Williams and Biesele 1978] joins the men who are cutting it up, after the heart is out because they are afraid that it is a thing which has (?)" (Bleek 1932a, 237). Lloyd's question mark leaves the word /ko:ode untranslated. Elsewhere, it is translated "magic power" (Bleek 1956, 320); it seems to mean a particularly intense and potentially dangerous concentration of potency. An association between eland and the shamanic dance appears even more explicitly in a !Kung avoidance word. The usual !Kung word for eland is n!; in ritual contexts, they call it tcheni, a word which means "dance" (Biesele, personal communication). The /Xam and the !Kung evidence thus suggests that, when hunting eland, men were also hunting power for the shamanic dance. Southern San rock paintings depicting men running after eland should probably be seen in the light of these associations. It is not just food that they are after; like the Meerkats, they are "hunting" supernatural potency. So, too, it seems clear that paintings of eland, singly or in herds, were not merely references to meat but to power (cf. Lewis-Williams and Dowson 1988; Lewis-Williams 1981a, 1990a).

Animals are, however, not the only source of potency. In another nineteenth-century account, the Mantis is said to have given the San the "song of this dance" (the trance, or curing, dance) (Orpen 1874, 10). "Medicine songs," as they are known (Marshall 1969), contain potency; they are named after powerful things, such as Sun, Eland, Giraffe, and, as we have seen, Honey. The bestowal of the "song" is another way of saying that the Mantis created and vouchsafed the potency that shamans harness. The potency, or song, that shamans most desire is that of the eland. Further, there is reason to believe that, when the San of the southeastern mountains were said to be "of the eland" (How 1962; cf. Vinnicombe 1976), it was the sharing of all the people, not just shamans, in eland potency that was being highlighted (Lewis-Williams 1988a). One of the principal points about the creation of the Eland is thus that, in making this mediatory, potent animal, the Mantis created the basis for /Xam shamanism.

The order of the Mantis's actions is significant. His creation of the foundation of shamanism followed his theft of /Kwammang-a's shoe. The Mantis thus first exposed the anomalous position of an affine within his family by revealing /Kwammang-a's pawed feet. He then began to prepare an answer to social tensions created by, among other things, the presence of affines by imbuing the eland with the potency that shamans would learn to harness.

The Mantis, it must be noted, did not make the Eland out of nothing. Part of the new creation had to come from another family, here represented by

/Kwammang-a and his shoe. The act of creation, or birth, is thus linked to sexual relations with affines and points away from incest. The sexual element in the narrative is developed in a further, equally oblique, way. When the shoe grew into the Eland, the Mantis fed it honey that he should have been taking home to his family. Both honey and fat are rich in sexual symbolism. The !Kung San use the phrases "to eat (or drink) honey" and "to eat (or drink) fat" as euphemisms for sexual intercourse (Biesele 1978). Feeding the Eland honey and moistening its flanks with honey are therefore probably references to sexual procreation. This component of honey symbolism is also expressed in Diä!kwain's statement that the Mantis used different kinds of honey to give the antelope their distinctive colors: For instance, "The Eland was the one to whom the Mantis once gave some wasps' honey; this is why he is dark" (Bleek 1924, 10). Different sources of honey produced different creatures. The shoe, then, came from an affine; the honey (probably a symbol of semen), on the other hand, belonged to the Mantis.

The first part of the myth may now be briefly summarized. The Mantis created the Eland by using his honey and something belonging to an affine, a shoe; in doing so, he created the potency on which the whole shamanic enterprise is posited. The act of creation took place in a waterhole, a point of breakthrough between realms, one of the points of access through which shamans reach the spirit realm. The Mantis moved from his camp to the waterhole for the process of transformation, and then back again. In the next part of the story he goes to the hunting ground and then, finally, back to his camp.

The Fight with the Meerkats

When /Kwammang-a learned about the Eland and what the Mantis was doing with the honey, he himself collected honey and went to the waterhole and there imitated the Mantis's call. When the Eland came out of the reeds, /Kwammang-a shot it, no doubt with a poisoned arrow, and it ran off to die out on the hunting-ground. /Kwammang-a went and spoke to his relatives, the Meerkats, and to Ki-ya-koe, who appears to be one of the Meerkats. They followed the Eland's spoor until they came to the carcass. Tracking an animal the day after it had been wounded with a poisoned arrow was a common San practice (Bleek 1932a, 233–40). After removing his arrow from the dead animal, /Kwammang-a returned home, leaving Ki-ya-koe and the Meerkats to cut up the Eland. Meanwhile, on finding that his Eland had been shot, the Mantis returned home, weeping. Then, it seems the next day, he tracked the Eland and found the Meerkats cutting it up. The fight ensued.

In the performance with which we are dealing, the fight with the Meerkats communicates on at least three levels. The first derives from /Xam hunting obser-vances. Hunters (the carnivorous Meerkats) have killed one of the Mantis's favor-ite animals, the Eland, and he is trying to punish the culprits (Lewis-Williams and Biesele 1978). In an account of /Xam hunting observances, Diä!kwain said that the Mantis does this by various ruses designed to cause the eland to survive (Bleek 1924, 11–12). Here, being thrown on the Eland's horns is probably an ironic inversion of one of the Mantis's ways of resuscitating a wounded eland. Diä!kwain put it like this: "He [the Mantis] goes and strikes the Eland's horn, and the Eland arises, the Eland eats, because it feels that it has come to life by means of the Mantis's doings, although it had nearly died" (Bleek 1924, 12). In the myth, instead of striking the animal's horn and so causing it to arise, the Mantis is himself thrown on to it, and it hurts him. His way of saving a wounded eland is frustrated.

On a second level, the Mantis attacked the Meerkats because they had taken his child. In San thought, hunting and mating are symbolically equivalent (Mar-shall 1959, 354; McCall 1970). In terms of this equivalence, /Kwammang-a's shooting of the Eland and the Meerkats' appropriation of it symbolize the mar-riage of the Mantis's Eland into the Meerkats' family. The Eland's "marriage" into the Meerkats' family is thus an inversion of /Kwammang-a's marriage to the Porcupine. In /Kwammang-a's marriage, he, the man, is legitimately performing bride-service for the Mantis. By contrast, the Meerkats' shooting of the Eland with an arrow violates the norms of bride-service in that 'she' goes to her hus-band's (the hunter's) camp. The Mantis was thus resisting the surrender of his child to a family of pawed creatures.

Third, the fight with the Meerkats is, like the creation of the Eland, explicable in terms of San shamanism. The Meerkats stole, not just an animal, but supernat-ural potency. The effect of this unauthorized appropriation is described in another performance of the myth; because of its crucial significance, I consider it in some detail. The narrator, Diä!kwain, said that the Mantis intended to "fight the Eland's battle" (Bleek 1924, 4). As translated by Lloyd, the sentence seems to mean that the Mantis intended to fight on behalf of the Eland, but this transla-tion is an example of the confusion that sometimes arose from Lloyd's unfamiliar-ity with /Xam shamanism; neither she nor Bleek, it should be remembered, actually witnessed /Xam rituals. The /Xam word that Lloyd translated as both the verb *fight* and the noun *battle* is /a. Those meanings are, in some contexts, correct, but Lloyd also gives /a as "danger." In Diä!kwain's performance of the death of the Eland (Bleek and Lloyd MS L.V.I.3640), a portion of which became part of Dorothea Bleek's "Second Version," the Mantis says, "It seems as if dan-ger has come upon my home" (Bleek 1924, 3). This is when he finds that the honey is "dry" and "lean." Lloyd also translated the word as "curse" (Bleek 1956, 267).

One of the meanings of the word is clarified by the way in which the !Kung use it. Although the !Kung and /Xam languages are largely lexically distinct, both have this particular word. In addition to "fight," /a can, for the !Kung, mean a potentially dangerous concentration of supernatural potency (Biesele, personal communication; Marshall 1962, 239, 1969, 351). Bearing this and the various uses of the word in the /Xam language in mind, I argue that the passage in question would be better translated to mean that the Mantis intended to fight against the Eland's great potency, which had been appropriated by the Meerkats (Lewis-Williams 1983d, 46–47). Then, when the Mantis shot at the Eland, his arrows were deflected back at him and he had to dodge them. The Eland's potency, now in the hands of the Meerkats, was too strong for him.

This interpretation is borne out by the observation that, in the Kalahari, the San like to dance next to the carcass of a freshly killed eland because, they say, the place is redolent with the antelope's scent and released potency, and they are able to harness it for a particularly effective trance dance (scent is thought to convey potency). A shaman who has special control of eland potency enters trance and cures all present of known and unknown ills. During such a dance, the spirits of the dead, attracted to the place by the beautiful dancing, shoot small, invisible arrows-of-sickness at people. The shamans, fortified by the eland's supernatural potency, deflect these arrows and remove any that may have penetrated people. I therefore argue that the image presented by //Kabbo's performance of the fight with the Meerkats is, in essence, that of a San curing dance.

Finally, and still on the shamanic level, I consider the curious role of the Eland's gall. In //Kabbo's performance, the Mantis angers the Meerkats by piercing the Eland's gall, and this act causes darkness. Other performances develop this episode at greater length. In them, the Mantis first leaps into the darkness created by the gall and later creates the moon. /Han≠kasso'o's performance gives the incident thus: "Then he pierced the gall, he made the gall burst . . . , and the gall broke covering his head; his eyes became big, he could not see. And he groped about feeling his way" (Bleek 1924, 9). Then, with an ostrich feather, the Mantis wipes the gall from his eyes. Finally, he throws the feather into the sky and it becomes the moon. Clearly, the gall is highly significant. When Diä!kwain was telling Lloyd about what happens to people after death, he said, "And, our gall, when we die, sits in the sky; it sits green in the sky, when we are dead" (Bleek and Lloyd 1911, 399). Here, it seems that gall is associated with the spirit of a person. The importance of an animal's gall is emphasized by !Kung shamans who sometimes eat the gall of a lion in the belief that it is the center of that animal's power. Further, lions eat people; by eating a lion's gall, and thus power, a shaman is, in a sense, consuming human flesh (Wilmsen, personal communication). Particularly powerful shamans are believed to have the ability to walk abroad at night in the form of a lion. This is another of the ways in which a shaman's ambivalence is expressed: On these nocturnal journeys, he bridges not only categories of being but also realms of existence.

Together, these beliefs and practices suggest that, when the Mantis pierced the gall, he was releasing the Eland's potency. In the performance of the myth in which he leaps into the resulting black cloud, he is immersing himself in the antelope's potency, and the way in which he gropes about in the darkness graphically suggests a man disoriented by trance.

We now move on to see how the Mantis used the potency after he had been humiliated. In the performance with which we are dealing, he simply left the scene of conflict and returned home. By omitting the incidents of the deflected arrows and the creation of the moon, //Kabbo was setting the stage for the denouement of a personal performance of the narrative. He had a different ending in mind, one in which the Mantis would not be defeated; after all, he was as /Han≠kass'o put it, "a Mantis man" (Bleek 1936, 143; for more on this phrase see Lewis-Williams 1996). According to //Kabbo, the tree with the Eland's meat and the Meerkats' belongings rose up, passed through the heavens, and settled next to him. Again, this episode communicates on different levels.

On the most straightforward level, the Mantis had his revenge by causing the tree to fly to his home. On a second level, the Meerkats' violation of the norms of bride-service was corrected: The "bride" returns to the Mantis's camp, albeit in the form of meat (cf. Biesele 1993). On a third level, the means by which the Mantis achieved his righting of an acceptable situation is crucial because it takes up a recurring theme that was present in the creation of the Eland, in the Meerkats' appropriation of the Eland, and in the Mantis's fight with the Meerkats.

To understand this theme as it is presented in the last part of the narrative we must examine //Kabbo's use of certain words; as elsewhere in the myth, they are the key to the significance of the passage. When the Mantis reached his camp, he lay down because his head ached. Then, said //Kabbo, he "trembled," and the tree traveled through the sky to his camp. The /Xam word translated "tremble" is !khauken (also !kauken and !kouken). The *Bushman Dictionary* (Bleek 1956, 425, 445) gives !khauken as "to tremble" and "to beat," but one of the examples that it gives points to a specific context in which the word was used: "When he returning comes in from the place to which he had gone on a magic expedition, he trembles." The "magic expedition" (/xau) is the out-of-body travel performed by shamans in dreams or during trance dances. In other /Xam narratives, !khauken similarly refers to the violent trembling of a shaman in trance: for example, "The others hold him down and rub his back with fat, as he beats (*!kauken*)" (Bleek 1935, 2); "He beats (*!kauken-i*) when he is snoring [curing] a person with his nose" (Bleek 1935, 2; the suffix *-i* signifies duration of action: Bleek 1928–1929, 168). Today, !Kung San shamans still tremble violently as they enter trance (Marshall 1962, 250, 1969, 370, 376; Katz 1976, 286, 1982, 65).

The potential confusion of "trembling in trance" with "beating" in the sense of "striking" is again evident in Lloyd's notes on another of the Mantis's adventures (Bleek and Lloyd MS L.II.22.1965–2042).[2] In this tale the Mantis fights the Cat. As it first appears, *!kauken* means "strike"—the Cat struck the Mantis. The second time the narrator used the word Lloyd was puzzled; her transliteration of the passage reads: "Therefore, thou didst get feathers, as thou beating stood . . . thou ascendest the sky" (Bleek and Lloyd MS L.II.22.1986). Lloyd noted her perplexity: "Can this be a passive (beaten)? JT [the narrator, //Kabbo] explains that the Mantis was beat*ing*. But I am not very sure, if I have the explanation rightly" (Bleek and Lloyd MS L.II.22.1987 rev.; Lloyd's emphasis). This is another instance of how Lloyd's unfamiliarity with Bushman shamanism, its physical effects and idioms among the /Xam sometimes resulted in uncertainty about exactly what the informants were saying to her. As we have seen, it is clear that the nineteenth-century /Xam sometimes used "tremble" to mean "to enter, or to be in, trance." Lloyd's narrator was therefore right: In the story of the Mantis and the Cat, it was through "beat*ing*," or "trembl*ing*" (i.e., entering trance), that the Mantis was able to grow feathers and escape from the Cat by flying through the sky, part of the spirit realm to which shamans have access (cf. the Mantis in "A Visit to the Lion's House," where "trembling" also leads to flight (Lewis-Williams 1996).

There is a final piece of evidence as to the significance of the Mantis's trembling. In a passage that Lloyd added after she had taken down the complete performance of "The Mantis, the Eland, and the Meerkats," //Kabbo elaborated on the flight of the tree together with its burden of meat and the Meerkats' belongings. Lloyd's translation of part of this addition is as follows: "It itself [the tree] mounts up into the sky, at night, of itself it goes to stand on the ground, because the mantis has ? conjured it" (Bleek and Lloyd MS L.II.4.511 rev.). Lloyd's question mark shows that she was again unsure of her translation of the /Xam word as "conjured." Using a concept with which she was familiar, she translated the worrisome /Xam word as best she could. The word that //Kabbo used was, however, *!khau-ka*, a form that seems to be cognate with *!khauken* (to tremble). The additional passage thus confirms my understanding of the episode of the tree: I argue that it was through entering an altered state of consciousness and employing his powers as a shaman that the Mantis was able to cause the tree to fly through the sky and to alight at his camp.

Exactly what the Mantis's shamanic intervention achieved is best understood, in the first instance, in terms of San sharing practices. Among the !Kung, an animal that has been shot is "owned" by the person to whom the fatal arrow belongs. He or she sees to the first distribution of large portions of meat. Thereafter, the meat is generally distributed along lines of kinship. In the end, everyone in the camp receives a portion (Marshall 1961). Thus, if the killing of the Eland had been a straightforward hunt, custom would have demanded that the Mantis receive a share of the meat by virtue of his relationship with /Kwammang-a. But the Meerkats denied their obligation to share meat with their affines, the Mantis and his family, when they beat him and drove him away. The Mantis then resorted to shamanic trance performance to right the wrong and to cause the meat to come to his camp. Because meat-sharing symbolizes kinship relations, the Mantis was symbolically restoring the social rupture caused by the Meerkats' refusal to share.

There is, however, a further dimension to the context of meat sharing. Among the San, it was and still is a frequent situation in which ill-feeling can be generated; if people feel they have been slighted by receiving a niggardly portion, arguments erupt. The kinship ties that meat distribution celebrates become strained and, if the strain is unchecked, it jeopardizes the survival of the social unit. It is therefore no coincidence that a shamanic dance often follows a substantial kill which attracts visitors (Marshall 1969), as the quagga meat attracted the Mantis, /Kwammang-a, and the Ichneumon to the Lion's camp in another of the /Xam myths (Bleek 1924, 15–18; Lewis-Williams 1996). The ill-feeling arising from inequitable distribution can be reduced by a shamanic dance.

All these events are played out on the stage of /Xam San cosmology. The Mantis returns to his home, the place of order, before he rights the wrong by means of his shamanic powers. The tale thus moves from his camp, to the hunting ground where the conflict with the Meerkats takes place, and then back to the camp where wrongs are righted and where shamanic dances usually take place. Further, when shamanic experience is evoked in this righting of wrongs, the realms are mediated: The tree leaves the mundane realm, travels through the realm above (the one through which shamans, too, fly), and then returns to the mundane realm. Like a waterhole, a tree itself is a mediator of realms in that its roots are below and its branches are above the plane of daily life.

In the reading I have given, "The Mantis, the Eland, and the Meerkats" asserts correct sharing along the lines of kinship and the Meerkats are punished for breaking the rules by losing their equipment and clothing. At the same time, a way of lessening conflict and righting wrongs is created.

Conflict Resolution

Tension between affines and the need to share scarce resources are dilemmas that cannot be resolved; they are inherent in San social structure and life (Biesele 1993). This is the sort of contradiction that Lévi-Strauss (1968) believes lies at the heart of many myths. All that can be hoped for is that such tensions be mitigated, and the mitigating mechanism posited by the /Xam myth is shamanic activity. The San still recognize that shamanic dances dissipate tensions. Indeed, they contrive to have men between whom there is animosity dance one behind the other, so that rhythmic unity can reestablish emotional amity (Biesele, personal communication). Marshall (1969) gives a dramatic example of the efficacy of shamanic intervention that she witnessed. A fight that threatened to spill over into really serious violence was interrupted by the women, who started singing a medicine song in full voice: "In minutes, two of the men from [one] group and one from the other group went abruptly into frenzied trance and soon fell unconscious." The tensions were dissipated (374).

Recognizing the importance of shamanic beliefs and rituals for the San, I argue that performances of "The Mantis, the Eland, and the Meerkats," especially those in which the narrator developed the shamanic episodes, served to reproduce acceptance of the key role of shamans in coping with social tensions. //Kabbo, himself a shaman, set up and elaborated the denouement of his performance so that the importance of shamans was foregrounded. For him, this and other San myths and their structures were not immutable givens; rather, they constituted a resource on which individuals could draw and which they could manipulate in the negotiation of their social statuses (cf. Giddens 1984; Lewis-Williams 1996).

Performances of the myth, elaborated in this manner, entrenched the positions of shamans in San communities. As the degree of contact with other peoples increased and became more conflictual, the positions of shamans became increasingly political: It was they, rather than the community's hunters and gatherers, who began to control access to resources through performing rainmaking rituals for their farming neighbors. As mediators of conflict both within their own communities and between their communities and their neighbors, the shamans held the balance of power. The shamanic tasks of rainmaking, healing, and tension reduction were, paradoxically, exploited in the negotiation of personal power. The performance of certain myths was one of the ways (rock painting was another; Dowson 1994) in which shamans consolidated and increased that power. People accepted that the myths derived from the ancient time when animals behaved as if they were people; as a result of their association with this primordial period, the myths were believed to embody incontrovertible truths, and the personally varied performances of them were consequently influential.

Notes

1. The *Bushman Dictionary* gives /ni as "ickneumon, Herpestes" (Bleek 1956, 348), and a translation in one of /Han≠kass'o's notebooks (L.VIII.I.6145) gives /ni as "slender tailed meerkat, Herpestes [*sic*]. There may be some confusion here because the ichneumon is the Egyptian Mongoose (*Herpestes ichneumon*). It is not found in the dry, central parts of southern Africa (Goss 1986; Smithers 1986).

2. Another performance of this tale (Bleek and Lloyd L.II.5.547–565) was published as "The Mantis and the Cat" (Bleek 1924, 19–21).

Extract from "The Mantis, the Eland, and the Meerkats: Conflict and Mediation in a Nineteenth-Century San Myth," in *Culture and the Commonplace: Anthropological Essays in Honor of David Hammond-Tooke*, ed. P. McAllister (Johannesburg: Witwatersrand University Press, 1997), 195–216. *African Studies* (special issue) 56 (2).

Retrospect

A point that is perhaps insufficiently emphasized in this analysis is the interlocking nature of San myth, cosmology, and spiritual experience. When San shamans enter an altered state of consciousness and travel to the spirit world, they do so within the framework of San cosmology that is, in turn, derived from and repeatedly validated by such experiences. In the spirit world they encounter personages and creatures that feature in myths. San ethnography from many communities and language groups shows that the people's principal source of knowledge about the spirit world and its beings comes from extracorporeal experiences of shamans—not from the unbridled imagination of people in general. The centrality of this source of spiritual knowledge does not mean that ordinary people cannot fashion tales and perform their own versions of myths, as they certainly do. But it does mean that most of their raw material comprises knowledge vouchsafed by shamans and conceived within the tiered cosmos.

Once the unity of San cosmology, myth, and spiritual experience is appreciated, it becomes clear that the received anthropological categories of mythology, religion, folktales, and so forth are unhelpful. They fragment a seamless unity and create unnecessary debate.

My analyses of "The Mantis, the Eland and the Meerkats" and "A Visit to the Lion's House" (Lewis-Williams 1996) merely scratch the surface of San mythology. The richness and complexity of that mythology became abundantly clear to me, if any such reinforcement were indeed needed, when I edited previously unpublished sections of the Bleek and Lloyd manuscripts (Lewis-Williams 2000). Much, much more remains to be done.

Through the Veil

Lift not the painted veil which those who live
Call Life; though unreal shapes be pictured there,
And it but mimic all we would believe
With colours idly spread: behind, lurk Fear
And Hope, twin destinies; who ever weave
The shadows, which the world calls substance, there.

—PERCY BYSSHE SHELLEY

To borrow Churchill's phrase once more, San rock art turned out to be "a riddle wrapped in a mystery inside an enigma." The answer to one question merely formulated another. Exploration of one field of evidence led to another. But this is surely what one would expect of a successful research approach in any discipline: An explanation that forever draws a line beneath itself is obscurantist.

Once it became apparent that the tiered, shamanistic San cosmology and the activities of shamans lay at the heart of San thought, that these matters were the fundamentals of all San life, it no longer seemed surprising that San rock art dealt largely with similar issues and within the same cosmological framework. Indeed, the centrality of shamanism for the San is hardly open to question: Its overwhelming importance comes through clearly in the nineteenth-century southern record as well as in the twentieth-century studies of the Kalahari San communities. Contrary to what some researchers believe, this key realization does not spell the end of research: It is not a final, monolithic "explanation" of San rock art. Rather, it opens up limitless possibilities for new and ever more detailed insights into the iconography and, as the previous chapter shows, into San mythology, cosmology, and social relations. Similarly, the realization that the stained glass windows in European cathedrals can be explained in terms of Christian belief, the

Bible, and church history in no way ends research into their iconography, social and political significance, and so forth. Certainly, one should not permit a successfully situating insight to blind oneself to other possibilities; this surely goes without saying.

Now, I show how the shamanistic explanation changed our ideas of the very essence of San rock art images, the significance of the rock face on which the images were executed, and the ways, beyond "viewing" in the Western art sense, in which the San related to the images. To address these questions it is necessary to introduce another source of insight, one that researchers began to explore in the 1980s. As I have argued, the word *shaman* implies some degree of universality; though it comes from the Tungus people of Central Asia, it is used worldwide to denote a belief system that, although it certainly has local variations, is strikingly uniform. A considerable portion of that uniformity derives from the ways in which the human nervous system behaves in altered states of consciousness. This is a point that assumes increasing importance in succeeding chapters.

The following article not only meshes San beliefs with the painted images, as have previous chapters; it also combines these two fields with the results of neuropsychological research on altered states of consciousness. We now have three, not just two, intermeshed cogwheels—images, San beliefs and rituals, and neuropsychology—and thus a more complex explanatory apparatus (Lewis-Williams 2001).

I wrote the article with Thomas Dowson, who was at that time a research officer in the Rock Art Research Institute; to underline our cooperation, I retain the first person plural.

Through the Veil: San Rock Paintings and the Rock Face

In the 1970s there was a move toward more anthropological studies of symbolism and an interest in polysemy. The eland, for instance, was recognized as a central, or key, symbol (Vinnicombe 1975, 1976). In some painted contexts the segment of its semantic spectrum that referred to girls' puberty was emphasized, while in other contexts it was boys' first-kill, marriage, or shamanistic associations that were highlighted (Lewis-Williams 1981a). Isolated and therefore apparently contextless depictions of eland were thought to reflect the whole "complex set of associations which constitutes the [eland's] implicational meaning" (Lewis-Williams 1981a, 130).

Although this ethnographic-anthropological approach differs sharply from earlier "readings" of rock art, there is nevertheless an important concept common to the two approaches. Both tacitly accept that the rock face, the support on which paintings were executed, was a tabula rasa; in other words, the support could carry pictures dealing with a range of topics and performing a range of functions. We now question the assumption that the rock face was a silent support.

In the first place, there are a priori reasons for doubting a neutral support. In Western thought, a blackboard, for example, is not neutral, despite the feeling one may have that anything can be written or drawn on it. Its associations strongly suggest a didactic purpose as well as an emphemerality that would be inappropriate for "works of art." A blackboard communicates its own message and circumscribes whatever is put on it. A framed canvas, on the other hand, at once implies that the images on it constitute a "work of art." An even more specific context is implied by stained glass windows in a church. They may be didactic, though in a different sense from blackboard drawings, but they inevitably imply religious associations, even though apparently secular objects, such as ships or animals, may be depicted. In Western art there is no such thing as an invisible support. The support makes its own, often vital, contribution to the meaning of the pictures on it; the support is in fact the most fundamental part of the context. Although all these examples come from Western art, an implication is that an understanding of the support is always necessary for a full understanding of a work of art (cf. Goodman 1976; Danto 1981).

These considerations lead us to ask: When San artists were painting, to what were they applying their paint? A Eurocentric answer is that paint was being applied to meaningless rock surfaces, because rock surfaces are not a recognized context for Western art. But, in addition to the a priori considerations we have mentioned, there are features of the art itself that suggest that the rock face was significant and in some sense part of the picture. Paintings frequently appear to enter and leave cracks and steps in the rock face. Others are "folded" into concave right angles; still others come off the edges of convex right angles. Some are fitted neatly into facets or hollows in the rock and a few incorporate nodules of rock. Some of these features also occur among rock engravings, but we do not consider them here (see Dowson 1990a). Instead, we concentrate on paintings that appear to enter and leave inequalities in the rock face.

Rock Paintings

We begin with the red lines that are frequently fringed with small white dots. One of the most compact and best preserved examples (figure 5.1) has been superimposed on an eland. It usefully illustrates a number of important features.

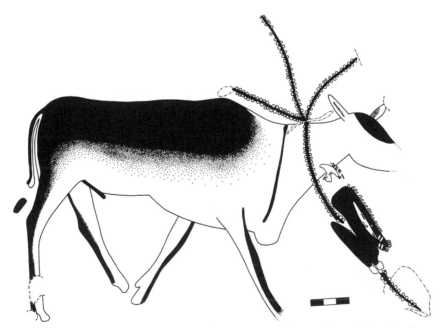

Figure 5.1.   Red lines fringed with white dots entering and leaving the rock face. The lines are superimposed on an eland. Northeastern Cape. The scale in this and other figures in this chapter is in centimeters. In all the figures in this chapter, broken lines represent cracks and other inequalities in the rock.

Four branches of the line emerge from, or enter into, a small 3-mm groove in the rock. Three of these branches end at very small, hardly noticeable steps in the rock face varying from 2 to 4 mm. The fourth simply ends on a smooth area. The lowermost branch is associated with a kneeling human figure: The line stops at the figure's stomach and then continues beyond its feet until it enters a small crack. White hairs are painted along its arm and on part of its body.

Sometimes these lines extend for many meters through a rock shelter, linking widely separated paintings and apparently weaving in and out of the rock face. Frequently, people and animals are depicted walking along sections of the line before it enters a tiny inequality on the rock or simply ends, only to reappear a few centimeters away (e.g., Pager 1975a; Vinnicombe 1976, fig. 152). In a particularly complex example from the ceiling of a Western Cape site (figure 5.2) the line is double and lacks fringing white dots. At first glance it may seem to depict paths, but a figure on the left is holding the line coiled as if it were a rope. Right of the central group the line touches a running man's foot and continues from his other foot. The central group introduces another way in which the rock face

Figure 5.2.   Double lines painted in red linking numerous human figures. In the center, a step in the rock has been outlined with red paint. Western Cape.

was used. This group is built around a small step in the rock that is about 15 mm at its deepest. Red paint has been applied around the step. A group of people stand within the hollow so formed, while another group approaches them from the left. Arrows fly between them. The double line on which the left-hand group is walking joins to the stave of a bow held by a man within the step. The double line leaves the bow string and leads to the bowman's face. Then it links the man's quiver to the face of another figure. Finally, the double line seems to appear to the right of the smeared red paint. Details like these show that the painting does not depict a "realistic" fight between two San groups, one of which is defending a rock shelter (Johnson and Maggs 1979, fig. 67). A second, roughly circular, area of paint has been placed to the left of the central group.

The even more elaborate painting in figure 5.3a develops a number of the ideas implied by figures 5.1 and 5.2. Black paint has been applied to a groove, or fold, in the rock face. At least one therianthrope and a number of other figures,

Figure 5.3a.   A cleft in the rock outlined with black paint. Therianthropes and other figures protrude from the cleft. The figures are associated with fish, eels, and tortoises or turtles. Northeastern Cape.

one of whom bleeds from the nose, rise up out of, or sink into, the cleft in the rock. Associated with at any rate the large therianthrope are a number of fish and what appear to be eels or snakes and two tortoises or turtles. There is also a cluster of at least ten flywhisks. Close by, the heads of two therianthropes emerge from an area of black paint that is not associated with a crack (figure 5.3b). This group seems to be constructed on the same principle as the roughly rectangular area of black paint from which fishtails protrude in figure 5.3a. These paintings thus show that not only lines but also therianthropes go in and out of the rock face and that "openings" were created by the application of paint.

Still other kinds of painting similarly interact with the rock. A Lesotho group shows two therianthropes, one superimposed on the other; both have flywhisks (figure 5.4). Their feet, or hooves, are on or close to the very small step in the rock. A fantastic serpent emerges from the upper extremity of this step, but part of the serpent has been painted so that it continues beyond the step. It thus appears to emerge partly from the step and partly from a smooth rock surface. The serpent has white "hairs" and two "tusks"; similar "hairs" and a single "tusk" are painted on one of the therianthropes: The link between the two depictions is clear.

Figure 5.3b.   Therianthropes protrude from an area of black paint. Approximately 110 mm from the crack in figure 5.3a.

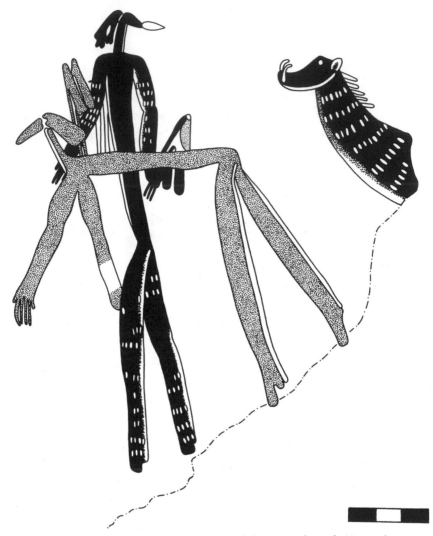

Figure 5.4.   A fantastic serpent emerges from a slight step in the rock. Next to it are two therianthropes. Lesotho.

Serpents are, in fact, commonly depicted entering or leaving cracks (e.g., Lewis-Williams 1981a, fig. 23). Vinnicombe (1976, 228, 235) describes snakes and fantastic serpents "slithering" from cracks in the rock. Some of these serpents have horns and antelope heads; a number bleed from the nose. An impressive example from the Northeastern Cape comes out of a crack and then undulates for 4 m across the rock before going behind a large boss of rock and emerging on the other side. It has antelope ears and bleeds from the nose (figure 5.5).

Another fantastic creature that emerges from the rock is the rain-animal. In a particularly fine example in the Northeastern Cape human figures clap while one

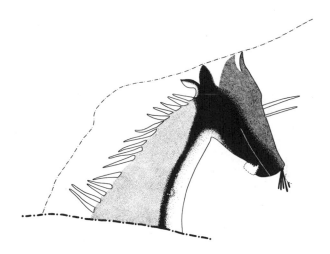

Figure 5.5.   Part of a large, fantastic serpent that enters and leaves the rock face. It has antelope ears and blood falls from its nose. Northeastern Cape.

plays a musical bow; some figures are therianthropic (Lee and Woodhouse 1970, fig. 193). To the left, a large spotted rain-animal emerges from a substantial step (Dowson 1990b, Dowson in preparation). Not all emerging creatures, however, are as obviously fantastic: Vinnicombe (1976, fig. 107) illustrates an eland emerging from a crack. Other paintings show antelope heads coming from steps or from blotches of paint. Figure 5.6 shows at least four antelope heads emerging from two sides of an inequality in the rock. Red paint has been smeared along the inequality and ochre dots have been added to it. Just above the heads and the smeared paint there is a figure in the same kneeling, arms-back posture as the one in figure 5.1. Within the hollow formed by the roughly oval inequality there is a figure standing in the arms-back posture and holding what are probably two flywhisks; another figure next to him runs with a bow and three arrows. Farther to the right, there is a line of walking figures, two of whom have large fantastic heads; one has antelope ears. They carry unidentifiable objects.

Another, and, as far as we know, unique, use of the rock surface is illustrated in figure 5.7. Here a white calcite run that emerges from the rock has been given white ears to create the impression of an animal head facing the viewer. A red zigzag has been painted on the calcite.

Finally, a few paintings seem to come out of the rock even though there is no step or smear of paint. A painting in Lesotho, for example, shows very clearly part of an animal (figure 5.8); it is well preserved, and there is no question of the missing part having faded. The painting seems to imply that the rest of the animal

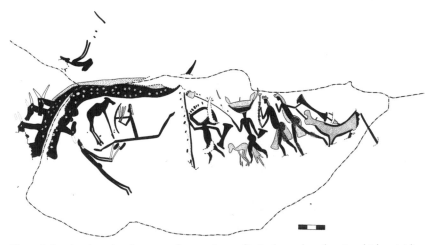

Figure 5.6.   Antelope heads emerge from an inequality in the rock surface to which paint has been applied. Eastern Orange Free State.

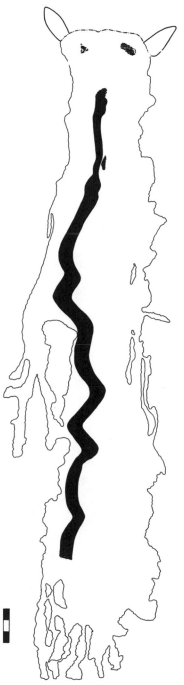

Figure 5.7. A white calcite run has had two white ears added to it. A red zigzag has been painted on the calcite. Northeastern Cape.

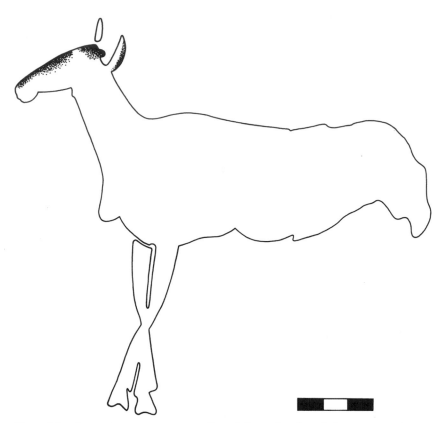

Figure 5.8.   An antelope seems to appear through the rock surface. Its legs are crossed as are the legs of numerous painted trance dancers (e.g., Vinnicombe 1976, figs. 102, 233, 234; Lewis-Williams 1981a, fig. 28). Lesotho.

is behind the rock face and out of sight of ordinary people. It recalls the way in which the red line with white dots weaves in and out of the rock face even though there are often no steps or other inequalities (figure 5.1).

These examples illustrate the principal ways in which San artists used the rock face to give the impression of depictions entering and leaving the wall of a rock shelter; many more examples can be found in the literature. To investigate the possible significance of the feature and what it implies about the support on which the paintings were executed we begin with what is now the most widely accepted understanding of the art's social context; we then develop a line of neuropsychological research that grew out of this understanding.

Culture and Neuropsychology

Ethnographic evidence shows that, whatever other associations or connotations the art may have had, it was essentially shamanistic (Lewis-Williams 1980, 1982, 1983d, 1988b; Lewis-Williams and Loubser 1986; Lewis-Williams and Dowson 1989a). It comprises symbols of the supernatural potency shamans harnessed to enter trance, depictions of hallucinations and activities associated with San shamanism, and metaphors of trance experience. Moreover, the detail of numerous hallucinatory depictions as well as ethnographic data suggest that, at least in many instances, the artists were themselves shamans and that they were depicting—for whatever reasons—their own spiritual experiences and insights (Lewis-Williams and Dowson 1989a). Studies in various parts of southern Africa from the Western Cape Province to the southeastern mountains and north to Zimbabwe have shown that many essentially shamanistic elements of the art were very widespread indeed (e.g., Huffman 1983; Maggs and Sealy 1983; Yates, Golson, and Hall 1985; Hall 1986; Garlake 1987a; Mazel 1989a).

The paintings we have described display a number of these elements. The kneeling human figures in figures 5.1 and 5.6 recall the posture shamans sometimes adopt when they fall semiconscious in trance (Marshall 1969, 376); shamans are often painted in this posture. Moreover, the figures have their arms in the backward trancing posture that some Kalahari shamans say they adopt when they are asking God for supernatural potency (Lewis-Williams 1981a, 88). The example in figure 5.1 also has a red line coming from its nose and sweeping back across its face; it probably represents the nasal hemorrhage experienced by San shamans (Arbousset and Daumas 1846, 246–47; Orpen 1874, 10; Bleek 1935, 12, 13, 35; Marshall 1969, 360, 374). The antelope in figure 5.8 has its legs crossed, as do a number of painted dancers.

Studies of the kind of connecting lines shown in figures 5.1 and 5.2 have suggested that they may represent supernatural potency or even be a transformation of the shaman himself; certainly, they are often associated with clearly shamanistic elements (Lewis-Williams 1981b; Dowson 1989). Serpents, which are often depicted with nasal blood (e.g., figure 5.5), may also be transformed shamans (Huffman 1983; Lewis-Williams and Dowson 1989a). Other transformations frequently found in the art include "hair" and "tusks" (figure 5.4). The activation of potency that brings about these transformations can take place in solitary circumstances or at a dance. Painted dancers frequently carry flywhisks (figures 5.3a, 5.4, and 5.6), artifacts that are closely associated with trance performance (Lee 1967, 31; Marshall 1969, 358).

To obtain a better understanding of the shamanistic experience implied by these paintings we turn to neuropsychological research into altered states of consciousness. Because the nervous system is a human universal, all people, no matter what their cultural background, experience similar kinds of hallucinations. This is true whether an altered state of consciousness is induced by psychoactive drugs, sensory deprivation, intense concentration, auditory driving, schizophrenia, hyperventilation, or sustained rhythmic movement (Klüver 1942; Horowitz 1964, 513–18; Siegel and Jarvik 1975; Asaad and Shapiro 1986). In certain altered states the nervous system becomes a "sixth sense" that produces its own, nonveridical, impressions that can be experienced alongside the impressions produced by the "normal" five senses. "Experiments point to underlying mechanisms in the central nervous system as the source of a universal phenomenology of hallucinations (Siegel 1977, 132; for more on neuropsychology and rock art, see Lewis-Williams and Dowson 1988; Dowson 1989).

The products of the nervous system are, however, only the raw material: Certain hallucinations are valued and cultivated while others are ignored. Writing of the Huichol use of the hallucinatory plant peyote, Furst (1972) says, "Beyond certain 'universal' visual and auditory sensations, which may be linked to the chemistry of the plant and its effect on the central nervous system, there are powerful cultural factors at work that influence, if they do not actually determine, both content and interpretation of the drug experience" (181–83). Despite common structural elements, hallucinations are essentially culturally controlled. Ultimately, "cultural determinants of hallucinations" (Siegel and Jarvik 1975, 136), not the nervous system, are paramount. In what follows we distinguish between "neurological" elements that are universal and "psychological" elements that are culture-specific. In doing so, we show that our dual approach enables us to address issues not referred to in the inevitably limited ethnography.

We remark first on a widely reported, virtually universal feature of trance experience that is neurologically determined. As subjects move into a deep stage of trance, they experience a vortex that seems to engulf them. Sometimes a bright light in the center of the field of vision creates this tunnel-like perspective. Subjects report "viewing much of their imagery in relation to a tunnel . . . images tended to pulsate, moving towards the center of the tunnel or away from the bright light and sometimes moving in both directions" (Siegel 1977, 134). Later, complex imagery of animals, people, and so forth appears to overlie the tunnel (Siegel and Jarvik 1975, 127–30; Siegel 1977, 136). One subject said, "I'm moving through some kind of train tunnel. There are all sorts of lights and colors, mostly in the center, far, far away, way, far away, and little people and stuff running around the walks [?walls] of the tube, like little cartoon nebishes, they're pretty close." Among fifty-eight reports of eight kinds of hallucinations, this sort of tunnel was found to be the most common (Siegel and Jarvik 1975, 139). Eventually, subjects are drawn into the vortex, and, being dissociated from their bodies, become part of their own mental imagery (Siegel and Jarvik 1975, 128; Siegel 1977, 136). It is at this stage that they feel themselves turning into animals (Klüver 1926, 505; Siegel and Jarvik 1975, 105) and that they experience other major transformations.

Westerners use culture-specific works like "funnels, alleys, cones, vessels, pits [and] corridors" (Siegel and Jarvik 1975, 113) to describe the vortex. In other cultures, it is often experienced as entering a hole in the ground. Shamans typically speak of reaching the spirit world via such a hole (Harner 1982b, 31). The Inuit of Hudson Bay, for instance, describe a "road down through the earth" that starts in the house where they perform their rituals (Rasmussen 1929, 124). The Bella Coola of the American Northwest Coast believe such a hole is "situated in each house between the doorway and the fireplace" (Boas 1900, 37). The Algonkians of Canada travel through layers of earth: "a hole leading into the bowels of the earth [is] the pathway of the spirits" (Vastokas and Vastokas 1973, 53). In Australia, shamans are said to "dive into the ground" and to travel through the earth (Elkin 1945, 107, 108). The Conibo of the Upper Amazon speak of following the roots of a tree down into the ground (Harner 1982b, 32).

The sensation of traveling through a tunnel is often associated with water, probably because of the rushing or roaring sound heard in certain altered states of consciousness. For Harner (1968), the acquisition of visions was closely associated with a waterfall. When the Inuit are living on the ice, the route to the underworld is through the sea: "He almost glides as if falling through a tube" (Rasmussen 1929, 124). The hole down which a Tavgi Samoyed shaman moves leads to a river with streams flowing in opposite directions (Harner 1982b, 33). Reports of culture-specific apprehensions of this universal, neurologically determined hallucination of subterranean and subaqueous travel could easily be multiplied.

It is therefore not surprising that underground and underwater imagery plays an important role in San shamanistic thought. An old !Kung shaman, K"xau, told Biesele (1980) how he reached the spirit world. First, the giraffe, his power animal, "took" him. Then Kauha (God) led him to a "wide body of water" which they entered. His teacher, an experienced shaman, told him that he would enter the earth, that he "would travel through the earth and then emerge at another place" (Biesele 1980, 56). "When people sing [medicine songs], I dance. I enter the earth. I go in at a place where people drink water. I travel in a long way, very far" (Biesele 1980, 61). The sensation of moving through a tunnel on this journey is suggested by K″xau's statement: "My sides were pressed by pieces of metal. . . . And in this way I traveled forward. . . . I was stretched out in the water" (Biesele 1980, 56).

Similar beliefs are evident in reports that Bleek and Lloyd recorded in the nineteenth century. The /Xam San of the Cape Province spoke of shamans going into a "waterpit" where the water was "alive"; there they captured the hallucinatory !khwa-ka xoro, the rain-animal, which they killed so that its blood and milk would fall as rain (Bleek 1935, 32; see also Lewis-Williams 1981a, 103–16). /Kaggen, the southern San trickster-deity, who was himself a shaman, dived into waterholes during trance episodes (Orpen 1874, 7; Bleek 1924, 17). In one myth he "descended into the ground and came up again" until he was close to an eagle whose honey he desired (Orpen 1874, 8).

These accounts and myths are clearly San versions of the worldwide shamanistic experience of reaching the spirit world through holes in the ground. They represent the San experience of neurologically determined sensations associated with altered states of consciousness. Kalahari shamans have these experiences in the center of the camp; they do not leave for some sacred or secluded spot. An old San woman, probably the last survivor of the southern San, described how shamans of the southern Drakensberg danced and entered trance in rock shelters (Jolly 1986; Lewis-Williams 1986b). We therefore argue that shamans often went into trance and experienced the underground journey in the presence of rock paintings. What would have been the effect of their altered states of consciousness when they looked at the wall of the shelter with its paintings?

Some idea of an answer to this question can be gleaned from accounts of trance vision obtained during laboratory experiments. In dealing with these accounts we continue to distinguish between universal, neurological elements and the Westerners' own cultural input. When a subject looked at a photograph of a waterfall that was opposite him on the wall, he saw "a remarkable brilliance" and a "three-dimensionality." "The picture appeared to have a depth found in stereoscopic pictures" (Cohen 1964, 133). Other subjects have reported similar changes in depth relations and the way in which two-dimensional objects are seen in three dimensions (Kieffer and Moritz 1968). Corridors often appear much longer than usual and objects can fluctuate in distance, approaching and receding from the viewer (Andersen and Rawnsley, cited by Hoffer and Osmond 1967, 13). Along with this effect goes a magnification of detail: Very small things increase in size and importance (Klüver 1966). Conversely, large objects, including the subject, can become very small. At the same time, hallucinations are projected onto walls or ceilings (Klüver 1926, 505, 506; Knoll et al. 1963, 208; Hoffer and Osmond 1967, 13). Significantly, Szuman (cited by Siegel and Jarvik

1975, 109) described this experience as "pictures painted before your imagination," and Siegel (1977, 134) likened it to "a motion picture or slide show." The Amazonian Tukano shamans similarly report images projected onto plane surfaces; these images include afterimages that may recur in this way for several months after the actual trance experience (Reichel-Dolmatoff 1978a, 8).

Because neuropsychological research and ethnographic reports show that three-dimensionality, magnification of detail, projection of mental imagery, and afterimagery are intrinsic to trance states, we argue that they played a role in the San understanding of the paintings we have described. For a San shaman in trance, the minute steps and cracks from which painted lines and other depictions sometimes emerge could have appeared much larger. Big steps and hollows and even the rock shelter itself could have become engulfing. In flickering firelight paintings of animals and people, like the photograph of the waterfall, probably assumed a three-dimensionality and life of their own. Along with vitalized paintings, shamans almost certainly saw their own mental imagery projected onto the walls and ceilings of the shelters. In the end, they would perhaps have not distinguished between paintings and projected hallucinations. Paintings and the hallucinatory "motion picture or slide show," to which Siegel refers, would have melted one into the other. Paintings themselves were, in this sense, hallucinations, contributing to and even inducing the shamans' visions. These and other effects of altered states of consciousness would have transformed the walls of rock shelters into animated screens of powerful imagery.

We argue that the walls of shelters and especially holes and inequalities in the rock surface may, under such conditions, have appeared to be entrances to tunnels leading to the spirit world. Shamans were drawn into these tunnels as they headed for the other realm. What lies at the end of the tunnel? Harner (1982b, 32) describes how the tunnel eventually opens out and a shaman finds himself or herself in "lands of forests, lakes and rivers, and strange cities bright as day, lit by a sun that has disappeared from the ordinary world above."

The San hallucinatory world is culturally determined, but it nevertheless incorporates similar elements of fantasy and the sense of another reality. Having passed through the tunnel, a San shaman ascends to the sky where the spirits of the dead live with God.

> People say there are leopards there. People say there are zebras. They say locusts. They say lions. . . . Elands are there. Giraffes are there. Gemsbok are there. Kudu are there. These things don't kill each other. They are God's possessions. (Biesele 1980, 59)

The presence of animals is also seen in a statement Orpen obtained. When he asked his San guide where /Kaggen was, the man replied:

> We don't know, but the elands do. Have you not hunted and heard his cry, when the elands suddenly start and run to his call? Where he is, elands are in droves like cattle. (Orpen 1874, 3)

But the spirit world is not pleasant. Kalahari San say that God and his wife have grotesquely enlarged genitalia. There is a frightening one-legged spirit and another "whose legs are all soft." He has horns and long hair hangs from his body. "A foul thing! A thing to make you run away." When people see God and these spirits, they "tremble with fear" (Biesele 1980, 58–59). Having had these experiences, the shaman returns to the mundane world via the tunnel: "You enter, enter, enter the earth, and then you return to enter . . . the skin of your body" (Biesele 1980, 60).

This journey to the spirit world involves physical changes. Old K"xau told Biesele (1980, 59) that a shaman had to make himself very small: "When you arrive at God's place, you make yourself small. You have become small." This seems to be part of the changes in size that are experienced in trance states. Significantly for an understanding of the paintings of serpents (figs. 5.4 and 5.5), it is sometimes necessary for a shaman to turn into a snake if he or she wishes to survive: "If you're a snake, friend, you'll stay alive. If you're a mamba, you'll stay alive" (Biesele 1980, 59).

Transformation into an animal is in fact part of San trance experience. It is represented in the art by therianthropes that combine human with, chiefly, antelope features, but occasionally with baboon, elephant, bird, or fish elements (Lewis-Williams and Dowson 1989a, 68–3). The antelope with its legs crossed (fig. 5.8) like those of trance dancers (Vinnicombe 1976, figs. 101, 102; Lewis-Williams and Dowson 1989a, fig. 20) may therefore be a transformed shaman emerging from the wall of the rock shelter.

If this is the sort of experience that lay behind the wall of the rock shelter and if that realm was reached by means of a tunnel through the rock, we can begin to form some idea of what the practice of painting meant to the San. Because shamans in trance shake too violently to hold a brush or to achieve the delicate, fine lines of the art (they are also often deeply unconscious), painting probably took place some time after, not during, trance experience. The effects of the passage of time on recollected mental imagery have been documented. After a period of five to twenty-six days, subjects tend to produce more elaborate and better-defined depictions than those done during an experiment. The memory of an hallucination does not necessarily fade like the memory of a dream. After five months, subjects produce even more generalized depictions rather than specific pictures (Knoll et al. 1963, 208–12). The effects of recollection probably explain the way in which some depictions of San rock art are bizarre yet carefully formed.

On the other hand, a more immediate relationship between mental image and painting may have obtained if San shamans experienced the sort of afterimage described by the Tukano and confirmed by neuropsychological research (Reichel-Dolmatof 1978b, 298). In these cases subjects are fully awake and in control of their faculties: Triggered by a change in body chemistry or an external stimulus, images simply float before them or are projected onto a surface.

Either way, some shaman-artists must have examined the rock face very carefully, seeking out the inequalities where they had entered the tunnel to the spirit world and through which they had returned with their visions. Other shaman-artists created "entrances" by applying paint to smooth areas of rock and then elicited from the paint what they had witnessed at the far end of the journey. Still others simply painted their mental images where they had been projected on the wall of the shelter, regardless of cracks, right angles, and other inequalities. San religion permits a wide range of idiosyncratic belief (Marshall 1962, 246, 1969; Biesele 1978, 1987; Katz 1982, 29; Guenther 1986, 221–22, 266–67), and this is reflected in their rock art (Dowson 1988, 1989; Dowson and Holliday 1989).

But what of the extremely unpleasant aspects of the spirit world? It is from that realm that malevolent shamans and the spirits of the dead, attracted by the beautiful singing and dancing, shoot small, invisible "arrows of sickness" into people. One of the shamans' tasks is to "confront these spirits and battle with them to save the people from sickness and death" (Katz 1982, 103). As Katz says, "The very performance of a dance calls for such a confrontation." Some paintings of fights probably depict these spiritual battles rather than "real" historical events (Campbell 1986). We suggest that this sort of conflict may explain part of the painting in figure 5.2: A group of malevolent shamans tries to emerge from the spirit world behind the rock face, while another group struggles to keep them and their flying "arrows of sickness" in the place where they belong and where they cannot harm people. The conflict centers around an opening to the spirit world, the step in the rock.

It is, however, not only malevolent spirits and shamans that a dance attracts. When Kalahari shamans dance, they say that animals are attracted to the place; they stand out in the darkness just beyond the firelight, spirit animals, but none the less real. They can be seen only by shamans, who draw each other's attention to them so that they can pool their visions and power. If people are dancing elephant potency, elephant come; if they dance eland potency, eland, the most powerful of all animals, approach (Biesele, personal communication). We have seen that the home of these animals is the spirit world, where God, a kind of Lord of the Animals, has all his possessions, and where "elands are in droves like cattle." We believe it is reasonable to suppose that, as spirit animals are attracted in the Kalahari, so the southern shaman-artists attracted spirit animals through the wall of the rock shelter and then caused them to be manifest for all to see. Everyone shares freely in the shamans' experiences (Biesele 1978, 937–38). Paintings of eland are probably not all depictions of "real" eland; many may be spirit eland brought back from the spirit realm by shaman-artists. There they stand, emerging from the rock, painted across cracks, folded into steps, because those steps and cracks hardly exist; shamans see beyond them as no ordinary person can.

Painting was thus a ritual act that employed two principal elements, each with its own range of significance: paint and rock face. These apparently purely technical elements cannot be separated from meaning.

First, the paint had its own power. When How (1962, 38) asked Mapote, an old man of Sotho and Pondomise descent who had learned to paint with San in their caves, to paint for her, he asked for *qhang qhang*, a glistening hematite dug out of the basalt mountains. It had to be prepared at full moon out of doors by a woman who heated it over a fire until it was red hot. After this it was ground to a fine powder. Mapote then said he needed "the blood of a freshly killed eland" with which to mix his paint. The ritual circumstances of making paint are clear (Vinnicombe 1975, 1976, 180), but the use of eland blood is particularly significant. The old San woman to whom we have referred confirmed the use of eland blood: Shaman-artists used the blood to infuse their paint with eland potency. She went on to explain that, as shamans danced, they turned to face the paintings when they wished to heighten the level of their potency (Jolly 1986; Lewis-Williams, 1986b). Paint was thus powerful and trance-inducing in itself; that is why it was sometimes applied to inequalities in the rock or used to make areas from which images could emerge. She also explained that a "good" person could place his or her hand on a painting of an eland and derive potency from it; a "bad" person would adhere to the rock and eventually waste away and die. Her remarks, taken together with the features of the art and San experience we have discussed, suggest a highly significant insight into the nature of San rock art. The paintings were not simply depictions of other things—animals, people, visions, and so forth; rather, they were things in themselves; they had a life and existence of their own. Probably, for shamans trancing in the rock shelters—and for ordinary people as well—the paintings *were* visions. Developing Marshall's (1969, 351) comparison of supernatural potency with electricity, we may say that many paintings were less like a zigzag symbolizing electricity on a fuse box than an electric wall plug to which appliances can be connected.

Second, we can see that the other major element in the act of painting, the rock face, was not a neutral tabula rasa to which paint was applied. The walls of rock shelters were rather the gateway to the spirit world and interacted with the ritual paint in ways we do not fully understand. Looking at the rock with its paintings, trancing shamans were drawn through the tunnel and into the world of God's animals, the rain-animal, and their own transformation into animals. There they remonstrated with God, fought against the spirits of the dead, captured a rain-animal, saw strange, wonderful, and frightening things, and then returned to the mundane world, again through the tunnel. The ritual act of painting lured those images through the rock face and fixed them there for all to see. Even unpainted rock may have been as pregnant as silences in music.

Conclusion

We have argued that the walls of rock shelters were in some sense a veil, a "painted veil," suspended between this world and the world of spirit (see also Lewis-Williams 1988b, 5.14). In some instances (e.g., figures 5.1, 5.2, 5.3a, 5.4, 5.5, and 5.6), small openings, steps, and other inequalities, enlarged in the shamans' trance vision, gave them an opportunity to penetrate the veil. In other instances (e.g., figures 5.2, 5.3b, and 5.6), the application of paint by smearing it on the rock facilitated access to the spirit world, and shaman-artists could cause their visions to come through these ritually created openings. In yet other cases (e.g., figure 5.8), it seems as if the veil was so diaphanous that an animal or a shaman could simply appear through it. Finally, marks on the rock could occasionally be transformed into mysterious creatures peering from the spirit world (e.g., figure 5.7).

A major implication of this argument is that the rock face constituted a shamanistic context for all paintings, much as stained glass windows in a church are a religious context. We therefore believe that nonshamanistic associations of the painted eland symbol (boys' first-kill, girls' puberty and marriage) formed only a penumbra, a background that contributed to the power of the symbol to move people but that was not highlighted. It was to shamanism that the multitude of eland and other depictions principally referred.

Ultimately, these eland and all the other images came from the spirit world hidden behind the walls of the rock shelters, invisible to ordinary people. Biesele

(1978) found that the Kalahari San shamans tell people about what is really going on in that world. The southern San shaman-artists went further and worked with paint and rock to reify their visions and insights so that, in addition to being symbols resonating on different levels, they became things in themselves, visible, tangible, and potent. part of the shaman-artists' mission was to make nonordinary reality a reality for ordinary people.

Note

From J. D. Lewis-Williams and T. A. Dowson, "Through the Veil: San Rock Paintings and the Rock Face," *South African Archaeological Bulletin* 45 (1990): 5–16.

Retrospect

Since the publication of this paper, research has suggested a more precise and persuasive explanation of the painted red lines fringed with white dots (Lewis-Williams et al. 2000). A remarkable aspect of southern African rock art research is that new ethnography is continually becoming available from communities living in the Kalahari Desert. Having read the new material, we are sometimes able to return to the finite, nineteenth-century southern ethnography and find in it evidence for San concepts that had previously escaped notice because they are referred to only obliquely. The new explanation of the red line motif is a case in point.

We now know that San shamans speak of "threads of light" that take them into and through the spirit world. They walk along, climb, or merely float effortlessly above these luminous threads as they pursue their transcosmological journeys. The threads also take them to distant parts of the desert so that they can find out how friends and relatives are faring. Sometimes, shamans speak of these threads as if they are made of n/om, supernatural potency. Sometimes, the threads are seen to enter into people.

The close parallels between the painted lines and San reports of threads of light strongly suggest that the shaman painters were depicting the means and the route that they traveled. That is why people are shown walking on the line, holding it as if it were a rope, dancing on it, or floating along it. Such contexts are not as contradictory as they may appear to us.

Perhaps most importantly, the lines weave in and out of the rock face. The route of shamans on out-of-body travel was through the rock face to the spiritual realm beyond. Rock shelters were, in this sense, portals to power and eternity.

A Dream of Eland 6

Was it a vision, or a waking dream?
Fled is that music:—do I wake or sleep?

—JOHN KEATS

URING THE 1980s and through the 1990s, despite the seemingly indelible impression of the San as fashioners of naiveté, the demonstrable fit between San beliefs and the images on the rock walls continued to provide explanations of otherwise opaque imagery. In particular, our expanding understanding of San religion and cosmology began to uncover unsuspected facets of belief and their expression in the art. The 1980s were especially exciting times. As we learned more about the vocabulary and syntax of San rock art, we were able to "read" increasingly complex painted texts. Or, to change the metaphor, we had a bunch of keys; now we had to see what lay behind a series of locked doors.

In a paper published in 1987, I tried to illustrate the potential of the ethnographic-neuropsychological method I advocated by discussing a hitherto unnoted component of San shamanism and leading my argument toward a painted panel that I considered to be one of the most remarkable in southern Africa. Today, I am even more astounded by the intellectual complexity of these images.

A Dream of Eland: An Unexplored Component of San Shamanism and Rock Art

Discussions of San rock art as part of shamanism have all emphasized the central role of the trance, or curing, dance (for extensive accounts of this dance see Lee 1967, 1968; Marshall 1969; Biesele 1975, 1978; Guenther 1975; Katz 1982). At a trance dance in the Kalahari today, women sing and clap the rhythm of medicine songs believed to contain supernatural potency. They sit around a central fire, also believed to contain potency, while the men, half of whom may be shamans, dance around them. As the dance intensifies, the men, usually without the aid of hallucinogens, tremble violently, stagger, and finally enter trance. In a state of controlled trance, they move around laying their trembling hands on all the people present and drawing known and unknown sickness out of them. In a deeper level of trance, the shamans collapse and experience hallucinations such as out-of-body travel. Some rock paintings depict similar circular dances, while others show dancers circling a patient (figure 6.1) or surrounded by clapping women. In yet other compositions the participants are arranged in no apparent order. In these less "realistic" paintings the men are often attenuated to express some of the sensations of trance, and others have extraordinary hallucinatory head forms and other distortions (figure 6.2).

Having acknowledged the importance of the trance dance, I now turn to a component of San shamanistic experience that has so far not received attention. The nineteenth-century Bleek collection of southern San (/Xam) ethnography records verbatim accounts of shamans experiencing dreams very similar to the hallucinations associated with the trance dance (for accounts of the Bleek Collection and its relationship to modern Kalahari San ethnography, see Lewis-Williams and Biesele 1978 and Lewis-Williams 1981a, 25–37). One of these accounts says that, when people hear a shaman shivering at night, they believe him to be combatting dangerous shamans (Bleek 1935, 13; see also Bleek 1936, 142–43). Lloyd, Bleek's collaborator, seems to have taken the passage to mean that the man was shivering as if from the cold. Because neither Bleek nor Lloyd had ever seen San shamans in action, they had only a vague understanding of what they did. Moreover, it is probable that neither had any conception at all of trance and its role in San shamanism. In any event, when Lloyd translated this passage she did not know that !khauken, the word she gave as "shiver," means to beat or to tremble, but especially to tremble in trance (Bleek 1956, 425). Thus, the informant was not referring to shivering from cold but to a shaman's physical reaction to an altered state of consciousness comparable to that experienced in the trance

Figure 6.1.   San rock painting of a curing dance. In the center, a kneeling shaman places his hands on a recumbent patient. The containing line may represent a hut or some unexplained concept. The scatter of arrows in the lower part of the panel may represent "arrows of sickness" that malevolent shamans were believed to shoot into people. Kwa Zulu-Natal Drakensberg. Colors: red and white. Scale in centimeters.

dance. The essence of the passage is that a shaman could protect the people in sleep just as he did in trance.

One informant developed this concept of a sleeping shaman's protective powers:

> Although he is asleep, he is watching the doings that occur at night, for he wants to protect the people from the things that come to kill them. Because of these things he watches over the people, for he is

Figure 6.2.   A complex group of shamans dancing with bows and sticks. Anatomical distortions and other features suggest the panel is hallucinatory. A large figure to the left has a line of dots along its back. This probably represents the "boiling" of potency in a shaman's spine. To the right, an eland, only partially preserved, has been superimposed on some of the dancers. Harrismith district. Colors: red and white. Scale in centimeters.

aware that other shamans walk by night to attack people at night. Therefore he protects them from these. (Bleek 1935, 26–27)

Such extracorporeal protecting and marauding was often accomplished in animal form, and the /Xam spoke of shamans turning themselves into creatures such as jackals (Bleek 1935, 15–17), birds (1935, 18–19), and lions (Bleek 1936, 131–33). One informant gave a long account of a female shaman becoming a lioness and visiting his camp "to see whether we were still well where we lived." He insisted that "fighting was not the reason why she had gone out" (Bleek 1935, 43–44). The modern !Kung San of northern Botswana believe that leonine marauding shamans can be seen only by other shamans (Katz 1982, 115, 227). Out-of-body travel is so closely associated with lions that the !Kung use the word for "pawed creature" (*jum*) to mean "to go on out-of-body travel" (Biesele, personal communication). Both malevolent and benevolent shamans are often depicted in feline form in the art (Lewis-Williams 1985c).

The means by which /Xam shamans accomplished these transformations and out-of-body journeys was also described by one of Bleek's informants: "He lies asleep by us, his magic walks about while we sleep here" (Bleek 1935, 30). The

/Xam word Bleek translated as "magic" is //ke:n; it means the supernatural potency San shamans possess and activate to enter trance. To dance the medicine (or trance) dance was "to do //ke:n." Dancing and sleeping shamans thus harnessed the same power. For the shamans, sleep was like the dance and therefore an active rather than a passive condition. Because the dreams I have described are so closely linked lexically (!khauken, //ke:n) and by substance (protection, out-of-body travel) to trance I call them *trance-dreams*.

A still closer link was described by /Han ≠ kass'o, one of Bleek's informants. He spoke of /Kannu, a shaman who had control of rain. The /Xam distinguished four overlapping categories of shamans, one of which comprised the *!khwa-ka gi:ten*, or "shamans of the rain." Their best-known technique was to enter trance and capture a hallucinatory "rain-animal," which they killed where rain was most needed (Lewis-Williams 1981a, 103–16). One of /Kannu's rainmaking techniques was to strike on his bowstring while the other members of his band were asleep (Bleek 1933b, 391). The vibrating bowstring recalls the trembling of trance, but /Han ≠ kass'o also said /Kannu and his friends dreamed "that rain would fall. Then they told the other people that they had dreamt that rain would fall. Then the rain came up" (389). This may, at first glance, appear to be a dreamed premonition or revelation, for these are also part of San belief (e.g., Bleek 1932b, 326; Biesele 1975, 1:4, 2:118, 123), but other accounts of dreaming suggest it was more than that. The /Xam word for dream, //kabbo, could be used in an active, transitive way in the sense of causing things to happen. This purposeful dimension is particularly clear in a statement given by //Kabbo, one of Bleek's most prolific informants. His name, Dream, is significant in the light of what he had to say. When he was staying with the Bleek family in Cape Town in 1871, he found gardening hard work. He therefore caused it to rain: "I dreamt that I told the rain to fall for me, for my arm ached, my chest ached. I therefore dreamt that I spoke. The rain assented to me, the rain would fall for me" (Bleek ms. L.II.6.625). Both //Kabbo and /Kannu were trance-dreaming to make rain. It is indeed possible that //Kabbo earned his name through such accounts and that he was himself a shaman and so a particularly valuable informant.

Causing things to happen by dreaming also occurs in myths about the Mantis, the /Xam trickster-deity. For instance, in one of the many tales about him, the Mantis was anxious for dawn to break: "The mantis dreamed the morrow, 'O day quickly break for me'" (Bleek ms. L.II.5.556; the published version, Bleek 1924, 20, obscures this literal translation). The Mantis was causing day to break, not just dreaming about it. In another narrative the Meerkats (a type of mongoose) killed the Mantis's eland. Greatly distressed, he returned home, leaving the

Meerkats cutting up the land and hanging its meat on the branches of a tree. Then the informant, again //Kabbo, said,

> He sleeps. He trembles as he lies. Then the tree comes out of the ground on which the eland meat is placed. The tree comes out of the ground, rises up, with all the things hanging on it. It goes through the heavens and comes down near the Mantis's head. When it descends near his head, it grows there making a home for him as he lies. (Bleek ms. L.II.4.511, 510 rev.)

Here the word translated "tremble" is again !khauken, to tremble in trance. By trance-dreaming, the Mantis caused the tree to uproot itself, and he thus regained possession of his antelope.

These and other accounts suggest that trance-dreaming was, for the /Xam, an important part of shamanistic practice and that they did not draw a clear distinction between it and the hallucinations of trance as experienced in the trance dance: trembling, manipulating potency, transformation into animals, rainmaking, and extracorporeal journeys were all part of both. On the other hand, the !Kung San speak of a variation on the /Xam experience. A !Kung shaman told Katz (1982, 218) that a shaman dreams of spirits trying to kill people. He then wakes up, enters trance, and kills them. In other societies too the distinction between dreams and shamanistic visions is not always clear (Eliade 1972, 33–66). Knoll (1985, 444) mentions the deliberate induction and manipulation of dream imagery in REM sleep, and it appears that this was part of /Xam shamanism. The shaman did not experience his dream passively; he actively engaged its imagery and manipulated it toward a desired end.

Unlike the medicine dance, which has a range of distinctive postures and associations, trance-dreaming is hard to depict. Nevertheless, the foregoing discussion of trance-dreaming places us in an advantageous position to elucidate the remarkable paintings with which this paper is principally concerned (figure 6.3). Apart from two slightly flaked eland, the panel comprises two almost identical parts, each of which has three elements: a standing eland, a superimposed hallucinatory form known as a trance-buck (also "flying buck," Woodhouse 1971; and "alites," Pager 1971), and, as it were between these two, a curled-up eland.

The order in which these paintings were executed is significant. The standing eland were painted first; then the trance-buck; and finally the two curled-up eland were added in halves to give the impression of being underneath the trance-buck. The horns and ears of the curled-up eland protrude from behind the humps of the trance-buck. Thus the artist tried, by painting the halves of curled-up eland,

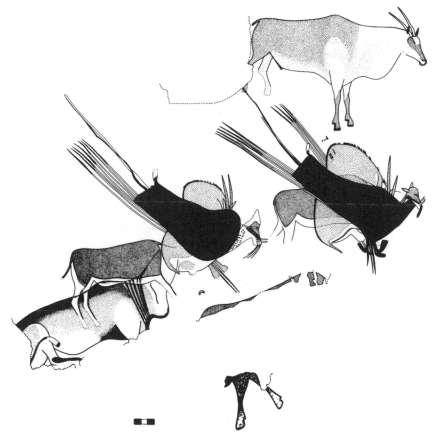

Figure 6.3.   A highly complex combination of eland and shamanic hallucinations. Harrismith district. Colors: red and white. Scale in centimeters.

to give the impression of superpositioning. Quantitative analyses of southern African rock art have suggested that superpositioning was a form of graphic syntax and that the painters favored certain combinations of subject matter and avoided others (Lewis-Williams 1972b, 1974b; Pager 1976b). This conclusion has been challenged (Willcox 1978a) and debated (Lewis-Williams, Butler-Adam, and Sutcliffe 1979). Whatever the merits of quantitative studies of superpositioning, this panel surely vindicates the view that San artists recognized superpositioning as a way of relating one painting to another. But to approach the meaning of the composition we must examine the twofold role of eland in San shamanistic beliefs.

In the first place, painted eland are symbols of the potency shamans harness to enter trance (Lewis-Williams 1981a, 75–101). In the Kalahari today this potency and its associated medicine songs are named after various "strong" things of which eland are particularly important. Eland are considered so potent that hunters like to "dance eland potency" next to the carcass of a freshly killed eland; they believe the place to be suffused with released potency (Lewis-Williams and Biesele 1978). A similar idea is contained in the /Xam myth about the Mantis and the Meerkats (Bleek 1924, 4). When the Mantis found the Meerkats cutting up his eland, he shot arrows at them, but the arrows flew back and he had to dodge them. The narrator said the Mantis intended "to fight the eland's battle." Again because she did not understand /Xam beliefs about shamanism, Lloyd took this to mean that the Mantis was fighting on behalf of the eland. It is, however, doubtful if /a, the /Xam word translated as both "fight" and "battle" (Bleek ms. L.V.I.3650), can, as a verb, mean anything other than "fight against." As a noun, /ā also means an extreme, perhaps dangerous, concentration of potency. Lloyd sometimes translated it "curse," the closest she could get to the San concept. The passage should read: "The Mantis intended to fight against the eland's potency." But the eland's potency, harnessed by the Meerkats, proved too strong, and his arrows were deflected. This potency also explains why /Xam hunters had to perform certain rituals when they approached a dead eland (Bleek 1932b, 237–38). The man who had shot the fatal arrow had to remain in the camp until his fellows had cut out the animal's heart, which was believed to possess a dangerous amount of potency. They then "beat" the carcass with its severed tail. Trance is suggested here by another use of !kauken (beat).

The eland's potency is one of the reasons why it is the most frequently depicted antelope in many parts of southern Africa. It is also the antelope on which the artists lavished the most care: It is painted in shaded polychrome and in a variety of postures more frequently than any other antelope (Maggs 1967; Pager 1971; Lewis-Williams 1972b, 1974b; Vinnicombe 1975, 1976). According to a descendant of the southern San, these eland paintings also contained potency. When shamans danced, she said, they turned to the depictions in the rock shelter to increase their potency (Lewis-Williams 1986b).

At a further level, shamans believed they actually became eland. Transformation into an animal seems to have been an essential part of /Xam shamanism. The Mantis, who was himself a shaman, could cause eland to escape hunters by entering into that antelope's bones; he also had a special affection for eland (Bleek 1924, 12). In another myth, he actually becomes "a large bull eland" (Orpen 1874, 5, 8). Prior to turning into the bull eland, the Mantis "descended into the ground three times." Going underground and underwater is so common in San and other shamanism that we may assume the Mantis effected his transformation while in trance.

In the art, transformation into an eland or other antelope is sometimes shown by blending human and antelope forms. These conflations fall into two broad categories: erect figures generally known as therianthropes and, second, kneeling trance-buck. The therianthropes have been interpreted as hunters wearing antelope masks, but numerous features count against this view (Pager 1975a; Lewis-Williams 198a, 75–101). For instance, they often carry flywhisks, an important accoutrement of the trance dance (Lee 1967, 31; Marshall 1969, 358), and have hooves in place of feet. In addition, many bleed from the nose. When a shaman entered trance he or she often bled from the nose and then rubbed the blood on a patient in the expectation that it would afford protection from evil and sickness. Nasal blood is indeed one of the most diagnostic features of painted shamans (Lewis-Williams 1981a, 75–101). In therianthropes the transformation of shaman into animal is sometimes at a half-man half-animal level, but in other paintings the transformation is complete or virtually complete and thus harder to detect. For example, some otherwise "realistic" paintings of eland have one or more red lines across the face (e.g., Vinnicombe 1976, figs. 102, 109, 247, 249), as paintings of shamans often do (e.g., Lewis-Williams 1981a, figs. 19, 20, 28, 38). Moreover, these lines are frequently associated with nasal blood in paintings of both eland and shamans. A less common link between shamans and eland is the flywhisk. At least one painting shows an otherwise "naturalistic" eland with a flywhisk protruding from the top of its head. Another painting shows a similarly realistic eland with a spray of lines curving from its hump (figure 6.4), a spot equivalent to a shaman's n//au, the "hole" in the nape of the neck through which sickness is expelled. Two small figures in a clapping posture also indicative of the trance dance are associated with the curving lines. The group of eland of which this one is part comprises two with lines on their faces and others that are apparently realistic. Compositions such as this lead one to suspect that all painted eland may be shamans as well as symbols of potency: In some cases the artists included extra features that confirm the antelope are transformed shamans, but in others they omitted these features. The "realistic" eland in figure 6.3 may thus be transformed shamans even though they lack nonrealistic features.

In addition to nonrealistic features the artists depicted specific aspects of animal behavior to suggest the intimate relationship between eland and shaman. San shamans are said to "die" when they enter trance, and the artists depicted an analogy between "dying" shamans and dying eland: Both tremble, sweat profusely, lower their head, stagger, bleed from the nose, and finally collapse unconscious.

Figure 6.4.   A group of painted eland some of which have nonrealistic features. Barkly East district. Colors: red, black, and white. Scale in centimeters.

In addition, a dying eland's hair stands on end. These behavioral characteristics of dying eland were used in the art to identify the many painted dying eland as shamans entering trance. Some paintings juxtapose dying eland with "dying" shamans who share some of their features (e.g., Lewis-Williams 1981a, fig. 28). The depiction of animal behavior was thus an important means of expressing concepts at the heart of San shamanism.

Behavioral symbolism of this kind is, I argue, also the key to understanding something of the meaning expressed by the curled-up eland in figure 6.3. Eland frequently sleep standing up or lying down with legs folded beneath them and head held high (M. Penrith and R. Smithers, personal communications; cf. eland at extreme left of figure 6.4). Both standing and lying down eland are common in the art. Because these may not be sleeping, it is impossible to say with any confidence that they represent a sleeping shaman. But another painted posture leaves no doubt: It is lying curled up with the head tucked in, as are the two in figure 6.3 (J. Kingdon and L. van Schalkwyk, personal communications). Even as depictions of dying eland are equivalent to shamans "dying" in trance, unequivocally sleeping eland may represent shamans in what I have called trance-dreaming.

This understanding helps to elucidate the complex forms that appear to overlie the sleeping eland. Each is a blend of a trance-buck and a hunting-bag containing an unstrung bow. Trance-buck are hallucinatory depictions of shamans fused with their animal potency. Some of their features include a kneeling posture or an absence of legs, blood falling from the nose, trailing "streamers," erect hair, and antelope heads (Lewis-Williams 1981a, 84–101). Here, the heads are particularly interesting because they both have a pair of tusks, an imperfectly understood feature of numerous hallucinatory depictions of shamans. Similarly, both have blood falling from the nose and also streaming back across the face in a way that recalls the red facial lines I have discussed. The trance-buck on the right has antelope ears, but the one on the left has a conical head. This type of head, often greatly exaggerated, probably depicts the sensation experienced in the crown of the head by people in altered states of consciousness. The San believe it is from this spot that a shaman's spirit leaves on out-of-body travel. Both trance-buck, but especially the one on the left, have humps reminiscent of an eland's dorsal line. Another feature common to both is the collection of items protruding from the chest. Those on the left are poorly preserved, but those on the right clearly include three flywhisks and a digging stick weighted with a bored-stone. A full discussion of this combination of male (flywhisks) and female (bored-stones) equipment in an hallucinatory painting lies beyond the scope of this paper. The "streamers" associated with each trance-buck are somewhat enigmatic. In depictions of trance-buck, such streamers probably represent potency entering the shaman or, sometimes, sickness being expelled. Here, the two sections of each streamer suggest link-shaft arrows, but in neither case do they appear to be in the bags; instead they seem to come from the sleeping eland.

Perhaps the most striking feature of these trance-buck is their fusion with hunting bags. Bags in general have great significance in San art, but here we are concerned specifically with hunting bags that are differently shaped from general purpose bags designed to be carried by hand. The proportions of ordinary bags tend to be square with rounded corners and they have a thong handle looped over the opening, but hunting bags are more oblong or slightly conical with a shoulder strap running the length of the bag and an opening at one end. When a San man goes out to hunt, he frequently places his quiver and bow in a hunting bag which he slings over his shoulder, a practice depicted in numerous paintings. The fusion of a hunting bag with a trance-buck probably refers to the fact that hunting is a further activity performed in trance. Sometimes trance-hunting is done in feline form, but it can also be accomplished with bow and arrow. A Nharo San shaman spoke of this when he said that, during a trance dance, he entered trance, went hunting, and shot an antelope. The next day, he claimed, he took his family to the place where he had killed the animal and they ate it (R. Matthews; personal communication). This "hunt" was experienced during a trance dance, but it seems probable that similar "hunts" could have been part of trance-dreaming.

Each trance-buck is thus a blend of diverse components: hunting bags, hunting equipment, antelope, a digging stick, flywhisks, and features of trance experience. Such bizarre combinations are characteristic of altered states of consciousness. Here, each trance-buck may be part of the trance-dream of a sleeping shaman, represented in this panel by the curled-up eland. The three components of each group are thus a standing eland (a shaman in eland form, or a symbol of potency), a sleeping eland (a shaman in a trance-dream), and, finally, an image of the shaman's trance-dream. The shaman, himself a sleeping eland, harnesses eland power and dreams of the eland hunt.

Although some of my explanation of these paintings is conjectural and incomplete, it should be clear that the essential elements and the location of the paintings within the domain of San shamanism are not in question. In establishing the provenance of these depictions, I have tried to show that the shamanistic view of southern San rock art is not, like some of its predecessors, a superficial explanation that does not confront individual paintings and the details within them. In contrast to earlier explanations, the shamanistic view forces us to address hitherto overlooked painted details and to explain these by drawing on well-documented San beliefs, experiences, and practices. The establishment of the art's association with shamanism is the beginning, not the end, of a long research project that will explore further components of San shamanism, decode increasingly complex painted panels, and thus help to reconstruct southern African Later Stone Age ideology (Lewis-Williams 1982, 1984b). Already southern African rock art provides an especially penetrating view into the heart of shamanistic experience. Eventually, we may be able to use these insights to formulate general principles of shamanistic rock art.

Note

Extract from J. D. Lewis-Williams, "A Dream of Eland: An Unexplored Component of San Shamanism and Rock Art," *World Archaeology* 19 (2) (1987): 165–177.

Retrospect

"[T]he beginning, not the end, of a long research project." Fourteen years later, the project is still underway—though, as the following chapters show, it has broadened considerably, conceptually and geographically.

One point needs emphasis. Today, it is clear that when San hunt large animals, such as eland, they are after potency as well as meat. This duality is well illustrated by the trance dance that they like to perform next to the carcass of a freshly killed eland. Prior to and during the hunt, shamans may well have harnessed that potency to ensure success. Do these points mean that we need to reconsider the old idea of "hunting magic" in the context of San beliefs?

More significantly, we note a blurring of a distinction between subsistence and religion. Can one be discussed without reference to the other?

Seeing and Construing 7

Though this be madness, yet there is method in't.

—HAMLET 2:2:205

B Y 1990, WHEN "Through the Veil" (chapter 5) was published, new problems were confronting rock art researchers, not only in southern Africa but
throughout the world. These issues had emerged during the second half of
the 1980s and had triggered considerable debate. Despite all the attention that
they have received since then, they are still not laid to rest.

The first concerned methodology, or the mode of argument that researchers
use to reach persuasive conclusions. Earlier work had been essentially empiricist:
Researchers believed that they could collect theory-free data and then, after a
process of "analysis," induce explanations from the data. The problems of inductivism and the ways in which they infiltrated so much rock art research, and, of
course, other archaeological investigations as well, had attracted my attention
(Lewis-Williams 1983a, 1984a). It was comparatively easy to expose the inducti-
vist (empiricist) nature of rock art research. It was more difficult to find an alternative. One way out of the dilemma at first seemed to be the method favored by
the New Archaeology and known as "multiple hypothesis testing." But that too
was fraught with problems that we need not go into now (Lewis-Williams and
Loubser 1986).

In the 1990s, these methodological studies seemed to be overtaken by various
brands of relativism. Arriving by way of a *reductio ad absurdum* argument, researchers
of a postmodern persuasion contended that sure knowledge was chimerical: We
can never know anything with any degree of certainty. Moreover, it was, in their
view, desirable to have as many explanations as possible and not to attempt to
discriminate between them, a position that seems to me obscurantist.

The second issue sparked more debate, sometimes entertainingly acrimonious, than did the problems of methodology—and it still does. The value of intermeshing San ethnography and art had, I believe, been demonstrated and had shown that the southern art was overwhelmingly shamanistic: It comprised images of powerful animal-helpers (especially the eland), metaphors of shamanistic experiences (such as "death" and "underwater"), therianthropic figures from the spirit world, representations of trance dances that are often shot through with nonmaterial entities, creatures and beings encountered in the spirit world, "threads of light" that conveyed shamans to the spirit world, rain-animals whose blood and milk could be made to fall as precipitation, idiosyncratic variations on many of these themes, and so forth. Then, as "Through the Veil" showed, the shamanistic experiences from which these images derived could be better understood if researchers consulted the voluminous literature on altered states of consciousness (Lewis-Williams 2001). Exactly how this third cogwheel could be built into the system of explanation was obviously crucial.

One way of tackling both these issues is through theoretical discourse, and that is a path that I followed. But it seems to me better to tread the path of theory and, *at the same time*, to produce persuasive, successful examples of an alternative approach. Theory and practical methodology need to be developed hand in hand. By the 1990s, much archaeological writing had become highly theoretical and lacking in substantive studies explicitly based on that theory, largely as a result of the Postprocessualist school of thought, then based at Cambridge University. The critiques that these writers produced of the New Archaeology were, in my view, welcome. Even better was their emphasis on ethnography and the possibility of a cognitive archaeology that, defying the strictures of the New Archaeologists, explored ancient thought, ritual, social issues, and cosmology. All this held out some hope that rock art research, at any rate as I envisage it, might find a new niche in a transformed mainstream archaeology—were it not for the crippling hypertheoretical and relativist component.

In a 1995 attempt to produce a persuasive example of what can be done beyond empiricism and multiple hypothesis testing, I turned to Bernstein and Wylie's notions of "cables and tacking." Here, I believe, is a way of circumventing pessimistic relativism, of intermeshing the three cogwheels (images, beliefs and rituals, neuropsychology), and of producing a persuasive explanation of an otherwise baffling San rock art motif.

Seeing and Construing: The Making and "Meaning" of a Southern African Rock Art Motif

Although they themselves may hesitate to use the words, archaeologists today seem to be increasingly polarized as theoretical optimists or pessimists. Four decades ago, Hawkes (1954) devised his now well known ladder metaphor to distinguish degrees, rather than poles, of archaeological optimism and pessimism. Recovering what ancient people thought and believed and how they conceived of the cosmos—today, "cognitive archaeology"—seemed to him an enterprise enjoying little chance of success; he consequently placed it at the vertiginous top of the ladder.

Present-day cognitive archaeologists are, of course, more optimistic than Hawkes, but even some of them continue to be pessimistic about recovering "meaning"—in any event a slippery and complex concept (cf. Garlake 1994, 353–54). Renfrew (1993) for instance, is "deeply sceptical of the claims by some non-processual archaeologists to reach the *meaning*, in a specific context, of individual symbols" (249, his emphasis). He goes on to claim that the "interpretive or hermeneutic approach" adopted by some archaeologists "sometimes offers supposed insights which cannot readily be distinguished from entirely imaginative and unbridled exercises." Just how such a distinction can be made is, of course, a crucial methodological question for cognitive archaeologists if they wish to distance themselves from the "unbridled exercises" of intuitive archaeologists. But this is nothing new. As an integral part of archaeology in general, cognitive archaeology faces the same methodological dilemmas as any other branch of the discipline (e.g., von Gernet 1993, 77; Lewis-Williams 1989a, 47).

The substantiation of knowledge claims about ancient cognition, like all archaeological knowledge claims, is caught between two philosophical poles. On the one hand, extreme objectivism postulates a discoverable past and ways of substantiating, incontrovertibly, statements about the past—optimism optimized. The problems with such an approach have been adequately exposed in the literature (e.g., Shanks and Tilley 1987b; for specific reference to rock art research, see Lewis-Williams 1983a, 1984a). On the other hand, extreme relativism—still alive and well—points in the direction of what many archaeologists see as a maelstrom of mutually incompatible explanations between which no one can discriminate. Relativism makes a virtue of pessimism.

The problem with contemporary archaeological relativism derives in part from a fashionable metaphor which, like Hawkes' ladder, should not be extended too far. Archaeological data are said to be like texts. Literary metaphor is, of course, not new to archaeology: The older locution, "the archaeological record," like the textual metaphor, implies that archaeological data are similar to written documents that can, in some sense, be "read" (e.g., Hodder 1986). But there is an important difference between the two metaphors. *Record* has, for optimists, congenial connotations of objectivity that *text* lacks; literary texts are open to more than one reading. Yet, even if archaeological data are, in some important ways, like a text that can be approached from different perspectives, they are, again like literary texts, not open to an infinite number of incompatible readings. Notwithstanding many plausible glosses, Hamlet was not a woman in disguise who was madly in love with Horatio. Used in an archaeological context, *text* should imply complementary and enriching perspectives, not an inability to discriminate between mutually exclusive interpretations.

In rock art research, the textual metaphor and its corollary the linguistic metaphor have more specific consequences. In the first place, *text* as a metaphor seems to be more fecund and alluring than *record:* It invites elaboration and freewheeling prose. Tilley (1991), for instance, develops the metaphor in such a way that it imputes categories and syntax to the rock art at Nämforsen: He writes of "chapters," "pages," "sentences," "words," and even "phonemes." True, he acknowledges that he is imposing these categories on the data, not deriving them from the data (Tilley 1991, 27); but he nonetheless writes as if at least some categories are self-evident and "reading" comes very close to inductivism.[1] In a case like this, the ramifications of the textual metaphor become more than an elegant nomenclature. There is a subtle interplay between Tilley's (selected) data, his unarticulated (rather than his articulated) criteria for categories, and connotations of the literary metaphor. Indeed, the metaphor subtly suggests and initiates a search for a particular kind of syntactical hierarchy where none may in fact exist; as Malmer (1993, 116) points out, some of the syntactical combinations that Tilley identifies at Nämforsen are more probably a function of motif frequencies. A search for a similar kind of linguistic syntax has been (pace Tilley 1991, 67) part of southern African rock art research (Lewis-Williams 1972b, 1974b; Lenssen-Erz 1989), but I now believe that the linguistic metaphor has not been very useful, perhaps even misleading (Lewis-Williams 1990b).

Be that as it may, it is another implication of the textual metaphor in rock art research that is especially relevant to the topic of this chapter. The notion of text directs attention to relationships between images, which are seen as "words" and "sentences" set on a meaningless "page." As I show in a later section, some southern African rock art images can be understood, not simply in their relationships to other images, but rather in their relationship to the rock face itself—the "page"—and what was believed to lie behind it. The "composition" of southern African rock art (and probably some other rock arts as well) was not only two-dimensional, as in literary texts: It was also three-dimensional.

In rock art research, then, the textual metaphor is problematic because it directs attention away from some significant features of the data and imputes to them a particular kind of syntax; it can also be incorrectly taken as license for incompatible, not just complementary, understandings of images. Because of their supposed parallels with language and, most significantly, their polysemy (Tilley [1991, 7] writes of their "infinitely expansive medium of discourse"), rock art images may seem to be ideal candidates for the institutionalized uncertainties of relativism.

In an attempt to go beyond extreme objectivism and extreme relativism Bernstein (1983) contrasts two types of argument: those that are like chains and those that are like cables. Briefly, a chainlike argument is conceived of as progressing, link by link, from observations to generalizations and explanations. Crucially, the metaphor suggests that the sundering, or the absence, of one link destroys the whole argument. By contrast, a cable-like argument intertwines distinct, separate strands of evidence. These strands can be mutually reinforcing in that each strand may point to a single conclusion despite their disparateness. At the same time, their independence ensures that they can be mutually constraining; certain strands can exclude specific conclusions and indeed whole classes of conclusions. Perhaps most importantly, a cable-like argument can be sustained despite a lacuna in one evidential strand if other strands can be shown to cover the gap. Wylie (1989) has taken Bernstein's metaphorical dyad of chains and cables into archaeology. The fragmentary and disparate nature of archaeological data suggests that concatenatory arguments are inappropriate. Even though there is no empirical bedrock, no ultimate grid—the objectivists' necessity— by which knowledge claims about the past may be evaluated, anarchic relativism is, Wylie argues, escapable if researchers construct cable-like arguments. Although such arguments do not, of course, "prove" anything, they can sometimes be powerfully persuasive, and that is the best for which archaeologists can hope.

Three Strands of Evidence

In this article I eschew relativism and the textual metaphor. Following Bernstein and Wylie, I intertwine three mutually constraining and reinforcing, yet distinct, strands of evidence in an attempt to understand at least something of the "meaning(s)" of a southern African San (Bushman)[2] rock art motif. The strands are the rock art itself, San ethnography, and neuropsychological research on altered states of consciousness.

First, San rock art, long conceived of as no more than an entirely enigmatic object of study, can now, contrary to what was formerly the case, be accepted as a strand of evidence in its own right. Today enough is known about the social and religious context in which the art was produced to permit the drawing of inferences from specific images and classes of images (cf. Dowson 1994; Garlake 1994). The general geographical validity of some of these inferences is supported by a marked degree of uniformity in San rock art across southern Africa. Indeed, the highly restricted nature of the subject matter was a point that the quantitative work of the late 1960s clearly established (e.g., Vinnicombe 1967; Lewis-Williams 1972b, 1974b; Smits 1971; Pager 1971). On the other hand, we must acknowledge that it is a "degree of uniformity" of which we speak. There are idiosyncratic San rock art images and also some clear distinctions between the imagery of different regions, such as the KwaZulu-Natal Drakensberg and the Western Cape Province, the two regions from which I take illustrative material for this paper (e.g., Van Riet Lowe 1941; Rudner and Rudner 1970). Sometimes highly unusual images and regional differences are constituted by unique, or nearly unique, subject matter, and sometimes by the ways in which familiar themes are uniquely varied (Dowson 1988; Dowson and Holliday 1989). Yet these idiosyncratic images and regional differences are embedded in a matrix of uniformity that suggests some subcontinental cognitive commonalities. The tension between cognitive continuities and the idiosyncrasy implied by some images constitutes a strand of evidence that, in itself, points to discriminations that may not be evident in the other two evidential strands. For these reasons there is a new respect for the art. Far greater care and much more time are expended on deciphering and recording poorly preserved painted details that, in earlier decades, escaped the notice or interest of recorders (e.g., Lewis-Williams, Dowson, and Deacon 1993). As I show in this chapter, these apparently insignificant features are often crucial for an understanding of the images.

Second, San ethnography is a multistrand cable in itself. The oldest ethnography comprises that collected by Arbousset and Daumas (1846) and Orpen (1874) in areas that are now part of the eastern Free State and Lesotho. Another nineteenth-century source is the material that Wilhelm Bleek and Lucy Lloyd took down from people who came from the central areas of the Cape of Good Hope (now Northern Cape Province). The Bleek and Lloyd Collection, compiled in the 1870s, is by far the largest corpus of San ethnography (e.g., Bleek and Lloyd 1911; Bleek 1933, 1935, 1936). It was recorded verbatim in phonetic script from people who lived some four hundred miles to the west of the area where Arbousset, Daumas, and Orpen worked (Lewis-Williams 1981a). These nineteenth-century sources are contemporary with the final phases of San rock art, the last depictions having been made toward the end of the nineteenth century or, in some areas, even in the first decade of the twentieth century. A more recent ethnographic strand is the twentieth-century ethnography on San people living in the Kalahari Desert some six hundred miles to the north of the Northern Cape Province (e.g., Lee 1968; Marshall 1969; Biesele 1978; Katz 1982). These Kalahari groups still speak languages that, though belonging to the same family of click languages, were not intelligible to the Northern Cape people with whom Bleek and Lloyd worked. The Kalahari people do not make rock art, nor do their myths and traditions preserve any recollection of painting or engraving on rocks. In any event, there are few rock surfaces in the sandy Kalahari Desert on which rock art could be made.

Despite significant separation in time and space and some linguistic diversity, all these ethnographies display conceptual commonalities that recall the geographical continuities of the rock art. They have led to the postulation of a "pan-San cognitive system" that does not, it must be noted, exclude regional variants (McCall 1970; Vinnicombe 1972b; Lewis-Williams and Biesele 1978; Lewis-Williams 1981a). In those specific areas of belief in which broad similarities can be clearly demonstrated, twentieth-century Kalahari ethnography can be cautiously used to fill lacunae in the nineteenth-century ethnographies.

Moreover, the close and detailed fit between, on the one hand, certain religious beliefs and rituals common to all the San groups for whom we have ethnographies and, on the other, specific classes of widely distributed rock art images led to the now generally accepted hypothesis that, although the images are richly polysemic, the making of the art was essentially associated with a form of shamanism (e.g., Lewis-Williams 1980, 1981, 1982; Lewis-Williams and Dowson 1989; Dowson 1992).[3] It is with the shamanic content of the art, rather than its many other significances, that this chapter is concerned.

The shamanic trance dance and curing rituals of twentieth-century Kalahari San communities are well known (e.g., Marshall 1969; Lee 1968; Guenther 1975; Biesele 1978; Katz 1982). The less well known nineteenth-century ethnographies (e.g., Arbousset and Daumas 1846, 246–47; Orpen 1874; Bleek 1933b, 1935, 1936) show that the southern San groups who made rock art practiced very similar trance rituals and held similar, though not identical, beliefs about the activities and supernatural powers of shamans (Lewis-Williams 1981a, 75–116). There is no record of San shamans using hallucinogens (but see Winkelman and Dobkin de Rios 1989); they induce trance by dancing, audio driving, intense concentration, and hyperventilation. Notwithstanding the polysemy to which I have referred, it is probably true to say that San rock art comprises principally a range of images that, in the first instance, have to do with diverse shamanic beliefs and rituals. These images include trance dances that sometimes blend ordinary observable entities, such as the dancers themselves, with "nonreal" elements that are "seen" by shamans only; shamans who are identifiable by a number of distinctive features, postures, and gestures; animals that were considered sources of supernatural potency, both in their real existence and in their depictions; "scenes" that appear to record historical events, but that sometimes incorporate shamanic elements; various activities that shamans conduct in the spirit world, such as out-of-body travel and rainmaking; shamans partially transformed into animals, the so-called therianthropes; and, perhaps most enigmatically, "abstract," geometric motifs (see Lewis-Williams 1981a; Campbell 1986; Lewis-Williams and Dowson 1989; Dowson 1992 for reviews of San rock art imagery).

Once the evidence for the shamanic context and content of the art had been accepted, some southern African rock art workers (e.g., Thackeray et al. 1981; Maggs and Sealy 1983; Lewis-Williams 1984b, 1986a; Lewis-Williams and Dowson 1988) began to examine what I take as a third evidential strand—neuropsychological research on altered states of consciousness. This neuropsychological research was conducted under laboratory conditions principally in the United States of America and Europe to identify types of visual, olfactory, somatic, and aural hallucinations; it was, of course, independent of southern African rock art research. Neuropsychological work on altered states of consciousness and the types of hallucinations associated with different levels, or stages, of altered consciousness therefore constitute a completely independent strand of evidence.

Neurologically Generated Mental Imagery

Neuropsychological research has shown that some types of hallucinations derive from the structure of the human nervous system (e.g., Eichmeier and Höfer 1974; Siegel and Jarvik 1975; Asaad and Shapiro 1986). These mental images are luminous, pulsating, expanding or contracting, blending, and changing geometric forms. They include zigzags, dots, grids, meandering lines, and U shapes. In the literature, they are variously called form constants, phosphenes, and entoptic phenomena (we take *entoptic* to mean "within the optic system," not just within the eye itself; Tyler 1978). Entoptic phenomena are experienced in an early, or comparatively light, altered state of consciousness, whether such a state is induced by means of psychotropic drugs, audio and rhythmic driving, sensory deprivation, hyperventilation, pain, or a variety of other factors (e.g., Siegel and Jarvik 1975).

The range of entoptic forms was established by laboratory experiments involving electrical stimulation of the cortex and ingestion of LSD and other hallucinogens. Subjects were asked to draw their visual imagery. The subjects who took part in these experiments were familiar with drawn geometric shapes and seem to have tried to make their depictions of their mental imagery as neat as possible. In more emotionally charged circumstances, such as religious rituals involving altered states of consciousness, subjects respond less "objectively" to their mental imagery. If they depict their imagery either during or after experiencing an altered state of consciousness, they are less interested in neatness and precision than are Western laboratory subjects and may rearrange constituent elements of entoptic phenomena according to their notions about the spirit world (e.g., Reichel-Dolmatoff 1978a).

Because the human nervous system is a universal, all people, no matter what their cultural background, are likely to "see" these geometric mental images (e.g., Reichel-Dolmatoff 1969, 1978a, b; Eichmeier and Höfer 1974; Hedges 1983; Lewis-Williams and Dowson 1988; Whitley 1988, 1992; for more on human universals, see Brown 1991; von Gernet 1993). Consequently, the largely shamanic context of San rock art suggests, simply on a priori grounds, that we should expect to find rock art images that, in some way, depict entoptic phenomena. Geometric motifs that are formally similar to certain entoptic elements are in fact common among the rock engravings (petroglyphs) of the central southern African plateau. These rock engravings occur on rocks scattered on open hilltops; in addition to geometric motifs, they include depictions of animals and, rarely, human beings. The engraved geometric motifs have been described by Dowson (1992, 30–52), who argues that many of them do indeed depict entoptic phenomena. Unlike engravings, rock paintings were executed on the walls of open rock shelters in the more mountainous areas of southern Africa. Geometric motifs are far less common among rock paintings; when they do occur, they are often integrated with "representational" art of animals and human beings (Lewis-Williams 1988b). It seems that the people who made the rock engravings were, by and large, more frequently interested in isolating the geometric imagery of an early stage of trance than were rock painters, who were more concerned with the iconic imagery of "deep" trance (Lewis-Williams and Dowson 1989a).

Nevertheless, it is with rock paintings that incorporate entoptic phenomena that this chapter is concerned. To understand some of the ways in which artists incorporated entoptic imagery in their paintings, we need to consider more closely how people respond to this sort of mental imagery. In certain states of consciousness the nervous system becomes a kind of "sixth sense" (Heinze 1986) that supplies to the brain an input of "nonreal" imagery that may include entoptic phenomena. The important question is: What does the brain do with these nonveridical, geometric images? Two factors come into play at this point: society and the individual.

First, socially established predilections and expectations cause people to ignore some entoptic images and to concentrate on others. The selected images are given meanings and significances that vary widely from society to society; form, not meaning, is encoded in the human nervous system. Second, there are always tendencies that cause some people to concentrate on entoptic elements that are ignored by others in the community and to associate novel versions of widely accepted beliefs with these elements.

The input of individuals is clearly evident in what may be seen as a second, or deeper, stage of altered consciousness (Lewis-Williams and Dowson 1988, 203–4). During this stage, subjects try to make sense of entopic phenomena by elaborating them into iconic forms of people, animals, and important or emotionally charged objects (Horowitz 1964, 514; 1975, 177, 181). The brain attempts to recognize, or decode, geometric entoptic forms by matching them against a store of experience, as it does normal sense impressions. Horowitz (1975, 177) links this process of making sense to the emotional state of the subject: For a Westerner, "the same ambiguous round shape on initial perceptual representation can be 'illusioned' into an orange (if the subject is hungry), a breast (if he is in a state of heightened sexual drive), a cup of water (if he is thirsty), or an anarchist's bomb (if he is hostile or fearful)." I call this process "construal." The four examples of construal that Horowitz gives are, of course, derived from the experiences of Western subjects; people who have different culturally established expectations of mental imagery in altered states of consciousness and different attitudes toward those states and images construe entoptic phenomena quite differently.

Navicular Entoptic Phenomena

I now focus on one of the "abstract" southern African rock art motifs. In attempting to explain the origins of this motif and something of what it may have signified to at least some of its original viewers, I intertwine the three evidential strands that I have briefly described: rock art images, ethnography, and neuropsychology. I argue that close attention to variations in the art suggests that individual San shaman-artists construed the motif in idiosyncratic yet related ways.

One of the most widely known entoptic phenomena (it is experienced by migraine sufferers; Sacks 1970; Richards 1971) is, in the simplest form recorded by laboratory subjects, a set of nested catenary curves (figure 7.1a). A more elaborate form, also recorded under laboratory conditions, comprises two elements: an outer arc characterized by iridescent flickering bars of light or zigzags (figures

Figure 7.1.   Three variations of the navicular entoptic phenomenon. After Siegel 1977.

7.1b and 7.1c), and, within this arc, a lunate area of invisibility, a sort of "black hole" that obliterates veridical imagery that falls within its confines. Indeed, people experiencing this entoptic phenomenon can cause objects or people before them to "disappear" by turning their heads so that the object or person is covered by the area of invisibility. Beyond the area of invisibility is the center of vision, marked by the dots in figure 7.1. These mental images are not static, but, like all entoptic phenomena, they shimmer and move; they slowly expand until they disappear beyond the periphery of vision. The general "boat shape" of the form leads me to call it the "navicular" entoptic phenomenon.

I shall deal first with what seem to be fairly straightforward and only slightly construed southern African rock art depictions of the navicular entoptic phenomenon (though, of course, these depictions were probably anything but straightforward for their makers and original viewers); I then move on to more complex construals. The minimally construed examples should, I argue, be seen in the light of the more complexly construed—and more informative—examples.

Minimally Construed Navicular Entoptic Phenomena

In the Western Cape Province there are rock paintings that are formally very similar to the navicular entoptic phenomenon as it is known from laboratory research (Maggs and Sealy 1983). One example comprises five nested curves; the outer and inner curves are corrugated, while the inner one also has two vertical lines supporting an undulating line (figure 7.2a). Another type does not have nested lines; instead, it is a solid lunate. In some examples the inner arc is corrugated (figure 7.2b); in others, the outer arc is surrounded by a zigzag line, and there are other zigzag lines above it (figure 7.2c). The two principal formal elements of the navicular entoptic phenomenon are thus present in these rock paintings—an arc and zigzag or denticulate margins.

It has been suggested that these paintings depict boats (Johnson, Rabinowitz, and Sieff 1959, figs. 38 and 39; cf. Holm 1987, 42–45). The one in figure 7.2a does indeed look somewhat like a boat with masts and rigging. Some other Western Cape Province boatlike paintings appear to have the heads of mariners emerging from them. The example in figure 7.2d is not particularly navicular in form (as I have used the word); instead, it has a long "prow" and an oblong "hull." Although it is easy to see how it could be taken as strong evidence that the whole set of paintings depicts boats, I argue later that it is not closely related to any of the other paintings shown in figure 7.2.

The maritime "reading" of the painted "text" finds ready acceptance in the colonial imagination, and Herodotus' account of Phoenician sailors possibly

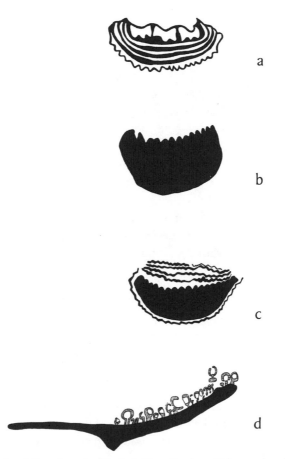

Figure 7.2.   Rock paintings from the Western Cape Province. Colors: red and white. After Maggs and Sealy 1983, figs. 5, 7, and 8; Johnson, Rabinowitz, and Sieff 1959, fig. 39.

rounding the Cape of Good Hope about 600 B.C. is sometimes invoked to account for the depictions. Similar thinking led the Abbé Henri Breuil (1948, 1955) to identify the famous rock painting known as the "White Lady of the Brandberg" as a Cretan or Minoan visitor to southern Africa (see also Schweiger 1912; Dart 1925; Breuil 1949). The identification of "first arrivals" in southern Africa, with or without boats, has long been a concern of historians and archaeologists of various political persuasions because of its supposed relevance to land rights (e.g., Holm 1987); rock art has played a role in these supposed identifications and consequently in the political agendas attached to them (Lewis-Williams and Dowson 1989a, 4–8; Lewis-Williams 1990b, 69–74, 1993).

If there were no ethnographic evidence showing that much San rock art was associated with shamanism, the formal parallels between these Western Cape painted images and the navicular entoptic phenomenon, rather than between them and boats, would not be especially persuasive (but see Lewis-Williams and Dowson 1993). But, given the independently and ethnographically demonstrated conclusion that many southern African rock art images derived from shamanic visions, and given the universality of the human nervous system and the entoptic mental imagery it produces in altered states, it seems probable that these paintings depict navicular entoptic phenomena experienced by San shamans (Maggs and Sealy 1983).

At present we have no direct evidence suggesting the meaning, or meanings, of these painted images, though it is possible that they were associated with some of the meanings implied by the depictions of more clearly construed navicular entoptic phenomena to which I now turn.

Moderately Construed Navicular Entoptic Phenomena

In contrast to the comparatively "simple" painted navicular forms, there are paintings in the Kwa Zulu-Natal Drakensberg that elaborate a basic U shape. One example comprises a set of five nested catenary curves painted in a reddish brown color (figure 7.3a); in another painting, similar curves are joined at one end (figure 7.3b). In both these paintings, tiny insects are individually and minutely drawn in red, each with a pair of white wings. By comparing paintings such as these with photographs of naturally formed U-shaped honeycombs, Pager (1971, 151, 347–52) was able to show that this is indeed what they depict and that the painted insects are bees. In some paintings, bees are represented by wingless red dots (figure 7.3b), some of which may originally have had white wings; white paint is more fugitive than other colors. Other paintings show bees by means of small crosses (e.g., Lewis-Williams and Dowson 1989a, fig. 28).

Writing at the beginning of the 1970s, Pager took these paintings to be unproblematic depictions of things in the real world and assumed that San painted them because they liked honey—which indeed they still do. While he was no doubt right in one sense, there was, I argue, more to the making of these depictions than simple representation of something the San enjoyed eating. In the light of the social and conceptual context of their production (a shamanic art that includes depictions of visions), the close formal resemblances between these paintings and the navicular entoptic phenomenon strongly suggest that some shaman-artists construed the navicular entoptic phenomenon as honeycombs, a familiar object in the "real" world. Two strands of evidence—one neuropsycho-

Figure 7.3a.   Rock painting from the KwaZulu-Natal Drakensberg. Colors: red and white.
After Pager 1971, figs. 387, 8b.

logical, the other ethnographic—probably explain why some Drakensberg rock painters construed their navicular visions in this way.

First, altered states of consciousness cause all the senses, not just sight, to hallucinate. A common aural experience is a buzzing or humming sound (e.g., Bootzin 1980, 343). Like entoptic phenomena, such aural experiences are open to a variety of construals, though cross-culturally their essential nature remains neurologically determined and therefore constant. The Amahuaca shamans of the Amazon Basin, for example, interpret the humming sound they experience while in trance as the calls of frogs, crickets, and cicadas (Lamb 1979, 144); other people construe it as wind, trickling water, or rain (Halifax 1979, 32; Lame Deer

Figure 7.3b.   Rock painting from the Harrismith district, northeastern Free State. Colors: red and white. Scale in centimeters.

and Erdoes 1979, 74; Neihardt 1979, 97; Munn 1973, 119; Christie-Murray 1978). The rock paintings I have described suggest that some San linked this aural experience to their simultaneous, flickering visual hallucinations of navicular entoptic phenomena, and thus believed that they were both seeing and hearing bees swarming over honeycombs.

Second, San beliefs, expectations, and emotional states explain why some sha-mans made this complex construal. As San shamans dance to the women's insis-tent clapping, a supernatural potency is said to "boil" in their stomachs, to rise up their spines, and to explode in their heads, thus catapulting them into the spirit world. This potency is closely associated with certain large animals. Some Kalahari !Kung San shamans therefore like to dance next to the carcass of a freshly killed eland. The dead animal is thought to release its potency so that the area around it becomes highly charged. Shamans say that they are able to harness this potency for a particularly efficacious spiritual experience. The !Kung also consider bees, said to be messengers of god, to have a great deal of potency (Wilmsen, personal communication). They like to dance when the bees are swarming because they believe that they can use "bee potency," even as they exploit eland potency. The !Kung in fact have a "medicine," or trance dance, song called "Honey" (Mar-shall 1962, 249). They do not, of course, actually dance in a swarm of bees, but it is easy to understand how the sight and sound of a glittering, loudly humming swarm could not only be associated with an altered state of consciousness but could, moreover, contribute to conditions that induce or intensify an altered state.

I therefore argue that some shaman-artists construed their combined visual and aural experiences as visions of very powerful and emotionally charged shamanic symbols—bees and honey. The neuropsychological and ethnographic evidential strands thus combine with features of the art itself to suggest a component of San shamanic belief and practice that could not be ascertained from one strand only.

Elaborately Construed Entoptic Phenomena

To approach what I argue are depictions of even more elaborate construals of the navicular entoptic phenomenon, I distinguish more clearly between the flickering outer arc and the inner area of invisibility and the ways in which shaman-artists perceived these two components. I then argue that the navicular entoptic phenomenon was, for some shaman-artists, conceptually associated with another widely reported, neurologically determined component of trance experience.

The first painted example (figure 7.4) of how some shaman-artists construed the outer arc comprises a single catenary curve and, arranged clockwise around the outer edge of the curve, six antelope heads facing the viewer, the profile of an antelope head and neck, the forequarters of an eland, and twelve antelope legs. Within the curve are the very faded remains of some earlier, now indecipherable, images and a cloud of white dots. The upper part of the painting is also poorly preserved, and the antelope heads are discernible only under optimal lighting conditions and then to skilled eyes only. Below the curved line is a running figure and the faded remains of some largely indecipherable paintings. The second example (figure 7.5) comprises a solid circular, rather than navicular, area of red paint, at least twenty-five antelope legs, the forequarters of an eland, and the hindquarters of two eland. The legs and the antelope are placed around the edge so that, although the area of solid paint is circular, they demarcate a semicircle. A white line leads from the painted circle to depictions of two human beings and a therianthrope; these figures appear to be walking along the line in the direction of the circle. Just beyond the righthand end of the line there are depictions of two jackals, one of which carries a bag as if it were a human being. The general form of the rock paintings shown in figures 7.4 and 7.5 parallels the simpler forms of the paintings in figure 7.2, but the flickering zigzag or denticulate margins of the simpler forms have been replaced by a "fringe" of antelope legs and other elements.

This replacement, or construal, may have been suggested to the artists by what

Figure 7.4.   Rock paintings from the Harrismith district, northeastern Free State. Colors: red and white. Scale in centimeters.

Figure 7.5.   Rock paintings from the Harrismith district, northeastern Free State. Colors: red and white. Scale in centimeters.

must have been a fairly common sight, one that is, I argue, depicted in the elegant painting shown in figure 7.6. To the left, five buck run and leap, while to the right six buck are massed one behind the other; all twenty-four legs of the six buck are shown. For those shamans who were believed to have the power to guide antelope herds toward the waiting hunters' ambush, the "shamans of the game" (Lewis-Williams 1981a, 77), the flickering arc of the navicular entoptic phenomenon, together with the humming sound simultaneously induced by their altered state of consciousness, may have recalled the emotionally charged experience of witnessing the flashing legs of galloping antelope at close quarters and hearing the drumming of their hooves. As shamans of the game, this was the very experience they sought in the spirit world where they controlled the movements of antelope herds. They (and, of course, other people as well) believed that this supernatural

Figure 7.6.   Rock paintings from the Harrismith district, northeastern Free State. Colors: red and white. Scale in centimeters.

experience could, in some way, bring about similar experiences in the real world and thereby ensure the success of a hunt. I therefore conclude that the placing of antelope legs in an arc in figures 7.4 and 7.5 is a zoomorphic construal of the flickering edge of the navicular entoptic phenomenon and, further, that this construal may have been related to the simultaneously experienced humming sound that, in these instances, was interpreted as the drumming of antelope hooves rather than the buzzing of bees.

In these zoomorphic construals, the legs and antelope bodies do not continue beyond the arc into the central area. In terms of the navicular entoptic phenomenon, this is an area of invisibility, the "black hole" that seems to cause things in the real world to disappear. For evidence pertaining to the way in which some San shaman-artists understood this "black hole"—a crucial element in an understanding of these paintings—I turn first to two highly complex depictions.

One of these paintings shows a red and white navicular form, on the outer edge of which are five white zigzags (figure 7.7). In this painting, a San shaman-artist has closely approached Western laboratory subjects' representations of the flickering arc as zigzags. Two therianthropic figures emerge from the inner arc and so recall the human heads that emerge from some of the Western Cape navicular depictions. One is covered with white dots, some of which spill over beyond the outline of its body and recall the cloud of white dots in figure 7.4. Emerging from the backs of both therianthropes are objects that comparison with other paintings suggests are flywhisks (Lewis-Williams and Dowson 1989a). Normally, in the Kalahari of today, a person may have one flywhisk; such a large number of them in the possession of one person would be highly unusual, so unusual as to suggest "nonreality." Indeed, flywhisks are closely associated with the nonreality of the spirit world: Shamans dance with them and manipulate them to deflect mystical arrows of sickness that nameless spirits of the dead and malevolent spirit-shamans are said to shoot into people. Whisks are seldom used in other circumstances.

The other example of a complex rock painting that is comparable with the navicular entoptic phenomenon is an inverted U shape painted in red and white (figure 7.8). Eight antelope heads are painted along the upper, or outer, arc. Along the inner arc there are six pairs of human legs. The shamanic context of this depiction is clearly established by the kneeling therianthropic figure to the left. It has its arms held behind its back in a posture that some Kalahari shamans adopt when they ask god to put more potency into their bodies so that they may enter the spirit world (Lewis-Williams 1981a, 88). Painted figures in this arms-back posture and also kneeling, known variously as flying buck (Woodhouse 1971), *alites* (Pager 1971), and trance-buck (Lewis-Williams 1981a), are fairly common

Figure 7.7.   Rock paintings from the Harrismith district, northeastern Free State. Colors: red and white. Scale in centimeters.

in the region from which this painting comes. They depict shamans partially transformed into animals (Lewis-Williams 1981a, 88–89).

The rock paintings shown in figures 7.7 and 7.8 have three points in common. First, both paintings are associated with features that clearly point to their shamanic context (flywhisks and trance-buck). Second, both include human or therianthropic figures that seem to disappear into what, in the navicular entoptic phenomenon, is an area of invisibility. Third and most important, transformation of human beings into animals is implied in both paintings. The painting shown in figure 7.7 has two therianthropic figures; in figure 7.8 there is a kneeling therianthrope, and, in addition, antelope heads are placed opposite human legs in such a way to imply some sort of connection between them. Transformation is also implied by elements in figure 7.5: As I have pointed out, a therianthrope walks along the white line in the direction of the antelope legs, and one of the two jackals on the extreme right carries a bag.

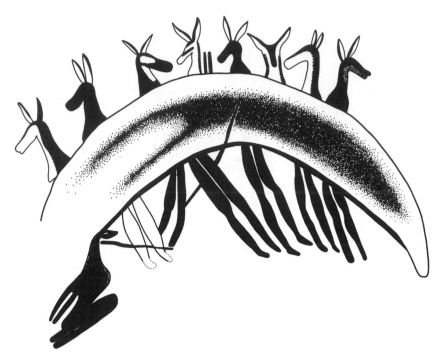

Figure 7.8.   Rock paintings from the KwaZulu-Natal Drakensberg. Colors: red and white. Scale in centimeters.

The Vortex

Disappearance into an area of invisibility and transformation into an animal, two concepts associated with these paintings, are, I argue, also components of one of the ways in which some San shamans understood another universally reported, neurologically generated feature of altered states of consciousness. After the second stage of trance, the one characterized by construal of entoptic phenomena, subjects enter the third and deepest stage. Laboratory research has shown that this deep level of trance is often approached via a vortex, or tunnel, into which subjects feel themselves drawn. Sometimes the sides of the vortex appear to be covered with a lattice, in the squares of which are the first iconic hallucinations; though entoptic forms persist peripherally into this third stage, some of the iconic images on the sides of the vortex soon become central to the subjects' experience (Siegel and Jarvik 1975). When subjects emerge from the far end of the vortex, they find themselves in a fantastic realm where they experience hallucinations of monsters and frightening or ecstatic events; they also feel themselves transformed, partially or completely, into animals. Their iconic hallucinations, though in some ways informed by the nervous system, derive from memory: They are therefore very largely culturally controlled. Subjects can now no longer observe their mental imagery in a detached way: They become part of their imagery, and all their senses hallucinate in the full sense of the word (Lewis-Williams and Dowson 1988).

The vortex that leads to this "other world" is variously understood in different cultures: Some shamans speak of entering a hole in the ground, others of following the roots of a tree, and so forth. Nineteenth-century San shamans spoke of diving into waterholes and traveling underground (Bleek 1933b, 1935)—their ways, I argue, of understanding the vortex. Subterranean travel is linked to transformation in one of the narratives that Orpen (1874, 8) recorded in the mountains of what is now Lesotho. /Kaggen ("Cagn" in Orpen's orthography), the San trickster-deity and himself a shaman, descended three times into the ground and came up at a different place each time. After the third leg of his subterranean journey, he came up transformed into a large bull eland. More recently, a !Kung San shaman, speaking of his underwater and underground journey to god, said, "My sides were pressed by pieces of metal . . . in this way I travelled forward" (Biesele 1979, 56). Having emerged from the distant end of this tunnel-like journey through what they believed to be the spirit world, nineteenth-century San shamans "saw" grotesque spirits of the dead, rain-animals, and god himself.

The southern San believed that, at least in some ritual contexts, this spirit world existed behind the walls of rock shelters (Lewis-Williams and Dowson 1990). The rock wall was like a veil suspended between the real and spirit worlds. In trance, shamans were able to see and to pass through this rupestral veil and to enter the spirit world. Some shaman-artists therefore painted images entering and leaving cracks, steps, and marks on the rock face: These mediatory images were partly in the world and partly in the spirit world, disappearing into a realm that ordinary people could not perceive. In some cases, shaman-artists smeared paint on cracks and folds in the rock face or simply applied a thick line or patch of paint to smooth rock. Therianthropic figures are sometimes shown disappearing into or emerging from these applications of paint. It is as if paint were a solvent that could dissolve hard, opaque rock and facilitate entrance into the spirit world; indeed, San ethnography suggests that some paint was believed to have its own intrinsic, mediating potency (Lewis-Williams and Dowson 1990). The two large therianthropes in the rock painting shown in figure 7.9 emerge from one of these applications of paint; in this case, paint has been applied to a deep fold in the rock. The subaquatic experience of trance is suggested by the painted fish, eels, and turtles (Lewis-Williams 1980, 472). The therianthropes are also associated with a large number of flywhisks and so recall the painting in figure 7.7. To the

Figure 7.9.   Rock painting from the Eastern Cape Province. Colors: red, black, and white.
Scale in centimeters.

right, four small human necks and heads emerge from the black paint; the blood
of trance experience (Arbousset and Daumas 1846, 246–47; Orpen 1874, 10;
Bleek 1935, 1, 20, 34; Lewis-Williams and Dowson 1989a, 40, 64, 73, 78, 80,
86, 94) falls from the nose of one of the heads. The placing of these heads in
relation to the smeared paint is similar to that in the Western Cape Province
painting shown in figure 7.2d, the one that appears to depict a "prow" and a long
"hull." Comparison with the painting in figure 7.9 suggests that the "boat" in
figure 7.2d is in fact a smear of paint; the painting in figure 7.2d is therefore
cognate with the one in figure 7.9 rather than with the others in figure 7.2.

There is, however, an important parallel between paintings that, I argue,
depicts the navicular entoptic phenomenon and those that feature paint applied
to inequalities in the rock face: Both incorporate depictions of therianthropes or
animals painted as if they are entering or leaving the plane of the rock face. The
ethnographically established shamanic context of San rock art in general and the
explicitly shamanic images in some of these paintings situate an explanation of

them. Given the way in which the navicular area of invisibility seems to be a "black hole" that obliterates elements of veridical perception, and given the evidence suggesting that the spirit world was believed to lie behind the rock face, I suggest that some San shaman-artists believed that the navicular entoptic phenomenon was like the vortex: It led to the spirit world and the transformations that awaited them there. Perhaps the strongest evidence for transformation taking place in the "black hole" of the navicular area of invisibility is provided by the painting shown in figure 7.8, where antelope heads and human legs are arranged on either side of the lunate. Such highly detailed paintings suggest that less elaborately construed painted navicular entoptic phenomena (figure 7.2) may also represent entrances to the underground journeys that took shamans into the spirit world, though the absence of explicit associated imagery means that this can be no more than a tentative suggestion.

These understandings of, first, both the vortex and the navicular entoptic phenomenon as entrances to another reality and, second, the disappearance of paintings into that alternative reality may have been repeatedly suggested to shamans during the performance of trance rituals. In the 1980s, an old woman of mixed San descent described how, at the end of the nineteenth century, her father, who was a shaman and a painter, had danced in the painted rock shelter to which she guided us (Jolly 1986; Lewis-Williams 1986b; Jolly and Prins 1994). When people felt that they needed more potency to carry them on their route to the spirit world, they turned to face the paintings because some of them contained potency, having been imbued with it by the addition of eland blood to the paint. Potency then flowed from these painted images into them.

The significance of this and the other ethnographic and neuropsychological evidence I have discussed is clear and important. If trancing shamans, turning to the paintings as the old San woman's father did, had at the same time experienced the navicular entoptic phenomenon, the area of invisibility would have blocked out some paintings or parts of paintings, thus creating precisely the effect depicted in figures 7.4, 7.5, 7.7, and 7.8. Moreover, the experience may have included sensations of being drawn through the rock face to the spirit world that existed behind it.

The mediating position of the rock face means that it was not simply a tabula rasa, a blank space on which artists could paint anything they wished. Unlike a page in a book, the rock possessed its own intrinsic, situating "meaning," and images placed on it related to it as much as they may have related to adjacent images; the textual/linguistic metaphor, with its emphasis on syntax between images, obscures the meaning of the "page," the rock face. Moreover, some of the painted images may relate not only to the rock face but also to (mental) images that were believed to be behind the rock and were therefore invisible to ordinary people. In other words, the "composition" of San rock art was, in at least some instances, three-dimensional. An axis that the textual/literary metaphor does not suggest stood at right angles to the more generally understood two-dimensional plane: vision ←→ rock face ←→ painted image ←→ viewer. Significantly, the only patterning that can be established quantitatively (Lewis-Williams 1972b, 1974b; Pager 1976a) existed along this right-angle axis. The ways in which paintings were superimposed upon one another followed, not a linguistic syntax in any usually understood sense, but a neuropsychological patterning established by the generation and projection of mental imagery. Full viewing and experiencing of a San rock art panel[4] thus involved dissociation from one's body and participation in the painted and the mental imagery of altered states of consciousness, not simply a detached "reading" of the arrested residues of other people's powerful religious experiences.

Universality and Individuality

Certain repeated, neurologically informed experiences of altered states of consciousness thus had the potential to animate rock art panels and to suggest travel to the spirit world through the "black hole" of the navicular entoptic phenomenon or via the vortex. It was not every San shaman-artist who explored the possiblities of depicting this experience; for reasons that we do not understand, many ignored the possiblity altogether and painted other kinds of images. But some idiosyncratically elaborated their mental imagery and their depictions, as a result of exceptional personal interest in the spirit world or aspects of it. Indeed, the more elaborate examples of these depictions may have been statements about personally obtained and possessed esoteric knowledge concerning spiritual things. The painters of these elaborate depictions may therefore have been making statements about their personal knowledge, power, and influence as shamans.

In certain historical circumstances, altered states of consciousness become a site of struggle: Groups and individuals compete for control of, and deeper insight into, "religious" mental imagery because possession of arcane knowledge sanctions political power (cf. Lewis-Williams and Dowson 1993; Dowson 1994; Freidel, Schele, and Parker 1993). The ways in which individuals modify and explore the mental imagery of altered states of consciousness is therefore often politically important. Their idiosyncratic mental imagery, as experienced and as depicted, can become associated with attempts to subvert political structures. Individuals negotiate their positions of power by delicately playing idiosyncrasy against socially sanctioned rituals, beliefs, and visions. They have to know how far they can go before they estrange those whom they wish to influence.

There is thus a tension between the feral human mind in altered states and the need to be understood and socially integrated. In general, San ritual and rock art, by their repeated formulae, work toward uniformity of religious experience; they thereby control and channel the development of personal power. San ritual and socially sanctioned art was therefore in constant conflict with the tendency of the human nervous system to produce novel visions and for people to construe universally experienced entoptic forms in novel ways. The elaborated navicular rock paintings from the southeastern mountains that I have described are, I argue, the product of this kind of tension, as it was set in the deteriorating political circumstances that the southern San experienced in the eighteenth and nineteenth centuries (Dowson 1994). The less elaborately construed Western Cape Province paintings derive from a different historical trajectory (Parkington et al. 1986) and will have to be examined in the light of their own changing historical circumstances.

In the wider perspective suggested by the universality of the human nervous system, the southern African rock art imagery with which this chapter has been concerned is, in some important senses, cognate with imagery experienced by shamans in other parts of the world: Everywhere, people in altered states of consciousness have the potential to experience the same entoptic elements (e.g., Reichel-Dolmatoff 1969, 1978a; Eichmeier and Höfer 1974; Hedges 1982, 1983; Bednarik 1984b; Sassen 1991; Dronfield 1993; Bradley 1989; Sales 1992; Boyd 1996). At the same time, ethnographic evidence shows that the meanings ascribed to these mental images and the ways in which they are construed are always culturally controlled and historically situated: Unlike entoptic forms and the progression of mental imagery in altered states of consciousness, meaning is not universal. Nevertheless, it seems that, despite cultural variation, one of the components of navicular entoptic phenomenon—the area of invisibility that obliterates veridical visual imagery—invites, by its very nature as a kind of "black hole," construal as an entrance to the spirit world, as does the vortex that leads to the deepest stage of trance.

Discriminating Reading

Each of the San rock art images that I have considered derived from a complex blend of universal neurological elements and culturally specific perceptions of those elements, as mediated by individuals in specific historical and political circumstances. Strands of evidence drawn from neuropsychology, ethnography, and San rock art itself thus combine in mutually reinforcing and constraining ways to suggest an explanation for some otherwise highly enigmatic rock paintings and to exclude a range of quite different explanations, including the reading that they depict boats.

The cable-like argument that I have developed in this case study thus reduces archaeological pessimism. Researchers' "restless explorations" of theory, method, and observations aim to eliminate, not celebrate, ambiguity; ambiguity (in the sense of mutually incompatible narratives rather than enriching multiple perspectives) is, after all, what research must, by its very nature, seek to reduce. Although I do not claim to have uncovered the exact, complete "meaning" of each painted image for each painter and viewer—there was surely a (restricted) range of readings and responses to the images even at the time when they were made—I argue, with tempered optimism, that we can place the paintings I have discussed in a broad context of meaning and ritual and that some readings *can* be excluded. It is therefore possible to reject extreme relativism and to discriminate between some (if not all) readings of the so-called archaeological text. Whatever antic dispositions he may have put on, transvestism was not one of Hamlet's masks.

Notes

1. Tilley (1991, 84) refers to what he calls "the very obvious relationships that exist between the carved *designs* on individual carving surfaces" and to "pages" that are "obviously and clearly differentiated in a physical sense" (1991, 23); he also claims that "the recognition of units and boundaries between the elements is usually readily apparent" (1991, 20). Observations that a writer claims are "readily apparent" or "very obvious" require close scrutiny, especially if he or she at the same time expresses reservations about empiricism.

2. Because San, or Bushman, communities speak many mutually unintelligible languages, there is no single indigenous word to cover all groups. "Bushman" is, in the view of some people, a pejorative and sexist word, although some San themselves do choose to use it. "San," a Nama (Khoenkhoen) word, is preferred by many, but by no means all, academic writers. Unfortunately, it means something like "vagabond" and is therefore also pejorative. There is no unanimity on which word should be used, and, as far as I can see, no way out of the dilemma with which history has presented us. In using "San," I explicitly reject any pejorative connotations.

3. For justification of the use of "shamanism" in the southern African context, see Lewis-Williams (1992). For the identification of shamanic imagery in various regions of southern Africa, see Garlake (1987), Huffman (1983), Yates, Parkington, and Manhire (1990), Kinahan (1991), Hall (1990), Yates, Golson, and Hall (1985), Deacon (1988), and Dowson (1992). For more on the polysemy of San rock art images see Vinnicombe (1976), Lewis-Williams (1981, 1990), Garlake (1987), Parkington (1989), Solomon (1992), and Deacon (1988).

4. Even during the period when such panels were being constructed by the addition and superimposition of new painted images, some viewers were no doubt unable to experience them in a fully shamanic way, but many of these viewers nonetheless knew that they were looking at images that were vivified in the experiences of shamans. For some people, therefore, the panels were to varying degrees exclusive, for others inclusive: "Meaning" is always nuanced.

"Seeing and Construing: The Making and 'Meaning' of a Southern African Rock Art Motif," *Cambridge Archaeological Journal* 5 (1) (1995): 3–23.

Retrospect

This article tried to do two things—which was, perhaps, not a good idea. Be that as it may, both points needed, and still do need, to be made. First, it *is* possible to distinguish between competing hypotheses. True, at certain stages in research one may not be able to discriminate because of a paucity of evidence, but that is a condition to be eliminated by a combination of theoretical and empirical work, not accepted as desirable or, worse, democratic and politically correct. Second, the findings of pure neuropsychological research demonstrably assist in explaining some otherwise opaque rock art motifs.

By and large, I now believe that the second of these two points is the more important and durable—the first is simply a boring philosophical sideshow. The fear that an approach that draws on neuropsychological research is inherently reductionist and eliminates social contexts is misplaced. Human beings have brains that function in discoverable ways, and they have to make sense of the self-generated products of their brains (e.g., dreams). Not only do they make sense of "aberrant" mental experiences, they go further and harness those experiences in daily social practice. These are some of the key points that the following chapters take up.

Building Bridges

8

Signs are small measurable things, but interpretations are illimitable.

—GEORGE ELIOT, *MIDDLEMARCH*

WE HAVE NOW REACHED a crucial stage on the journey from the rock art of southern Africa to the cave art of Upper Paleolithic western Europe. The methodological bricks have been fired in the furnace of practical explanatory southern African examples (e.g., Lewis-Williams 1985c, 1986a, 1986b, 1988a, 1988b, 1992, 1993, 1995; Lewis-Williams and Blundell 1997), but to build an explicit methodological bridge to the Upper Paleolithic they need to be articulated in new ways.

In 1972, I visited a number of Upper Paleolithic cave sites in the Dordogne, through the kindness of André Leroi-Gourhan. This experience, longed for since 1968 when I read his book *The Art of Prehistoric Man in Western Europe* (1968a), did not simply confirm my fascination with the underground images; it also persuaded me that there must surely be some, at that moment unknown, ways of moving from the southern African rock art to these images so remote in time and space. This kind of extension from a twentieth-century ethnographically known art to such ancient images was, I knew, taboo in archaeological and anthropological circles. Indeed, Leroi-Gourhan himself struggled to avoid what were (pejoratively) called "ethnographic analogies," and I fully appreciated the danger of such analogies' turning the past into a carbon copy of the present. But if all researchers were deterred by received, academically sanctioned opinion there would be few, if any, advances in human knowledge. Leroi-Gourhan's bid to avoid ethnographic analogies was right for its time: Too many analogies, such as Breuil's, were indeed naive and misleading. But, if we eschew analogy, what do we put in its place? As we have seen, pure empiricism will not work. In any event, despite his avowed intention, *did* Leroi-Gourhan avoid analogy?

Later, in the 1980s, a way forward opened, one which would reduce the dangers of ethnographic analogies: The brains of anatomically modern Upper Paleolithic people were wired in the same way as those of all people living in the twentieth century. Once the explanatory potential of neuropsychological research on the brain and altered states of consciousness was evident, it became necessary to construct a model of those experiences that would facilitate reaching beyond San rock art and indeed beyond all those rock arts for which there is relevant ethnography. In the temporally remote Upper Paleolithic of Franco-Cantabria, for which there is, of course, no ethnography, the ethnographic cogwheel would have to be abandoned—at least temporally—and a new approach essayed.

Working again with T. A. Dowson, I attempted to construct a methodological bridge from the present to the Upper Paleolithic. But, in doing so, he and I made a grave error, the effects of which we seem doomed to endure to our dying days. As we began work on what we would call the "neuropsychological model," we envisaged two papers: The first was to deal with the entoptic phenomena experienced in an early stage of altered consciousness (chapter 7 provides an example), while the second would deal with deeper levels of altered consciousness. In the event, we resolved to combine the two proposed papers, but we erred in retaining the title of the first, seduced, I have to admit, by its euphony. Certainly, "The Signs of All Times" is a phrase that lodged in readers' minds, but it gave the impression that the utility of the neuropsychological model depended entirely on the universality of entoptic phenomena, which, as a thorough reading of the paper itself shows, is not the case.

Then, eighteen years after my first experience in the Dordogne caves, I was invited to speak at a conference held in Montignac to mark the fiftieth anniversary of the 1940 discovery of Lascaux. The French did the occasion proud: It was a grand national celebration of France's position in the genesis of "art," complete with fireworks, laser displays, and a visit by the president. As a special concession, President Mitterrand was taken into the sacred, underground chambers of Lascaux. Later, after he had completed his prepared address to the conference, he folded up his notes, put them in his pocket and spoke movingly of his experience earlier in the day. Those of us who had also enjoyed the privilege of exploring Lascaux sensed that he was speaking beyond the political requirements of the celebration.

My presentation to the conference dealt, in large measure, with the bridge that I felt could be built from the twentieth century to the Upper Paleolithic. As events turned out, the conference proceedings were not published. But an English recension of what I believed the southern African research could offer was published the following year in the *South African Journal of Science*. That article contained a drastically shortened version of the neuropsychological model. In what follows, I have substituted for that summary the fuller description of the model that appeared in the ill-named 1988 *Current Anthropology* article; those sections remain in the first person plural.

Upper Paleolithic Art in the 1990s:
A Southern African Perspective
and
The Signs of All Times: Entoptic Phenomena
in Upper Paleolithic Art

The Upper Paleolithic art of western Europe presents one of the greatest archaeological challenges. Made between, roughly, 10,000 and 32,000 years ago, it comprises engraved and carved bone, ivory, antler, and stone art *mobilier*, as well as the better-known painted and engraved cave art, some of which was executed deep underground in dark passages, halls, and even small *diverticules* into which only one person can fit—and then only with difficulty.

The first major cave art discovery took place in 1879, when Don Marcelino Sanz de Sautuola's daughter, perhaps bored by her father's excavations in the Spanish cave Altamira, happened to glance up at the ceiling and saw the magnificent painted bison. Though cautious, de Sautuola believed he had found genuine Upper Paleolithic art, but for the next two decades a fierce controversy raged over the authenticity and antiquity of the Altamira art until, in 1902, the influential prehistorian Emile Cartailhac published his "Mea culpa d'un sceptique." De Sautuola was vindicated, but, unhappily, he had died a frustrated man in 1888.

Lascaux, discovered on September 12, 1940, is perhaps the best-known and most striking of the painted and engraved caverns. It contains approximately 600 paintings and nearly 1,500 engravings (Leroi-Gourhan and Allain 1979). In the Rotunda, the largest of its chambers, two brilliantly colored converging cavalcades of animals—horses, aurochs, stags, and a strange imaginary creature—glisten spectacularly on the calcite-covered walls, while in the small Apse hundreds of animals and geometric "signs" have been engraved one on top of the other in a confusing palimpsest.

Lascaux, Altamira, and the approximately 260 other decorated caves in Europe (Bahn and Vertut 1988, 35, 39) have long defied convincing interpretation. How can twentieth-century archaeologists explain why people of the Upper Paleolithic braved the dangerous subterranean labyrinths to make pictures of animals, "signs," and, very occasionally, of people?

Ethnographic and Structuralist Explanations
During the first half of the twentieth century, interpretive work was based on simple ethnographic analogies drawn largely from Australia. Writers such as

Salomon Reinach, noting descriptions of Aboriginal practices, claimed that Upper Paleolithic people made the art in order to control the animals they hunted or to ensure their fertility. As new finds came to light, they were forced to fit this explanation. For instance, when depictions of felines and other dangerous animals were found, the Abbé Henri Breuil, for fifty years an authority on Paleolithic art, argued that the artists hoped to acquire the strength and ferocity of these creatures. But, as discoveries mounted up, it eventually became clear that sympathetic or hunting magic was too simple an explanation.

After disillusionment with the hunting-magic hypothesis, workers felt that they should concentrate exclusively on Upper Paleolithic data and avoid all ethnographic analogies. Accordingly, Leroi-Gourhan (1968) and Laming-Emperaire (1962) attempted to induce a new kind of explanation from what they saw as the objectively determined distribution of motifs within the caves. Influenced by the heady structuralist thought of the 1950s and 1960s, they argued that the cave art was constructed on the binary opposition male : female; the animal species and the signs could, they claimed, be divided into these two categories, and the categories were placed in predetermined sections of the caves. Bison and aurochs, for Leroi-Gourhan both so-called female animals, were said to be concentrated in the central parts of caves, while horses, "male" animals, were scattered through the entrance, central, and deeper zones; felines, bears, and rhinoceroses, "dangerous" animals, appeared to be clustered in the most remote parts of caves. The "male" and "female" signs were said to follow the same pattern. Leroi-Gourhan and Laming-Emperaire believed that the underlying binary formula lasted throughout the Upper Paleolithic. Then, in the 1970s and 1980s, empirical and statistical work, combined with growing recognition of the greatly varied topography of the caves, weakened their hypothesis.

At the beginning of the 1990s, the structuralist "grand scheme" has been virtually abandoned, and there is an interpretative void. Many archaeologists still fear that a return to ethnographic analogies will reduce the complex Upper Paleolithic societies to a simplistic reflection of a single society presently living in marginal circumstances and having a long history that included contact with other cultures. After all, it is generally acknowledged that no exact equivalents of Upper Paleolithic societies exist today or existed when the earlier ethnographies were compiled.

Because of their rejection of ethnography, modern researchers run into two problems. First, they set out to be purely empirical; that is, their work is directed to Upper Paleolithic data rather than to explicitly theoretical and methodological concerns. Indeed, the view is widely expressed that theoretical matters and explanations must wait until the old data have been reexamined and new, theory-free data have been brought to light. Although this sounds sensible enough, researchers are not in fact working, as they believe themselves to be, in a theory-free vacuum; rather, they are moving in the direction of empiricism, the scientific method that advocates the induction of explanations from supposedly objective, unbiased, theory-free data. The serious logical and methodological problems inherent in empiricism have been amply exposed in the philosophical literature (e.g., Chalmers 1978; Copi 1982; Hempel 1966; Gibbon 1989), and its debilitating role in southern African rock art research has also been criticized (e.g., Lewis-Williams 1983a, 1984a; Lewis-Williams and Loubser 1986; for an extension of these criticisms to Alexander Marshack's Upper Paleolithic research see Lewis-Williams and Dowson 1989b). At the same time it must be noted that criticisms of *empiricism* do not deny the value of the good *empirical* work that is presently being done on Upper Paleolithic art. On the contrary, it is only the belief that explanations can be logically inferred, or will simply emerge, from supposedly theory-free data that is in question. As Shanks and Tilley (1987) put it, "It is important to distance being empirical—considering data in all its potential fullness and complexity—from being empiricist—granting primacy to that data."

Second, the rejection of all ethnographic analogies inevitably leads to the use of an "ethnography" that is vague, tacit, poorly formulated, and, ultimately, derived from Western constructs of the "savage" and the "primitive" in human history. Explanations that have no counterparts in these largely ideological and unarticulated constructs are automatically excluded. In this way outright rejection of ethnographic analogy as an explanatory tool merely tightens the grip of Western concepts and values on the past.

By contrast, my own view of Upper Paleolithic art must inevitably be colored by the ethnographic instance with which I am most familiar, the San, or Bushman, rock art of southern Africa. Despite the legitimate misgivings of some researchers, I argue that it is possible to draw on some southern African material without turning Upper Paleolithic people into nineteenth- or twentieth-century San. Escape from what is sometimes called the "tyranny of ethnography" lies in part— and only in part—in neuropsychological research on altered states of consciousness. In the first place, southern African rock art research combined with neuropsychological work has yielded general theoretical and methodological insights that reach beyond San art; second, it has provided clues to a specific interpretation of Upper Paleolithic art that proposes that the painted and engraved images were in some sense and in some ways associated with practices that we may loosely yet legitimately call shamanistic.

I now consider three of the broad theoretical and methodological issues: the notion of the archaeological context of Upper Paleolithic art; the ordering of depictions within a cave or a single panel; and, last, the oft-drawn functional distinction between sacred cave art and secular mobile art. I then move on to clarify a number of points raised by the shamanistic interpretation of Upper Paleolithic art.

Theory and Method

Context

The current moratorium on explanation has placed renewed emphasis on the archaeological context of Upper Paleolithic art. A similar emphasis is evident in southern Africa: Books on San art sometimes start with accounts of geology, climate, zoology, and the Later Stone Age lithic sequence (for a review article on such a book, see Lewis-Williams 1990a). Without in any way denying the intrinsic interest of these concerns, I argue that what constitutes an "archaeological context" is not, as the illusion of positivist, empiricist archaeology suggests, a given. On the contrary, it is a value-laden construct of selected observations compiled by archaeologists working within a particular theoretical framework. Simply to say that the art must be placed in its context thus begs the question of what that context actually might comprise.

In considering this problem it is useful to distinguish between at least two kinds of archaeological context. One comprises a whole range of circumstances that obtained when the art was made; these include geology, climate, stone artifacts, and so forth. But when writers invoke this sort of context, they do not say explicitly how specific components of the context informed specific features of the art. Rather, this sort of context does no more than provide a backdrop to descriptions of the art that remain essentially detached from it. Perhaps more seriously, one of the dangers of a backdrop context is that it tends to control the type of explanation that may be considered appropriate. Therefore, emphasis on climate and zoology tends to lead to an ecological, adaptationist explanation: The art is seen as an adaptive response to the environmental conditions of its "context." Indeed, ecological contexts are constructed in the expectation that the environmental data they incorporate had some direct, causative, and formative (though usually still to be explicated) bearing on the production and content of the art.

A different type of context is what we may call the informing context ("inform" in the sense of "to put into form or shape," S.O.D.). Unlike a backdrop context, it comprises only those features of the past that actually influenced the art and its production in some definable way. In reconstructing the informing context we enquire about the social relations and cognitive processes that gave rise to the art and that imparted meaning to its images and significance to their placement in the social and natural environment. The social processes that such a context includes go beyond the division of labor (men hunt; women collect plant foods). Rather, it incorporates the "invisible" relationships into which people enter to provide the material basis for life, the (somewhat variously understood) relations of production, as well as the ideology that articulates with and naturalizes these relations (e.g., Shanks and Tilley 1987a; Godelier 1977, 1978; on the social context of San rock art see Lewis-Williams 1982).

There is, of course, a catch here that arises from the very nature of empiricism. Researchers cannot begin to construct the informing context until they know the art's "meaning" or social role. If they have no idea of the art's meaning or its social role, they can have no idea of just where it fitted into the social formation. In other words, they cannot even start collecting data until they know which data are relevant to the context and therefore worth collecting.

In southern Africa this methodological dilemma was largely resolved when, in the late 1960s and early 1970s, researchers started to examine the large corpus of nineteenth- and twentieth-century San ethnography that had been virtually ignored until then. This new ethnographic initiative showed that San rock art, though polysemic (Lewis-Williams 1981a, 1990a), is essentially shamanistic (e.g., Lewis-Williams 1982, 1936; Lewis-Williams and Dowson 1989a; Yates, Golson, and Hall 1985; Huffman 1983; Garlake 1987b). As a result of this work we now know that, for example, changes in the sizes of stone artifact types are not germane to an understanding of the paintings and engravings—unless the changes can be shown to have been associated with changes in the relations of production and ideology (Lewis-Williams 1985b; Wadley 1987; Mazel 1909). Further, researchers found that, notwithstanding important local variations, the art was shamanistic over diverse ecological zones from the semiarid Kalahari Desert to the much better watered Drakensberg over 1,000 km to the southeast. The potential of an adaptationist explanation for San rock art was thus seriously reduced, and the futility of constructing an environmentalist context in the belief that it was an informing context was exposed.

Establishing the informing context of Upper Paleolithic art must therefore follow, not precede, formulation of some notion of its "meaning," or "meanings," and its place in society. Working the other way around runs the risk of predetermining its significance(s) and social role(s). Researchers are reluctant to take the first of these two routes because they distrust explanations of any aspects of the past that go beyond subsistence and technology. They are trapped on the lowest rungs of Hawkes's notorious ladder of inference that postulates a steadily (perhaps exponentially) increasing lack of confidence as we move "up" from technology to economy, to social forms, and, finally, to religion. They believe, incorrectly, that economy can be empirically determined; they do not realize that "an economy" is as much an abstract construct as "a religion." It is only pieces of stone, bone, and plant material that they dig up; "economy" is an abstract model inferred from the physical data. "Economy" exists in archaeologists' heads, not in the palms of their hands.

The methodological dilemma involved in the creation of an informing context is, however, less intractable than it may at first appear. The impasse is created by rigid adherence to empiricism and its corollary, the rejection of all ethnographic analogies. A different methodological route can, I argue later, lead to some idea of the art's significance(s) and social role(s) and from there on to reconstructing the informing context in which it was made.

Order

The problems encountered in constructing an informing archaeological context are akin to those experienced in attempts to grapple with the second methodological/theoretical issue to which I shall refer: determining the topographic or "compositional" order in Upper Paleolithic parietal art. Laming (1962), Leroi-Gourhan (1968a), and, currently, Vialou (1986) have had to deal with this dilemma.

All attempts to discern and understand the placing of depictions within a cave or within a single panel must start with the creation of categories. Certain groups of depictions or attributes of depictions have to be established before counting them and plotting them on a map of the cave can commence. But the categories (like "context") are not "given"; researchers create them in the hope that some sort of pattern will be evident once the counting and plotting have been completed. Thus, all categorical distinctions, be they between geometric motifs and representational depictions, "feminine" and "masculine" signs, bovids and horses, or "safe" and "dangerous" animals, derive from the researchers' minds, not from Upper Paleolithic art itself. Indeed, all bodies of data can be categorized in a variety of ways. The categorization adopted must be justified by the goal at which the research aims. If the categories are not set up with this goal in mind, they run the risk of being (indeed, probably are) inappropriate and misleading.

This difficulty emerged in southern African rock art research in the late 1960s when a number of researchers adopted quantitative techniques (e.g., Vinnicombe 1967; Maggs 1967; Pager 1971; Lewis-Williams 1972b, 1974b; Willcox 1978b). They categorized paintings according to species and a wide range of blindly selected attributes and then set about using computer programs, punch cards, and intuition to seek patterns in the data. There is some controversy over the usefulness of this work. When the data were plotted topographically according to sites and then within sites, no clear and intelligible order emerged. Indeed, comparisons between some art sites could have led researchers to suppose that the different sites were associated with completely different San activities. For example, some sites comprise almost entirely geometric motifs; others have only representations of people and animals. Later it became apparent that both kinds of sites were created within the framework of San shamanism, whatever the non-significant differences might mean. Similarly, all attempts to analyse panels according to the placement of, for instance, species—whether they face left or right, whether they are high up or low down, and so on—failed to produce any evidence for a repeated "compositional" order.

Once it became known that the art was shamanistic, the futility of much of this work was apparent. For one thing, many of the attributes of depictions that we now know to be significant were unknown and therefore unnoticed and unrecorded in the 1960s. The vast inventories compiled in the 1960s are therefore fundamentally flawed: They omit some highly important features and, conversely, include many that now appear to be trivial. By contrast, the shamanistic explanation allows researchers to address the differences between sites and between panels by selecting discriminating features of known meaning.

Moreover, it now seems that the kind of "compositional" order researchers were then seeking in painted panels and which they tried to accommodate in their categories is essentially Western and inappropriate to a study of San rock art. The order (or, more correctly, one of the orders) in San rock art is not a matter of left/right balance or complementary between what we may see as major themes (e.g., antelope, felines, people). Such orders presume a more or less flat, two-dimensional surface on which motifs are deployed according to an accepted aesthetic of composition. The concept of order is rather to be approached from an entirely different perspective because, in San art, order also obtains at right angles to the rock face, not just across it as in Western pictures. The right-angle order extends beyond the rock face in both directions. Starting behind the rock face, it can be summed up thus: spirit world ⟷ rock face ⟷ depiction (or manifestation of vision) ⟷ the "real" world. This right-angle, two-way order was created every time shaman-artists passed through the rock face to the spirit world and then returned to this world to fix, by the act of painting, their spiritual visions (Lewis-Williams and Dowson 1990). As panels accumulated over centuries, painted visions piled up and thus created a distribution of images that appears chaotic to a Westerner who sees only the paintings and knows nothing about what was believed to lie behind the rock face or how the shaman-artists obtained and then manifested their visions. The superpositions that this right-angle order created were not random. For reasons at present unknown, San shaman-artists favored certain combinations and tended to avoid others (Lewis-Williams 1972b, 1974b; Pager 1976b; see Willcox 1978 and Lewis-Williams, Butler-Adam, and Sutcliffe 1979 for debate).

This is not to say that there is no order on the plane of the rock face; some depictions appear to be related to others by activities, such as dancing, walking in a file, and, less commonly, hunting. But these relationships are only part of the aggregation of images and cannot be understood by themselves. San rock art is in essence three-dimensional in the sense that its "meaning" and its "composition" lay in part beyond and in front of the rock face in dimensions invisible to Western viewers.

The complexities and "foreignness" of San rock art shows that the concept of order needs careful thought when we are studying arts other than Western art. We could easily impose on Upper Paleolithic art Western and entirely inappropriate notions of what constitutes order or confusion, whether within a single aggregation of motifs or within the topography of a cave. Indeed, as I now briefly suggest, much evidence implies that Upper Paleolithic order was closer to (though not necessarily identical with) San rock art than to Western artistic "compositions."

In the first place, the superimposition of one depiction on another, especially in such locations as the Apse in Lascaux, recalls densely painted San rock art panels. One explanation that has been advanced for this sort of Upper Paleolithic superpositioning is that the artists simply ignored earlier images because the act of depiction mattered more than the depiction itself (Ucko and Rosenfeld 1967, 40, 161–64). But other evidence suggests that this may be too simple an explanation. A great many depictions of animals make use of natural features to delineate a dorsal line or a leg, or of small marks and nodules to represent an eye. It is as if the animal is hiding in or behind the rock; the "artist" has to release it or lure it out by carefully adjusting the position of his or her lamp and then adding a few strokes. In other instances natural rock features have been used to suggest faces looking out from behind the rock; the "masks" in Altamira (Leroi-Gourham 1968a, figs. 402–4) and the horse's head painted on a flint nodule in Rouffignac spring to mind. Clearly, an argument can be made for Upper Paleolithic cave art being as three-dimensional as San art: The leaving of natural rock to represent parts of a depiction suggests that the animal remains intimately linked to its hinterland, possibly an animal-filled spirit world that, like the realm San shamans visit, lay behind the rock wall. In the Upper Paleolithic caves we are probably dealing with shamanistic mental images becoming graphic images and piling up on earlier glimpses through the rock face into a spirit world. In the Magdalenian, these glimpses were facilitated initially by entry into a cave and a subterranean journey; physical penetration into the chthonian realm was thus preparatory to psychic penetration of the rock itself.

Function

The strangeness for Westerners of three-dimensional order in what appears to be a "flat" art is only one part of the problem of dealing with Upper Paleolithic imagery. My third theoretical/methodological point concerns the ways in which Westerners tend to use categories of their own that unwittingly divide Upper Paleolithic art into spurious functional types. For decades there has been much talk of sacred and secular, or domestic and ritual, art. Writers have often acknowledged that depictions in the deep, barely accessible parts of caves may have been sacred or ritual, and the places where they were executed may have been sanctuaries. On the other hand, art executed in daylight contexts or on pendants and other portable items is said to be domestic or secular. This distinction has, in turn, given rise to debate about the significance of footprints in the caves. Prints that seem to have been made by youths are said to imply puberty rituals conducted in sacred decorated areas; at the same time, the footprints of children are sometimes said to imply that the depths of caves were not sacred.

The root of this problem lies in the lexical and conceptual dichotomies of Western languages. Southern African ethnographic work has shown that some of the oppositions used in rock art research are intrinsically Western and derive from capitalist ideology that postulates distinctions between supposed economic, political, and religious institutions.

To illustrate the problems created by the sacred/secular, ritual/domestic distinctions I turn to the San's most important ritual, the trance, or curing, dance. This ritual is conducted in the camp. While women clap the rhythm and sing powerful medicine songs, the men dance in a circle around them. As the intensity of the dance increases, the shamans enter trance. Today, about half of the men and a third of the older women are shamans. As the shamans stagger in a light trance and shriek violently at the spirits of the dead or fall cataleptic in deep trance, children run around and sometimes playfully mimic the behavior of the trancers. If, centuries later, the impressions left in the sand by such an occasion were to be studied according to the ritual/domestic dichotomy, no useful, unequivocal results would be achieved. The circular rut left by the dancers may suggest some ritual activity, but the random mixture of adult, child, and even dog footprints would tip the balance in favor of a secular explanation. The truth of the matter is that the San do not recognize a distinction between sacred and

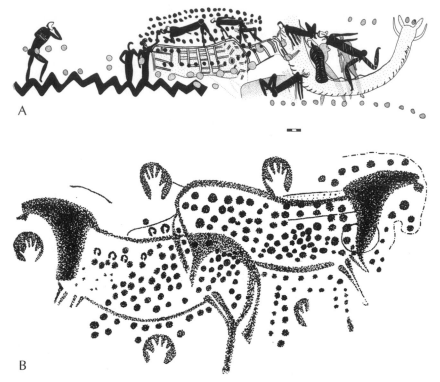

Figure 8.1.   Similarities between southern African and Upper Paleolithic art probably derive from the universality of the human nervous system and the way it reacts in altered states of consciousness. These two paintings, one (A) from the Eastern Cape Province and the other (B) from Pech Merle, France, comprise similar hallucinatory elements. In the southern African painting two sets of dots, each in a different color, and a zigzag are entoptic elements seen in the first stage of altered consciousness. In a deeper level of trance such geometric elements combine with hallucinations of animals and people, as the grid has been combined with the eland. The eared serpent issues from a step in the rock. The human figures are in typical trancing postures. In constructing the Pech Merle painting, the artist, or artists, painted the right-hand horse, the "shrunken" head of which is outlined by a natural rock formation, and then filled it in with dots and placed dots around it. Later, the left-hand horse was painted and filled in with a second set of dots (Marshack 1985). The artists also added stenciled handprints, a circle on the chest of the right-hand horse, and a fish, only partially shown in this copy, along the dorsal line of the same horse.

secular places in the same way that Westerners do. Rituals were conducted in the domestic arena. The evidence of occupation in southern African painted rock shelters therefore does not have any bearing on the ritual or domestic function of the art on the walls of those shelters.

Researchers often jokingly say that archaeologists label whatever they cannot understand as "ritual" rather than domestic, economic, or technological. The southern African ethnographic evidence suggests that we can go further and say that our understandings of Upper Paleolithic data in terms of rigid lexical dichotomies such as ritual/domestic, sacred/secular are probably misleading. The fact that Upper Paleolithic caves may have been visited by all sorts of people need not have made them any less appropriate for "religious" observances. I consider a corollary of abandoning our long-standing distinction between ritual and domestic activities in the following section.

Shamanism

Although the points I have discussed so far arise from fairly general ethnographic and methodological considerations arising from San ethnography and rock art research, I have referred again and again to the shamanistic interpretation of Upper Paleolithic art. The suggestion that at least some Upper Paleolithic art may have been associated with shamanistic practices is, of course, not new. Shamanism, in the broad sense of rituals during which a person enters an altered state of consciousness to divine the future, change the weather, cure the sick, go on out-of-body journeys, and control animals (for more on definitions of shamanism see Dobkin de Rios and Winkelman 1989 and Bourguignon 1989), is a universal, or nearly universal, feature of hunting and gathering societies (cf. Eliade 1972, La Barre 1975, and Winkelman 1986). This universality is in itself evidence for the high antiquity of the practices and for common neuropsychological origins of many shamanistic experiences. As Lommel (1967a), Eliade (1972), La Barre (1972), and many others have argued, shamanism was probably the ur-religion of the Upper Paleolithic.

To test this hypothesis in a more rigorous way than had previously been undertaken, Dowson and I constructed a three-stage model of altered states of consciousness that derives entirely from neuropsychological research, not from ethnography or rock art research.

Entoptic Phenomena

The strong evidence that chimpanzees, baboons, monkeys, cats, dogs, and other animals hallucinate suggests that altered states of consciousness and hallucinations are a function of the mammalian, not just the human, nervous system (Siegel and Jarvik 1975, 81–104) and that "nonreal" visual percepts were experienced long before the Upper Paleolithic. Indeed, australopithecines probably hallucinated. Be that as it may, the nervous system is a human universal, and we accept that, by the Upper Paleolithic, it was much the same as it is now. The content of early human mental imagery is, however, more problematic than its existence, because cultural expectations inform the imagery to a considerable extent. For a conservative beginning to an investigation of possible Upper Paleolithic mental imagery we therefore comment less on culturally informed hallucinations than on a feature of altered states completely controlled by the nervous system.

Under certain circumstances the visual system generates a range of luminous percepts that are independent of light from an external source (e.g., Klüver 1926, 1942; Knoll et al. 1963; Horowitz 1964; Oster 1970; Richards 1971; Eichmeier and Höfer 1974; Siegel and Jarvik 1975; Siegel 1977, 1978; Asaad and Shapiro 1986). Although there was interest in these visual percepts in the nineteenth century and at the beginning of the twentieth, it was not until the 1920s that Heinrich Klüver began the systematic analysis of the phenomena. Working under laboratory conditions, Klüver (1926, 1942, 177) concluded that these percepts were not just visual "dust"; they had form. Abstracting redundant form elements from his subjects' reports of altered states of consciousness, he arrived at four groupings of the percepts. Some years later, Horowitz (1975, 178), unaware of Klüver's work, similarly abstracted redundant form elements from reports of altered states. He then found that his elements, despite their "indescribableness" (Klüver 1926, 503), corresponded very largely with Klüver's categorization. Other workers (e.g., Knoll 1958; Horowitz 1964; Richards 1971; Eichmeier and Höfer 1974; Siegel 1977) have confirmed these findings and identified further recurring form elements. Their research has shown that these visual phenomena, although complex and diverse, take geometric forms such as grids, zigzags, dots, spirals, and catenary curves. All these percepts are experienced as incandescent, shimmering, moving, rotating, and sometimes enlarging patterns; they also grade one into another and combine in a bewildering way (Klüver 1942, 176). Because they derive from the human nervous system, all people who enter certain altered states of consciousness, no matter what their cultural background, are liable to perceive them (Eichmeier and Höfer 1974; Reichel-Dolmatoff 1978a).

These geometric visual percepts can be induced by a variety of means. Under laboratory conditions, electrical stimulation (e.g., Knoll and Kugler 1959; Knoll et al. 1963; Brindley 1973; Eichmeier and Höfer 1974) and flickering light (Young et al. 1975) produce them, but, although flickering firelight may have played a role in the past, we clearly have to look elsewhere to explain prehistoric experience. Psychoactive drugs generate the percepts, but fatigue, sensory deprivation, intense concentration, auditory driving, migraine, schizophrenia, hyperventilation, and rhythmic movement are some other generating factors (Klüver 1942;

Horowitz 1964, 512–18; Sacks 1970; Siegel and Jarvik 1975). Much more research will have to be done before it can be established whether specific geometric forms are associated with particular circumstances of generation (but see Knoll et al. 1963).

Nomenclature for these visual percepts poses some problems. Hoping to avoid a diversionary logomachy, we follow Tyler (1978, 1633) in using *entopic phenomena* (from the Greek, "within vision") to mean visual sensations derived from the structure of the optic system anywhere from the eyeball to the cortex. This term covers two classes of geometric percept that appear to derive from different parts of the visual system—phosphenes and form constants. *Phosphenes* can be induced by physical stimulation, such as pressure on the eyeball, and are thus entophthalmic ("within the eye"; Walker 1981). *Form constants* derive from the optic system, probably beyond the eyeball itself (Knoll et al. 1963; Siegel 1977). We distinguish these two kinds of entoptic phenomena from *hallucinations*, which have no foundation in the actual structure of the optic system. Unlike phosphenes and form constants, hallucinations include iconic visions of culturally controlled items such as animals, as well as somatic and aural experiences. These definitions are somewhat complicated by similarity between certain phosphenes and form constants and the simultaneous experience of form constants and hallucinations and, moreover, by a tendency for writers to use *hallucination* to cover phosphenes, form constants, and hallucinations as now defined. One of us (JDL-W) has been guilty of such confusion, but we feel that greater definitional clarity should be sought if we are to attain more precision in our understanding of shamanistic experience. Nevertheless, at the present stage of research it is premature to distinguish between phosphenes and form constants (cf. Hedges 1983, 59), and we therefore use only the generic term *entoptic phenomena* (or *entoptics*) for the largely geometric visual percepts. We reserve *hallucinations* for more complex iconic visions (Siegel 1977, 134; Reichel-Dolmatoff 1978a, 12–13).

A Neuropsychological Model

The universality of entoptic phenomena encourages us to construct a model of the ways in which mental imagery is perceived by people in certain altered states of consciousness. Ultimately, such a model should be relevant to all arts derived from these altered states. Because we are concerned principally with entoptics, we say less about iconic hallucinations, but the intimate relationship between the two must be clarified by any model that seeks to explain the imagery of altered states. We distinguish three components within our model: types of entoptic phenomena, principles governing their perception, and stages in the progression of altered states of consciousness.

Entoptic Forms

Although there are numerous entoptic forms, certain types recur. We have selected six of the commonest types from the range established by neurologists and psychologists (see, for example, Klüver 1942, 172–77; Knoll and Kugler 1959; Horowitz 1964; Oster 1970; Richards 1971; Eichmeier and Höfer 1974; Siegel 1977). (An important omission is the spiral or vortex, but we feel this deserves special treatment.) These are (1) a basic grid and its development in a lattice and expanding hexagonal pattern, (2) sets of parallel lines, (3) dots and short flecks, (4) zigzag lines crossing the field of vision (reported by some subjects as angular, by others as undulating), (5) nested catenary curves (in a developed form the outer arc comprises flickering zigzags), and (6) filigrees or thin meandering lines. Because these phenomena are mercurial, we do not suppose our six categories to be as rigid as this list seems to imply. Nevertheless, we take the six entoptic types to be fundamental because they were established by abstracting redundant elements from a large number of reports.

Principles of Perception

According to neuropsychological studies, the ways in which subjects perceive both entoptic phenomena and iconic hallucinations are many and varied. We have, nevertheless, formulated seven general principles that govern their perception: replication, fragmentation, integration, superpositioning, juxtapositioning, reduplication, and rotation.

When a subject perceives an entoptic phenomenon in one of the fundamental forms, we speak of *replication*, our first principle. The entoptics subsumed under this principle are, in a sense, unmistakable; those covered by the second principle, *fragmentation*, are less so because research has shown that an entoptic phenomenon may be broken down into minimal components (Horowitz 1975, 178). A grid, for example, may be fragmented into a ladder-like form. The third principle, *integration*, moves in the opposite direction and blends images to build up complex patterns (Klüver 1942, 177; Siegel 1977, 134). For instance, a grid may blend with a series of zigzags. Two less intimate ways of bringing together visual images are *superpositioning* and *juxtapositioning*. One entoptic form may be projected against another (Knoll et al. 1963, 205, 208, 214; Walker 1981, 148) or simply appear next to it. The next principle is *reduplication*. What may start as a single image becomes a series of duplicated images, such as festoons of catenary curves (Klüver 1942, 177, 182, 187; Reichel-Dolmatoff 1972, 92; Siegel 1977, 134). Finally, entoptic phenomena *rotate* in the field of vision (Klüver 1926, 504, 505; 1942, 181; Knoll et al. 1963, 204–6).

Although we have referred to only entoptic phenomena, these seven principles also apply to iconic hallucinations and in some cases link the two kinds of percept. In such an experience a grid, for example, may be integrated with an animal; in other instances an animal may be blended with characteristics of another species. The principles are necessarily a simplification of the many distortions and alterations experienced in mental imagery (Klüver 1942, 187), but, after the identification of entoptic forms, they are a second step in building a neuropsychological model of the ways in which mental imagery is apprehended.

Stages in the Development of Mental Imagery

As a third step we examine three broadly conceived stages in the progression of mental imagery during altered states of consciousness.

In stage 1 subjects experience entoptic phenomena alone (Siegel and Jarvik 1975, 111; Siegel 1977, 132). These are perceived with the eyes open or closed (Klüver 1942, 503; Siegel 1977, 132) and tend to be located at reading distance (Siegel 1977, 139), though they also appear to recede and advance. The phenomena cannot be consciously controlled; they seem to have a life of their own (Klüver 1926, 504; Siegel 1977, 132). They are, furthermore, characterized by varied and saturated colors (Knoll et al. 1963; Siegel 1977, 132). Sometimes a bright light in the center of the field of vision obscures all but peripheral images (Klüver 1926, 503; Siegel 1977, 134). The rate of change of the phenomena seems to vary from one hallucinogen to another (Knoll et al. 1963, 221) but is generally rapid. Laboratory subjects new to the experience find it difficult to keep pace with the rapid flow of imagery, but, significantly, training and familiarity with the experience increase their powers of observation and description (Siegel 1977, 134).

In stage 2 subjects try to make sense of entoptics by elaborating them into iconic forms (Horowitz 1964, 514; 1975, 177, 178, 181). In a normal state of consciousness the brain receives a constant stream of sense impressions. A visual image reaching the brain is decoded (as, of course, are other sense impressions) by being matched against a store of experience. If a "fit" can be effected, the image is "recognized." In altered states the nervous system itself becomes a "sixth sense" (Heinze 1986) that produces a variety of images including entoptic phenomena. The brain attempts to recognize, or decode, these forms as it does impressions supplied by the nervous system in a normal state of consciousness. Horowitz (1975) links this process of making sense to the disposition of the subject: "Thus the same ambiguous round shape on initial perception can be 'illusioned' into an orange (if the subject is hungry), a breast (if he is in a state of heightened sexual drive), a cup of water (if he is thirsty), or an anarchist's bomb (if he is hostile or fearful)" (177).

As subjects move from this stage into stage 3, marked changes in imagery occur (Siegel 1977, 132). Many laboratory subjects report experiencing a vortex or rotating tunnel that seems to surround them, and there is a progressive exclusion of perceptual information (Horowitz 1975, 178). The sides of the vortex are marked by a lattice of squares like television screens. The images on these "screens" are the first spontaneously produced iconic hallucinations; they eventually overlie the vortex as entoptics give way to iconic images (Siegel and Jarvik 1975, 127, 143; Siegel 1977, 136). The iconic images appear to derive from memory and are often associated with powerful emotional experiences (Siegel and Jarvik 1975, 111; Siegel 1977, 136). This shift to iconic imagery is also accompanied by an increase in vividness. Subjects stop using similes to describe their experiences and assert that the images are indeed what they appear to be. They "lose insight into the differences between literal and analogous meanings" (Siegel and Jarvik 1975, 128). Nevertheless, even in this essentially iconic stage, entoptic phenomena may persist: Iconic imagery is "often projected against a background of geometric forms" (Siegel 1977, 134).

These three stages are not necessarily sequential. Some subjects appear to move directly into the third stage, while others do not progress beyond the first. It does, however, appear that exclusively entoptic imagery is characteristic of the first stage. Nor should the stages be considered discrete. Construal, for instance, may occur in stage 3, with construed entoptics accompanying true iconic hallucinations. Although entoptics still occur in stage 3, they are secondary and tend to frame the principal iconic elements (Reichel-Dolmatoff 1978a, 147). The three stages we propose should therefore be seen as cumulative rather than sequential.

This three-stage progression was established by research using mescaline and LSD. We do not know if the trajectory of mental imagery is identical for all drugs and for non-drug-induced states, but we believe that a broad similarity can be accepted. This assumption is partially justified by the identification by the Tukano of the Colombian northwestern Amazon of three stages in their *yajé*-induced visual experiences (Reichel-Dolmatoff 1978a, 12–13). They speak of an initial stage in which "grid patterns, zigzag lines and undulating lines alternate with eye-shaped motifs, many-coloured concentric circles or endless chains of brilliant dots" (Reichel-Dolmatoff 1978b: 291–92). During this stage they watch "passively these innumerable scintillating patterns which seem to approach or to retreat, or to change and recombine into a multitude of colourful panels." We emphasize that these forms are depicted by the Tukano and identified by them as elements in their *yajé* visions. Reichel-Dolmatoff (1972, 1978a, b) has demonstrated their isomorphism with entoptic phenomena established quite independently by laboratory experiments. In the second stage recognized by the Tukano there is a diminution of these patterns and the slow formation of larger images. Together with these they perceive recognizable shapes of people, animals, and monsters. The intense activity of this stage gives way to more placid visions in the final stage. The Tukano's stages 1 and 2 conform to our stages 1 and 3, respectively.

The model we propose thus comprises a set of six entoptic forms, seven principles governing the perception of entoptic phenomena and iconic hallucinations, and three stages in the progression of altered states of consciousness.

To establish the utility of this model, Dowson and I applied it to southern African rock paintings and engravings because, as we have seen, there is independent ethnographic evidence that this art is shamanistic (figure 8.2). We found that images referable to all three stages are present. The same is true of Tukano bark and house paintings and North American Coso rock art, two other arts known independently to be shamanistic (Reichel-Dolmatoff 1969, 1978a; Whitley 1988). Conversely, if the model is applied to arts known not to have been associated with altered states of consciousness (such as Goya's portraits), it does not fit. The model can thus confirm or reject the hypothesis that the images of at least many arts derived from the visions and experiences of altered states of consciousness.

Encouraged by the model's discriminatory potential, we applied it to Upper Paleolithic art. Here again we found evidence for all three stages of altered consciousness. Many (but not all) of the so-called signs are similar to stage 1 entoptic forms; some seem to have been construed as animals in the manner of stage 2 hallucinations, though this is more difficult to demonstrate; and there are monsters, therianthropes, and other features of the third and deepest stage of trance. The puzzling co-occurrence of geometric and representational depictions throughout the Upper Paleolithic is thus explained. They are not two evolutionary categories or two parallel kinds of art. Rather, they are two kinds of universally experienced mental percepts. As neuropsychological research shows, we should expect to find both of them in an art derived from altered states of consciousness.

At this stage it is important to emphasize that the argument is not based on a simple ethnographic analogy with San rock art, but on the presence of a constellation of features linked by strong relations of relevance (Lewis-Williams 1991b). A relation of relevance is some causal or otherwise determining relationship between two elements in the source of an analogy; here it is the link between certain altered states of consciousness and the types of hallucination that have

ENTOPTIC PHENOMENA		SAN ROCK ART		COSO	PALEOLITHIC ART			
		ENGRAVINGS	PAINTINGS		MOBILE ART		PARIETAL ART	
A	B	C	D	E	F	G	H	I
I								
II								
III								
IV								
V								
VI								

Figure 8.2.   Six categories of entoptic phenomena compared with San and Coso rock art depictions. Redrawn from the following: (I)A, Siegel (1977, 138a); B, Richards (1971, 93); C, Thackeray et al. (1981, fig. 3); D, Manhire, Parkington, and Yates (1985, fig. 4); E, Grant (1968, 82). (II)A and B, Siegel (1977, 138d and c); C, Fock and Fock (1984, fig. 258); D. Pager (1971, fig. 307); E, Grant (1968, 102). (III)A and B, Siegel (1977, 138b and k); C, Fock (1979, pl. 100); D, Lewis-Williams (1981a, fig. 20); E, Wellmann (1979, pl. 164). (IV)A, Siegel (1977, 138e); B, Horowitz (1975, fig. 2); C, Fock and Fock (1984, fig. 259); D, Pager (1971, fig. 338); E, Grant (1968, 66). (V)A, Siegel (1977, 138j); B, Richards (1971, 91b); C, Wilman (1968, pl. 59); D, Lewis-Williams (1995b); E, Grant (1968, 28). (VI)A, Horowitz (1975, fig. 2); B and C, Fock and Fock (1984, fig. 251); D, Lewis-Williams (1981b, fig. 2); E, Grant (1968, 101). Six categories of entoptic phenomena compared with Upper Paleolithic mobile and parietal art depictions. Redrawn from the following: (I)F, Marshack (1972, fig. 34); G, Marshack (1979, fig. 34); H, Marshack (1985, fig. 17); I, Leroi-Gourhan (1968a, fig. 73). (II)F and G, Marshack (1972, figs. 4 and 36); H and I, Leroi-Gourhan (1968a, figs. 157 and 126); (III)F, Marshack (1972, fig. 12); G, Marshack (1972, fig. 36); H and I, Leroi-Gourhan (1968a, figs. 64 and 165). (IV)F, Marshack (1972, fig. 43); G, Marshack (1972, fig. 200); H and I, Leroi-Gourhan (1968a, figs. 152 and 710). (V)F, Marshack (1979, fig. 29); G, Marshack (1972, fig. 84); H, Leroi-Gourhan (1968a, 277); I, Marshack (1977, pl. 45). (VI)F and H, Marshack (1977, pl. 10 and 32).

been established by neuropsychological research. If one element of a relation of relevance is identified in the archaeological record, the relation of relevance strongly suggests that the other was also present, provided, of course, that the linking mechanism obtained in the past. Therefore, the presence in Upper Paleolithic art of images referable to all three stages of altered consciousness, together with the generally accepted assumption that Upper Paleolithic people's nervous systems were essentially modern, suggests very strongly that the production of at least some of the images was associated with altered states and hallucinations. Given the foraging economy of Upper Paleolithic societies, it seems highly likely that these states and hallucinations and their depictions were at least in some ways associated with what we may call shamanism.

Mention of shamanism understandably raises fears of another "grand scheme," such as Leroi-Gourhan's structuralism, that will obscure temporal and spatial differences in Upper Paleolithic art and that will, by its very blandness, accommodate any new data, as the sympathetic magic hypothesis was adjusted to cover depictions of felines. The shamanistic hypothesis, however, rests on quite different foundations from the earlier ethnographic explanations. It is not based only on the presence of a few geometric motifs. Nor is it a simple ethnographic parallel, but, as I have shown, it is based on features of the universal human nervous system (Lewis-Williams 1991b). More important, it emphasizes complexity and diversity and opens up the way to more productive multiple ethnographic analogies based on strong relations of relevance (for more on analogy, see Lewis-Williams 1991b; Wylie 1985, 1988). To allay fears that the shamanistic explanation may be insensitive to Upper Paleolithic diversity, I now consider some of the complexities of the hypothesis.

Types of Altered Consciousness

In the first place it is necessary to distinguish between different altered states of consciousness. Very broadly, altered states of consciousness can be conceived of as graded along a horizontal scale. At one end, there are light, mildly altered states such as those experienced when one's awareness of one's surroundings is diminished while speaking on a telephone or day-dreaming. Next comes a number of deeper levels during which subjects have less control over their commitment to the experience; these include euphoric conditions induced by such drugs as marijuana. At the other end, there are deep trance states in which subjects experience vivid and engulfing visual hallucinations as well as aural, somatic, olfactory, and gustatory hallucinations.

Both light and deep trance may be induced by a variety of means. Although ingestion of hallucinogens is perhaps the best-known technique, sensory deprivation, auditory driving, intense concentration, hyperventilation, pain, fasting, and other conditions are also important. It is possible that all these techniques were used at different times, in different places, and for different purposes during the Upper Paleolithic.

Various techniques of induction as well as different levels of trance may have been associated with different kinds of shamanistic experience. For instance, in some shamanistic societies, such as those of North America (but not southern African San), initial visions are sought during a vision quest conducted in a secluded spot, sometimes a cave. Here the initiate fasts, endures the pain of self-mutilation, and exposes his body to the elements until he "sees" the animal that will become his spirit helper. Such ethnographic reports raise the possibility of similar means of induction in the Upper Paleolithic, particularly in the isolated, dark, silent, and cold *diverticules* of the caves. Having achieved his vision, the Upper Paleolithic quester may have made a depiction of it at once or at a later time, perhaps on a second visit; we must remember that in some societies shamans go on regular vision quests, not just one.

Altered states of consciousness may also be induced in more social circumstances in which the dancing and singing of the group propels the shamans toward the spirit world, as is the case among the southern African San. The chambers of some Upper Paleolithic caves with large, communally produced paintings,

Figure 8.3.   Upper Paleolithic signs not covered by the neuropsychological model: (A) spear-like signs superimposed on a horse, Lascaux (after Marshack 1972, fig. 115); (B) spearlike signs with zigzags, Polesini (after Marshack 1969, fig. 38); (C) claviforms, Villars (after Leroi-Gourhan 1968a, 515), Le Gabillou (after Leroi-Gourhan 1968a, 515); (D) tectiforms, Bernifal (after Leroi-Gourhan 1968a, fig. 33), Font-de-Gaume (after Sieveking 1979, fig. 64b).

such as the Rotunda at Lascaux, may have been the scene of such preparatory rituals before the vision quester ventured alone into the deeper, isolated parts of the cave. In neuropsychological terms, the communally produced art created expectations and informed the content of the subsequent visions; an emic view may have been that the communally produced art exhibited and introduced a quester to the power animals. In some socially and historically specific contexts the quester may, in this introductory stage, have already been in an initial, light state of altered consciousness induced by singing and dancing.

Upper Paleolithic "Spiritual" Experience

Neuropsychological research also helps us to understand something of what Upper Paleolithic people experienced as they moved along the trajectory that leads from light trance to the overpowering and often terrifying experiences of stage 3. As laboratory subjects move into the deeper third stage they report experiencing a vortex or tunnel into which they are pulled by forces beyond their control. Some Western subjects say that the sides of the vortex are covered with "television screens" on which there are animated pictures. Others report seeing their visions projected onto their surroundings rather like a side show or a film (Klüver 1926, 505–6; Siegel and Jarvik 1975, 109; see also Reichel-Dolmatoff 1978a,b). This experience sounds very much like moving from the larger vestibules of some Upper Paleolithic caves into the narrow painted and engraved passages and *diverticules*. In Upper Paleolithic circumstances visions and already existing depictions would have merged into a single powerful, animated experience (cf. Lewis-Williams and Dowson 1990).

During all these kinds of trance, subjects are not necessarily totally oblivious of their surroundings: They may be able to walk about and to some extent perceive what is around them. Indeed, one kind of hallucination, the afterimage, may be experienced while the subject is fully awake. Afterimages may recur months after an hallucinatory experience when they are triggered by a change in body chemistry or some external stimulus (Reichel-Dolmatoff 1978b, 298–99). They float in the subject's vision or are projected onto a surface for a few seconds or for as much as some minutes. In this way, images acquired initially under what Westerners may regard as the "sacred" circumstances of the deep caves may have been carried into daily or "secular" life, for they can recur at any time. Inevitably, this kind of experience and other factors militate against the formation of a sacred/secular dichotomy that, as we have seen, is a culturally constructed distinction.

Polysemy

The afterimage experience leads us to the polysemic nature of symbols and its relevance to the distinction between mobile and parietal art. While Upper Paleolithic mobile and parietal art have much in common, the two art forms do not share identical imagery. Animal species, for instance, receive differential numerical emphasis in the two contexts (Bahn and Vertut 1988; Ucko and Rosenfeld 1967). At first glance the differences seem to suggest totally distinct art forms, one sacred and associated with the caves and the other purely decorative and associated with personal adornment and secular, technological life. As we shall now see, this distinction underestimates the complexity of shamanism.

The animals of shamanistic experience are complex, polysemic symbols with a range of associations, only some of which are emphasized in any given set of circumstances. This kind of polysemy is illustrated by San beliefs. San shamans desire to possess the potency of animals, such as eland, giraffe, and gemsbok; most shamans in fact possess two kinds of potency. During a trance dance, the women's singing and clapping combine with the shamans' intense concentration, hyperventilation, and rhythmic dancing to alter their state of consciousness. As one San shaman put it, the giraffe, his personal power animal, came and took him to the spirit world (Biesele 1980). This may be the principal, or central, context of animal symbolism, but the eland, the trickster-deity's favorite animal, and the one believed to have more supernatural potency than any other creature, is also invoked in the San girls' puberty ritual, the so-called Eland Bull Dance, in boys' first-kill scarifications, and in marriage observances (Lewis-Williams 1981a). In each of these superficially disparate contexts a different segment of the eland's symbolism is emphasized. While supernatural potency is paramount during the trance dance, fertility and rain are highlighted during the girls' puberty rituals. But even there shamanistic visions play a role because some San say that at the height of the girls' puberty dance they see an eland running up to them, a "good thing," they say, sent by God (Lewis-Williams 1981a, 41–54). At this time the other social and psychological associations of the key symbol are present, but in the background. A specific context thus highlights a segment of a symbol's semantic spectrum without eliminating other segments. The polysemic semantic and affective penumbra created by its diverse associations gives a symbol its power to move people (cf. Turner 1967).

The most prominent animals of Upper Paleolithic art almost certainly had comparably wide-ranging associations, as indeed do symbolic animals in all societies, not just forager groups. A horse depicted in an Upper Paleolithic cave may have been a symbol of shamanistic potency. But on a pendant a horse may have invoked fertility or prophylactic power. Personal decoration is never random or purely aesthetic; it is always significant of social status, attitudes, and so forth. Its imagery is selected from the repertoire of social symbols and adjusted to personal position and nuances. The *art mobilier* horse heads from Mas d'Azil or the engraved plaquettes from Enlène could not have been conceptually *entirely* divorced from the painted and engraved parietal horses of the same period. Indeed, the fact that the heads of some painted horses are "too small" while those in the *art mobilier* are more realistic may point to different emphases within the animal's symbolic spectrum created by emphasizing or attenuating parts of the body.

The association of parietal and mobile depictions would thus not have been entirely unrelated; all the imagery would have been caught up in a complex system of shamanistic belief and symbolism. Ultimately, it is the multidimensional "power" of animals that is important, however that concept may have been conceived.

New Decade, New Research

The subtle, complex symbolism of shamanism permeates all areas of hunter-gatherer life. Though diverse, various social and ritual contexts are held together by a web of symbolism (Lewis-Williams 1981a). Ethnography shows that this kind of linking took place in different ways in different shamanistic societies; similarly, the reticulated symbolism of the Upper Paleolithic probably operated differently at different periods and in different places: The 20,000 or so years of the Upper Paleolithic was a time of change, not stagnation. This is one of the reasons why it is impossible to use a single, simple ethnographic analogy of the kind employed by Reinach when, in 1903, he cited Australian Aboriginal beliefs and practices.

Instead, we must start, in the 1990s, with the human universals suggested by neuropsychology and then employ multiple ethnographic analogies with strong relations of relevance (Wylie 1988, 147) to reconstruct the informing context and the diverse shamanistic experiences of particular times and places in the Upper Paleolithic. Above all, we must remember that Upper Paleolithic shamanism, at any particular time and in any specific place, would not necessarily have closely resembled any single ethnographic instance of shamanism.

The discovery of Lascaux in 1960 not only aroused great interest among the general public; Lascaux also stimulated renewed and vigorous research. Now, many years later and with over 260 known sites, it is not so much the discovery of new caves like Lascaux that is required—exciting though that would be. Rather, it is new approaches to the data that will open up research. The devising of flexible methodologies for piecing together humankind's first "religious" concepts and experiences is the challenge of the new decade.

Note

J. D. Lewis-Williams, "Upper Paleolithic Art in the 1990s: A Southern African Perspective," *South African Journal of Science* 87 (1991): 422–429; and J. D. Lewis-Williams and T. A. Dowson, "The Signs of All Times: Entoptic Phenomena in Upper Paleolithic Art," *Current Anthropology* 29 (1988): 201–245.

Retrospect

The suggestion that some form of shamanism may have informed the cognitive and social context of Upper Paleolithic cave art elicited divided opinion. Some researchers saw that the hypothesis makes sense of numerous otherwise puzzling features of the art; others took issue with, first, the very notion of shamanism and, second, any attempt to project so far back in time what they believed to be a late, historically situated, Western construct that has no foundation in cross-cultural studies.

It is hard to tell how much the use of *shamanism*, admittedly a central Asian Tungus word, to describe religious complexes throughout the world and as old as those of the Upper Paleolithic was the cause of the trouble. Some researchers seem to be fascinated by arid logomachies: They do not see that an argument about an appellation is not the same as an argument about the content of a socio-religious complex. As a result, time and energy are wasted on nonissues. *Shamanism*, along with *entoptic phenomena*, has become a millstone around my neck.

But I am unrepentant. There have been and still are many other researchers who believe that some form of shamanism was the first attempt to deal with functions of the brain, humankind's ur-religion; by no means do I stand alone. We must not become so obsessed by differences between communities and their beliefs that we do not see fundamental continuities. Of course, there is always a danger of reducing the past to the present. Of course, the kinds of shamanism that were practiced in Franco-Cantabria through the millennia of the Upper Paleolithic were probably not identical to any presently observable manifestation of shamanism. Of course, Upper Paleolithic shamanism did not remain utterly unchanged throughout the period, nor was it always uniform across the whole of western Europe. Yet these are not totally debilitating reservations.

What was needed after the publication of "The Signs of All Times" was better definition of *shamanism* and, as I have repeatedly argued, practical, specific examples of how theoretical notions make sense of data. The next chapter attempts to answer both these needs. It and the one that follows it are too recent to warrant retrospection.

Harnessing the Brain

9

O the mind, mind has mountains; cliffs of fall
Frightful, sheer, no-man fathomed.

—GERARD MANLEY HOPKINS

P UBLICATION OF THE neuropsychological model and an assault on Upper
Paleolithic art launched from distant southern Africa raised a good deal of
controversy, much of it healthy, some of it more emotional than rational.
The debate that accompanied the *Current Anthropology* article was a useful foretaste
of what was to come. For one thing, it became clear to me that there was considerable misunderstanding of the neuropsychological model itself and of the role that
the southern African research played in the overall argument. The presence in
Upper Paleolithic art of geometric images homologous with entoptic phenomena
was not the beginning and the end of the argument, as so many researchers
seemed to believe. Nor was the argument a simple ethnographic analogy with
southern African rock art. I addressed some of the logical issues in "Wrestling
with Analogy: A Methodological Dilemma in Upper Palaeolithic Art Research"
(Lewis-Williams 1991b; reprinted in Whitley 1998). Other components of the
debate required more precise definitions and, especially, confirmatory research.

The problems with a definition of *shamanism*, a term that is persistently associated with Mircea Eliade's (1972) compendious and influential book *Shamanism:
Archaic Techniques of Ecstasy*, clearly needed to be laid to rest. Moreover, researchers'
fears that talk of a universal, loosely defined shamanism would eliminate significant differences between shamanisms and would mask the diversity of social contexts in which shamanism flourished would have to be allayed.

Those initial tasks would shore up the foundations of the argument that
Upper Paleolithic religion could be broadly termed shamanistic. But more was
required; the simple statement that shamanism was present in various forms

during the west European Upper Paleolithic was no more than a first step, crucial but insufficiently explored. For instance, we needed to ask: What features of Upper Paleolithic art, *other than the images themselves*, does the shamanistic explanation clarify? What social role did Upper Paleolithic shamanism play? What connections existed between shamanistic beliefs, social distinctions, and the embellished caves? Can we begin to distinguish regional and temporal shamanisms in Upper Paleolithic western Europe? Is the shamanistic explanation a key to a range of questions? Does it open up new avenues of research? How does it compare with other explanations of Upper Paleolithic imagery?

This chapter and the one that follows come from papers that began to address these questions.

Harnessing the Brain: Vision and Shamanism in Upper Paleolithic Western Europe

A glance at a bibliography of recent publications reveals something of the character of present-day Upper Paleolithic art research—or, as some writers prefer to say, Upper Paleolithic "image-making" or, still more circumspectly, "mark-making." Two to three decades ago more researchers would have been interested in the grand sweep of Upper Paleolithic art—despite some of its inappropriate connotations, I retain the handy monosyllable. Art for art's sake, totemism, sympathetic magic, and binary oppositions, all explanations for the art as a whole, would have been debated. Then, following the death in 1986 of the eminent French prehistorian Andre Leroi-Gourhan, there was a feeling that research of this kind had attempted to fly too high. Tacitly, a moratorium on explanation was declared. Certainly no one was prepared to attempt another grand scheme to replace Leroi-Gourhan's and Annette Laming-Emperaire's binary structuralist hypothesis (Leroi-Gourhan 1968a; Laming-Emperaire 1962); indeed, the very notion of an all-encompassing explanation was discredited. Attention therefore began to focus on empirical issues.

Data and Explanation

West European Upper Paleolithic research has produced and still is producing data that are indispensable to new hypothesis construction, and nothing I say here should be seen as critical of good empirical work. Research requires both theory and data. But, in this post–Leroi-Gourhan age, we have to guard against what Richard Bradley (1985, 86) has called Mr. Micawber archaeology: Keep at it long enough and something is bound to turn up. When we have "enough" facts their meaning will become evident: In other words, data precede and lead to theory. Empiricism, the philosophical name for Micawberism is, however, not an infallible program for the production of explanations (for discussions of empiricism in rock art research, see Lewis-Williams 1984a, 1989b, 1990b; Lewis-Williams and Loubser 1986; Tilley 1991). We need some other methodological routes to the uncovering of "meaning."

In southern Africa, a historical trajectory markedly different from the European one led not to a moratorium but to an intensification of work aimed at explaining rock art. This difference between European and southern African research is partially explained by the existence of directly relevant southern African ethnography. It was a close reading of this ethnography that led to an understanding of the art that has, in the first place, specific and detailed explanatory power and, second, broad methodological implications that extend beyond southern Africa.

In short, the demonstrably multiple fit between aspects of nineteenth- and twentieth-century San ethnography and the highly detailed rock art images of the subcontinent led to a concomitantly detailed explanation: San rock art was, at any rate in large measure, associated with the beliefs, cosmology, experiences, diverse rituals, notions of supernatural power, changing social relations, metaphors, and symbols of San shamanism (e.g., Lewis-Williams 1980, 1981a; Lewis-Williams and Dowson 1989a; Dowson 1994). At first there was some resistance to this view because two classic interpretations, art for art's sake and sympathetic magic (both inherited from European Upper Paleolithic art research), were deeply entrenched in popular thought and political strategies (Lewis-Williams 1995c). Today, however, the shamanic interpretation is widely accepted, though healthy debate continues on just how much of the art is shamanic and in what sense it is shamanic, and, further, on the nature of other meanings that may be encoded in the art (see papers in Lewis-Williams and Dowson 1994).

But the southern African research trajectory did not end with that specific, ethnographic explanation. Two simple yet crucial points with wider methodological implications became apparent. First, all shamanism is posited on certain kinds of institutionalized altered states of consciousness. Second, the nervous system that produces those states is a human universal. Because all human beings have the same nervous system, they have the potential to experience similarly structured visual, aural, somatic, olfactory, and gustatory hallucinations, though the meanings ascribed to hallucinations and much of their content are, of course, culturally and historically contingent (Knoll et al. 1963; Klüver 1966; Bourguignon 1974; Eichmeier and Höfer 1974; La Barre 1975; Siegel and West 1975; Siegel 1977; Asaad 1980; Asaad and Shapiro 1986). I argue that the southern African work that led to these two observations established a methodology that, together with the empirical work that is now being done in western Europe, will allow us to escape from a purely empiricist approach to Upper Paleolithic art and enable us to essay a bold conjecture, or hypothesis, that is empirically based and that can be evaluated (Lewis-Williams 1991b).

The methodology to which I refer eschews the empiricist notion that research moves linearly from data to explanation; instead, this methodology consists in the intertwining of independent, mutually constraining, and reinforcing strands of evidence (Wylie 1989). In western European research, these strands include Upper Paleolithic empirical data of many different kinds, neuropsychological research on altered states of consciousness, and multiple analogical arguments that draw on a range of hunter-gatherer ethnography and are founded on strong relations of relevance (Wylie 1982, 1985, 1988). Because this methodology has been published elsewhere (Lewis-Williams 1991b, 1995b), I do not rehearse its details here. In essence, it has informed the argument that much Upper Paleolithic parietal imagery was, in some measure, in some ways, shamanic.

This explanation is, of course, not new; it has long been in the air (e.g., Reinach 1903; Levy 1963; Lommel 1967a; La Barre 1970; Eliade 1972; Marshack 1972, 280, 1976, 278–79; Eichmeier and Höfer 1974; Furst 1976; Halifax 1980, 3, 17; Pfeiffer 1982; Hedges 1983; Bednarik 1984b, 1986; Bahn and Vertut 1988, 157–58; Goodman 1988; Smith 1992). Yet it has never been generally accepted, as were art-for-art's-sake, sympathetic magic, or, more recently, Leroi-Gourhan's and Laming-Emperaire's structuralist interpretations. The reasons for the relegation of the shamanic interpretation to the periphery of academic interest are no doubt numerous and complex. I simply mention four. First, it has lacked a powerful, articulate, and charismatic proponent, like the Abbé Henri Breuil, who remained for many decades committed to the sympathetic magic explanation. Second, in more recent times the position has run counter to an important trend in Upper Paleolithic research—adaptation. Rather than granting social, individual, and, much worse, psychological factors a prominent formative position, adaptationist writers have preferred to see the making of art as a response to Upper Paleolithic climatic conditions and resultant demography. Third, the shamanic view has never meshed as neatly with contemporary Western philosophical thought as did (at least for a while) Leroi-Gourhan's and Laming-Emperaire's structuralism. Finally and most important, the shamanic view has never been fully developed, its exact implications made clear and the arguments in favor of it—especially those recently derived from neuropsychological research—fully set out.

I begin this broad overview by listing the principal features of shamanism; this provides some overall orientation for the sections that follow. Then, having given reasons for suspecting some sort of shamanism in the Upper Paleolithic, I assess the potential of the explanation by considering four specific features of the underground parietal imagery of southwestern France. Next, I comment briefly on some of the ways in which Upper Paleolithic shamans exploited the widely varying topographies of the caves. Finally, I consider, in a preliminary way, the role of shamanism in the changes that took place during the Upper Paleolithic.

Shamanism

Although societies practicing other modes of production sometimes evince elements of shamanism (e.g., the Maya; Freidel, Schele, and Parker 1993), I narrow the field to hunter-gatherers and propose ten central characteristics of shamanism as it is practiced in such societies.

In the first place, hunter-gatherer shamanism is fundamentally posited on a range of institutionalized altered states of consciousness. Second, the visual, aural, and somatic experiences of altered states of consciousness give rise to conceptions of an alternative reality that is frequently tiered. Third, people with special powers and skills, the shamans, are believed to have access to this alternative reality. Fourth, the behavior of the human nervous system in certain altered states creates the illusion of dissociation from one's body (less commonly understood in hunting and gathering shamanic societies as possession). Shamans use dissociation and other experiences of altered states of consciousness to achieve at least four ends; these ends constitute the next four features of hunter-gatherer shamanism. Shamans are believed to contact spirits and supernatural entities; they heal the sick; they attempt to control the movements and lives of animals; they are believed to have the ability to change the weather. Ninth, these four functions of shamans, as well as their entrance into an altered state of consciousness, are believed to be facilitated by a variously conceived supernatural potency, or power. Last, this potency is commonly associated with animal-helpers that assist shamans in the performance of their tasks.

In compiling these ten characteristics of hunter-gatherer shamanism I have excluded features that some writers consider important, if not essential, for the classification of a religion as shamanic. I do not, for instance, link shamanism to mental illness of any sort, though some shamans may well suffer from epilepsy, schizophrenia, migraine, and a range of other pathological conditions. Nor do I stipulate the number of religious practitioners that a shamanic society may have; some societies have many, others only a few, often politically powerful, shamans. Nor do I stipulate any particular method or methods for the induction of altered states of consciousness. Altered states may be induced by ingestion of psychotropic drugs, rhythmic and audio driving, meditation, sensory deprivation, pain, hyperventilation, and so forth.

If we allow only the ten distinguishing features I have given, the word *shaman* can be freed from its central Asian Tungus origin and be more widely applied (cf. Eliade 1972; Lewis-Williams 1992), even, I argue, to the Upper Paleolithic of western Europe.

Upper Paleolithic Shamanism

There are two major reasons for suspecting some form of shamanism in the Upper Paleolithic.

First, there is evidence to suggest that the ability of the human nervous system to enter altered states and to generate hallucinations is of great antiquity. We do not, of course, know exactly what chimpanzees, baboons, monkeys, cats, and dogs experience, but they and many other creatures apparently do hallucinate, not only when psychotropic drugs are administered to them but also sometimes under natural circumstances (Siegel and Jarvik 1975, 81–104). The ability to hallucinate is therefore probably a feature not just of the human but of the mammalian nervous system. Consequently, it seems likely that australopithecines hallucinated, highly probable that Neanderthals hallucinated, and certain that at least some of the anatomically modern human beings of the Upper Paleolithic also hallucinated. What australopithecines, Neanderthals, and Upper Paleolithic people made of their hallucinations is another question altogether.

Second, I point to the ubiquity of shamanism among hunter-gatherer communities (see, among many others, Eliade 1972; Winkelman 1986; Harner 1973; Vitebsky 1995). Whatever differences there may be, hunter-gatherer communities throughout the world and on all continents have religious practitioners who enter altered states of consciousness to perform the tasks I have listed. The widespread occurrence of shamanism results not from diffusion but (in part) from universal neurological inheritance that includes the capacity of the nervous system to enter altered states and the need to make sense of the resultant hallucinations within a foraging community. There seems to be no other explanation for the remarkable similarities between shamanic traditions worldwide. It is therefore probable that some form of shamanism—not necessarily identical to any ethnographically or historically recorded type of shamanism—was practiced by the hunter-gatherers of Upper Paleolithic Europe.

That probability is increased by a more specific consideration of some of the features of Upper Paleolithic imagery. We need to know if components of the imagery of Upper Paleolithic art have anything in common with the mental imagery of altered states of consciousness. I leave aside mobile and open-air art and concentrate on parietal cave art.

Entirely independently of work on Upper Paleolithic art, neuropsychological research on altered states of consciousness has identified types of mental imagery and the sequence in which the types are often, but not ineluctably, experienced (see Lewis-Williams and Dowson 1988 for an overview). In the first and "lightest" stage of altered consciousness people may experience geometric visual percepts that include dots, grids, zigzags, nested catenary curves, and meandering lines (e.g., Klüver 1926; Eichmeier and Höfer 1974; Siegel and Jarvik 1975; Asaad and Shapiro 1986). These percepts flicker, scintillate, expand, contract, and combine with one another; they are independent of light from an exterior source. They can be experienced with the eyes closed; with open eyes, they are projected onto and partly obliterate veridical visual perception. Because they are wired into the human nervous system, all people, no matter what their cultural background, have the potential to experience the same forms. They are known variously as phosphenes, form constants, and entoptic phenomena (on nomenclature, see Tyler 1978). As subjects go further, or deeper, into altered consciousness they enter a second stage in which they sometimes try to make sense of these geometric forms by seeing them as objects or experiences familiar or important to them (Horowitz 1964, 514, 1975, 177, 178, 181). This process of construal is, unlike the forms themselves, culturally situated. The third and deepest stage is frequently entered via a vortex or tunnel (Siegel 1977; Horowitz 1975, 178). In this stage, the geometric forms are peripheral to but sometimes combined with iconic images of animals, people, monsters, and highly charged emotional situations (Siegel and Jarvik 1975, 127, 143; Siegel 1977, 136). The animals, people, and objects seen in this stage are often distorted in various ways, but they can also have a startling, lifelike "reality." Eventually, subjects become part of their own imagery, and they feel themselves to be blending with both geometric and iconic imagery (Klüver 1942, 181, 182). It is in this final stage that people sometimes feel themselves to be turning into animals (e.g., Siegel and Jarvik 1975, 105) and undergoing other frightening or exalting transformations.

The utility of the neuropsychological model to identify graphic imagery derived from altered states of consciousness may be assessed by slotting it against arts known ethnographically, and therefore independently, to be associated with shamanic altered states of consciousness, such as southern African San rock art (Lewis-Williams 1980, 1981a; Lewis-Williams and Dowson 1989a), the rock art of the Cosos (Great Basin, North America; Hedges 1982; Whitley 1987, 1988, 1992, 1994a, 1994b), the art of the Tukano (South America; Reichel-Dolmatoff 1972, 1978a) and Huichol art (Central America; Berrin 1978). In the iconography of each of these four arts there are geometric motifs isomorphic with the geometric forms of stage 1, construed geometrics referable to stage 2, and stage 3 iconic images that are sometimes therianthropic and sometimes combined with geometric forms (Lewis-Williams and Dowson, 1988). Arts known independently to be associated with shamanic altered states of consciousness thus display a complex set of features—not merely geometric motifs—that fits the set of features established by laboratory research on the mental imagery of altered states of consciousness. If the model is tested against an art not associated with altered states of consciousness, say Rembrandt's work, no such fit will be found (cf. Dronfield 1994, 1995).

Having supported the utility of the neuropsychological model, we can apply

it to Upper Paleolithic parietal art, an art that is, of course, not known a priori
to be shamanic. Because this has been done in detail elsewhere (Lewis-Williams
and Dowson 1988, 1992; Lewis-Williams 1991b), I give only a brief summary
of the main points. In the first place, many of the so-called signs of Upper Paleolithic art are referable to one or other category of stage-I geometric mental percepts: Dots, zigzags, grids, meandering lines, and, less frequently, nested catenary
curves (so-called festoons) occur in Upper Paleolithic parietal art. On the other
hand, some Upper Paleolithic motifs that are at present usually classified as
"signs" do not appear to be derived from geometric mental percepts. These
include spearlike forms and the so-called claviforms and tectiforms (Lewis-
Williams and Dowson 1988, fig. 3). What these excluded motifs may represent
does not concern us at the moment, but it needs to be said that their exclusion
points to a strength rather than a weakness in my argument because it renders
invalid the potential criticism that virtually any mark can be interpreted as having
been derived from a geometric mental percept.

In any event, the fit between neuropsychologically identified elements of mental imagery and the motifs of Upper Paleolithic parietal art does not end with
geometric forms. Upper Paleolithic images referable to stage 2 and, especially,
stage 3 are also present. By their very nature, stage-2 construals are difficult to
identify because, if the construal is far advanced, the original geometric form is
masked by the representational image into which it is transformed. Possible
Upper Paleolithic examples of contrual include depictions of ibexes with greatly
exaggerated curved horns that recall the nested catenary curves of stage I. Again,
it must be emphasized that the meaning or meanings of such depictions is another
issue altogether. Stage-3 Upper Paleolithic images are clearer. They include therianthropes, anthropomorphs, and, of course, animals, many of which are superimposed on or by and juxtaposed with geometric forms—a characteristic of stage-
3 mental imagery. Sometimes depictions show distorted animals and "monsters,"
but many images are, on the other hand, markedly "realistic" (Clottes, Garner,
and Meury 1994). Comparable realism also characterizes much southern African
San rock art (Vinnicombe 1976; Lewis-Williams 1981a); yet a small, easily overlooked feature sometimes suggests that a San image does not depict a "real" animal, as a superficial glance may suggest (Lewis-Williams and Dowson 1989a). It
is important to note that the argument I am outlining does not concern geometric
motifs alone. It is the presence in Upper Paleolithic parietal art of imagery referable to all three stages that makes the argument compelling (Lewis-Williams
1991b).

In sum, the antiquity and ubiquity of altered states of consciousness, the widespread occurrence of shamanism among hunter-gatherers, and formal parallels

between elements and the mental imagery of altered states and Upper Paleolithic parietal imagery are three points that suggest that at least some—not necessarily all—parietal art was probably associated with institutionalized hallucinations. In other words, it seems highly probable that some yet to be precisely defined forms of shamanism were present at, probably, all periods of the Upper Paleolithic of western Europe. This very general conclusion contributes significantly and economically (in the sense of economical explanations) to an understanding of numerous otherwise puzzling features of Upper Paleolithic art. I refer to four such features.

Explanatory Power

The first has exercised researchers for a long time. It is indeed one of the key features of Upper Paleolithic parietal art. Frequently, depictions of animals are adjacent to, superimposed by, or superimposed on geometric "signs." Panels, such as the Apse at Lascaux (Leroi-Gourhan and Allain 1979) or parts of the Sanctuary at Les Trois Frères (Bégouën and Breuil 1958), are so densely covered with both representational and geometric images that some sort of relationship between the two types of image seems inescapable. At one time it was thought that representational imagery evolved out of geometric imagery, but it is now accepted that both types continued to be made throughout the Upper Paleolithic. The contemporaneity of the two kinds of image has led to the suggestion that they derived from two distinct, parallel, perhaps complementary, graphic systems (e.g., Leroi-Gourhan 1968a; Marshack 1972). In terms of this view, geometric and representational images are comparable to text and graphs in a book: Both may be saying the same thing, though in different ways. Although there may be an element of truth in this two-systems explanation, it does not explain why people maintained the two systems throughout the Upper Paleolithic, why the two types of image crowd one on top of another in a way that baffles and confuses modern Western viewers, nor, significantly, why both geometric and representational images are found in shamanic arts throughout the world.

The answer to the problem is, I argue, straightforward. As we have seen, in certain altered states, the human nervous system produces these two kinds of images—geometric and representational—and they are sometimes superimposed and blended with one another (Siegel 1977, 134). The two types are therefore not as different as they appear to modern Westerners: Both derive from the same source—the nervous system in certain altered states. Their intimate association in a shamanic art is therefore not a surprise; on the contrary, as the neuropsychological model I have outlined suggests, it is to be expected.

This observation resolves the postulated dichotomy between geometric and representational Upper Paleolithic imagery that has formed the basis and starting point for all classifications of Upper Paleolithic art hitherto devised. Both types of image are in fact representational, for they both represent (by way of complex processes) mental imagery. If a taxonomic distinction is to be drawn between them, it should be posited on the different stages of altered consciousness in which the nervous system generates them and the iconographic contexts that those states create, not on a supposed distinction between their "representational" and "nonrepresentational" functions.

The second feature of Upper Paleolithic art that the shamanic hypothesis explains is the placing of some parietal images deep underground. Some images are in or near entrances to caves, in shallow rock shelters, or in the open air (Bahn 1995) and must therefore have been well or partially lit by natural light; during the Upper Paleolithic, before weathering processes took their toll, there were doubtless many more than there are today. Other images, especially (but not exclusively) those of the Magdalenian, are found a kilometer and more underground in totally dark and silent chambers and passages. Sometimes these images are in small *diverticules* and chimneys that are hard to find and to which access is sometimes extremely difficult. Moreover, the danger involved in getting to some remote locations should not be underestimated: Deep chasms have to be avoided, and labyrinthine passages have to be negotiated. Upper Paleolithic people had, of course, to traverse these routes assisted by only flickering torches or tallow lamps. These remote, subterranean images have to be seen in the context of shamanic cosmology.

To speak of shamanism in the Upper Paleolithic is to make a statement about cosmology, not just religious belief. All life, economic, social, and religious, takes place within and interacts reciprocally with a cosmology. As I have mentioned, the shamanic cosmos is conceived, in the first instance, as comprising two realms, this world and a spirit world. Often, the spirit world is immanent, interdigitating with the real world. At the same time, these two realms are frequently conceived of as subdivided and layered, the more complex the shamanic society, the more tiered subdivisions of the cosmos (Eliade 1972). I argue that the widespread shamanic notions of a spirit world and a layered cosmos derive, in the first instance, from experiences of altered states of consciousness that are universal: They include a whole range of hallucinations and dreams as well as sensations of flying, rising up, entering a vortex, and passing underground and through water. Altered states of consciousness thus not only create notions of a tiered cosmos; they also afford access to and thereby validate the various divisions of that cosmos. The shamanic cosmos and "proof" of that cosmos constitute a closed system of experiential creation and verification. Universal neurologically generated and veri-fied experiences account, at least in part, for the ubiquity of the shamanic cosmos in one manifestation or another.

The layers of the shamanic cosmos are accessible to shamans as they explore their altered states of consciousness in pursuance of their various tasks. The route of their explorations, what anthropologists sometimes call the *axis mundi* (e.g., Eliade 1972), is conceived of differently in different shamanic societies; it may, for instance, be thought of as a hole in the ground at the back of a shaman's dwelling, the roots of a tree, or, significantly, a cave. Always it is some sort of tunnel, a notion that derives, I argue, from the neurologically produced vortex that seems to draw subjects into the third and deepest stage of trance, the stage in which they inhabit a vivid, hallucinatory, but for them intensely real, world. I argue that the neurologically generated concepts of a tiered cosmos and entry into a vortex or tunnel make it highly probable that entry into a cave was, for Upper Paleolithic people, entry into part of the spirit world.

Further, the constriction and sensory deprivation of narrow subterranean pas-sages may not only have replicated the vortex; they may also have contributed to the induction of altered states. Under such circumstances, the experience of the passage and the experience of the vortex may have become inextricably interwoven as "spiritual" experiences were given topographical materiality. Here is one of the reasons why Western binary oppositions of spirituality and reality, sacred and profane, a material realm and a nonmaterial realm, together with all their various permutations, probably did not obtain in the Upper Paleolithic.

The subterranean passages and chambers were therefore places that afforded close contact with, even penetration of, a spiritual, nether tier of the cosmos. The images that people made there related to the chthonic world. Images were not so much taken underground and "placed" there as obtained there and fixed there. The hallucinatory, or spirit, world, together with its painted and engraved imag-ery, was thus invested with materiality and precisely situated cosmologically. Moreover, acts of image making did not merely take place in the spirit world: They also informed and incrementally created that world. There was thus a com-plex interaction between the topography of the caves, mental imagery, and histori-cally situated image making by individuals and groups that, through time, built up and changed the spirit world both conceptually and materially.

This understanding brings me to a third and related feature of Upper Paleo-lithic art that is difficult to explain outside of the shamanic hypothesis. One of the best-known and most consistent features of Upper Paleolithic art is the use that artists made of features of the rock surfaces on which they placed their images (e.g., Graziosi 1960; Ucko and Rosenfeld 1967; Bahn and Vertut 1988). Almost every cave contains examples; I cite but a few.

At Labastide, for instance, the natural contours of the rock provide the dorsal line of a bison; the rest of the animal has been suggested by the addition of a few features (figure 9.1: Omnès 1982, fig. 154; see also fig. 147, Pl.XIX, no. I). Upper Paleolithic depictions are also sometimes placed so that a small, seemingly insignificant nodule or protuberance forms the eye of an animal. Some of these nodules are so insignificant that one suspects that they were identified and selected by touch rather than by sight. Fingers lightly exploring the walls may have discovered a nodule, and the mind, prepared for the discovery of animals, took it to be an eye.

On a larger scale, a natural rock shape at Comarque seems to have suggested a remarkably realistic horse's head, complete with nostrils and mouth (Leroi-

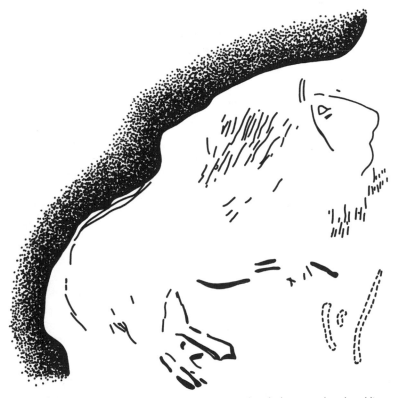

Figure 9.1.   Labastide (Hautes-Pyrénées, France). Natural rock shape used as dorsal line of a bison. Redrawn from Omnès 1982, fig. 154.

Gourhan 1968a, fig. 13); an engraver completed and added details to the form. Human figures occasionally also make use of natural features of the rock. At Le Portel, for example, two red outline human figures are painted so that protuberances become their penes (Bahn and Vertut 1988, fig. 52).

The importance of natural features of the rock is particularly clear at Castillo where a depiction of a bison has been painted to fit undulations in the surface of a stalagmite: The back, tail, and hindleg of the depiction fit the shape of the rock. But in order to use the rock in this way the artist had to position the bison vertically (figure 9.2; Bahn and Vertut 1988, fig. 53). In doing so, he or she expressed a highly significant difference between the animals of mental imagery and the animals of the real world that, in the nature of things, normally assume horizontality. What was important to the Castillo artist was fitting the bison into the natural features of the rock, not orienting the image so that it would call to mind a real, standing bison.

So far, I have described depictions that present, principally, lateral views of animals. By contrast, in the Salon Noir at Niaux an artist added antlers to a hole in the rock that looks something like the head of a deer as seen face on (figure 9.3; Clottes 1995, fig. 142 and 164). At Altamira, in one of the deepest sections of the cave, natural shapes in the rock have been transformed by the addition of painted eyes and, in one case, a black patch that may represent a beard (Leroi-Gourhan 1968a, figs. 402–4; Freeman et al. 1987, 224–33). The same technique has been employed at Gargas (Breuil 1952, fig. 271). At Montespan, a natural rock formation has been similarly transformed into what appears to be an animal head (Leroi-Gourhan 1968a, pl. 36). The same effect has been achieved at Rouffignac where a remarkable horse's head has been painted on a flint nodule that juts out from the wall of the cave; the body of the horse seems to be behind the wall (figure 9.4). For a final example I cite a depiction in the Chimney at Bernifal: Eyes, nostril, and mouth have been added to a natural edge to produce a human face. The effect created by all these images is of human and animal faces looking out of the rock wall, the rest of their bodies being concealed behind the surface of the rock. The figures are not merely painted onto the surface; they become part of and, at the same time, construct the walls of the caves in specific ways.

All the examples I have so far described point to an interaction between the maker of an image and natural features of the rock face. My last examples are especially important because they imply interaction between, not just makers of images and their handiwork, but also between viewers and images. Sometimes an undulation in the rock surface becomes the dorsal line of an animal if one's light is held in a specific position; an artist added legs and some other features to the shadow. By moving one's lamp the image can be made to disappear and reappear.

Figure 9.2.   Castillo (Santander, Spain). Natural shape of stalagmite used to give form to a vertical bison. Redrawn from Ripoll, in Bahn and Vertut 1988, fig. 53.

At Niaux, for example, an undulation in the rock has been used as a bison's back; this is especially clear when the light source is held to the left of and somewhat below the image. An artist added a head, legs, a belly line, and a tail. But, like the bison at Castillo, this Niaux animal is positioned vertically in order to exploit natural features of the rock (Clottes 1995, figs. 177 and 180). On a larger scale, the head of one of the well-known "spotted horses" at Pech Merle is suggested

Figure 9.3.   Niaux (Midi-Pyrénées, France). Antlers added to natural cavity to give effect of a deer seen from the front. Redrawn from Clottes 1995, figs. 120, 142, 164.

by a natural feature of the rock, especially when the source of light is in a certain position (figure 9.5). But, in this case, the artist distorted the painted horse's head, making it grotesquely small; the rock shape is in fact more realistically proportioned than the painted head. It is as though the rock suggested "horse," yet the artist painted not a "real" horse but a distorted horse, perhaps a "spirit-horse." Many further examples could be given. Indeed, Freeman (Freeman et al. 1987) points out that the technique of using shadows to complete a depiction "is more common than is usually supposed" (105).

An important reciprocality is implied by these images born of shifting chiaroscuro. On the one hand, the creator of the image holds it in his or her power: A movement of the light source can cause the image to appear out of the murk; another movement causes it to disappear. The creator is master of the image. On the other hand, the image holds its creator in its thrall: If the creator (or subsequent viewer) wishes the image to remain visible, he or she is obliged to maintain

Figure 9.4.   Rouffignac (Dordogne, France). Horse's head painted on a flint nodule that juts out of the cave wall. Redrawn from Graziosi 1960, pl. 202d.

a posture that keeps the light source in a certain position. Relax, and the image retreats into the Stygian realm from which it was coaxed. Perhaps more than any other Upper Paleolithic images, these "creatures" (creations) of light and darkness point to a complex interaction between person and spirit, artist and image.

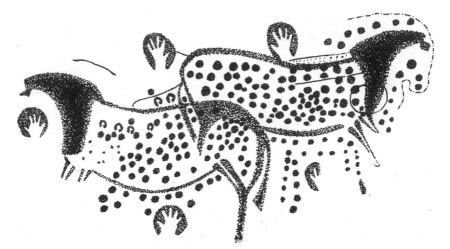

Figure 9.5.   Pech Merle (Lot, France). Natural shape to right (broken line) suggests a horse's head. Redrawn from Leroi-Gourhan 1968a, fig. 64; Graziosi 1960, pl. 196; and other photographs.

All the intimate and complex relationships between images and rock surfaces that I have described, together with the placing of these images in subterranean locations, are understandable in the light of ethnographically known practices. In some shamanic societies, such as those of North America, but not in others, such as that of the San, the notion of a vision quest is crucial to becoming a shaman, and, sometimes, repeated vision quests are required to sustain a shaman's power. A North American quester usually repairs to a remote, isolated place, sometimes a high cliff top, sometimes a cave (Eliade 1972, 50–51, 110–14; Halifax 1980, 6), to fast, meditate, and induce the altered state of consciousness in which he or she will "see" the animal helper that will impart the power necessary for shamanic practice. When the vision of the sought-after animal comes, it bestows shamanic power. It is a vision, it should be noted, that bestows the power, not a real animal.

Upper Paleolithic evidence suggests that parts of the caves, especially the deep passages and small, hidden *diverticules,* were places where vision quests took place (cf. Hayden 1993; Pfeiffer 1982). Certainly, the sensory deprivation afforded by the remote, silent, and totally dark chambers, such as the Chamber of Felines in Lascaux, induces altered states of consciousness (La Barre 1975, 14; Walker 1981, 146; Pfeiffer 1982, 211; Siegel and Jarvik 1975). In their various stages of altered states, questers sought, by sight and touch, in the folds and cracks of the rock face visions of powerful animals. It is as if the rock was a membrane between them and one of the lowest levels of the tiered cosmos; behind the rock lay a realm inhabited by spirit-animals, and the passages and chambers of the cave penetrated deep into that realm.

Such beliefs and rituals also account for the fourth feature of Upper Paleolithic art to which I refer: the various ways in which the walls of numerous Upper Paleolithic caverns were touched and otherwise treated. In some sites, such as Grotte Consquer, finger-flutings cover most of the walls and parts of the ceilings to a considerable height (Clottes et al. 1992, 586; Clottes and Courtin 1994). At Hornos de la Pena the so-called finger-flutings are more restricted in distribution: A finger-traced "grid" surrounds and appears to issue from a natural cavity (Ucko 1992, pl. 9). In another remarkable treatment of cave walls, cavities at Hornos de la Pena were filled with mud and then punctured, apparently with fingers or sticks (Ucko 1992, 158, pls. 10 and 11). Ucko remarks, "It is . . . inconceivable to us today to understand the nature of such action" (158). But, if we allow that Upper Paleolithic people believed that the spirit world lay behind the thin, membranous walls of the underground chambers and passages, the evidence for this and much otherwise incomprehensible behavior can be understood in rational, if not absolutely precise, terms. In a variety of ways, people touched, respected, painted, and otherwise ritually treated the cave walls because of what existed behind their surfaces. The walls were not a meaningless support. They were part of the images, a highly charged context.

The four features of Upper Paleolithic art that I have discussed are thus economically explained by a hypothesis that invokes altered states of consciousness and a shamanic cosmos. Moreover, features that may otherwise be considered unrelated are shown, economically, to be manifestations of a single religious activity—some form of shamanism.

Space and Time

As I pointed out at the beginning of this chapter, there is today an understandable reluctance to accept explanations that purport to cover the entire span of Upper Paleolithic art in all its diversity. Such comprehensive explanations are rightly dismissed as "monolithic." Conkey (1987, 414–15) remarks that "there can no longer be a single 'meaning' to account for the thousands of images, media, contexts, and uses of what we lump under the term 'Paleolithic art.' " I have therefore confined my discussion to west European cave art and have not considered portable art or the arts of other regions. But it also needs to be shown that the shamanic explanation, even within western Europe, is sensitive to temporal, geographical, social, and iconographic diversity. Indeed, the shamanic explanation is an effective tool for uncovering and exploring such diversity, not for concealing it. To demonstrate the heuristic potential of this explanation and its sensitivity to diversity, and so refute a potential charge of monolithism, I briefly consider, first, geographical diversity and then temporal diversity.

Individual Caves

Upper Paleolithic people did not "process" caves in a rigid, formularistic way, as Leroi-Gourhan (1968a) suggested. Rather they explored and adapted each cave in accordance with its peculiar topography (cf. Vialou 1982, 1986) and, most importantly, the particular expression of shamanic cosmology and social relations as it existed at a given time and in a given region. At the same time, we must recognize that the prehistoric entrances to caves are not always known. Moreover, in some caves, the distribution of imagery as it is found today is a palimpsest resulting from changing exploitation of the topography of the cave and changing shamanic beliefs and social relations, as, for example, the dating of the discoveries at Grotte Cosquer shows (Clottes et al. 1992). It also seems that, even at a given time, Upper Paleolithic people did not adhere rigidly to a single set formula; as in many shamanic societies, there were always idiosyncratic interventions (cf. Dowson 1988). In some instances new dating techniques will sort out what is a function of the passage of time and what is contemporary idiosyncrasy, but the chronological resolution in many instances will not be fine enough to make the necessary discriminations.

Le Gabillou (Dordogne) serves as a fairly simple example of how the distribution of imagery within caves may be understood in terms of the shamanic explanation. This cave is said to date to the early Magdalenian and so to be contemporary with Lascaux (Breuil 1952, 310–11; Gaussen 1964; Leroi-Gourhan 1968a, 317). Unlike many caves that are divided into complex interlinking passages, chambers, and *diverticules*, Le Gabillou comprises only an entrance chamber, which was probably at least partially open to natural light in prehistoric times, and a single straight tunnel that extends from the entrance chamber for approximately thirty-three yards (Leroi-Gourhan 1968a, 317; Gaussen et al. in *L'Art des Cavernes* 1984, 225–31). The two parts of the cave need to be considered separately.

It seems that the entrance chamber (now partly destroyed by the construction of a cellar) was decorated with carefully painted images as well as some "simpler" engravings. Some of the painted images may have been communally produced, various classes of people participating ritually and differently, perhaps hierarchically, in the procurement of pigment and binders, mixing the paint, and applying it to the rock (Lewis-Williams 1995a; see also Vandiver 1983). This seems almost certainly to have been the case in Lascaux, where the remains of scaffolding have been found near very large paintings (Leroi-Gourhan and Allain 1979). The entrance chamber at Le Gabillou may therefore have been a kind of vestibule in which group ceremonies were performed. These communal ceremonies and the paintings themselves may, on some occasions, have prepared the minds of vision questers for what they were to see at the climax of their initiation. The culturally informed component of the deepest stage of trance derives from memory, and the novices were being shown not just pictures of animals but recreations of spirit-animals of the kind that they themselves hoped to see. Their memories were being stocked with desirable images. The entrance chamber was therefore a staging post on the route from this world to the lower tier or tiers of the cosmos.

The tunnel that leads off the entrance chamber at Le Gabillou was excavated in recent times; during the early Magdalenian visitors to the passage were obliged to crawl, and movement was very restricted. The passage images are engraved, often with only a few, sure strokes. There are no elaborately painted images in the passage, although there do appear to be some patches of ocher that may be the remains of paint. The comparatively "simple" execution of the passage images implies that less time was expended on them than on the imagery in the entrance chamber. If, as I suggest, communal, preparatory rituals took place in the entrance chamber, it seems that solitary vision quests were undertaken in the narrow tunnel, where questers, isolated from the community, made more swiftly executed engravings.

The engravings in the tunnel are, moreover, strung out along its entire length. Some sections of the tunnel are slightly more densely engraved than others, but, although some images are overlain by other marks (said by some to be "magical strokes"; Breuil 1952, 311), no section is nearly as densely engraved as, say, the Apse at Lascaux.

During the Magdalenian, the Apse was reached by means of a painted and engraved 15-m passage in which it was necessary to crawl or crouch very low (Leroi-Gourhan and Allain 1979, fig. 42). This passage led from the large, richly decorated Hall of the Bulls, into which the prehistoric entrance almost certainly led and in which communal rituals probably took place, past the Apse and on to the Nave and, finally, the very narrow Chamber of Felines, the most remote part of the cave (Leroi-Gourhan and Allain 1979, fig. 313). The Apse was thus an alcove, or side chamber, on the way from the Hall of the Bulls to the Chamber of Felines, a route that may have been fully traversed only rarely. The Apse is moreover, situated above the Shaft (Leroi-Gourhan and Allain 1979, fig. 53), at the bottom of which is the celebrated group comprising an apparently bird-headed anthropomorph, a "wounded" bison, what may be a bird-headed staff, and other images (for a shamanic interpretation of this "scene" see Davenport and

Jochim 1988; some researchers now question whether the Apse was connected to the Shaft during the Magdalenian).

In the Apse there seems to have been a determined and sustained effort to place principally engraved but also some painted images in a single area. The complexity of the superimpositions in the comparatively small Apse suggests that the people who made the images were sharing, or desired to share, the acquisition of a special, topographically situated power (Leroi-Gourhan and Allain 1979, 220–88). This power was, I argue, related in complex ways to the different kinds of images in the other, topographically and iconographically distinct, areas of Lascaux.

By contrast, the separated images in the tunnel at Le Gabillou suggest that the acquisition of visions there was of a more individual nature: The people at Le Gabillou did not seek to associate their visions intimately with the visions of others. The different ways of placing imagery in the Apse and the Le Gabillou tunnel thus point to different kinds of social relations between vision questers themselves and, by extension, between shamans and the wider community.

The approach that I advocate is thus able to suggest the different uses to which parts of Le Gabillou (and other caves) may have been put and how various parts of the cave related to the shamanic cosmos.

Image and Change

Social contexts are, of course, not immutable. As the Upper Paleolithic progressed, the historically and geographically situated forms of shamanism changed, and the associated practice of making imagery came to be linked to growing social complexity. Evidence for such change may be found in Upper Paleolithic art and its placement in the caves.

At the beginning of the Upper Paleolithic, Aurignacian "artists" engraved and painted their images in the entrances to caves or, at any rate, as far in as light penetrated, though the deep art at La Grotte Chauvet shows that much variation existed even at that time (Chauvet, Deschamps, and Hillaire 1995). At this time, access to religious imagery (if not the actual experience) may have been open to all, and the shamanic cosmos may not have been conceived of as tiered. Later, they ventured into totally dark depths, and, certainly by the Magdalenian a few people were traveling considerable distances underground in order to make images, sometimes squeezing through narrow openings or scaling slippery chimneys to reach hidden niches (e.g., Bahn and Vertut 1988; Ucko and Rosenfeld 1967). The leaving of daylight areas to go deeper into the dark caves suggests growing interest in and insistence on spatially distinct ritual areas. The source of increasingly esoteric religious knowledge was being placed farther and farther away from daily life: The deeper into the caverns, the more restricted the access to altered states of consciousness or, more precisely, to those altered states that were defined as the ones that really mattered, a tendency that probably paralleled growing social differentiation (cf. Bender 1989; Thomas 1991) and increasing cosmological complexity. The spectrum of altered states of consciousness, ranging from "light" euphoria to deeply hallucinatory conditions, was being divided and socially allocated. Upper Paleolithic shamanism was developing through time.

In many instances, it seems that the more structured the social dimension, the more likely it is that the deeper altered states of consciousness will be regarded as dangerous (Douglas 1973, 104). Certainly, it is hard to imagine that penetration of the deep Upper Paleolithic caves could have been regarded as anything but perilous. Increasing the physical danger and discomfort further restricted access to the ultimate religious experience and the power that this experience bestowed. At the same time, the markedly restricted movement that some of the smaller decorated areas (e.g., the tunnel at Le Gabillou, the Chamber of Felines in Lascaux, and the Chimney in Bernifal) permit suggests increasing restrictions on the ways in which ideologically defined altered states of consciousness might be experienced and a concomitant codification of beliefs concerning such states. Access to certain altered states, and hence to certain kinds of knowledge, was being restricted. Altered states were being appropriated, defined, and differentially allocated in attempts to reproduce and to transform relations of power (Lewis-Williams 1995a).

The essential historicity of this process explains why the making of shamanic rock art was not a universal practice, despite the universality of shamanic mental imagery. In southern Africa, for instance, some shamanic San communities made rock paintings and engravings, while others, such as those living in the Kalahari Desert, did not. There are, of course, few rock surfaces in the flat, sandy Kalahari on which rock art could be made, but the shamanic functioning of the San communities that live there does not, even today, seem to be impaired by an absence of image making. The experiences of altered states of consciousness are, in fact, a necessary but not a sufficient condition for the making of shamanic art. Those experiences and their associated mental imagery constitute a resource that, under certain historically specific social circumstances, can be exploited. As Bourguignon (1974, 234) pointed out, visions acquired in altered states of consciousness are "raw materials for potential cultural utilization." The need to reify on rock these experiences and visions is not ineluctable: There is no neuropsychological imperative. In some communities, shamans weave their experiences into tales, songs, and mythology; sometimes they also depict them on perishable materials, such as skin drum coverings and clothing (e.g., Brodzky, Danesewich, and Johnson 1977). Each instance of the making of rock art is therefore a specific historical question. Neuropsychological research into altered states of consciousnes clarifies the substance and nature of a resource, not the social conditions under which that resource is accessed. Why people living at the beginning of the west European Upper Paleolithic began to make rock art is a question that still needs to be addressed. The reasons why they continued to make rock art throughout the Upper Paleolithic may well have changed as historical circumstances changed.

The historical specificity of each Upper Paleolithic image and the kind of shamanic context in which it was made point to an important mechanism for change in the cosmological, social, religious, and iconographic frameworks of the period. Each painted or engraved image should be seen as an individual or group intervention. Human agency (see, for example, Bourdieu 1977; Giddens 1984; Johnson 1989), not impersonal, hardwired cognitive structures, accounts for change. As I have pointed out, altered states of consciousness are a resource on which actors can draw as they negotiate their social and political statuses. Unfortunately, it is a resource that is usually omitted from archaeological accounts of change, perhaps because of current values in Western academia and a (one hopes implacable) resolve to exclude "New Age science" with which "mystical" things such as altered states are associated. The seriousness of this omission is highlighted by those studies that do consider altered states. For instance, in an account of change in the iconography of southern African rock art, Dowson (1994) argues that different types of images were manipulated by politically emergent shamans to negotiate new statuses. Citing Barth (1987), Riches (1994) makes a similar point. Religious specialists among the Mountain Ok of New Guinea effect incremental shifts in the connotations of particular symbols. In Riches's apt phrase, the shaman is a "cosmology maker." I argue that, as individual Upper Paleolithic shamans pursued their personal and group interests, the cosmology that they created and modified (partly by their art) both constrained and enabled social change.

A Way Ahead

As I pointed out at the beginning of this chapter, there is today a deep and justifiable suspicion of all-encompassing explanations for Upper Paleolithic art—those that cover all the different forms of art that people made during the entire 20,000-year span of the period. In demonstrating the explanatory power of the shamanic hypothesis, I have therefore considered only the parietal cave art of western Europe. I have, moreover, emphasized spatial and temporal diversity.

There are, of course, unresolved problems, and the explanation and its implications need to be fully worked out. But that is true of the most abundantly confirmed and widely accepted hypotheses; evolutionary theory is a case in point. One does not have to explain everything in order to explain something.

I simply argue that no other explanation currently before researchers has equal evidential support. Nor does any other explanation have comparable explanatory power and potential; the shamanic explanation resolves some of the most intractable problems of Upper Paleolithic research in a parsimonious way. In doing so, it creates an entirely new way of categorizing Upper Paleolithic images and addressing their changing deployment within the caves. Moreover, it places all Upper Paleolithic activity, whether economic, social, or ritual, within an evolving cosmology.

By intertwining diverse empirical data, multiple ethnographic analogies with strong relations of relevance, and the results of neuropsychological research on altered states of consciousness, the approach that I advocate breaks out of the current impasse created by the collapse of earlier explanations and by a tendency to think that new data, by themselves, will ultimately provide explanations. The despair of ever understanding at least something about Upper Paleolithic art that characterizes much writing on the period is unjustified.

Note

J. D. Lewis-Williams, "Harnessing the Brain: Vision and Shamanism in Upper Palaeolithic Western Europe," in *Beyond Art: Pleistocene Image and Symbol,* ed. M. W. Conkey, O. Soffer, and D. Stratmann (Berkeley: University of California Press, 1997), 321–342.

Agency, Altered Consciousness, and Wounded Men

10

> *. . . down the labyrinthine ways*
> *Of my own mind.*
>
> —FRANCIS THOMPSON

TWO MAJOR POINTS have emerged from the approach to rock art that I have developed in previous chapters. They apply to both the southern African and the Franco-Cantabrian Upper Paleolithic images. First, such arts played a social role. It is therefore not enough to decode the images and to provide statements about what they may have meant to the original makers and viewers. We need to elucidate the ways that the images functioned in society. But general statements derived from theoretical positions are not acceptable. To assert, for instance, that Upper Paleolithic cave art was a semiotic, signifying system or to state that the images were a form of interband communication is meaningless. What, exactly, did the images *say* and what did they *do*? What did people do with them? Second, explanations need to be tied to features of specific images—as I have repeatedly argued. If an explanation does not enable us to stand before a panel of images and to see and comprehend features that had hitherto escaped our notice or were meaningless, then it is futile.

At the root of such issues is the distinction between individuals and the society that they constitute. Can we in any way discern the hand, the agency, of individuals as, by making images, they reproduced and subverted their own society?

Agency, Art, and Altered Consciousness: A Motif in French (Quercy) Upper Paleolithic Parietal Art

In 1989 Matthew Johnson made a sobering point: "The individual has been triumphantly reinstated at the centre of the stage in theory, but quietly relegated to the wings, or written out of the script altogether, in practice" (Johnson 1989, 190). Since then, the situation has not changed radically, at least in the publication of persuasive case studies (but see, for example, De Marais, Castillo, and Earle 1996; Joyce and Winter 1996; Mithen 1996).

In response to the lacuna that Johnson identifies, I lead my argument to a rock art motif that is known in Upper Paleolithic art research as "the wounded man" or "the vanquished man." After briefly situating the present study in the development of rock art research, I explore the notion of agency in five cumulative sections. First, I discuss, in a preliminary way, the role that altered states of consciousness can play in the construction of selfhood. Second, I describe some clinically and ethnographically reported somatic hallucinations. I then draw on these reports in a specific case study, the San. I show that certain somatic hallucinations were construed and manipulated in different ways by shamanic San rock painters. Next, drawing on principles and material adumbrated in my first, second, and third sections I examine formal aspects of the "wounded man" figures. Finally, I essay an explanation of these Upper Paleolithic images that takes cognizance of human agency and the construction of selfhood.

The Role of Agency in Rock Art Research

The study of Franco-Cantabrian Upper Paleolithic art has, at different times, placed markedly different emphases on the role of human individuality. Soon after the high antiquity of the art was established, the images were seen as the artistic products of artists: *Art pour l'art*, as an explanation for the making of images, emphasized the activities and volitions of talented Upper Paleolithic individuals who responded to innate compulsions to express themselves. This first phase of explanation did not last. Before long ethnographic analogies led to the proposal of hunting and reproductive magic as a more plausible explanation. In this understanding of the art, influentially advocated by the Abbé Henri Breuil, individuals were believed to have made the images in order to sustain the material basis of life.

Individualism was eclipsed with the advent of Annette Laming-Emperaire's (1962) and André Leroi-Gourhan's (1968a) structuralism. These writers postulated a "mythogram," or conceptual template, that persisted throughout the Upper Paleolithic and that informed the subject matter and the placing of images within the caves. This mythogram derived from the supposed universal binary pattern of human thinking proposed by Claude Lévi-Strauss. Lévi-Strauss (e.g., 1963) argued that myths think themselves through the minds of people; for Laming-Emperaire and Leroi-Gourhan, it was the (comparably binary) mythogram that thought itself through the minds of people into the art. Although the association has not, to my knowledge, been explored, Laming-Emperaire's and Leroi-Gourhan's structuralism marched well, at least in one respect, with the adaptationist and processual archaeological approaches of the time. On the one hand, human volition and art were seen to be the products of a suprahuman mythogram; on the other, human life was similarly reduced to the product of inexorable economic and ecological laws. In both cases, human agency was thought to be of little consequence.

At the beginning of the 1980s, a growing interest in what became known as cognitive archaeology (Renfrew 1982) proved congenial to renewed archaeological concern with agency (e.g., Hodder 1982a; Shanks and Tilley 1987b). In the new interpretations of the past, adaptationist and "vulgar Marxist" theories began to give way—at least for some writers—to Pierre Bourdieu's theory of practice and Anthony Giddens's related structuration theory (Bourdieu 1977; Giddens 1984). Central to the work of both Giddens and Bourdieu is the resolution of the dichotomy between the individual and society. Bourdieu and Giddens argue that individuals are not pawns moved across an ecological checkerboard by transcendent forces. Rather, at least some individuals know a great deal about the workings of society and are able to manipulate the rules and resources of society; but at the same time individuals are not completely free agents capable of doing exactly as they desire. Their actions are both enabled and constrained by the rules and resources that they manipulate. Despite these theoretical innovations in archaeology, the role of agency and the complex interplay between constraint and enablement in the making and purpose of Upper Paleolithic art has not been much explored (but see Bender 1989; Hayden 1990; Lewis-Williams and Dowson 1993).

The trajectory of research on southern African San rock art has in some ways paralleled that of west European Upper Paleolithic research, but in other ways it has diverged markedly. During the first six decades of the twentieth century various forms of art for art's sake and sympathetic magic were imported from western Europe, partly as a result of Breuil's visits to southern Africa. Although there was a tentative attempt in the early 1970s, the heady days of structuralism, to challenge the *art pour l'art* explanation by the detection of binary oppositions in San rock art (Lewis-Williams 1972b, 63–64), Laming-Emperaire's and Leroi-Gourhan's mythographic interpretation did not take hold in southern Africa. The major divergence from the course of west European research, however, came in the late 1960s and early 1970s when workers began to heed nineteenth- and twentieth-century San ethnography. The multiple and empirically verifiable fit between this ethnography and specific features of San rock art opened up hitherto unrecognized avenues of interpretation that, because of an absence of ethnography directly and historically relevant to Upper Paleolithic art, were not possible in western Europe. Soon a new explanation began to gain ground in southern Africa: It was argued that San rock art was, in large measure though not exclusively, associated with shamanic rituals, symbols, notions of supernatural power, and spiritual experiences (e.g., Lewis-Williams 1980, 1981a, 1990a; Lewis-Williams and Dowson 1989a, on the use of *shaman* in the southern African context, see Lewis-Williams 1992). Following up this interpretation, Dowson (1994) has explored the role of agency in the production of specific classes of shamanic images. Drawing on historical and ethnographical reports, as well as on the images themselves, he argues that the comparatively egalitarian status of San shamans was challenged by "shamanic consortia," small groups of shamans who banded together to extend their influence, and also by "preeminent shamans" who exploited their religious functions in order to acquire political power.

Recently, a broadly conceived shamanic explanation has been argued for west European parietal art on the basis of principles developed during the course of the southern African work: On both continents, so the argument runs, the making of rock art was largely, but not exclusively, associated with institutionalized, ritualized altered states of consciousness, a central feature of shamanism.

It is not my purpose here to rehearse the arguments in favor of this explanation or to explicate the principles on which those arguments are based; they have been set forth elsewhere. Suffice it to say that, although this particular methodological thrust was initially developed in southern Africa, the argument does not consist in a simple analogy between the San and the people of the west European Upper Paleolithic. Rather, the argument points to the similar (but not identical) ways in which human neurological universals of altered states of consciousness are manifested in different historical circumstances. Drawing on these universals, the shamanic interpretation provides a parsimonious explanation for a constellation of puzzling features of Upper Paleolithic parietal art; these include: therianthropic figures (a common component of hallucinations); the placing of many images deep underground (sensory deprivation induces altered states); the varied and intimate relationships between images and subterranean surfaces (surfaces were a permeable "membrane" between those who ventured into the caves and spirit-animals in a subterranean realm); the various ways in which the walls of subterranean chambers and passages were touched and otherwise treated (in the establishment of diverse interactions with the spirit world); the ways in which parts of caves were differentially exploited (in the course of various shamanic rituals); and the co-occurrence of representational images and geometric "signs" (two kinds of hallucination).

Altered States of Consciousness and the Construction of Selfhood

Altered states of consciousness can, of course, be understood only in relation to some sort of "normal" consciousness. It is this dynamic and complex relationship that opens up discussion of agency in the Upper Paleolithic. "Consciousness" is a notoriously difficult concept to define (Edelman 1994, 111 ff); everyone thinks that they know what the word means—until they try to articulate its meaning. Michel Foucault (1965) recognized the social nature of definition when he argued that the "normal" self, the "normal" consciousness, is constituted by the various ways in which communities define and treat altered consciousness and madness. If there is at least one assumption about the Upper Paleolithic that we can make confidently, it is that "altered" consciousness and "madness" were defined and accommodated differently from the ways in which they are defined and accommodated in late twentieth-century Western society. The construction of Upper Paleolithic "selves," and hence the foundation of human agency, consequently proceeded along routes that were peculiar to that time and that no doubt changed during the course of the 20,000-year period.

All communities are obliged to formulate definitions of consciousness, various kinds of altered consciousness, and madness, whether explicitly or implicitly, for these mental conditions are inseparably part of being human. At the same time, those definitions are always a site of contestation. The resources on which Upper Paleolithic individuals drew in the construction and transformation of acceptable and powerful social identities therefore doubtless included definitions of various kinds of consciousness. As in many societies and subcultures today, altered, or ecstatic, states of consciousness were a manipulatable resource. Indeed, any account of the past that omits consideration of altered states of consciousness is likely to be incomplete (cf. Sherratt 1991, 52). The hostility of some researchers to discussion of altered states is obscurantist.

The construction of Upper Paleolithic selves and associated human agency can be examined within the framework of shamanism and the various ways in which altered states of consciousness can be defined because the human nervous system and some of its experiential products are common to all people: All human beings have the potential to experience similarly structured visual, somatic, aural, olfactory, and gustatory hallucinations. The neuronal structure of the brain informs

1. The progression of mental imagery from light to deep altered states (though progression through each and every stage is not ineluctable);
2. The forms of pulsating, iridescent geometric imagery (known as phosphenes, form constants, or entoptic phenomena) experienced principally in the first stage of altered consciousness and that persist into subsequent stages;
3. Entry into a vortex, or tunnel; and
4. The nature of deep state experiences, such as the blending of forms (e.g., human and animal), synesthesia (confusion of the senses), a sense of dissociation from one's body, and, above all, the sense of being in another realm that has its own rules of order and causality and that is therefore very different from the material world (for a summary, see Lewis-Williams and Dowson 1988).

These neurologically generated commonalities account, in large measure, for the striking and often surprising similarities of shamanism worldwide. Further shamanic commonalities are generated by the setting of shamanism in foraging societies that depend on the hunting of animals, the avoidance of dangerous predators, appropriate weather conditions for hunting and the growth of plants (in some regions other factors, such as seasonal salmon runs, may be included here), and various forms of social cooperation and social networks.

By contrast, much of the content of shamanic beliefs, visions, and experiences is culture-specific and therefore varies from society to society. Dealing with universals and specifics, Weil (1986, 29; see also Siegel 1985, 248) emphasizes the importance of "set" (individual expectations and personality) and "setting" (the physical and social environment) in determining how an altered state of consciousness is experienced. Shamanic experience is generated by an interplay between neurological universals and cultural and personal realizations of those givens.

Shamanism is a complex, not monolithic, category. Within any given instance of shamanism, shamans experience different kinds of hallucinations, perform various "supernatural" tasks, participate in a range of rituals, and engage in diverse power struggles. From this uncontroversial proposition there flows an important yet largely overlooked observation. For the human agent, both the universal and the cultural components of altered states of consciousness have the potential to become, in Giddens's terms, a resource capable of manipulation for personal and group ends. In some shamanic societies the making of art that is associated with and that in some ways defines altered states is one of the most important resources available to human agents (Lewis-Williams and Dowson 1989, Dowson 1989; Dowson 1994; Solomon 1994). As is now widely accepted, material culture, taken to include art, does not merely reflect culture and society; in the hands of human agents, it also constitutes culture and society (e.g., Miller 1987; Shanks and Tilley 1987b, 122–34, 1992; Conkey 1991). Individual image makers—including rock artists—actually did things and achieved ends with material culture.

Somatic Hallucinations

Up to the present, the neuropsychological contribution to research on west European Upper Paleolithic parietal art has concerned only visual hallucinations and their possible depiction in the art. By contrast, southern African research has also attended to somatic hallucinations (I take *somatic* to include haptic, or tactile, and synesthetic hallucinations), such as the sensations of attenuation and polymelia (having extra limbs or digits; e.g., Lewis-Williams and Dowson 1989a). Somatic hallucinations may occur in varying ways and to varying degrees, whether the subjects' altered state is induced by ingestion of psychotropic substances, sensory deprivation, or other extraneous factors, or by pathological conditions such as temporal lobe epilepsy and schizophrenia (Siegel 1977; Brindley 1973, 593).

Somatic hallucinations occur in various parts of the body. For instance, schizophrenic patients report alarming stretching of the scalp; sometimes parts of the scalp seem to be pulled as much as 12 inches beyond the head (Pfeifer 1970, 57). Less dramatic somatic hallucinations are more common and occur in variously induced altered states of consciousness. They include tingling, prickling, and burning sensations. Although such sensations may be experienced in various parts of the body, they seem to be concentrated over the scalp, neck, shoulders, sternum, the outsides of the arms, hands and feet, stomach, and the front of the upper legs. But there is a problem in determining these locations because, in general, the sensations are ambiguously experienced, and subjects sometimes find it difficult to report exactly where they are located. A schizophrenic invoked this difficulty to explain differences between her reports and the reports of other patients (Pfeifer 1970, 58). This potential variety facilitates individual manipulation and the personalization of experiences.

Subjects, both Western and non-Western, seem to refer to somatic hallucinations less frequently than to visual hallucinations. In their very nature, visual hallucinations are more striking than hallucinations that are experienced in the other senses and that, in any event, often seem to be subsumed under and informed by visual hallucinations, as the examples I give below show. Consequently, neuropsychological research seems to have concentrated on the forms and progression of visual hallucinations at the expense of other kinds.

The ratio between visual hallucinations and hallucinations in other sensory modalities may, in some instances, be affected by the cause of the altered state of consciousness in which they occur. Lysergic acid diethylamide (LSD), for example, is said to induce predominantly visual hallucinations, whereas the pathological condition schizophrenia usually elicits a greater degree of auditory and somatic hallucinations (Winters 1975, 54). In schizophrenia, tactile hallucinations are rarely reported independently of auditory or visual hallucinations (Asaad 1980). Like LSD, psilocybin and peyote induce visual hallucinations minutes after ingestion, but auditory hallucinations are frequently experienced some two hours later; other kinds of hallucinations occur only sporadically (La Barre 1975, 12–13). The issue is further complicated by the observation that hallucinations experienced in one sensory modality can, by the process known as synesthesia, be perceived in terms of another: For instance, a sensation felt on the skin (somatic) may be perceived as "blue" (visual) (Klüver 1942, 199; Fischer 1975, 222; La Barre 1975, 10; Emboden 1979, 44; Cytowic 1994).

Attempting to clarify the relationship between visual hallucinations and somatic hallucinations, Siegel (1978) argues that there is "an orderly progression of hallucinations from simple snow lights through geometric forms to tactile sensations" (313). Some subjects, however, speak of tactile, or somatic, experiences in earlier stages than those that Siegel specifies. To clarify this apparent contradiction, it is useful to distinguish between somatic sensations and somatic hallucinations. In an early stage of altered consciousness, subjects may experience sensations of itching and tingling in various parts of the body. Because subjects do not "illusion" these sensations they are known as pseudohallucinations. With pseudohallucinations, subjects know that the similes they employ to describe their sensations are no more than similes. In a deeper state of altered consciousness subjects lose the ability to discriminate between veridical and hallucinatory impressions. At this point, they no longer compare their physical sensations to something else; the sensations *are* what the hallucination dictates. Similes become realities.

This progression can be detected in reports by Western subjects. Harner, for instance, gives a detached, somewhat clinical account of a physical sensation that he experienced after one cup of the South American hallucinogen *ayahuasca:* "A hyper-excitation is felt in the body, which produces a pleasant agitation in the epiderm" (Harner 1973a, 156). Siegel, who ingested peyote while on a visit to the Central American Huichol, gives a more dramatic, but still "objective," account, even if he does employ a metaphor: "Another 'Ping!' My skin prickled with electricity" (Siegel 1992, 29). For Westerners, electricity seems to be a ready metaphor; elsewhere, Siegel (1978, 313) records a subject as saying that the sensations were like "electricity running through the skin." These subjects are perfectly aware that they are using similes to describe their sensations. In deeper altered states, such as chronic cocaine addiction, subjects are less able to distinguish between reality and somatic hallucinations. One patient tore off his skin and, looking in the bottom of the wound, believed he was pulling out microbes with his fingernails and with the point of a pin (Magnon and Saury, quoted by Siegel 1978, 309–10). The modern Western setting that includes fear of contracting disease as a result of infection by invisible germs here led to the patient's attribution of his sharp sensations to the presence of microbes. In this case, the "pleasant agitation" that Harner describes became a terrifying hallucination. Other subjects report "the hallucination of small animals moving in the skin" (Freud, quoted by Siegel 1978, 309). At the same time as these subjects hallucinate the tingling sensation as small animals or insects on or under the skin, a condition known as formication (Asaad 1980), they experience zoopsia (visual hallucinations of animals), thus combining two sensory modalities.

By contrast, in highly charged religious contexts Western subjects sometimes seem to be ambivalent about whether they are speaking in similes or not. Their statements are nevertheless clearly informed by their setting, that is, their supportive emotional circumstances and the sort of imagery in use in those circumstances. Goodman (1972, 58) reports that charismatic Christians, delighting in the ecstasy of heightened religious experience, tell of a "gentle rain coming down on neck and shoulders and penetrating the chest"; the sensation extends down into the legs and the middle of the back. This sort of language reflects the notion of "showers of blessing", the outpourings of divine grace for which they yearn. Although Goodman does not mention the point, references to divine blessing in the form of rain are common in the Bible, written as it was in an arid and semiarid environment. For instance, Ezekiel (34:26), with characteristic eloquence, represents the Lord as saying, "And I will make them and the places round about my hill a blessing; and I will cause the shower to come down in his season; there shall be showers of blessing." Clearly, this sort of imagery informs the somatic sensations triggered by charismatic Christians' altered states of consciousness. But whether they believe that the "rain" is real or metaphorical is not entirely clear; a lack of language sophistication can lead to the suppression of "as if" in descriptions of hallucinations (Sarbin 1967, 371). Either way, these somatic experiences are a resource that individuals manipulate to achieve religious and social prominence.

The Western experiences that I have so far described range from variously successful attempts to observe one's own reactions objectively to the overwhelming experiences of pathological conditions. Non-Western shamans who experience the same universally neurologically structured somatic hallucinations do not attempt to assess their experiences objectively. Instead, they construe them in culturally contingent ways that are often different from Western reports of "microbes," "electricity," or "divine rain." For instance, in the 1920s Marius Barbeau recorded the experience of Isaac Tens, a Gitksan Native American shaman. Tens spoke of frequently falling spontaneously into a trance and of how, after he had undergone training, powerful chants forced themselves out of him, the phenomenon known as glossolalia. Speaking of one of these experiences, he said, "The bee-hive's spirit stings my body. . . . In my vision, I went round in a strange land which cannot be described. There I saw huge bee-hives, out of which the bees darted and stung me all over my body" (Barbeau, in Halifax 1980, 189). The hallucination that developed out of Isaac Tens's somatic sensations in trance was thus similar to the hallucinations of Westerners who speak of insects crawling over them. The sharpness of Tens's sensations, however, together with the zoopsia produced a complex multisensory hallucination of bees stinging him. Tens was able to use this hallucination to entrench his shamanic status.

For the Jivaro of the Amazon Basin, sharp, pricking sensations lead to a different hallucination. Jivaro shamans believe that they can keep magical darts in their stomachs indefinitely and regurgitate them at will. These darts bear a supernatural potency that can also take the form of spirit helpers, or *tsentsaks,* that enable shamans to perform their tasks (Harner 1973b, 17). The Jivaro notion of mystical darts is developed in beliefs about *pasuks,* another kind of spirit helpers who aid malevolent bewitching-shamans by shooting their own objects into victims (Harner 1973b, 21–22). While in an altered state of consciousness, curing-shamans can shoot a *tsentsak* into an eye of a threatening *pasuk,* the eyes being the *pasuks'* only vulnerable area. Apart from *tsentsaks,* there are other supernatural darts that can kill or injure people; they are called *anamuk.* They are invisible to people who are not under the influence of the hallucinogen *natemä.* In complex hallucinations, a shaman's darts sometimes take the form of animals that protrude from his skin. The darts also cover a trancing shaman's body as a protective shield (Harner 1973b, 24). The Miwok of the Central Sierra Nevada, California, held very similar beliefs. "Poison doctors," *tu yu ku,* rubbed various kinds of poison on a pinlike stick or porcupine quill and then, by magical means, shot or threw the poisoned dart at a person who may have been as far as fifty miles away (Bates

1992, 101–2). Among the Jivaro and the Miwok, then, the sharpness of the prickling experienced universally during altered states of consciousness contributes to beliefs about and hallucinations of pointed missiles and, recalling the Western subjects' reports, creatures under and coming out of the skin (formication). Jivaro and Miwok shamans weave these experiences into accounts of their prowess and, like Isaac Tens, thus enhance their social positions.

As numerous writers have pointed out, the attainment of extrahuman shamanic power and concomitant social status is frequently situated in the midst of an ordeal and an encounter with death. Often, it seems, the more horrific and painful the ordeal, the greater the prestige and power that accrue to the initiate. Death, suffering, excarnation, dismemberment, transformation, and rebirth are indeed common elements of shamanic initiation (Eliade 1972). Piercing is frequently a part of that experiential sequence. A Siberian Tungus shaman, for instance, told how his shaman ancestors initiated him: "They pierced him with arrows until he lost consciousness and fell to the ground; they cut off his flesh, tore out his bones and counted them; if one had been missing, he could not have become a shaman" (Eliade 1972, 43). In a comparable account, Eliade (1972) notes that the souls of a Siberian Buryat initiate's ancestors "surround him, torture him, strike him, cut his body with knives, and so on" (43). During this initiatory torture, the neophyte "remains for seven days and nights as if dead" (Eliade 1972, 44). A Kazak Kirgiz initiate of southern Siberia spoke of five spirits in heaven who cut him with forty knives and pricked him with forty nails (Eliade 1972, 44).

Halifax (1982) sums up the suffering of the shaman in the title of her book, *Shaman: The Wounded Healer.* For the frontispiece she chose a photograph of an Inuit greystone, ivory, and bone carving of a shaman harpooning not a seal but himself: He holds a harpoon that goes right through his body (figure 10.1). According to Halifax (1982), this carving of a pierced figure "captures the essence of the shaman's submission to a higher order of knowing" (5). The carving, I argue, is also an expression of the widely reported hallucination of piercing and so a visible, tangible guarantee of the "higher order of knowing" that sets the shaman apart from others.

Somatic Hallucinations and San Rock Art

I now show that the somatic hallucinations that I have described constitute a resource that San shamans manipulated, and still manipulate, in a number of ways. I argue that certain San rock paintings represent some of those manipulations and point to a possible explanation for the west European "wounded man" figures.

Figure 10.1.   Inuit carving of a shaman with a harpoon through his body. Halifax 1982, frontispiece, redrawn by R. McLean.

Today San shamans do not resort to hallucinogens (but see Schultes 1976; Dobkin de Rios 1986); they achieve an altered state of consciousness through intense rhythmic dancing, audio driving, concentration, and hyperventilation. They speak in a variety of ways about the kinds of somatic sensations and hallucinations that are thereby induced. For instance, Old K″au, a !Kung shaman (*n/um k″au*, owner of supernatural potency), spoke of flies clustering all over his sides when he was in god's presence. There were, he said, also mambas, pythons, bees, and locusts: "When you go there, they bite you. Yes, they bite you (gestures to his legs). . . . Yes, they bite your legs and bite your body" (Biesele 1980, 57). I argue that Old K″au was construing his tingling, prickling somatic sensations and his visual hallucinations of extracorporeal travel and animals and insects. Only the greatest !Kung shamans actually reach god's house, and Old K″au was manipulating and developing his hallucinatory experiences to achieve that status.

Bees, one of the creatures that Old K″au mentioned, are closely associated with god. Both the twentieth-century !Kung and the nineteenth-century /Xam are recorded as saying that god's wife is "the mother of the bees" (Marshall 1962, 226, 245; Bleek 1924, 47). God himself likes bees and, if people burn bees when they are trying to smoke them out of a hive, he will send sickness to them; Marshall (1962, 245) heard of two men who were said to have died because they burned bees. God, moreover, can change himself into honey and place himself in a tree like a honeycomb. If he wants to kill someone, he attracts that person to the honey; if the person eats the honey, he or she dies (Marshall 1962, 245). Not surprisingly, "Honey" is the name of a medicine, or trance dance, song (Marshall 1962, 249). Such songs are believed to be imbued with the supernatural potency that shamans are said to "own" and that they activate in order to enter trance. The !Kung of the northern Kalahari like to dance when the bees are swarming, though not, of course, actually in a swarm (Wilmsen personal communication); they believe that bees are vehicles for potency (Katz 1982, 94).

An association between bees and trance dancing is evident in an Eastern Cape Province rock painting, part of which is shown in figure 10.2. Here bees are depicted by means of small white crosses; in other paintings they are depicted with red bodies and tiny white wings (figure 10.2, inset; Pager 1971, figs. 187–89, 191, 387, 1973). Some of the bees in figure 10.2 seem to be issuing from a roughly quadrilateral form that may represent a hive, or, if !Kung beliefs are taken into account, perhaps god himself. In addition, a swarm is depicted over the heads of the dancing figures to the right. Some of these dancers have red lines on their faces that probably represent the flow of nasal blood that San shamans sometimes experience in trance (Lewis-Williams 1981a, 95–97, 98–99); at the far right, blood falls from a figure that bends forward and wears the eared cap that /Xam San informants associated with shamans who were believed to have the ability to control the movements of game (Bleek 1935, 1936, 144). This dancer reaches out to what is probably an hallucinatory creature that holds dancing sticks, bleeds from the nose, has red lines on its face, erect hair on its back, and two trailing "streamers" (for explanations of these features, see Lewis-Williams 1981a, Lewis-Williams and Dowson 1989a). None of the bees is depicted actually on any of the human figures.

By contrast, the complex somatic and visual experience of which Old K"au spoke—bees stinging (biting) him—is, I argue, depicted in a small number of rock paintings. One such painting is in the KwaZulu-Natal Drakensberg. The large panel comprises many depictions, among which are two swarms of bees that, like those in figure 10.2, are represented by small crosses, though in this case the crosses are painted in red. One of the swarms is associated with dancing figures and an hallucinatory "elephant" with toes, a bifurcating trunk, and possibly

Figure 10.2. Part of a painted panel in the Eastern Cape Province. Inset: Painted bees, after Pager (1971, fig. 387.3). Colors: red and white.

human hind legs (Lewis-Williams 1983d, fig. 74). One hundred sixty centimeters to the right there are seven elaborately painted human figures with white crosses on their red legs (figure 10.3); they seem to be running in the direction of the swarms. The crosses on these figures, like those of similar size that are painted in swarms, probably represent bees, but here the bees are crawling on and possibly stinging a number of shamans.

In the Eastern Cape Province, a painting shows a similar association of bees with the human body, but it places this association in a highly unusual congeries of motifs. At the left there is a standing figure with eighteen red crosses painted on its legs; there is also one cross on its body (figure 10.4). Given the San ethnography and painted examples that I have cited, these crosses almost certainly again

Figure 10.3.   Three running figures selected from a complex panel. KwaZulu-Natal Drakensberg. Colors: red and white.

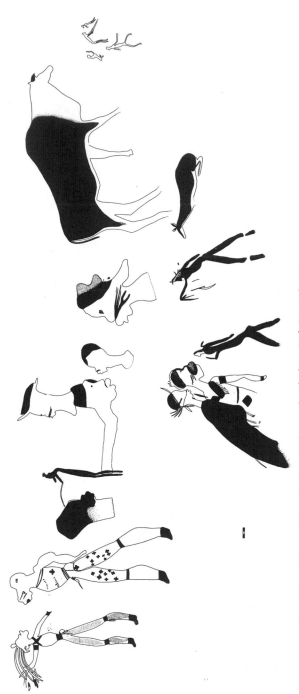

Figure 10.4. Painted panel, Eastern Cape Province. Colors: red and white. Scale in centimeters.

represent bees crawling on and possibly stinging a shaman's body. Nearby is a markedly attenuated figure that, in a typical trance dancing posture, bends forward and holds a stick. Attenuation is a somatic hallucination that is frequently depicted in San rock art (Lewis-Williams and Dowson 1989a, 76–77). This figure and the figure with the crosses are associated with other images that include five highly unusual depictions of human heads. Four of these heads have white faces with red lines at the nose; the lines on the head farthest to the right are the most numerous and most clearly suggest the nasal hemorrhage of San trance experience. The trance dance itself is explicitly suggested by the four white figures at the extreme right, one of which holds two dancing sticks and bends forward in the frequently painted and ethnographically reported dancing posture. Two antelope are also depicted. The recumbent one is probably a rhebuck; the standing or walking one is an eland, the creature most closely associated with supernatural potency (Lewis-Williams 1981a). There is a great deal more of interest in this remarkable panel. Here I note only the numerous indicators of San shamanism and hence altered states of consciousness. The somatic component of those states is represented by the attenuated figure and by the crosses on the large standing figure.

These paintings of human figures with crosses on their legs and bodies strongly suggest that a culturally situated understanding of universally, neurologically structured somatic and visual hallucinations was expressed in San rock art. But the differences between these paintings and between both of them and the dance shown in figure 10.2 are highly significant for an understanding of the ways in which somatic hallucinations can become a resource that shamans can manipulate. In figure 10.2, the bees are associated with a large number of dancing figures, not with an individual or small group of individuals. Moreover, no one figure stands out in any striking way. The power of the bees seems to be open to all the dancers. This group is probably what Dowson (1994) calls a "communal group." By contrast, the running figures in figure 10.3 suggest that a small group of shamans chose to identify itself with a particular kind of shamanic hallucination. I know of no similar paintings in this area, and the unusualness of this kind of painting suggests that some shamans sought a novel group identity. Dowson (1994) calls such cooperative groups "shamanic consortia." In yet greater contrast, the panel shown in figure 10.4 carries the notion of individuality further, first by the depiction of individual heads and, second, by the placement of bees on the legs and body of a single, large figure. The singularity and prominence of this figure suggest that an individual shaman appropriated one component of somatic experience in order to establish his special status (cf. Dowson 1988, 1994).

I now turn to another way in which San shamans understood sharp, pricking somatic sensations of altered states and in which San artists exploited those understandings. A !Kung shaman, a man, said, "In !kia, around your neck and your belly you feel tiny needles and thorns which prick you. Then your front spine and your back spine are prickled by these thorns" (Katz 1982, 46).

!Kung women who enter trance describe a similar experience: They say that their "middle feels as if it is full of thorns" (Katz 1982, 165). The pricking of needles and thorns is, I argue, two San construals of the somatic sensation experienced universally in certain altered states of consciousness.

As the Jivaro beliefs about supernatural darts show, a hallucination cognate with pricking thorns readily suggests itself in the setting of hunting and gathering societies that hunt with bows and arrows, darts, and spears. San shamans describe the shooting of what they call arrows-of-potency that are small and invisible to ordinary people. Some of these mystical arrows-of-potency are sent by god or the spirits of the dead; they cause sickness and death (Bleek 1935, 5, 7). If people allow the central fire at a trance dance to die down, they say, "God's arrows will strike us and make our skin painful" (Katz 1982, 120). It is the shamans' task to remove these arrows during a medicine dance and to hurl them back at the spirits and nameless malevolent shamans who lurk beyond the firelight.

Other, benign, arrows-of-potency are shot by an experienced shaman into a novice's //gebesi ("stomach"; Katz 1982, 168). A !Kung shaman said, "You fire them in and fire them in until these arrows of n/um, which are a lot like long thorns, are sticking out of your //gebesi." The informant went on to give a vivid and highly significant description of how this appears: "Your abdomen is like a pin cushion, with arrows sticking out in all directions" (Katz 1982, 214). Even if the peculiarly Western pincushion metaphor was contributed by Katz, the statement gives a vivid impression of a St. Sebastian–like figure and recalls the other ethnographic reports that I have cited.

This visual construal of a physical sensation is probably represented in some San rock paintings. One such painting (figure 10.5) shows an isolated recumbent person wearing the sort of eared cap that was associated with shamans who were said to have power over game (cf. figure 10.2; Bleek 1935, 45, 1936, 144). The figure is impaled and surrounded by many short lines that are clearly not "realistic." The painting certainly recalls the remark about feeling like a pincushion. The short lines may represent arrows-of-sickness or, perhaps, mystical "thorns," but, because the figure lacks a painted context, it is difficult to say whether the "arrows," if so they be, are carrying sickness or beneficial potency. (For further examples of "impaled" figures in southern African rock art, see Garlake 1987a, fig. 67, 1987b, fig. 6, 1995, fig. 185; Bond 1948.)

Figure 10.5.   Supine impaled figure, eastern Free State. Scale in centimeters.

Although it is tempting to interpret such paintings as historical narrative (per-haps a murder), the large number of arrows piercing the figure, the eared cap, and the nature of southern African rock art in general suggest they have to do with spiritual experiences. I argue that those experiences were associated with the tin-gling and pricking sensations that were experienced in certain altered states of consciousness and that the San themselves describe.

In sum, I argue that San paintings of figures with bees on their bodies and those apparently pierced by arrows negotiated desired status by, first, their novelty and, second, their factuality. Their novelty was a challenge to the ordinary run of images; although they drew on widespread San beliefs about bees, arrows, and supernatural potency, they constituted a contestation of the San iconographic canon. At the same time, the factuality of the images (Lewis-Williams and Dowson 1990; Lewis-Williams 1995a) consisted in a reification, not just a "picture" or "representation," of an unusual ineffable experience, cultivated, very probably, for social and political ends. As powerful things-in-themselves (Lewis-Williams 1990a), these and many other southern African rock art images were more than mere statements about personal experiences. As palpable reifications of those experiences they aspired to incontrovertibility. One cannot argue with such a reified spiritual experience without challenging the whole belief and ritual system and thereby undermining one's own status. We can therefore speak of the experiences of altered states of consciousness and certain items of material culture—here rock art images—as a resource. The images had the potential to be instruments of human agency, not merely reflecting beliefs and society in a vague and general way but being used by individuals and interest groups to act upon social and political structures. Ethnographic and historical studies have shown that shamans do indeed play an active role in social and political change (e.g., Guenther 1975; Hitchcock 1982; Aldenderfer 1993; Thomas and Humphreys 1996). Here I have identified one of the ways in which they can achieve their ends.

The "Wounded Men" of Upper Paleolithic Art

The empirical neuropsychological, ethnographic, and painted evidence that I have so far adduced lays a firm foundation for a consideration of the Upper Paleolithic "wounded man" figures (figure 10.6).

Anthropomorphic images are far less numerous in west European Upper Paleolithic parietal art than they are in San art. Leroi-Gourhan (1982, 50) estimated that there are about only seventy-five anthropomorphic figures in all Upper Paleolithic parietal art, a number that would constitute a very small percentage indeed of the (unknown) total number of images. Recent discoveries have not materially affected that percentage. By contrast, quantitative surveys of rock paintings in defined geographical areas in southern Africa suggest that human figures constitute 50 percent to 75 percent of all representational images in those areas (Maggs 1967; Vinnicombe 1976; Pager 1971; Lewis-Williams 1972b, 1974b). This striking difference may seem to count against any argument based on the universality of the human nervous system; I therefore point out that the apparent contradiction derives from a misleading generalization.

While it is true that there are many depictions of human beings in southern African rock painting sites (located largely, but not exclusively, in the more

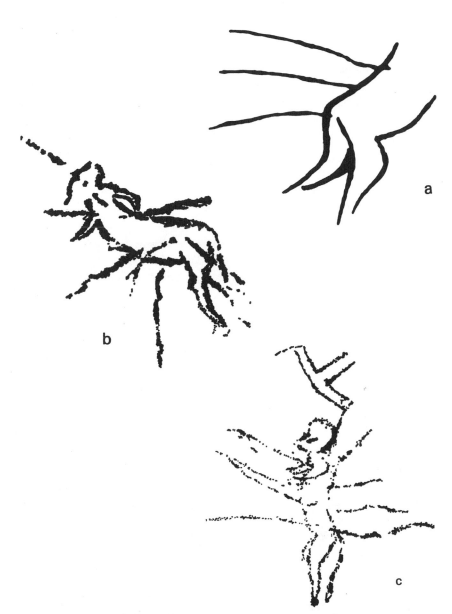

Figure 10.6. "Wounded man" figures: (a) Cougnac, after Méroc and Mazet (1977, pl. 11); (b) Cougnac, after Lorblanchet (1984a, fig. 7); (c) Pech Merle, after Lorblanchet (1984b, fig. 10).

mountainous regions of the subcontinent), most rock engraving sites (located on the plains of the interior plateau) have hardly any. In one section of the Vaal and Gariep River basins Fock and Fock (1989, 143) found that only 5 percent of the representational engraved images were anthropomorphic. Yet it has been persuasively argued that both the engravings and the paintings were associated with shamanic practices (Deacon 1988; Dowson 1992; Lewis-Williams 1988b, Lewis-Williams and Dowson 1989a). A stipulated proportion of human to animal depictions is not, in fact, a crucial component of the hypothesis that an art is largely associated with ritualized altered states of consciousness. The proportion is historically contingent: For whatever reasons, some communities seem to be principally interested in the geometric mental imagery of the early stages of altered states of consciousness, while other groups are more concerned with the iconic imagery of deep trance—the animals, monsters, and spirits of the "other world." Then again, some societies focus on animals as sources of power or as "helpers," while others emphasize anthropomorphic depictions of people or spirits.

The Upper Paleolithic human figures known as "wounded men" occur at Cougnac and Pech Merle, two sites in the Quercy district of France. The images are of human figures with three or more lines radiating from their bodies (figure 10.6). Leroi-Gourhan (1982, 54, chart xxviii) places these "wounded" figures in a larger category that he calls "vanquished man" and in which he includes depictions of men who appear to have been knocked down by a bear or bison. Clottes and Courtin (1996, 155–61) call the category "L'Homme Tué," "the killed man." They too extend the category beyond the Quercy figures and include the recently discovered figure in Le Grotte Cosquer on the Mediterranean coast (1996, fig. 158), a figure in Sous-Grand-Lac (1996, fig. 166; Bahn and Vertut 1988, 152), and three figures in Le Grotte de Gabillou (Clottes and Courtin 1996, figs. 167, 168). All these figures are certainly associated with lines, one in the case of the supine Cosquer figure, more in the other depictions, but the lines do not seem to emanate from the bodies of the figures as clearly as they do in the Quercy examples; nor are the lines in most cases as numerous. I therefore concentrate on the Quercy figures; they constitute a clear, unambiguous group.

The sex of the Quercy figures is difficult to establish unequivocally: With the possible exception of the image shown in figure 10.6c, which may have a penis, primary sexual characteristics are not depicted. Yet, if these images are compared with those Upper Paleolithic parietal images that are clearly female, such as the figures on the ceiling at Pech Merle, the "reclining women" at La Magdeleine (Leroi-Gourhan 1968a, figs. 501, 502) or the profile figure at Les Combarelles (Leroi-Gourhan 1968a, fig. 514), their general form seems to be male rather than female. I therefore retain the current phrase "wounded man" but add that the sex of the figures is, in any event, not crucial to my argument.

Méroc and Mazet (1977, 35–37, 70) describe the three examples at Cougnac. The first, painted in black, is part of a large painted panel. It appears to be running toward the right and has three lines emerging from its lower back and buttocks (figure 10.6a). The torso of the figure appears to lean forward slightly, and this posture gives, at any rate to modern viewers, a sense of movement, perhaps of fleeing. The head and upper parts of the body are not depicted. It is placed near to depictions of large-horned deer (megaceri) and ibexes (Leroi-Gourhan 1968a, fig. 383). It is, in fact, placed on the lower chest of a megaceros, the throat and chest line of which follows a natural contour of the rock face. The second "wounded man" figure is part of another panel. It has seven or eight lines emerging from various parts of its body and has short arms without hands; no feet are depicted (figure 10.6b). It bends toward the left and its head seems to be fitted into the head of a mammoth that, like the megaceros, is partially defined by the natural contours of the rock. The figure is surrounded by double applications of paint perhaps made with two fingers (Leroi-Gourhan 1968a, fig. 384). Below it, there is another but smaller mammoth that is partly superimposed on the larger one; to the right is an ibex. The group of images is painted near the entrance to a low side chamber that contains painted dots. A third figure, described by Méroc and Mazet (1977) as the oldest and as being painted in a dark redish color, is said to have three lines, two in the breast and one in the back. This figure is, however, very difficult to make out: Certainly, I cannot decipher it.

A further example is at Pech Merle, some 30 km away (figure 10.6c). Painted on a sloping ceiling, it is more erect than the others, and, like one of the Cougnac figures, it has vestigial arms. It has nine lines protruding from it, but one of these may represent a penis. A significant feature of this figure is that one of the so-called brace signs is painted just above it so that the righthand "arm" of the brace touches the back of its head. Given the ample space available, a connection between the figure and the sign seems to be intended. At Cougnac there is a panel of such signs. There may be eight or more of them, but some are now very fragmentary (Lorblanchet 1984a, fig. 8). This Cougnac panel is some 35 m from the "wounded men." Nevertheless, the brace signs, like the "wounded men," clearly suggest some sort of link between the two sites, and the way that the sign at Pech Merle touches the back of the "wounded man's" head in turn suggests a link between these human figures and brace signs.

The bending-forward posture of one of the Cougnac figures and the slightly less bent position of another require comment. Leroi-Gourhan (1982) notes that "an important number" of all human figures have the body bent forward "to around 30–45°" (53). This sort of posture may be occasioned by one of the physiological effects of some altered states of consciousness. When a San informant was describing the pricking of "needles and thorns," he went on to say, "Your //gebesi tightens into a balled fist" (Katz 1982, 46). This painful experience causes San trance dancers to bend forward until their bodies are almost at right angles to their legs (Marshall 1969, 363-64). Southern African rock paintings often depict trancers in this position (e.g., figure 10.2; see also Lewis-Williams 1981a, figs. 19, 20, 23, 28, 32; Lewis-Williams and Dowson 1989a, figs. 15, 16c, 17, 20, 28, 32a). Similarly, in the "wounded man" figures, as well as in other Upper Paleolithic human figures (e.g., the female figures from Lalinde [Marshack 1972, figs. 181, 182] and the Les Trois Frères "sorcerer" [Leroi-Gourhan 1968a, fig. 57]), this posture may represent a physical response to the prickings and contractions induced by some altered states of consciousness. This interpretation does not, of course, derive from a simple ethnographic parallel with the San (Lewis-Williams 1991b). Rather, it is based on what is a common physiological response that is governed, at least in part, by the human nervous system.

Indeed, as is often remarked, there is no directly relevant ethnography to guide the interpretation of Upper Paleolithic art, as there is for San rock art. Writing of all four examples, Méroc and Mazet (1977) categorize the depictions with paintings of "wounded animals" and argue for "*la magie de la destruction*" (36). One context for this kind of magic and image may, they go on to argue, have been conflict over territory, the images having been made and ritually "pierced" prior to a real fight between competing communities. Méroc and Mazet, however, doubt this explanation, arguing that, if it were correct, the makers of the images would have depicted the heads of the figures as faithfully as possible. Pointing to the nonhuman or animal-like faces of three of the figures and the absence of the fourth's head, they suggest that the putative magic was more probably related to the exorcism of malicious demons rather than to the defeat of adversaries. Similarly, Clottes and Courtin (1996, 160–61) argue that the imprecision and incomplete nature of the figures was deliberate and may have constituted a safeguard of some sort. In a comparable explanation, Graziosi (1960) argues for "magic death practices" (182). Méroc and Mazet, Graziosi, and, to a lesser extent, Clottes and Courtin, thus argue that the images were made by individuals to secure economic or personal survival.

On the other hand, Breuil (1979), in a literal "reading," suggested that figure 10.6c depicts a masked man pierced by "many arrows, unless he is carrying them" (272). Similarly, Leroi-Gourhan (1982, 54) sees the Quercy figures, together with the other images in his "vanquished man" group, as the most "pictographic" (narrative) in Upper Paleolithic art, but he allows that the different aggression themes supposedly expressed by the images in this category—killed by animals or by humanmade artifacts—could have had different "mythographic" (symbolic) messages. He cites Laming-Emperaire's observation that male human beings most often occur in what appear to be scenes of a tragic character (Leroi-Gourhan 1968a, 130). This is, of course, a Western "reading" of the images. In his descriptions of all the "impaled" figures in his "vanquished man" category, Leroi-Gourhan takes as unproblematic the interpretation that they are, literally, pierced by spears. Clottes and Courtin (1996, 160–61), too, argue that the most plausible explanation is that the lines represent spears of some sort. They conclude that the supine figure in La Grotte Cosquer that is traversed by a single horizontal line indisputably depicts a slain man (1996, fig. 158). For Clottes and Courtin, this conclusion lends support to the view that the Quercy figures also represent people struck by projectiles of some sort.

Smith (1992) has formulated an alternative explanation. He argues that the multiple lines represent "life forces" that link shamans to animals. "Life forces," a generalization that Smith draws from his survey of shamanism worldwide, is an explanation that has some merit, but, by itself, it seems too vague a concept to provide a firm basis for an explanation of the "wounded man" figures. The empirically established experiences generated by the human nervous system in altered states that I have described hold out the hope of more precision and may provide, though in a different way, support for Smith's suggestion that the lines do not represent spears.

An ethnographic example illustrates this point. When San trancers experience a tingling sensation in the top of the head, they ascribe it to the soul, or spirit, leaving on extracorporeal travel (they explain trance by spirit loss, not by spirit possession). Some San shaman-artists depicted this experience by drawing long lines emanating from the head of trancing figures (Vinnicombe 1976, figs. 109, 152, 247; Lewis-Williams 1981a, figs. 31, 38; Lewis-Williams and Dowson 1989a, figs. 22, 32a, 32b, 33b, 65b). Similarly, Upper Paleolithic shamans may have construed the pricking sensations felt in various parts of the body not as being caused by sharp lances but by some sort of potency or spirit entering or leaving the body; they may then have depicted such a concept by the lines emanating from the Cougnac and Pech Merle figures. But, as Clottes and Courtin (1996, 160) point out in their argument against Smith's explanation, the "wounded man" figures irresistibly call to (our Western) mind a person struck by projectiles, especially in the case of the apparently fleeing figure in Cougnac (figure 10.6).

There is at any rate one point on which writers agree: The "wounded man" figures are not easily interpreted. Clottes and Courtin (1996, 161) believe that, without some extraordinary discovery, it will be impossible to achieve certainty, and Leroi-Gourhan (1982) concludes that the figures pose "serious problems that we are not yet capable of resolving except through hypotheses which have little foundation" (54). I leave aside inappropriate notions of proof or certainty; as with most archaeological explanations we shall have to relinquish a desire for absolute proof (whatever that may consist in) and content ourselves with degrees of confidence as constituted by evidence, logic, internal consistency, analogies with strong relations of relevance, and so forth. I argue that a hypothesis derived from the ideas and data that I have developed in previous sections of this chapter moves from a well-attested foundation toward a persuasive resolution of at least some of the problems posed by the "wounded man" figures.

First, the "pictographic," or "realistic," nature of the images must be questioned. The partial representation of the human body in all the examples, the possibly zoomorphic aspect of the head of two of the examples, and, especially, the larger number of "lances" in the figures are features that suggest that the Quercy paintings are not literal depictions of real, violent events. At the same time, it should be noted that concepts of "realism" and "nonrealism" are culturally situated and not universal. They may be handy labels if loosely applied, but they probably obscure other and more complex notions of what may constitute reality. A rigid distinction along the lines of Western concepts of what is real and what is not seems unlikely to have obtained in the Upper Paleolithic.

Second, as the clinical and ethnographic examples that I have given show, Upper Paleolithic people's understanding of somatic sensations and hallucinations would have been as much controlled by their set and setting as are Westerners' or the San's. Yet, the fact that Upper Paleolithic people were hunter-gatherers suggests that there may have been similarities between the ways in which shamans of that time and San, Gitksan, Jivaro, and Miwok shamans interpret their somatic sensations and hallucinations.

Indeed, the two informing factors that I have emphasized—the universality of the human nervous system and the shamanic hunter-gatherer setting—suggest that the artists who painted the Cougnac and Pech Merle figures may have experienced the pricking sensations of trance and have hallucinated them as multiple stabbings with sharp pointed lances. So while the radiating lines may represent spears, they are not "literal" spears, and the images do not depict violent incidents. Rather, they represent spiritual experiences. The possible ritual setting of those experiences is the next question to be addressed.

As I have shown, beliefs in missiles of some sort that carry potency and pierce a shaman are a widespread concomitant of one of the physical experiences of some trance states. Moreover, a context in which piercing is commonly reported is shamanic initiation. Shamans must suffer before they can heal, die before they can bring life to their people. The ethnographic examples of initiatory piercing that I cited and indeed the title of Halifax's survey of shamanism worldwide, *Shaman: The Wounded Healer* (1982), inevitably recall the Upper Paleolithic images of what seem to be people pierced by spears. The "wounded man" figures may, I argue, represent a form of shamanic suffering and initiation that was closely associated with somatic hallucinations.

This interpretation can be extended by a consideration of the locations sometimes chosen for shamanic initiations. In central Australia, an aspirant Aranda "medicine man" goes to the mouth of a cave where he "falls asleep"; spirits then throw invisible lances at him, piercing his neck and cutting off his head (Eliade 1972; 46). Similarly, a Smith Sound Inuit initiate must go to a cliff containing caves: "If he is predestined to become a shaman, he will enter a cave. . . . As soon as he has entered the cave, it closes behind him and does not open again until some time later" (Eliade 1972, 51). A particularly vivid North American account of subterranean shamanic initiation combines visual and auditory hallucinations. A fifty-year-old Paviotso man wishing to become a shaman entered a cave and prayed. He tried to sleep but was prevented by strange noises—the grunts and howls of bears, mountain lions, and deer. When he finally did fall asleep, he saw a healing ceremony. Then the rock split open and a "man appeared in the crack. He was tall and thin. He had the tail feather of an eagle in his hand." He taught the initiate how to cure (Eliade 1972, 101). The wall of the cave was but a thin membrane between the initiate and the spirits, both animal and human, of the underworld (cf. Lewis-Williams 1995a; Clottes and Lewis-Williams 1996). In citing these and numerous other ethnographic instances of shamanic initiation, Eliade (1972, 50–53) emphasizes the importance of caves and the fact that the "death" of an initiate often involves a descent to the lowest realm of the shamanic cosmos.

These and other instances of piercing and entry into caves add a further dimension to the explanation that I propose: The "wounded men" of Upper Paleolithic Quercy art may, together with other images, have been associated with chthonic shamanic initiation (cf. Pfeiffer 1982; Hayden 1990). The neuropsychological and ethnographic evidence that I have adduced strongly suggests that, in these subterranean images, we have an ancient and unusually explicit expression of a complex shamanic experience that is informed by altered states of consciousness: That experience comprised isolation and sensory deprivation by entrance into an underground realm, "death" by a painful ordeal of hallucinatory multiple piercing, and emergence from those dark regions of an inspired, reborn shaman. Ritualized altered states of consciousness and these images were thus intimately associated with the construction of social *personae*. We are now in a position to consider the role of human agency in the making of the "wounded man" Upper Paleolithic images.

Art and Agency

First, we must note that the group of figures that I have defined was made in a restricted geographical area and, probably, within a comparatively restricted period (Clottes and Courtin 1996, 159). Their existence therefore points to an historically situated event or complex of events.

Something of the nature of those events is suggested by the placing of the novel "wounded man" images in the "traditional" shamanic Upper Paleolithic contexts of subterranean chambers and painted panels comprising depictions of animals and "signs." These two contexts, topographic and iconographic, suggest that the "wounded man" images were associated with a social and cognitive movement situated within and accepting (at least in part) of existing cosmology. As I have argued, all novelty is a form of contestation. But, like the making of the southern African paintings that I described, the making of the "wounded man" figures was probably not, despite their originality, an attempt to challenge the entire cosmology. Rather, it was probably an attempt to manipulate the resources of existing cosmological, social, religious, and iconographic frameworks so that the novel images and what they represented would be acceptable to at least some people. Cosmological, social, religious, and iconographic frameworks are not immutable givens. They are reproduced through complex processes and forms of representations and are therefore always open to negotiation.

It is not clear if the contestation implied by the "wounded man" figures came from emergent individuals or from interest groups in some ways similar to Dowson's (1994) "shamanic consortia." The notion of an individual is complex and always historically and culturally situated (for a range of ideas on this point, see Carrithers, Collins, and Lukes 1985). Without exploring the philosophical implications of the notion of personhood, we can draw a distinction between large, complex paintings that must have been communally produced (such as the well-known ones in the Rotunda and elsewhere in Lascaux) and those simpler images that were probably made by individuals (such as the images in the Cabinet de Félines, Lascaux; Leroi-Gourhan and Allain 1979, figs. 314–50). Communally produced art in large chambers was probably associated with group rituals, while smaller and more remote images may have been made by individual initiates or vision questers (cf. Bender 1989; Hayden 1987; Lewis-Williams and Dowson 1993). The making of personal images was probably associated with rituals that were different from those that attended the making of communal images (Lewis-

Williams 1994, 1995a). Although all Upper Paleolithic individuals probably had to have some following in order to get to the point of making images in the subterranean chambers, it seems likely that self-differentiating individuals played a key role in the making of the novel "wounded man" images. Indeed, entry into the caves, as well as the preparation of paint and the making of images, was probably part of a series of interrelated, socially differentiating ritualized contexts (Lewis-Williams 1995a, 2002; see also chapter 11).

Individuality that was opposed to a dominant social and religious order is suggested by the fact that the images are not of "otherness"—animals, animals as sources of power, visionary animal-helpers, and so forth. On the contrary, I argue that the "wounded man" images are probably highly manipulated representations of the subjects themselves. In these self-images, the subject is foregrounded. The distinctive "wounded man" images were therefore probably an answer or challenge to the general paucity of human figures in Upper Paleolithic parietal art. What that paucity meant is a difficult question. The hegemony of animals in the (representational) symbolling systems of the time may have tended to place the source of supernatural and, in all probability, political power outside of the human sphere. In these depictions of (albeit transformed) human beings, we may have evidence for a particular, historically situated challenge to the locus and control of supernatural and political power: Some people were wishing to become a visible part of the interrelated symbolling and power systems but in a new way, and this desire meant that new representations had to be fashioned out of the existing and potentially divisive religious experiences.

Conclusion

In mounting challenges to the status quo individuals adopt roles that are different from their familial and economic roles. In seeking initiation as a shaman, an intimate hopes to don a new persona that has specific social advantages. Drawing on the dramaturgical origins of *persona*, Hollis (1985, 222) discusses the difficulty of separating out the "fusion of man and mask": Self and role become intertwined. I argue that this fusion is particularly closely achieved when the act of adopting a new persona involves altered states of consciousness, because those states are situated within an individual's conception of him- or herself: Role becomes reality in the same way that simile can become metaphor, and metaphor can become "reality."

Fusion and transformation are unusually clear in the "wounded man" figures. In one powerful image they represent person and role, a new kind of shamanic role made possible by a conscious, deliberate decision to highlight a distinctive and, at that time, unrepresented component of altered states—piercing somatic hallucinations. The individuals who made the images were, I argue, manipulating a resource (altered states of consciousness) to advance their own religious, social, and political positions. They were presenting their religious experiences as related to, yet different from, the experiences of others; probably, they were emphasizing their personal suffering as a superior road to advancement. The contestation of the Upper Paleolithic iconographic canon that the images constituted is therefore an example of how material culture can, in the hands of human agents, play an active, formative role.

Note

J. D. Lewis-Williams, "Agency, Art, and Altered Consciousness: A Motif in French (Quercy) Upper Palaeolithic Parietal Art," *Antiquity* 71 (1997): 810–830.

The Social Production and Consumption of Rock Art   11

> *There is a history in all men's lives,*
> *Figuring the nature of the time deceas'd,*
> *The which observed, a man may prophesy,*
> *With a near aim, of the main chance of things*
> *As yet not come to life, which in their seeds*
> *And weak beginnings lie intreasured.*
> *Such things become the hatch and brood of time.*

> —*II HENRY IV* 3:1:80–86

IN THIS CONCLUDING CHAPTER, I return to our geographical starting point: southern African San rock art. Having developed ideas about the social production and consumption of rock art in the Upper Paleolithic of western Europe, and having, through close analysis of San ethnography, found out much about the place of San rock art in its makers' cosmology and daily life, I ask if it is possible to propose some exploratory model for the manufacture and use of both arts.

The differences between southern African San rock art and the temporally and spatially remote west European Upper Paleolithic art are, after all, to be expected; it is the ways in which the arts resemble one another that is striking and that require explanation. I have suggested that part of that explanation lies in the functioning of the human nervous system in a spectrum of states of consciousness that range from alert, rational consciousness, through introversion and daydreaming, to sleep dreaming, and on to deeply altered states characterized by hallucinations in all the senses. But that cannot be the whole explanation. In the societies with which we are dealing, foraging—hunting animals and gathering plant foods—provided the material necessities of life, as well as being interwoven with cognitive and social matters. How, we need to ask, did the making of imagery on rock shelter and deep cave walls constitute and subvert human social relations? I adumbrated part of that social process in the previous chapter.

Now, to conclude our journey, I draw southern African and west European rock art together in a tentative model of the social production and consumption of rock art images. The unravelling of iconography is, I argue, a necessary first step in the study of a rock art. Now we need to build on that foundation as we explore social issues.

Modelling the Production and Consumption of Rock Art

The production and consumption of rock art was embedded, as indeed all arts are, in the social, economic, and intellectual circumstances of the community in which the images were made.[1] Like other genres of material culture, rock art did not merely reflect the society in which it was made, its economy, power structures, myths, and so forth. It also constituted, reproduced, and sometimes subverted social relations and beliefs. In that sense, the making of each rock art image by an individual or interest group was a sociopolitical intervention. This understanding enables rock art researchers to address the issue of human agency, that is, the manipulation of, among other things, material culture by people who, in many cases, have a clear conception of what they wish to achieve and the means by which it can be achieved. In communities that made rock art, the intervention of human agents was based, often, on the possession of arcane knowledge and attempted to shift the locus, nature, or object of divine sanction. Exactly what those social relations, bodies of knowledge, and sanctions were and exactly how any given rock art image reproduced or subverted them are specific historical issues. (On material culture and agency, see, for example, Hodder 1982b, c; Shanks and Tilley 1987a, see also Giddens 1984 and Bourdieu 1977; on agency and southern African rock art, see Dowson 1994, 2000.)

Historical questions that deal with the link between received theory about material culture and actual instances are, however, seldom easily handled. Merely to assert that material culture constitutes social relations is one thing; to explain how and why specified items of material culture, when manipulated by individuals or interest groups, have the power to accomplish such ends is another altogether (Johnson 1989). Rock art images are no exception. To understand their reproductive and transformative power, it is necessary to situate them in the social and ritual milieu of their time and, at the same time, to form some idea of their original ontological status. Researchers need to elucidate to what extent and in what ways rock art motifs, as well as the contexts in which they were made and used, were open to manipulation by social agents (cf. Conkey 1993).

To this end I construct a model that isolates and defines a progressive series of manipulable contexts and thereby focuses attention on key stages in a complex process; the model enables the exact points at which rock art imagery was implicated in social processes to be determined. Although the model has the potential, in a slightly varied form, to deal with both rock paintings and rock engravings, I concentrate on paintings alone. The four stages of the model are (1) the acquisition of imagery, or motifs; (2) the making of paint; (3) the painting of images; (4) the subsequent use of images.

These stages are interrelated: What happened in one stage had the potential to affect what happened in subsequent stages. Yet each stage was, in itself, an arena for the negotiation of social relations. Because the production and consumption of images was, at any rate in certain circumstances, implicated in rituals that involved dancing, singing, and other activities, there were diverse opportunities for negotiation beyond the images themselves. Indeed, it seems probable that, in each of the stages, different individuals and interest groups within and outside the community that made the art would have had at their disposal different kinds of opportunities. Further, it needs to be noted that the consumption of rock art images may have implicated relationships in ways not planned by the makers of the images. Contemporary or subsequent debate on the significance of images may sometimes have gone against the manifest intention of the artist or artists. But that is, of course, the essence of negotiation: Success is not guaranteed.

To illustrate the utility of the model I apply it to the production and consumption of rock art in a comparatively well understood ethnographic instance, the San. I begin with a brief overview of San shamanism to provide a context for my stage-by-stage demonstration of the utility of the model. This illustrative use of San rock art should not be mistaken for a thorough study of all the possibilities that the model opens up in southern African time and space. Rather, I show in a brief and preliminary way that rituals associated with the acquisition of imagery, as well as the making and use of the paintings, were deeply embedded in social relations and that both these rituals and the painted images themselves had the potential to constitute and, in some instances, to mold those relations (see, more generally, Conkey 1993; Dobres and Hoffman 1994). Finally, I use the model in a consideration of some broad implications for the study of an art for which there is no direct ethnographic record, the parietal art of western Europe. I argue that the same four stages were implicated in the negotiation of Upper Paleolithic social relations.

The San Shamanic Context

Broadly speaking, San rock art comprises a range of motifs most of which are referable to one or another aspect of San shamanism, though not exclusively to explicitly shamanic values. These depictions include trance dances; shamans identifiable by a number of features, postures, and gestures; polysemic animals, such as the eland, that were, among their associations, considered sources of supernatural potency but were not necessarily visionary; "scenes" that appear to record historical events, but that sometimes incorporate shamanic elements; various activities that shamans conducted in the spirit world, such as out-of-body travel and the capture of a rain-animal; shamans partially transformed into animals (therianthropes); other experiences, including shamanic hallucinations; and "abstract," geometric motifs that probably depict the geometric entoptic mental images experienced in an early stage of trance (for reviews of these various classes of painted imagery, see, for example, Lewis-Williams 1981a, 1990a; Yates, Golson, and Hall 1985; Campbell 1986; Lewis-Williams and Dowson 1989a; Yates and Manhire 1991; Dowson 1992). It would therefore be wrong to assume that each and every San rock art image derived from a specific ecstatic vision. Similarly, it would be wrong to assume that every South African rock art image was made by a shaman.

The Four-Stage Model and San Art

The diverse subject matter of San rock art throughout southern Africa suggests that it was concerned not with a single, monolithic "meaning" but rather with closely interrelated sets of meanings, a broad diversity situated within an essential unity (Lewis-Williams 1981a). This tension between diversity and unity is one of the factors that create for the art the possibility of a sociopolitical role (Dowson 1994). Further, the association of the art with altered states of consciousness is another fundamental and powerful feature that facilitates sociopolitical exploitation. As Bourguignon (1974) has pointed out, visions acquired in altered states of consciousness are "raw materials for potential cultural utilization" (234). Indeed, rituals involving altered states of consciousness were implicated, directly or obliquely, in all four stages of the production and consumption of San rock art.[2] I now consider the stages in turn to show in what ways each was open to manipulation by individuals and interest groups.

Stage 1: The Acquisition of Imagery

There were at least four contexts in which San shamans acquired insights into the spiritual world: the trance, or curing, dance; special curing rituals that did not entail a large-scale dance; viewing rock art; and dreams. Each of these was associated with two related oppositions that had the potential for sociopolitical exploitation: first, society and the individual; second, socially informed and sanctioned visions and the novel, unexpected visions that altered states of consciousness inevitably produce.

The trance dance was the principal San shamanic ritual; it brought together all people no matter what their age or gender. One of the earliest accounts we have of such a dance was recorded by Arbousset and Daumas in the 1830s. It is, of course, an "outsider's" view and is shot through with these missionaries' manifest distaste for indigenous beliefs and rituals. The dance, they said, was performed by moonlight and consisted of "irregular jumps. . . . They gambol together till all be fatigued and covered with perspiration" (Arbousset and Daumas 1846, 246–47). The dance was so "violent" that some dancers fell to the ground "exhausted and covered with blood which pours from the nostrils." These "exhausted" dancers were cared for by some of the women. About forty years later, Orpen (1874, 10) recorded a similar dance which, he said, was circular. He too noted that dancers fell down "as if mad and sick" and that blood ran from the noses of some.

The wider importance of blood in San ritual and art will become apparent as I proceed. Here I note only that Bleek and Lloyd found that /Xam shamans suffered nasal hemorrhages and that they rubbed their blood on those whom they wished to heal; they believed that its smell would keep evil spirits at bay. Twentieth-century researchers in the Kalahari did not encounter much nasal bleeding among shamans, but they were told that a shaman may bleed in especially challenging or dangerous circumstances (Marshall 1960, 374; Lewis-Williams 1981a, 81). The depiction of nasal hemorrhage is one of the distinguishing features of paintings of trancing shamans. Neither Arbousset and Daumas, nor Orpen, nor Bleek and Lloyd seem to have had any real understanding of altered states of consciousness, but today it is clear that, in their use of "exhausted" and "as if mad and sick," these early writers were in fact describing trance dances similar to those still performed in parts of the Kalahari Desert (e.g., Lee 1968; Katz 1982; Lewis-Williams 1992).

During the course of a present-day trance dance in the Kalahari, when a number of shamans are in trance, one may draw the others' attention to what he or she believes he or she can see, perhaps a number of spirit-eland standing in the semidarkness beyond the light of the fire. The others look in the direction indicated, and then they too see the same visions. There is thus a sharing of insights that makes for commonality of visions. Moreover, the describing of visions after everyone has returned to a normal state of consciousness is a further powerful influence on what people "see" in future trance experiences. People tend to hallucinate what they expect to hallucinate.

At the same time, there are forces pulling in the opposite direction. No matter how powerful the informing social influences may be, the human brain in an altered state of consciousness always produces novel, or aberrant, hallucinations. In all societies, most people ignore these sports of the human nervous system because they are seeking specific kinds of visions that they can understand and that will make them feel part of a social group. But some people seize upon hallucinatory novelties and then present them to others as specially privileged insights that set them above others or, more forcefully, that challenge the whole structure of power relations. In some circumstances, the individual visionary thus opposes social constraints. Both these attitudes to the mental imagery of altered states of consciousness are found among the San. In the past, the tension between socialized and idiosyncratic mental imagery presented shaman-artists with an opportunity to negotiate their social positions by manipulating, within socially accepted parameters, certain classes of mental imagery and their associated painted images.

The choreography of the dance is one of the factors that focus attention on shamans and their visions. The form of the dance is, however, open to manipulation, even as the visions themselves are. Southern rock paintings show what appear to be a number of ways in which participants arranged their relative positions. One trend observable in the painted record seems to have been a development in some areas from a dance form that placed a number of shamans on an equal footing to one in which a single prominent shaman was surrounded by smaller figures. As Dowson (1994) argues, these different kinds of paintings are evidence for the manipulation of rock art imagery by groups and by individuals.

In a "special curing," the second context in which shamans achieve insights into spiritual things, one or two shamans may enter trance without the women's supportive clapping and singing. This happens when a person is deemed to be particularly ill. Under these circumstances, a shaman may "see" into the body of a patient and discern the cause of illness. The cause is then removed by the laying on of hands. First, it is drawn into a shaman's body; then it is expelled through a "hole" in the back of the neck, a supernatural event that is visible to shamans only and that appears in some rock paintings. Some shamans become renowned for their curing abilities and may be summoned from afar to cure a sick person. Special curings are thus a particularly fertile context for social differentiation.

The viewing of rock art probably also gave shamans insights that could become part of their own experiences in altered states. There was, therefore, probably a recursivity between some rock art images and visions.

The role of individual San shamans is also evident in the ways that they understand dreams, the fourth and most personal of all contexts in which they obtain visions. The Bleek and Lloyd collection records the ways in which nineteenth-century shamans made rain and went on out-of-body journeys while in a dream (Lewis-Williams 1987a). In a particularly striking and well-documented twentieth-century instance, Beh, a Kalahari !Kung woman, dreamed of galloping giraffes (Biesele 1993). When she awoke, she was able to discern in the rhythm of their pounding hooves the meter of a song. She was not herself a shaman, but when she sang the song to her husband, who was a shaman, he instantly recognized it as a new source of animal potency. In a comparatively short time, the giraffe "medicine song" had spread across the Kalahari and was being sung alongside older songs, such as eland and gemsbok. Beh and her husband became well known, though not politically powerful, people. As I have said, all people experience unusual visions and dreams, but only a few seize upon them and recognize their potential.

This tension between personal revelations and socially sanctioned visions is evident in the rock art (Dowson 1988; Dowson and Holliday 1989). Many rock art motifs are widespread. The eland, for instance, is the most frequently depicted animal in most regions of southern Africa (Maggs 1967; Pager 1971; Smits 1971; Lewis-Williams 1972b, 1974b; Vinnicombe 1972a, b, 1976). Yet, idiosyncratic motifs do occur. For these motifs to have been intelligible to other people they must have fallen within the broad, general framework of San symbolism and experience. An apparently unique painting of crabs, for instance, develops the San metaphor of being underwater, a way of expressing the sensations of trance experience (Dowson 1988). Crabs, as a painted motif, did not become accepted by other artists, so we can probably conclude that the artist who painted these unique images retained, unlike Beh and her husband, the special insight; the prestige of having acquired a unique insight into "underwater" experience was not dissipated among shamans in general. Whether the prestige that accrued from this insight developed into political power is a question that we cannot now answer.

So far, I have considered only imagery that clearly derives from visions. As I have pointed out, much other rock art imagery is concerned with symbols and metaphors of San shamanic belief. Some paintings, such as those of shamanic dances, combine observable reality (such as dancers and dancing rattles) and spiritual reality that was "seen" by shamans only (such as expelled sickness, supernatural potency, and physical transformations). But even some images that appear, at first glance, to be "realistic" are in fact problematic. Apparently "realistic" depictions of eland, for instance, that could easily be taken to represent real, individual animals sometimes have features that suggest that another, nonreal, element is present (e.g., Lewis-Williams 1987a, fig. 5). It seems that too rigid a distinction between purely visionary images and purely realistic images would be a Western imposition and unhelpful. In San rock art, reality is a shifting, elusive notion that differs from the Western idea of reality.

Stage 2: The Manufacture of Paint

The second stage of the model, the making of paint, can also be illustrated by reference to the San. Very little was recorded about the ways in which San artists prepared their paint. Perhaps early writers considered this too prosaic a matter to warrant their attention. There is, however, an important account that strongly suggests that the making of paint was far from prosaic.

In the early 1930s Marion Walsham How was able to converse with a seventy-four-year-old southern Sotho man, Mapote, who, as a young man, had learned to paint with San in their caves. He was a son of the chief Moorosi, and he had half-San stepbrothers, the sons of Moorosi's San wives (How 1962, 33). According to Mapote, the "true" San painted at one end of the cave, while he and his half-San stepbrothers painted at the other end. A distinction between paintings at opposite ends of rock shelters has not been observed, so we do not know how general this separation may have been or, indeed, how many southern Sotho people were taught how to paint. It may have been something that happened very seldom, though, as Mapote implied, the relationship between the San and the southern Sotho was clearly close. Either way, Mapote's statement implies that the San whom he knew maintained a distinction between their own paintings and paintings done by other people: Painting, as they saw it, was an essentially San activity.

When How produced some red pigment that a friend had given her some time before she met Mapote, he declared it to be authentic San pigment known as *qhang qhang*; it "glistened and sparkled" in contrast to commercially available ochre which was dull by comparison. *Qhang qhang* was dug out of the high basalt mountains, and many southern Sotho people regarded it as a "powerful medicine" that would ward off lightning and hail (How 1962, 34). Not only the San themselves but also neighboring people thus believed one of the pigments to have supernatural powers (Lewis-Williams 1981a, 116). This is one of many shared beliefs (cf. Jolly 1995).

The transformation of this highly prized pigment into paint was, according to Mapote, accompanied by ritual procedures. He said that a woman had to heat the *qhang qhang* out of doors at full moon until it was red hot. It was then ground between two stones until it was a fine powder. The production of red pigment was, therefore, at least in certain circumstances, a collective enterprise in which people possessed different kinds of technical expertise. The control of this expertise was probably implicated in the negotiation of social power (cf. Dobres 1988).

The role of a woman in the preparation of pigment recalls the part played by women at a trance dance. Although up to a third of the women in a Kalahari San camp may be shamans, they generally sit in a circle with all the other women around a central fire; some may dance with the men for a while. It is all the women together who supply the vital singing of "medicine" songs and the complex rhythmic clapping that helps the dancing shamans to enter trance and thus perform curings and acquire visions. Within the contexts of both the dance and the preparation of paint men and women cooperated. So constituted, the dance and the preparation of paint were both potential ritual arenas for the negotiation of gender roles: The contribution of women to shamanic rituals was crucial, and individual women could no doubt have manipulated these gender relations and their participatory technical acts to their own advantage (cf. Parkington 1989; Solomon 1992, 1994; Stevenson 1995; Wadley 1997; see also Dobres and Hoffman 1994). In the Kalahari in recent times women's trance rituals have begun to emerge (Katz and Biesele 1986), and similar movements may have taken place in the past as well.

In any event, after some commercial ochre (How deemed her piece of *qhang qhang* too precious to be used) had been ground to a powder, Mapote asked for another highly significant ingredient for his paint: "the blood of a freshly killed eland" (How 1962, 37). *Qhang, qhang,* he said, was the only pigment that the San mixed with eland blood; other pigments were mixed with other media. If the blood were not fresh, it would coagulate and not soak into the rock. As How observes, the need for fresh blood implies that painting took place after a successful eland hunt. Significantly, a large kill is one of the occasions that trigger a communal trance dance. Mapote then set about painting an eland because, as he put it, "the Bushmen of that part of the country were of the eland" (How 1962, 38). Perceptively, Vinnicombe (1976) took the title of her book from Mapote's observation (for more on the phrase "of the eland," see Lewis-Williams 1988a).

The importance of eland blood as an ingredient in the manufacture of red paint was confirmed and enlarged upon in the early 1980s by an old woman of partial San descent, known as "M," who was living just to the south of the Drakensberg (Jolly 1986; Lewis-Williams 1986b; Prins 1990). Her father had been a shaman-artist, and she pointed out paintings that he had made. Her elder sister, who had died a few years before she was interviewed, had been taught her father's shamanic (though not artistic) skills and had been well known locally as a rainmaker. According to M, the whole sequence of events started with a ritualized eland hunt. She explained that a young girl accompanied a group of hunters who went out after an eland. This girl "hypnotized" the eland by pointing an arrow at it; on the arrow was "medicine" that had been prepared by shamans. The participation of a young girl in a hunt again recalls the participation of both men and women in trance dances and suggests a further arena for the negotiation of gender as well as social and political relations. Although M did not specify the age of the young girl, it is worth noting that the /Xam spoke of a girl at puberty as having supernatural power (Lewis-Williams 1981a, 52). The preparation of ochre by a "woman" and participation in the hunt by a "young girl" may suggest differential participation by females.

When the girl had exercised her power, the dazed eland was led back, again by supernatural means (though the movements of exhausted or wounded eland can in fact be fairly easily controlled), to a place near the rock shelter where the people were living and where the paintings were to be made (Jolly 1986). The people then prepared a mixture of eland blood and fat. M explained that eland blood contained supernatural potency (Jolly 1986, 6); she used the Xhosa word *amandla*. Used in scarification rituals, this mixture of blood and fat imbued the recipient with eland potency. She went on to say that eland blood was also used in the preparation of paint, and thus confirmed Mapote's statement. Her words and actions suggested that a painting made with eland blood was a kind of store-house of potency.

Further, it should be noted that a dying eland bleeds from the nose and foams at the mouth, even as a shaman who, in the San's own phrase, is "dying" in trance bleeds from the nose. Qing implied this parallel when he told Orpen (1874, 2) that the therianthropic figures in the art (shamans partially transformed into animals; Lewis-Williams 1981a) had been "spoilt [entered trance] at the same time as the elands and by the dances of which you have seen paintings" (for a fuller explanation and interpretation of Qing's highly complex statement, see Lewis-Williams 1980).

Two kinds of blood were thus involved in the production of rock paintings. First, shamans bled from the nose when they entered trance to obtain visions of the spirit world. At this time, their "dying" in trance and bleeding paralleled the nasal bleeding of a dying eland. Second, the potent blood of an eland was, at least sometimes, used in the making of rock art images. Moreover, the accounts provided by Mapote and M corroborate one another in suggesting that different interest groups, men and women, were involved in various ways in the provision of blood and the manufacture of paint.

The whole process of manufacturing paint was thus open to manipulation. Different interest groups and individuals could be differentially involved in the process, and this variability could be used to contain or challenge the circle of power (cf. Dobres and Hoffman 1994). At the same time, it appears that different kinds of paint were recognized, some with eland blood, some without, and, possibly, other kinds of which we now know nothing. The ritualized obtaining of eland blood and *qhang qhang* and their use to imbue certain paintings with potency was similarly a rich field for the negotiation of social relations and associated manipulation of supernatural sanctions through technical means. Clearly, for the San, rock paintings were far more than mere pictures and the processing of pigments more than just a material technique.

Stage 3: The Making of Rock Paintings

The ways in which San artists applied paint to rock surfaces has been much debated. They achieved remarkably fine lines and delicate detail; the lines are often as fine as those made by a thin lead pencil. How (1962, 33) noted that Mapote made small brushes from feathers and tiny reeds, but it seems that the very finest lines must have been made with something even finer, perhaps a quill or a sharp bone point.

The delicate workmanship and sureness of line that are evident everywhere in southern Africa suggest that it is most unlikely that all shamans painted; it seems more likely that only some acquired this special skill. That being so, the making of rock art images would have been potentially an arena for the negotiation of social status. At some times and in some places, the making of rock paintings may have bestowed a privileged status on those who possessed the necessary skills (cf. Riddington 1988; Ingold 1993).

Nor does it seem likely that shamans painted while in deep trance; if not actually unconscious, they tremble violently. More probably, they painted while in a normal state of consciousness, recalling their vivid glimpses of the spirit world and making powerful images of those visions and of the animals that were their principal sources of potency. Probably, the very act of painting assisted in the recall, re-creation, and reification of otherwise transient glimpses of spiritual things. Like Wordsworth's observation on poetry, San rock art should be seen as powerful emotion recollected in tranquility.

In the Kalahari today, people listen intently as, the day after a dance, shamans recount their spiritual experiences; each account is accepted as a revelation, even if it seems—to ordinary people who have not experienced the kaleidoscopic world of trance—to contradict someone else's account (Biesele 1978). The fluidity of San belief opened up a potential for social differentiation. Under certain historical circumstances, that potential was exploited (Dowson 1994).

Rock paintings depicting therianthropes, greatly elongated human figures, bizarre animals, and so forth were part of that fluidity. They may, in some sense (but, of course, not exactly), have paralleled the modern San shamans' verbal reports of spiritual things. By looking at these paintings, people could obtain a vivid idea of the variety of things that shamans saw in the spirit world. This parallel between paintings and verbal accounts of trance experience should, however, not be taken too far. The potent ingredients qhang qhang and eland blood caused some paintings to be powerful "things-in-themselves" and thus sanctioned certain images and the social relations to which they pointed.

The status of rock art images as something more than mere pictures is further seen in the way in which some of them enter or leave cracks, steps, or other inequalities in the rock face. Sometimes an antelope, a snake, or a rain-animal is painted in such a way that it seems to be emerging from behind the rock surface. This feature of the art is probably related to the San belief that the spirit world is reached by means of an underground journey. For some nineteenth-century shamans this journey started by diving (in their trance experience) into waterholes (Bleek 1935; cf. Biesele 1978). It seems probable that rock shelters were also sometimes seen as potential entrances to the spirit world and that the rock face was a kind of "veil" suspended between this world and that other world (Lewis-Williams and Dowson 1990). Shaman-artists used their technical and esoteric skills to coax the animals and other inhabitants of the spirit world from behind the rock and then, using ritually prepared, potent paint, to fix these visions on the rock for all to see.

Unfortunately, we do not know if this fixing of mediating visions was accompanied by rituals or how a shaman-artist prepared him- or herself for the task. For instance, was the fixing of visions considered as dangerous as spiritual journeys to the other world? Perhaps, like the dance in which visions were acquired, this fixing of visions was also considered an appropriate occasion for the singing of "medicine songs" to strengthen shamans in their work. If the task of "materializing" visions was considered hazardous and in need of communal support in varying degrees, this was another circumstance in which social relations could be reinforced or challenged. Whatever the case, it seems unlikely that San artists were anything like the detached ascetics of the Western Romantic fiction.

Stage 4: The Use of Rock Paintings

Once made, many San images seem to have continued to perform significant functions. The rock shelters were not simply "galleries," as writers on rock art often call them, where people could view "works of art." As I have already argued, many of the paintings were "things-in-themselves," not just pictures of things that existed elsewhere. Some were, moreover, made with special, ritually prepared paint and thus became reservoirs of supernatural potency.

Again, there is, unfortunately, little ethnographic information on precisely what happened to these potent images after they had been made. Given the three stages I have so far described, it seems unlikely that paintings would have simply dropped out of the ambit of San ritual and belief. On the contrary, such evidence as we do have suggests that they continued to play an important function.

For instance, M said that, if a "good" person placed his or her hand on a depiction of an eland, the potency locked up in the painting would flow into the person, thus giving him or her special powers. To demonstrate how this was done, she arranged my fingers so that my entire hand was on a depiction of an eland. As she did so, she cautioned that if a "bad" person did this, his or her hand would adhere to the rock and the person would eventually waste away and die.

The importance of touching, and not merely looking at, rock paintings is supported by evidence from the Western Cape Province where there are patches of paint that have been rubbed smooth (Yates and Manhire 1991). It is not entirely clear what the patches were rubbed with, but the smoothness of the rock, particularly in the center of the patches, is easily discerned. Similarly, the making of the positive handprints that are common in some parts of the Western Cape was probably closely associated with ritual touching of the rock rather than with the making of "pictures" of hands (Lewis-Williams and Dowson 1989a, 108).

There is thus evidence that some of the paintings were not made merely to be looked at. After they had been made, they continued to be involved in rituals in ways that we do not fully understand. It does, however, seem that physical contact with some of the images facilitated the acquisition of supernatural potency. M's remarks suggest that the touching of paintings was not open to everyone and that for some people it could be hazardous, at least under certain circumstances. Significantly, she was implying differential access to the art and concomitant social differentiation.

In addition to physical contact, the images were important visually as well, but, again, not simply as Western notions of art might suggest. This contention was borne out by M. She demonstrated how, long ago, San people had danced in the painted rock shelter to which she took Jolly and me and how they had raised their arms and turned to the paintings when they wished to intensify their potency. As they danced and looked at the paintings, potency flowed from the images and entered into them. This was, I believe, her way of saying that the sight of the paintings deepened the dancers' trance experience.

More than that, the fixed visions already on the rock face probably contributed to the dancers' hallucinations, informing and constraining the stream of mental images that the human nervous system produces in altered states of consciousness. The painted images became part of a complex ritual of dancing, singing, and clapping that controlled the spiritual, or hallucinatory, experiences of shamans and, possibly, other people as well.

As I have suggested, there was probably a recursivity in the ritual sequence of making and using rock paintings: The paintings impacted the formation of mental images, some of which were destined to be "fixed" on the rock face. Yet the recursive loop was not ineluctable. Rather, the recursivity was mediated and manipulated by shaman-artists in specific historical circumstances. The "distance" between new painted images and older ones was crucial in establishing the social position of the makers. Similarities said one thing, differences another.

As time went by, certain rock shelters acquired more and more of these spiritual images, in some shelters paintings were done one on top of another, thus building up multiple layers of images, the oldest ones fading into a blurred red background. In some instances, paintings were carefully overpainted apparently in an effort to renew them visually and spiritually (Vinnicombe 1976, 141, 161, 164, 170, 180, 185, 187, 236, 329, 330; Yates and Manhire 1991). Exactly which paintings were chosen for renewal and which were not probably had social significance, and the most densely painted and "renewed" rock shelters were probably regarded as places of exceptional personal or group power (cf. Deacon 1988; Dowson 1994).

The roles played by these places and the images in them no doubt varied according to the social circumstances of their viewing. For example, when viewed from within a San community, images would have reinforced or challenged social relations between San individuals and various interest groups. When people from outside the San community were present, for whatever reasons, images that would otherwise have been divisive may, for the San, have performed a unifying role in the face of the contestation implied by the outsiders. That is why it is necessary always to situate the production–consumption trajectory as precisely as possible.

So far, I have demonstrated the utility of the four-stage model by applying it to San rock art. The model facilitates identification and discussion of the many and varied opportunities for manipulation that were present in the differential production and consumption of this art. I now move on to apply the model to an art for which there is no direct, historically relevant ethnography.

Upper Paleolithic Parietal Art

The thought that Upper Paleolithic art (approximately 10,000 to 33,000 years B.P.) may, in some measure, in some ways, have been associated with beliefs and rituals that may be called shamanic has long been in the air.[3] My own arguments that the Upper Paleolithic parietal art of Franco-Cantabria was essentially, rather than incidentally, shamanic have been set out elsewhere and need not be repeated here (Lewis-Williams and Dowson 1988, 1992, 1993; Lewis-Williams 1991a, 2002; Clottes and Lewis-Williams 1996, 1998). They derive from neuropsychology and ethnographic observation. The explanatory power of the shamanic explanation may be judged by the numerous features of Upper Paleolithic parietal art that it clarifies, such as the placing of images in the depths of caves, therianthrope figures, the intimate relationship between many images and the surfaces on which they were placed, and the co-occurrence of representational and "geometric" images.

Discussion of Upper Paleolithic shamanism and art must, however, take full cognizance of temporal and geographical diversity. The 20,000-year period must not be homogenized into a replica of any single, ethnographically observed society, San or other (Conkey 1984, 1993). Rather, multiple analogies and interpretations are required to build up a multicomponent mosaic that fits the diverse Upper Paleolithic evidence. That task would require too much detail for a chapter such as this. My purpose is rather to demonstrate the utility of the four-stage model with reference to an art for which there is no directly relevant ethnography. I show that the model focuses attention on the multicomponent potential of Upper Paleolithic parietal art and associated rituals and technologies to be implicated in the negotiation of social relations by individuals and interest groups (Conkey 1993).

Stage 1: The Acquisition of Imagery

During the course of the Upper Paleolithic, the rituals of image acquisition almost certainly varied considerably in, first, the ways in which these rituals were socially situated and, second, the ways in which altered states were induced and experienced.

At some times (especially but not exclusively at the beginning of the Upper Paleolithic) and in some places these rituals of image acquisition were probably communal. They may have taken place in the presence of painted and engraved images in the open air, in open rock shelters, or in large chambers not far from cave entrances. Like the San trance dance, these rituals probably brought together large numbers of people, and shamans (who may or may not have been full-time specialists) obtained their visions in the midst of society, witnessed not only by other shamans but also by ordinary people. Under such circumstances, there was a direct, visible association between the acquisition of visions and the body social. Ordinary people supported the shamans and encouraged them in the face of spiritual hazards. Such power relations as were underwritten by the possession of visions were thus reproduced and entrenched by direct relations between shamans and ordinary people. The ecstasy of shamans was visible evidence for their special powers.

In such communal circumstances, the various participants would have experienced a range of altered states of consciousness. Those who were most intensely seeking visions may have used psychotropic drugs to induce deep trance. Others, caught up in the ritual dancing and music, believed that they could share some but not all of the insights that the leading shamans were experiencing. Still other people, on the fringe of the activity, were probably less intensely swept along by the ritual; they experienced euphoria but did not themselves see visions. On the other hand, some people may have felt themselves to be opposed to the social significance of the whole ritual procedure and may have attempted to reprogram the rituals in order to foreground themselves, as, under specific historical circumstances, some San shamans did (Dowson 1994). Altered states of consciousness and the material production of the art thus constituted a variable resource that could be harnessed in the reproduction or subversion of social relations.

Further, hierarchical social relationships are suggested by the different places in which images may have been acquired. Those images that were placed and may, in some instances, have been acquired deep underground imply social statuses different from those implied by large, communally made images near cave entrances, such as the Hall of the Bulls at Lascaux. Often, more remote images are so placed that they can be viewed by only a few people, sometimes by only one person at a time, such as the Chamber of the Felines at Lascaux (Bender 1989; Lewis-Williams and Dowson 1993). These images imply something like a vision quest, as practiced by, for instance, North American shamanic groups (cf. Whitley 1992, 2000), but not by the San. Especially during the Magdalenian, shamans in search of repeated visions and novices seeking them for the first time seem to have separated themselves from society and, in the remote, dark, silent recesses of the caverns, sought the altered states of consciousness that could provide their visions. In some instances, the often hastily executed rock art images of the remote areas may have been made in a light state of altered consciousness as the questers' mental imagery was projected onto rock surfaces rather like a slide or film show (Lewis-Williams and Dowson 1988); in other cases the questers probably made images after they had reverted to a normal state of consciousness, as did the San. These images should be seen not as "pictures" but as recreated, fixed visions.

Hayden (1987), too, emphasizes the role of altered states of consciousness in ethnographic and Upper Paleolithic rituals. He argues that the Franco-Cantabrian art may have been associated with initiation rituals leading to membership of secret societies. The deep caves, he argues, would have created "emotionally binding experiences during the initiation of adolescents or others into adult status" (Hayden 1993, 130; cf. Pfeiffer 1982). Some art, he goes on to say, could have been "related to status display," while other images were possibly associated with "the acquisition of animal allies in personal visionary experiences" (Hayden 1993, 138).

Stage 2: The Manufacture of Paint

At least some of the paint that vision questers took with them into the depths of the caves, as well as that used to make large, communal images nearer the entrances, was probably considered to have special, supernatural properties, as were some of the San's paints. At present we know that Upper Paleolithic people took great care with the manufacture of paint and that they used different recipes (e.g., Vandiver 1983; Ballet et al. 1979; Leroi-Gourhan and Allain 1979; Clottes, Menu, and Walter 1990; Lorblanchet et al. 1990; cf. Conkey 1993). These recipes should be considered to see if they contain any evidence for rituals.

Whatever such a study may reveal, it seems likely that Upper Paleolithic people would have considered the materials necessary for the fixing of visions to have properties commensurate with the potency of the visions themselves and that the preparation of paint would have become hedged around with prohibitions and rituals that would have defined social relations. Who collected pigments and media, who mixed paint and who applied it to rock surfaces may, in some instances, have been related to different interest groups (Conkey 1993; Dobres and Hoffman 1994, 234). In other instances, all these tasks may have been the work of one person in the pursuit of individual status and power.

Stage 3: The Making of Rock Paintings

Upper Paleolithic paintings were made by a variety of techniques: Paint was sometimes applied as a wash and sometimes blown onto the rock surface; in other instances outlines were drawn with charcoal or a piece of ocher. These different techniques held potentially different "meanings" and manipulation by different social groups (Conkey 1993).

The sheer quantity of paint needed to make large images seems to imply a series of divisionally arranged tasks and, possibly, social differentiating rituals. The large images in the Hall of the Bulls and the Axial Gallery at Lascaux, for instance, demanded considerable quantities of paint and the construction of scaffolds (Leroi-Gourhan and Allain 1979). The making of these images therefore most likely involved the active participation of a large number of people. These large, imposing images in chambers that can hold fair numbers of people may have, as Hayden (1993, 138) argues, been related to the status of the whole group that depicted them. They need not necessarily have derived from individual, personal visions.

The rituals that attended the actual making of these large and complex paintings were, I argue, different from those performed in the depths of the caves, as, for example, in the Chamber of the Felines at Lascaux, where most images were delineated by only a few engraved strokes. What appears to be communally produced art therefore needs to be distinguished from what was more likely individually produced art; both kinds of art imply rituals that define and reproduce social relations, but they do so in different ways.

The distinction between communally and individually produced images and their locations must have been based on a particular kind of cosmology. As in many shamanic societies, including the San, the Upper Paleolithic cosmos was probably conceived of as tiered. Within such a cosmology, part of the spirit world was probably believed to be underground, and journeys into caves were probably believed to be journeys into that realm. Rituals formalizing the acquisition of imagery, the manufacture of paint, and the making of painted images were probably all posited on differential access to a subterranean, animal-filled realm that held the supernatural potency that sustained the universe and, more especially, that shamans sought and harnessed for the good of society and themselves in society (Lewis-Williams 2002).

Although there were almost certainly major differences between the rituals associated with paintings and engravings near or at the entrances to Upper Paleolithic caves and those situated in the depths, numerous images in all parts of the caves display a characteristic that flows from belief in a chthonic, animal-filled realm. Artists exploited natural features of rock surfaces in ways that imply that they believed the animals they were depicting existed behind the rock face; their task was to entice these spirit-animals through the rock so that they could establish a spiritual relationship with them that would empower them to perform their shamanic tasks (La Barre 1972a, 401–2; Lewis-Williams 2002). Importantly, this relationship was probably achieved by touch as well as by painting, as the exploitation of convolutions and small nodules in the rock face suggests.

Access to the chthonic realm was probably protected and reserved for limited numbers of people. It seems that, during the course of the Upper Paleolithic, as the depths of the caverns were increasingly explored, society became more and more complex and hierarchical, with political power being increasingly concentrated in the hands of a few shamans (Bender 1989; Lewis-Williams and Dowson 1993), though I do not argue for a straightforward linear development from simple to complex societies. The Chauvet cave (c. 31,000 B.P.), for instance, may have been associated with an unusually early but ephemeral flowering of social complexity (Chauvet, Deschamps, and Hillaire 1995; Clottes et al. 1995).

Stage 4: The Uses of Upper Paleolithic Parietal Art

A further implication of the production–consumption model concerns the no doubt numerous ways in which painted and engraved images were used. The large, impressive images in such places as the Salon Noir at Niaux (Clottes 1995) probably performed a function similar to many San rock art images. Placed at or within comparatively easy reach of the entrances to Upper Paleolithic caves, these images probably prepared questers on some occasions for the visions that they would see in the depths of the caves. As I have said, people hallucinate what they expect to hallucinate (or what they have been deliberately led to believe they will hallucinate), and we may postulate the performance of preparatory rituals that dramatically revealed communally made entrance art to vision seekers (and to others as well) in an attempt to inform the hallucinations they would experience in remote solitude. Such rituals would have reduced the personal element by controlling, to some extent, the range of hallucinations that the nervous system generates and by alerting questers to only certain kinds of mental imagery. Indeed, social control of altered states of consciousness lies at the heart of shamanism.

Another common component of ritual deserves mention. Sound plays an important role in shamanic rituals, not only among San groups but worldwide (for a brief review, see Dobkin de Rois and Katz 1975). Rhythmic and audio driving induce altered states of consciousness and provide a framework for a visionary's concentration. Musical instruments are also used to imitate sounds made by animals and birds and thereby to create multimedia, multisensory experiences.

There is evidence that music, or at any rate sound, was a component of Upper Paleolithic rituals. A number of "flutes" have been found in west and east European Upper Paleolithic sites. Further, Huyge (1991) argues that the "horn" held by the so-called Venus of Laussel is a scraped idiophone. These and other possible instruments, such as bull roarers and drums, could have been used to suggest the presence of animals as well as to provide a hypnotic rhythm (see also Waller 1993). The role that such sounds would have played in the control of mental imagery is clear enough.

Moreover, Reznikoff and Dauvois (in Scarre 1989) suggest a topographical association between sound and art. They argue that there is a correlation in some Ariège caves between areas of resonance and the presence of rock art. Maximum resonance, they claim, is achieved by the human voice, and this leads them to suggest that chanting may have been part of rituals that were associated with rock art.

Given the Upper Paleolithic understandings of the underworld and the rock face that I have considered, the suggestion that sounds were produced by striking stalactites is particularly interesting (cf. Needham 1967; e.g., Tuzin 1984; Dams 1984, 1985; Clottes and Simonnet 1990; Clottes 1995, 78–81). I argue that the striking of stalactites would, in itself, have been a way of arousing and communicating with the spirit world that would have worked together with painting, singing, and dancing to constitute complex ritual sequences. The stalactites themselves would have been part of the spirit-filled underworld; perhaps the sounds that they emitted were deemed to emanate from that world, even as the pendant stalactites themselves did.

Conclusion

I have developed a four-stage model of the production and consumption of rock art, and illustrated its utility by applying it to the production and consumption of San rock paintings. All four stages were embedded in rituals that, together with the motifs themselves, had the potential to reproduce and create San social relations. Within this framework there was, nevertheless, room for individual San shamans to acquire novel visions and to exploit these visions, the representations that they made of them (and of other, nonvisionary subjects), and the uses to which the images were subsequently put to subvert social relations for their own ends.

The same four interrelated stages probably obtained in Upper Paleolithic western Europe. There, too, each stage was probably set in a ritual context; indeed, it would be hard to imagine that the "fixing" and the subsequent use of the subterranean images was not ritualized. Importantly, the series of rituals associated with the production and consumption of Upper Paleolithic art would have been open to manipulation in the negotiation of social relations.

The production and consumption of both San and Upper Paleolithic parietal art thus constituted a complex, multimedia resource on which people could draw in the establishment of their social positions: Indeed, the principal significance of both arts consisted in their potential for manipulation in sociopolitical interventions. As the San example shows, the constitutive role of rock art images need not be merely assumed in the light of current material culture theory: The mechanisms and processes whereby rock art images achieved social and political ends can be identified.

Notes

1. This chapter includes some material that was published in the Spanish journal *Complutum* (5:277–89 1994) under the title "Rock Art and Ritual: Southern Africa and Beyond." I am grateful to Dr. T. Chapa and Dr. M. Menéndez, editors of *Complutum*, for permission to include that material.

2. A fifth stage, the recycling of San rock art motifs in late twentieth-century South Africa, does not concern us here.

3. See, for example, Reinach 1903; Levy 1963; Lommel 1967a; Eliade 1972; La Barre

1972a, b; Marshack 1972, 280, 1976, 278–79; Eichmeier and Höfer 1974; Furst 1976; Halifax 1980, 3, 17; Pfeiffer 1982; Hedges 1983; Bednarik 1984b, 1986; Bahn and Vertut 1988, 157–58; Goodman 1988; Smith 1992.

J. D. Lewis-Williams, "Modelling the Production and Consumption of Rock Art," *South African Archaeological Bulletin* 50 (1995): 143–154.

Prospect

This book has charted a journey from the San rock art of southern Africa to the Upper Paleolithic images of western Europe (for an up-to-date review of world rock art research see Whitley 2001). With the benefit of hindsight, the end point (or, rather, the present point) with its emphasis on social issues (Lewis-Williams 2002), can perhaps be discerned in its "weak beginnings," when the complexity of San rock art was becoming increasingly apparent. But can we, by "Figuring the nature of time deceas'd . . . prophesy . . . the main chance of things As yet not come to life"? Where will the study of rock art go in the next decade?

I cannot answer those questions. Long-term rock art research projects, those that require many years of data collection, analysis, and explanation, seem doomed to remain unfinished. Goals of explanation that seemed so attractive at one time are often overtaken by theoretical and methodological innovations and begin to appear old hat. By the time new questions are formulated, the gathered data seem no longer relevant. Long-term research planning is the refuge of unthinking, nonproductive empiricism.

The future of the discipline is forged in the heat of practical work, not in contemplation of either past or future. Research is a real-life wrestling in the here and now. True, there are lessons to be learned from the past. So many of the old debates now seem, at least to me, to be based on misunderstandings and semantic gymnastics. If they can be left behind, the future will be more attractive, though I doubt that a convivial Utopia lies ahead. It would be idle to await a Kuhnian revolution in rock art research, though future historians may well identify some point in the past half-century as a revolution. That point may turn out to be the time when the old gaze-and-guess approach to rock art gave way to explicit methodology and theory and so opened up a long, hard slog, but one that at least produced results.

All in all, there is one thing of which I am certain. Advances will be made when, and only when, theory and empirical (not empiricist) work go hand in hand. Any suspicion of a distinction between those who deal in theory and adjudicate others' results and those who do hands-on research needs to be eliminated. We cannot have thinkers and doers. Nor can we have data gatherers and data users. Those distinctions are the source of much misunderstanding. It is in the messy, rather than neatly ordered, daily practice of research, the to-ing and fro-ing between theory and data, and the adventurous intertwining of disciplines, that the future lies "intreasured."

References

Alexander, J. E. 1837. *A narrative of a voyage of observation among the colonies of western Africa.* London: Colburn.

Anati, E. 1981. The origins of art. *Museum* 33: 200–210.

Applegate, R. B. 1975. The Datura cult among the Chumash. *Journal of California and Great Basin Anthropology* 2: 7–17.

Arbousset, T. 1846. *Narrative of an exploratory tour of the north-east of the Cape of Good Hope.* London: John Bishop.

Arbousset, T., and F. Daumas. 1846. *Narrative of an exploratory tour of the north-east of the Cape of Good Hope,* trans. J. C. Brown. Cape Town: Robertson.

Asaad, G. 1980. *Hallucinations in clinical psychiatry: A guide for mental health professionals.* New York: Brunner/Mazel.

Asaad, G., and B. Shapiro. 1986. Hallucinations: Theoretical and clinical overview. *American Journal of Psychiatry* 143: 1088–97.

Bahn, P. G. 1978. Water mythology and the distribution of Palaeolithic parietal art. *Proceedings of the Prehistoric Society* 44: 125–34.

———. 1986a. Comment on: Parietal finger markings in Europe and Australia, by R. G. Bednarik. *Rock Art Research* 3: 54–55.

———. 1986b. No sex, please, we're Aurignacians. *Rock Art Research* 3: 99–120.

———. 1995. Cave art without caves. *Antiquity* 69: 231–37.

Bahn, P. G., and J. Vertut. 1988. *Images of the Ice Age.* London: Windward.

Ballet, O., A. Bocquet, R. Bouchez, J. M. D. Coey, and A. Cornu. 1979. *Étude technique de poudres colorées de Lascaux inconnu.* Paris: Centre National de la Recherche Scientifique.

Barrow, J. 1801. *An account of travels into the interior of southern Africa.* London: Cadell & Davies.

Barth, F. 1987. *Cosmologies in the making.* Cambridge: Cambridge University Press.

Barthes, R. 1967. *Elements of semiology.* London: Cape.

Bates, C. D. 1992. Sierra Miwok shamans, 1900–1990. In *California Indian shamanism,* ed. L. J. Bean, 97–115. Menlo Park, Calif.: Ballena Press.

Battiss, W. W. 1939. *The amazing Bushman.* Pretoria: Red Fawn Press.

———. 1948. *The artists of the rocks.* Pretoria: Red Fawn Press.

Battiss, W. W., G. H. Franz, J. W. Grossert, and H. P. Junod. 1958. *The art of Africa.* Pietermaritzburg: Shuter and Shooter.

Bednarik, R. G. 1979. The potential rock patination analysis in Australian archaeology. Part I. *Artefact* 4: 14–38.

———. 1984a. Die Bedeutung der Paläolithischen Fingerlinientradition. *Anthropologie* 22: 73–79.

————. 1984b. On the nature of psychograms. *Artefact* 8: 27–32.

————. 1986. Parietal finger markings in Europe and Australia. *Rock Art Research* 3 (1): 30–61.

Bégouën, H., and H. Breuil. 1958. *Les cavernes du Volp. Trois-Frères. Tuc d'Audoubert. Ö Montesquieu-Avantäs (Ariäge).* Paris: Arts et Métiers Graphiques.

Bender, B. 1989. The roots of inequality. In *Domination and resistance,* ed. D. Miller, M. Rowland, and C. Tilley, 83–93. London: Unwin and Hyman.

Bernstein, R. J. 1983. *Beyond objectivism and relativism: Science, hermeneutics, and praxis.* Oxford: Blackwell.

Berrin, K. 1978. *Art of the Huichol Indians.* New York: Abrams.

Biesele, M. 1975. Folklore and rituals of !Kung hunter-gatherers. Ph.D. diss., Harvard University.

————. 1978. Sapience and scarce resources: Communication systems of the !Kung and other foragers. *Social Science Information* 17: 921–47.

————. 1980. Old K"xau. In *Shamanic voices: A survey of visionary narratives,* ed. J. Halifax, 54–62. Harmondsworth: Penguin.

————. 1987. "Anyone with sense would know": Tradition and creativity in !Kung narrative and song. In *Contemporary studies on Khoisan,* vol. 1, ed. R. Vossen and K. Keuthmann, 83–106. Hamburg: Helmut Buske Verlag.

————. 1993. *"Women like meat": The folklore and foraging ideology of the Kalahari Ju/'hoan.* Johannesburg: Witwatersrand University Press.

Blackburn, T. 1977. Biopsychological aspects of Chumash rock art. *Journal of California and Great Basin Anthropology* 4: 88–94.

Bleek, D. F. 1924. *The Mantis and his friends.* Cape Town: Maskew Miller.

————. 1927. The distribution of Bushman languages in South Africa. In *Festschrift Meinhof.* Hamburg: Freiderichsen de Gruyter.

————. 1928–29. Bushman grammar. *Zeitschrift für Eingebovenen-Sprachen* 19: 81–98 and 20: 161–74.

————. 1932a. Customs and beliefs of the /Xam Bushmen. Part III: Game animals. *Bantu Studies* 6: 233–49.

————. 1932b. Customs and beliefs of the /Xam Bushmen. Part IV: Omens, wind-making, clouds. *Bantu Studies* 6: 321–42.

————. 1932c. A survey of our present knowledge of rock paintings in South Africa. *South African Journal of Science* 29: 72–83.

————. 1933a. Beliefs and customs of the /Xam Bushmen. Part V: The rain. *Bantu Studies* 7: 297–312.

————. 1933b. Beliefs and customs of the /Xam Bushmen. Part VI: Rain-making. *Bantu Studies* 7: 375–92.

————. 1935. Beliefs and customs of the /Xam Bushmen. Part VII: Sorcerors [*sic*]. *Bantu Studies* 9: 1–47.

————. 1936. Beliefs and customs of the /Xam Bushmen. Part VIII: More about sorcerors [*sic*] and charms. *Bantu Studies* 10: 131–62.

————. 1956. *A Bushman dictionary.* New Haven, Conn.: American Oriental Society.

Bleek, W. H. I. 1874. Remarks on Orpen's "Mythology of the Maluti Bushmen." *Cape Monthly Magazine*, n.s., 9: 10–13.

―――. 1875. *A brief account of Bushmen folklore and other texts.* Cape Town: Government Printers.

Bleek, W. H. I., and L. C. Lloyd. 1866–77. Unpublished manuscripts. Jagger Library, University of Cape Town.

―――. 1911. *Specimens of Bushman folklore.* London: George Allen.

Boas, F. V. 1900. The mythology of the Bella Colla Indians. *Memoirs of the American Museum of Natural History* 2: 25–127.

Bond, G. 1948. [Cover design.] *South African Archaeological Bulletin* 3 (11).

Bootzin, R. R. 1980. *Abnormal psychology.* Toronto: Random House.

Borcherds, P. B. 1861. *An autobiographical memoir.* Cape Town: Robertson.

Bordes, S. 1969. Os percé moustérien et os grave acheuléen du Pech de l'Azé II. *Quarternaria* 2: 1–6.

Bourdieu, P. 1977. *Outline of a theory of practice.* Cambridge: Cambridge University Press.

Bourguignon, E. 1974. Cross-cultural perspectives on the religious uses of altered states of consciousness. In *Religious movements in contemporary America*, ed. I. Zaretsky and M. Leone. Princeton, N.J.: Princeton University Press.

―――. 1989. Trance and shamanism: What's in a name? *Journal of Psychoactive Drugs* 21: 9–15.

Boyd, C. E. 1996. Shamanic journeys into the Otherworld of the Archaic Chichimec. *Latin American Antiquity* 7: 152–64.

Bradley, R. 1985. *Consumption: Change and the archaeological record.* Edinburgh: University of Edinburgh, Department of Archaeology.

―――. 1989. Deaths and entrances: A contextual analysis of Megalithic art. *Current Anthropology* 30: 68–75.

Brentjes, B. 1969. *African rock art.* London: Dent.

Breuil, H. 1930. Premiers impressions de voyage sur la préhistoire Sud-Africaine. *L'Anthropologie* 40: 209–23.

―――. 1948. The White Lady of the Brandenberg, southwest Africa, her companions and her guards. *South African Archaeological Bulletin* 3: 2–11.

―――. 1949. Some foreigners in the frescoes on rocks in southern Africa. *South African Archaeological Bulletin* 4: 39–50.

―――. 1952. *Four hundred centuries of cave art.* Montignac, France: Centres d'Etude et de Documentation Préhistoriques.

―――. 1955. *The White Lady of the Brandenberg.* London: Trianon Press.

―――. 1979. *Four hundred centuries of cave art.* Montignac, France: Centre d'Etude et de Documentation Préhistoriques.

Brindley, G. S. 1973. Sensory effects of electrical stimulation of the visual and paravisual cortex in man. In *Handbook of sensory physiology*, vol. 7, part 3B, ed. R. Jung, 583–94. New York: Springer-Verlag.

Brodzky, A. T., R. Danesewich, and N. Johnson, eds. 1977. *Stones, bones and skin: Ritual and shamanic art.* Toronto: Society for Art Publications.

Brown, D. E. 1991. *Human Universals.* New York: McGraw-Hill.

Bryden, H. A. 1899. *Great and small game of Africa.* London: Rowland Ward.

Burkitt, M. C. 1928. *South Africa's past in stone and paint.* Cambridge: Cambridge University Press.

Callaway, G. 1969. *The fellowship of the veld: Sketches of Kafir life in South Africa.* New York: Negro University Press.

Campbell, C. 1986. Images of war: A problem in San rock art research. *World Archaeology* 18: 255–68.

——. 1987. Contact period rock art of the south-eastern mountains. Master's thesis, University of the Witwatersrand, Johannesburg, South Africa.

Campbell, J. 1815. *Travels in South Africa.* London: London Missionary Society.

Carrithers, M., S. Collins, and S. Lukes, eds. 1985. *The category of the person: Anthropology, philosophy, history.* Cambridge: Cambridge University Press.

Carter, P. L. 1970. Late Stone Age exploitation patterns in southern Natal. *South African Archaeological Bulletin* 25: 55–58.

Chalmers, A. F. 1978. *What is this thing called science?* Milton Keynes: Open University Press.

Chapman, J. 1868. *Travels in the interior of South Africa.* 2 vols. London: Bell and Daldy.

Chase, P. G., and H. L. Dibble. 1987. Middle Palaeolithic symbolism: A review of current evidence and interpretations. *Journal of Anthropological Archaeology* 6: 263–96.

Chauvet, J.-M., E. B. Deschamps, and C. Hillaire. 1995. *La grotte Chauvet, à Vallon-Pont-d'Arc.* Paris: Èditions du Seuil.

Chomsky, N. 1957. *Syntactic structures.* The Hague: Mouton.

Christie-Murray, D. 1978. *Voices from the gods.* London: Routledge and Kegan Paul.

Clarke, J. D. 1962. L'Abbé H. Breuil. *South African Archaeological Bulletin* 17: 21–22.

Clottes, J. 1995. *Les Cavernes de Niaux: Art préhistorique en Ariäge.* Paris: Èditions du Seuil.

Clottes, J., and J. Courtin. 1994. *La grotte Cosquer: Peintures et gravures de la Caverne Engloutie.* Paris: Èditions du Seuil.

——. 1996. *The cave beneath the sea: Paleolithic images at Cosquer.* New York: Abrams.

Clottes, J., and J. D. Lewis-Williams. 1996. *Les chamanes de la préhistoire: Transe et magie dans les grottes ornées.* Paris: Le Seuil.

——. 1998. *The shamans of prehistory: Trance and magic in the painted caves.* New York: Harry Abrams.

Clottes, J., and R. Simonnet. 1990. Retour au Réseau Clastres (Niaux, Ariège). *Bulletin de la Société Préhistorique de l'Ariège* 45: 51–139.

Clottes, J., M. Garner, and G. Meury. 1994. Magdalenian bison in the caves of the Ariäge. *Rock Art Research* 11: 58–70.

Clottes, J., J. Menu, and P. Walter. 1990. New light on the Niaux paintings. *Rock Art Research* 7: 21–26.

Clottes, J., A. Beltran, J. Courtin, and H. Cosquer. 1992. The Cosquer cave on Cape Morgiou, Marseilles. *Antiquity* 66: 583–98.

Clottes, J., J. M. Chauvet, E. Brunel-Deschamps, C. Hillaire, J. P. Daugas, M. Arnold, H. Cachier, J. Evin, P. Fortin, C. Oberlin, N. Tisnerat, and H. Valladas. 1995. Les peintures paléolithiques de la Grotte Chauvet-Pont-d'Arc, à Vallon-Pont-d'Arc (Ardèche, France): Datations directes ed indirectes par la méthode du radiocarbone. *Comptes-Rendus de l'Académie des Sciences* 320: 1133–40.

Cohen, S. 1964. *The beyond within: The LSD story.* New York: Atheneum.

Conkey, M. W. 1980. The identification of prehistoric hunter-gatherer aggregation sites: The case of Altamira. *Current Anthropology* 21: 609–30.

————. 1983. On the origin of Paleolithic art: A review and some critical thoughts. In *The Mousterian legacy: Human biocultural change in the Upper Pleistocene*, ed. E. Trinkaus, 201–27. British Archaeological Reports International Series 164.

————. 1984. To find ourselves: Art and social geography of prehistoric hunter-gatherers. In *Past and present hunter-gatherer studies*, ed. C. Schrire, 253–76. New York: Academic Press.

————. 1987. New approaches in the search for meaning? A review of research in "Palaeolithic art." *Journal of Field Archaeology* 14: 413–30.

————. 1991. Contexts of action, contexts for power: Material culture and gender in the Magdalenian. In *Engendering archaeology: Women and prehistory*, ed. J. M. Gero and M. Conkey, 57–92. Oxford: Basil Blackwell.

————. 1993. Humans as materialists: Image making in the Upper Palaeolithic. In *The origin of humans and humanness*, ed. D. T. Rasmussen, 95–118. Boston: Jones & Bartlett.

Cooke, C. K. 1983. More on San rock art. *Current Anthropology* 24: 538.

Copi, I. M. 1968. *Introduction to logic.* New York: Macmillan.

————. 1982. *Introduction to logic.* 6th ed. New York: Macmillan.

Currlé, L. C. 1913. Notes on the Namaqualand Bushmen. *Transactions of the Royal Society of South Africa* 3: 113–20.

Cytowic, R. E. 1994. *The man who tasted shapes.* London: Abacus.

Dams, L. 1984. Preliminary findings at the "organ" sanctuary in the cave of Nerja, Málage, Spain. *Oxford Journal of Archaeology* 3: 1–14.

————. 1985. Palaeolithic lithophones: Descriptions and comparisons. *Oxford Journal of Archaeology* 4: 31–46.

Danto, A. C. 1981. *The transfiguration of the commonplace: A philosophy of art.* Cambridge, Mass.: Harvard University Press.

Dart, R. A. 1925. The historical succession of cultural impacts upon South Africa. *Nature* 115: 425–29.

Davenport, D., and M. A. Jochim. 1988. The scene in the Shaft at Lascaux. *Antiquity* 62: 558–62.

Davis, W. 1982. Comment on: The economic and social context of southern San rock art, by J. D. Lewis-Williams. *Current Anthropology* 23: 440–41.

————. 1986a. The origins of image making. *Current Anthropology* 27: 193–215.

————. 1986b. Reply [to B. Delluc and G. Delluc]. *Current Anthropology* 27: 515–16.

Deacon, J. 1988. The power of a place in understanding southern San rock art. *World Archaeology* 20: 129–40.

Deacon, J., and T. A. Dowson, eds. 1996. *Voices from the past: /Xa, Bushmen and the Bleek and Lloyd collection.* Johannesburg: Witwatersrand University Press.

Delluc, B., and G. Delluc. 1978. Les manifestations graphiques aurignaciennes sur support rocheux des environs des Eyzies (Dordognes). *Gallia Préhistoires* 21: 213–438.

————. 1985. De l'empreinte au signe. *Dossiers Histoire et Archéologie* 90: 56–62.

————. 1986. Comment on: The origins of image making by W. Davis. *Current Anthropology* 27: 371.

De Marais, E., L. J. Castillo, and T. Earle. 1996. Ideology, materialization, and power strategies. *Current Anthropology* 37: 15–86.

Dickson, B. 1990. *The dawn of belief: Religion in the Upper Palaeolithic of southwestern Europe.* Tucson: University of Arizona Press.

Dobkin de Rios, M. 1986. Enigma of drug-induced altered states of consciousness among !Kung Bushmen of the Kalahari Desert. *Journal of Ethnopharmacology* 15: 297–304.

Dobkin de Rios, M., and F. Katz. 1975. Some relationships between music and hallucinogenic ritual: The "jungle gym" in consciousness. *Ethos* 3: 64–76.

Dobkin de Rios, M., and M. Winkelman. 1989. Shamanism and altered states of consciousness: An introduction. *Journal of Psychoactive Drugs* 21: 1–7.

Dobres, M.-A. 1988. The underground world of the Upper Paleolithic on the central Russian plain: Social organization, ideology and style. Master's thesis, State University of New York, Binghamton.

Dobres, M.-A., and C. R. Hoffman. 1994. Social agency and the dynamics of prehistoric technology. *Journal of Archaeological Method and Theory* 1 (3): 211–58.

Dornan, S. S. 1917. The Tati Bushmen (Masarwas) and their language. *Journal of the Royal Anthropological Institute* 47: 37–112.

Douglas, M. 1973. *Natural symbols: Explorations in cosmology.* Harmondsworth: Penguin.

Dowson, T. A. 1988. Revelations of religious reality: The individual in San rock art. *World Archaeology* 20: 116–28.

―――. 1989. Dots and dashes: Cracking the entoptic code in Bushman rock paintings. *South African Archaeological Society, Goodwin Series* 6: 84–94.

―――. 1990a. *Major rock engravings of southern Africa.* Johannesburg: Witwatersrand University Press.

―――. 1990b. 19th and 20th century Bushman ethnography and rock art: A rain making "scene" from the eastern Cape. Poster presented at the Sixth International Conference on Hunting and Gathering Societies, May 27–June 1, Fairbanks, Alaska.

―――. 1992. *The rock engravings of southern Africa.* Johannesburg: Witwatersrand University Press.

―――. 1994. Reading art, writing history: Rock art and social change in southern Africa. *World Archaeology* 25: 332–45.

―――. 2000. Paintings as politics: Exposing historical processes in hunter-gatherer rock art. In *Hunters and gatherers in the modern world: Conflict, resistance, and self-determination,* eds. P. P. Schweitzer, M. Biesele, and R. K. Hitchcock, 413–26. New York: Berghahn.

Dowson, T. A., and A. L. Holliday. 1989. Zigzags and eland: An interpretation of an idiosyncratic combination. *South African Archaeological Bulletin* 44: 46–48.

Driver, H. E. 1937. Cultural element distributions. 6. Southern Sierra Nevada. *Anthropological Records* 1: 35–154.

Dronfield, J. 1993. Ways of seeing, ways of telling: Irish passage tomb art, style and the universality of vision. In *Rock art studies: The post-stylistic era or Where do we go from here?,* ed. M. Lorblanchet and P. G. Bahn, 179–93. Oxford: Oxbow Books.

―――. 1994. Subjective visual phenomena in Irish passage-tomb art: Vision, cosmology and shamanism. Ph.D. diss., University of Cambridge.

―――. 1995. Subjective vision and the source of Irish megalithic art. *Antiquity* 69: 539–49.

Earle, Timothy K. 1994. Preface. In *New light on old art: Recent advances in hunter-gatherer rock art research,* ed. D. S. Whitley, i–ii. Institute of Archaeology, UCLA, Monograph 36.

Edelman, G. 1994. *Bright air, brilliant fire: On the matter of the mind.* London: Penguin.

Eichmeier, J., and O. Höfer. 1974. *Endogene Bildmuster.* Munich: Urban and Schwarzenberg.

Eliade, M. 1972. *Shamanism: Archaic techniques of ecstasy.* New York: Routledge. and Kegan Paul.

Elkin, A. P. 1945. Aboriginal men of high degree. *John Murtagh Macrossan Memorial Lectures of 1944, University of Queensland.* Sydney: Australasian Publishing.

Emboden, W. 1979. *Narcotic plants.* New York: Macmillan.

Evans-Pritchard, E. E. 1940. *The Nuer: A description of the modes of livelihood and political institutions of a Nilotic people.* Oxford: Oxford University Press.

————. 1956. *Nuer religion.* Oxford: Oxford University Press.

Faris, J. C. 1983. From form to content in the structural study of aesthetic systems. In *Structure and cognition in art,* ed. D. K. Washburn, 90–112. Cambridge: Cambridge University Press.

Fischer, T. 1975. Cartography of inner space. In *Hallucinations: Behaviour, experience, and theory,* ed. R. K. Siegel and L. J. West, 197–239. New York: John Wiley.

Fock, G. J. 1971. Review of Holm, E. 1969. *Die Felsbilder Südafrikas: Deutung und Bedeutung. South African Archaeological Bulletin* 26: 93–95.

————. 1979. *Felsbilder in Südafrika.* Vol. I: *Die gravierungen auf Klipfontein, Kapprovinz.* Köln: Bohlau Verlag.

Fock, G. J., and D. Fock. 1984. *Felsbilder in Südafrika.* Vol 2: *Die gravierungen auf Linderdam und Kalahari.* Köln: Bohlau Verlag.

————. 1989. *Felsbilder in Südafrika.* Vol. III: *Die Felsbilder im Vaal-Oranje Becken.* Köln: Bohlau Verlag.

Foucault, M. 1965. *Madness and civilization.* New York: Random House.

Fourie, L. 1928. The Bushmen of South West Africa. In *The Native tribes of South West Africa,* ed. C. Hahn. Cape Town: Cape Times.

Freeman, D., J. G. Echegerey, F. Bernaldo de Quiros, and J. Ogden. 1987. *Altamira revisited and other essays on early art.* Chicago: Institute for Prehistoric Investigations.

Freidel, D., L. Schele, and J. Parker. 1993. *Maya cosmos: Three thousand years of the shaman's path.* New York: William Morrow.

Frobenius, L. 1931. *Madsimu Dsangara.* Berlin: Atlantis-Verlag.

Furst, P. T. 1976. *Hallucinogens and culture.* Novato, Calif.: Chandler & Sharp.

————, ed. 1972. *Flesh of the gods: The ritual use of hallucinogens.* New York: Praeger.

Gamble, C. 1980. Information exchange in the Palaeolithic. *Nature* 283: 522–23.

————. 1982. Interaction and alliance in Palaeolithic society. *Man* 17: 92–107.

————. 1983. Culture and society in the Upper Palaeolithic of Europe. In *Hunter-gatherer economy and prehistory: A European perspective,* ed. G. Bailey, 210–11. Cambridge: Cambridge University Press.

Garlake, P. S. 1987a. *The painted caves: An introduction to the prehistoric rock art of Zimbabwe.* Harare: Modus.

————. 1987b. Themes in the prehistoric art of Zimbabwe. *World Archaeology* 19: 178–93.

————. 1990. Symbols of potency in the paintings of Zimbabwe. *South African Archaeological Bulletin* 45: 17–27.

————. 1994. Archetypes and attributes: Rock paintings in Zimbabwe. *World Archaeology* 25: 346–55.

————. 1995. *The hunter's vision: The prehistoric art of Zimbabwe.* London: British Museum Press.

Garvin, G. 1978. Shamans and rock art symbols. In *Four rock art studies*, ed. C. W. Clewlow Jr., 65–87. Ramona, Calif.: Ballena Press.

Gaussen, J. 1964. *La grotte Ornée de Gabillou*. Memoir 4. Bordeaux, France: Inst. de Préhistoire de l'Univeristé de Bordeaux.

Gibbon, G. 1989. *Explanation in archaeology*. Oxford: Basil Blackwell.

Giddens, A. 1984. *The constitution of society: Outline of the theory of structuration*. Cambridge: Polity Press.

Gilman, A. 1984. Explaining the Upper Palaeolithic revolution. In *Marxist perspectives in archaeology*, ed. M. Spriggs, 115–26. Cambridge: Cambridge University Press.

Godelier, M. 1977. *Perspectives in Marxist anthropology*. Cambridge: Cambridge University Press.

———. 1978. Infrastructures, society and history. *Current Anthropology* 19: 763–71.

Gombrich, E. H. 1961. *Art and illusion*. Princeton, N.J.: Bollingen Series.

Goodman, F. D. 1972. *Speaking in tongues: A cross-cultural study of glossolalia*. Chicago: University of Chicago Press.

———. 1988. *Ecstasy, ritual, and alternate reality: Religion in a pluralistic world*. Bloomington: Indiana University Press.

Goodman, N. 1976. *Languages of art*. Indianapolis: Hackett.

Goodwin, A. J. H. 1936. Vosburg: Its petroglyphs. *Annals of the South African Museum* 24: 163–210.

———. 1945. Method in prehistory. In *South African Archaeological Society Handbook No. 1*. Claremont: South African Archaeological Society.

Goss, R. 1986. *Maberly's mammals of southern Africa: A popular field guide*. Johannesburg: Delta Books.

Grant, C. 1965. *The rock paintings of the Chumash: A study of a California Indian culture*. Berkeley: University of California Press.

———. 1968. *Rock drawings of the Coso Range*. China Lake, Calif.: Maturango Press.

Graziosi, P. 1960. *Palaeolithic art*. London: Faber and Faber.

Guenther, M. G. 1975. The trance dancer as an agent of social change among the farm Bushmen of the Ghanzi district. *Botswana Notes and Records* 7: 161–66.

———. 1975–1976. The San trance dance: Ritual and revitalization among the farm Bushmen of the Ghanzi district, Republic of Botswana. *Journal of the South West Africa Scientific Society* 30: 45–53.

———. 1986. *The Nharo Bushmen of Botswana: Tradition and change*. Hamburg: Helmut Buske Verlag.

———. 1999. *Tricksters and trancers: Bushman religion and society*. Bloomington: Indiana University Press.

Gulbrandsen, O. 1991. On the problem of egalitarianism: The Kalahari San. In *The ecology of choice and symbol: Essays in honour of Fredrik Barth*, ed. R. Gronhaug, G. Haaland, and G. Henriksen, 82–110. Bergen: Alma Mater Forlag.

Halifax, J. 1979. Shaman song. In *Shamanic voices: A survey of visionary narratives*, ed. J. Halifax, 29–33. Harmondsworth: Penguin.

———. 1982. *Shaman: The wounded healer*. New York: Crossroad.

———, ed. 1980. *Shamanic voices: A survey of visionary narratives*. Harmondsworth: Penguin.

Hall, S. L. 1986. Pastoral adaptations and forager reactions in the eastern Cape. *South African Archaeological Society, Goodwin Series* 5: 42–49.

———. 1990. Hunter-gatherer-fishers of the Fish River Basin: A contribution to the Holocene prehistory of the eastern Cape. Ph.D diss., University of Stellenbosch, South Africa.

———. 1994. Images of interaction: Rock art and sequence in the eastern Cape. In *Contested images: Diversity in southern African rock art research*, ed. T. A. Dowson and J. D. Lewis-Williams, 61–82. Johannesburg: Witwatersrand University Press.

Halverson, J. 1987. Art for art's sake in the Palaeolithic. *Current Anthropology* 28: 63–89.

Hammond-Tooke, W. D. 1972. *The structuring of chaos*. Johannesburg: Witwatersrand University Press.

———. 1974. The Cape Nguni witch familiar as mediatory construct. *Man* 9: 128–36.

———. 1975. The symbolic structure of Cape Nguni cosmology. In *Religion and social change in southern Africa*, ed. M. G. Whisson and M. West. Cape Town: David Philip.

———. 1977. Lévi-Strauss in a garden of millet: The structuralist analysis of a Zulu folktale. *Man* 12: 76–86.

———. 1981. *Patrolling the Herms: Social structure, cosmology and pollution concepts in southern Africa*. Johannesburg: Institute for the Study of Man in Africa.

———. 1983. Reply to A. R. Willcox. *South African Archaeological Bulletin* 38: 5–6.

———. 1992. Twins, incest and mediators: The structure of four Zulu folktales. *Africa* 62: 204–20.

Harner, M. J. 1968. The sound of rushing water. *Natural History* 77 (6): 28–33, 60–61.

———. 1973a. Common themes in South American Indian *Yage* experiences. In *Hallucinogens and shamanism*, ed. M. J. Harner, 155–75. New York: Oxford University Press.

———. 1982b. *The way of the shaman*. Toronto: Bantam Books.

———, ed. 1973. *Hallucinogens and shamanism*. New York: Oxford University Press.

Hawkes, C. F. C. 1954. Archaeological theory and method: Some suggestions from the Old World. *American Anthropologist* 56 (1): 155–68.

Hayden, B. 1987. Alliances and ritual ecstasy: Human responses to resource stress. *Journal for the Scientific Study of Religion* 26: 81–91.

———. 1990. The cultural capacities of Neandertals: A review and re-evaluation. *Journal of Human Evolution* 24: 113–46.

———. 1993. The cultural capacities of Neandertals: A review and re-evaluation. *Journal of Human Evolution* 24: 113–46.

Hedges, K. 1973. Rock art in southern California. *Pacific Coast Archaeological Society Quarterly* 9: 1–28.

———. 1976. Southern California rock art as shamanistic art. In *American Indian rock art*, vol. 2, ed. K. Sutherland, 126–38. El Paso, Calif.: El Paso Archaeological Society.

———. 1982. Phosphenes in the context of Native American rock art. In *American Indian rock art*, vol. 7/8, ed. F. G. Bock, 1–10. El Toro: American Rock Art Research Association.

———. 1983. The shamanic origins of rock art. In *Ancient images on stone: Rock art in the Californias*, ed. J. A. van Tilburg, 46–59. Los Angeles: Rock Art Archive, UCLA.

Heinz, H.-J. 1966. The social organization of the !Kõ Bushmen. Master's thesis, University of South Africa, Pretoria.

———. 1975. Elements of !Kõ Bushman religious beliefs. *Anthropos* 70: 17–41.

Heinze, R.-I. 1986. More on mental imagery and shamanism. *Current Anthropology* 27: 154.

Heizer, R. F., and M. A. Baumhoff. 1959. Great Basin petroglyphs and game trails. *Science* 129: 1904–5.

―――. 1962. *Prehistoric rock art of Nevada and eastern California.* Berkeley: University of California Press.

Hempel, C. G. 1966. *Philosophy of natural science.* Englewood Cliffs, N.J.: Prentice Hall.

Hewitt, R. L. 1986. *Structure, meaning and ritual in the narratives of the southern San.* Hamburg: Helmut Buske Verlag.

Hitchcock, R. K. 1982. Patters of redentism among the Basarwa of Botswana. In *Politics and history in band societies,* eds. E. Leacock and R. Lee, 223–67. Cambridge: Cambridge University Press.

Hodder, I. 1982a. Sequences of structural change in the Dutch Neolithic. In *Symbolic and structural archaeology,* ed. I. Hodder. Cambridge: Cambridge University Press.

―――. 1982b. *Symbols in action.* Cambridge: Cambridge University Press.

―――. 1982c. Theoretical archaeology: A reactionary view. In *Symbolic and structural archaeology,* ed. I. Hodder, 1–16. Cambridge: Cambridge University Press.

―――. 1986. *Reading the past: Current approaches to interpretation in archaeology.* Cambridge: Cambridge University Press.

Hoffer, A., and H. Osmond. 1967. *The hallucinogens.* New York: Academic Press.

Hollis, M. 1985. Of masks and men. In *The category of the person: Anthropology, philosophy, history,* ed. M. Carrithers, S. Collins, and S. Lukes, 217–33. Cambridge: Cambridge University Press.

Holm, E. 1987. *Bushman art.* Pretoria: De Jager-HAUM.

Horowitz, M. J. 1964. The imagery of visual hallucinations. *Journal of Nervous and Mental Disease* 138: 513–23.

―――. 1975. Hallucinations: An information-processing approach. In *Hallucinations: Behaviour, experience and theory,* ed. R. K. Siegel and L. J. West, 163–95. New York: John Wiley.

How, M. W. 1962. *The mountain Bushmen of Basutoland.* Pretoria: Van Schaik.

Hudson, T., and G. Lee. 1984. Function and symbolism in Chumash rock art. *Journal of New World Archaeology* 6: 26–47.

Huffman, T. N. 1983. The trance hypothesis and the rock art of Zimbabwe. *South African Archaeological Society, Goodwin Series* 4: 49–53.

Hultkrantz, A. 1981. Accommodation and persistence: Ecological analysis of the religion of the Sheepeater Indians in Wyoming, U.S.A. *Temenos* 17: 35–44.

Hunchak, J. F. 1980. Hypnotic induction by entoptic phenomena. *American Journal of Clinical Hypnosis* 22: 223–24.

Huyge, D. 1991. The "Venus" of Laussel in the light of ethnomusicology. *Archeologie in Vlaanderen* I: 11–18.

Ingold, T. 1993. Technology, language and intelligence: A consideration of basic concepts. In *Tools, language and cognition in human evolution,* ed. K. Gibson and T. Ingold, 449–72. Cambridge: Cambridge University Press.

Inskeep, R. R. 1982. Comment on: The economic and social context of southern San rock art, by J. D. Lewis-Williams. *Current Anthropology* 23: 441–42.

Jenkins, T., and P. V. Tobias. 1977. Nomenclature of population groups in southern Africa. *African Studies* 36: 49–55.

Jochim, M. A. 1983. Palaeolithic cave art in ecological perspective. In *Hunter-gatherer economy and prehistory: A European perspective*, ed. G. Bailey, 212–19. Cambridge: Cambridge University Press.

Johnson, M. H. 1989. Conceptions of agency in archaeological interpretation. *Journal of Anthropological Archaeology* 8: 189–211.

Johnson, T., and T. M. O'C. Maggs. 1979. *Major rock paintings of southern Africa*. Cape Town: David Philip.

Johnson, T., H. Rabinowitz, and P. Sieff. 1959. *Rock-paintings of the southwest Cape*. Cape Town: Nasionale Boekhandel.

Jolly, P. 1986. A first generation descendant of the Transkei San. *South African Archaeological Bulletin* 41: 6–9.

———. 1994. Strangers to brothers: Interaction between south-eastern San and southern Nguni/Sotho communities. Master's thesis, University of Cape Town.

———. 1995. Melikane and Upper Mangolong revisited: The possible effects on San art of symbiotic contact between south-eastern San and southern Sotho and Nguni communities. *South African Archaeological Bulletin* 50: 68–80.

Jolly, P., and F. Prins. 1994. M.—a further assessment. *South African Archaeological Bulletin* 49: 16–23.

Jones, T. 1982. Comment on: The economic and social context of southern San rock art, by J. D. Lewis-Williams. *Current Anthropology* 23: 442– 43.

Joyce, A. A., and M. Winter. 1996. Ideology, power, and urban society in pre-Hispanic Oaxaca. *Current Anthropology* 37: 33–86.

Katz, R. 1976a. Education for transcendence. In *Kalahari Hunter-gatherers*, ed. R. B. Lee and I. DeVore, 281–301. Cambridge, Mass.: Harvard University Press.

———. 1976b. The painful ecstasy of healing. *Psychology Today*, December, 81–86.

———. 1982. *Boiling energy: Community healing among the Kalahari !Kung*. Cambridge, Mass.: Harvard University Press.

Katz, R., and M. Biesele. 1986. !Kung healing: The symbolism of sex roles and culture change. In *The past and future of !Kung ethnography: Critical reflections and symbolic perspectives. Essays in honour of Lorna Marshall*, ed. M. Biesele, R. Gordon, and R. Lee, 195–230. Hamburg: Helmut Buske Verlag.

Kieffer, S. N., and T. B. Moritz. 1968. Psychedelic drugs. *Pennsylvania Medicine* 71: 57–67.

Kinahan, J. 1989. Pastoral nomads of the central Namib Desert. Ph.D. diss., University of the Witwatersrand, Johannesburg, South Africa.

———. 1991. *Pastoral nomads of the central Namib Desert: The people that time forgot*. Windhoek: Namibia Archaeological Trust and New Namibia Books.

Kirkland, F., and W. W. Newcomb. 1967. *The rock art of the Texas Indians*. Austin: University of Texas Press.

Klüver, H. 1926. Mescal visions and eidetic vision. *American Journal of Psychology* 37: 502–15.

———. 1942. Mechanisms of hallucinations. In *Studies in personality*, ed. Q. McNemar and M. A. Merrill, 175–207. New York: McGraw-Hill.

———. 1966. *Mescal and mechanisms of hallucinations*. Chicago: Chicago University Press.

Knoll, M. 1958. Anregung geometrischer Figuren und anderer subjektiver Lichtmuster in elektrischen Feldern. *Zeitschrift für Psychologie* 17: 110–26.

Knoll, M., and J. Kugler. 1959. Subjective light pattern spectroscopy in the encephalographic frequency range. *Nature* 184: 1823–24.

Knoll, M., J. Kugler, O. Höfer, and S. D. Lawder. 1963. Effects of chemical stimulation of electrically induced phosphenes on their bandwidth, shape, number and intensity. *Confinia Neurologica* 23: 201–26.

Knoll, R. 1985. Mental imagery cultivation as a cultural phenomenon: The role of visions in shamanism. *Current Anthropology* 26: 443–61.

Kroeber, A. L. 1925. *Handbook of the Indians of California.* Bureau of American Ethnology Bulletin 78.

Kubler, G. 1985. Eidetic imagery and Palaeolithic art. *Journal of Psychology* 119: 557–65.

La Barre, W. 1972. Reprint. *The Ghost Dance: Origins of religion.* London: Allen & Unwin. Original edition, Garden City, N.J.: Doubleday, 1970.

———. 1972. Hallucinogens and the shamanistic origins of religion. In *Flesh of the gods: The ritual use of hallucinogens,* ed. P. T. Furst, 261–78. New York: Praeger.

———. 1975. Anthropological perspectives on hallucination and hallucinogens. In *Hallucinations: Behaviour, experience, and theory,* ed. R. K. Siegel and L. J. West, 9–52. New York: John Wiley.

Lamb, F. B. 1980. Manual Córdova-Rios. In *Shamanic voices: A survey of visionary narratives,* ed. J. Halifax, 140–48. Harmondsworth: Penguin.

Lame Deer and R. Erdoes. 1980. Lame Deer. In *Shamanic voices: A survey of visionary narratives,* ed. J. Halifax, 70–75. Harmondsworth: Penguin.

Laming-Emperaire, A. 1962. *La signification de l'art rupestre Paléolithique.* Paris: Picard.

Layton, Robert. 2000. Review feature: Shamanism, totemism and rock art: *Les Chamanes de la Préhistoire* in the context of rock art research. *Cambridge Archaeological Journal* 10: 169–86.

Lee, D. N., and H. C. Woodhouse. 1964. Rock paintings of flying buck. *South African Archaeological Bulletin* 19: 71–74.

———. 1968. More rock paintings of flying buck. *South African Archaeological Bulletin* 23: 13–16.

———. 1970. *Art on the rocks of southern Africa.* Cape Town: Purnell.

Lee, G. 1977. Chumash mythology in paint and stone. *Pacific Coast Archaeological Society Quarterly* 13 (3): 1–14.

Lee, R. B. 1967. Trance cure of the !Kung Bushmen. *Natural History* 76 (9): 31–37.

———. 1968. The sociology of !Kung Bushman trance performance. In *Trance and possession states,* ed. R. Prince, 35–54. Montreal: R. M. Bucke Memorial Society.

———. 1993. *The Dobe Ju/'hoansi.* New York: Harcourt Brace College Publishers.

Lee, R. B., and I. de Vore, eds. 1976. *Kalahari hunter-gatherers.* Cambridge, Mass.: Harvard University Press.

Leeuwenberg, J. 1970. A Bushman legend from the George district. *South African Archaeological Bulletin* 25: 145–46.

Lenssen-Erz, T. 1989. Catalogue. In *Rock paintings of the upper Brandburg,* Part I, *Amis Gorge,* by H. Pager. Cologne: Heinrich Barth Institute.

Leroi-Gourhan, A. 1968a. *The art of prehistoric man in western Europe.* London: Thames & Hudson.

———. 1968b. Les signes parietaux du Paléolithique supérieur franco-cantabrique. In *Simposia internacional de art rupestre,* 67–77. Barcelona: Instituto de Prehistoria y Arqueología.

————. 1982. *The dawn of European art: An introduction to Palaeolithic cave painting.* Cambridge: Cambridge University Press.

Leroi-Gourhan, A., and J. Allain. 1979. *Lascaux inconnu.* Paris: Centre National de la Recherche Scientifique.

Levine, M. H. 1957. Prehistoric art and ideology. *American Anthropologist* 49: 949–64.

Lévi-Strauss, C. 1963. The structural study of myth. In *Structural anthropology*, ed. C. Lévi-Strauss, 206–31. Harmondswoth: Penguin.

————. 1966. *The savage mind.* London: Weidenfeld & Nicolson.

————. 1967. The story of Asdiwal. In *The structural study of myth and totemism*, ed. E. Leach. London: Tavistock.

————. 1968. The structural study of myth. In *Structural anthropology*, ed. C. Lévi-Strauss. Harmondsworth: Penguin.

Levy, G. R. 1963. *Religious conceptions of the Stone Age.* New York: Harper & Row.

Lewis, I. M. 1971. *Ecstatic religion.* Harmondsworth: Penguin.

Lewis-Williams, J. D. 1962. The Tarkastad rock-engravings. *South African Archaeological Bulletin* 17: 24–26.

————. 1972a. The Drakensberg rock paintings as an expression of religious thought. *Actes du Ier Symposium International sur Les Religions de La Préhistoire.*

————. 1972b. The syntax and function of the Giant's Castle rock paintings. *South African Archaeological Bulletin* 27: 49–65.

————. 1974a. Rethinking the South Africa rock paintings. *Origini* 68: 229–56.

————. 1974b. Superpositioning in a sample of rock-paintings from the Barkly East district. *South African Archaeological Bulletin* 29: 93–103.

————. 1975. The Drakensberg rock paintings as an expression of religious thought. In *Les religions de la préhistoire*, ed. E. Anati, 413–26. Capo di Ponte: Centro Camuno di Studi Preistorici.

————. 1977a. Ezeljagdspoort revisited: New light on the enigmatic rock painting. *South African Archaeological Bulletin* 32: 165–69.

————. 1977b. Led by the nose: Observations on the supposed use of southern San rock art in rain-making rituals. *African Studies* 36: 155–59.

————. 1977c. *Believing and seeing: An interpretation of symbolic meanings in southern San rock paintings.* Ph.D. thesis, University of Natal, Durban.

————. 1980. Ethnography and iconography: Aspects of southern San thought and art. *Man* 15: 467–82.

————. 1981a. *Believing and seeing: Symbolic meanings in southern San rock paintings.* London: Academic Press.

————. 1981b. The thin red line: Southern San notions and rock paintings of supernatural potency. *South African Archaeological Bulletin* 36: 5–13.

————. 1982. The economic and social context of southern San rock art. *Current Anthropology* 23: 429–49.

————. 1983a. Introductory essay: Science and rock art. *South African Archaeological Society, Goodwin Series* 4: 3–13.

————. 1983b. Reply [to C. K. Cooke and A. R. Willcox]. *Current Anthropology* 24: 540–45.

————. 1983c. Review of: *Rock art of the Spanish Levant,* by A Beltran (Cambridge: Cambridge University Press, 1982) and *The dawn of European art: An introduction to Palaeolithic cave painting,* by A. Leroi-Gourhan (Cambridge: Cambridge University Press, 1982). *South African Archaeological Bulletin* 38: 100–101.

————. 1983d. *The rock art of southern Africa.* Cambridge: Cambridge University Press.

————. 1984a. The empiricist impasse in southern African rock art studies. *South African Archaeological Bulletin* 39: 58–66.

————. 1984b. Ideological continuities in prehistoric southern Africa: The evidence of rock art. In *Past and present in hunter-gatherer studies,* ed. C. Schrire, 225–52. New York: Academic Press.

————. 1984c. Reply [to H. C. Woodhouse]. *Current Anthropology* 25: 246–48.

————. 1984d. The rock art workshop: Narrative or metaphor? In *Frontiers: Southern African archaeology today,* ed. M. Hall, G. Avery, D. M. Avery, M. L. Wilson, and A. J. B. Humphreys, 323–27. British Archaeological Reports International Series 207.

————. 1985a. The San artistic achievement. *African Arts* 18 (3): 54–59.

————. 1985b. *Social theory in southern African archaeology.* Paper presented at South African Association of Archaeologists conference, Grahamstown.

————. 1985c. Testing the trance explanation of southern African rock art: Depictions of felines. *Bolletino: World Journal Rock Art Studies* 22: 47–62.

————. 1986a. Cognitive and optical illusions in San rock art research. *Current Anthropology* 27: 171–78.

————. 1986b. The last testament of the southern San. *South African Archaeological Bulletin* 41: 10–11.

————. 1987a. A dream of eland: An unexplored component of San shamanism and rock art. *World Archaeology* 19 (2): 165–77.

————. 1987b. Paintings of power: Ethnography and rock art in southern Africa. In *The past and future of !Kung ethnography: Critical reflections and symbolic perspectives,* ed. M. Biesele, R. Gordon, and R. Lee, 231–73. Hamburg: Helmut Buske Verlag.

————. 1987c. The San rock art debate. *Man* 22: 173–75.

————. 1988a. "People of the eland": An archaeo-linguistic crux. In *Hunters and gatherers: Property, power and ideology,* ed. T. Ingold, D. Riches, and J. Woodburn, 203–11. Oxford: Berg.

————. 1988b. Reality and non-reality in San rock art. Twenty-fifth Raymond Dart Lecture. Institute for the Study of Man in Africa, Johannesburg, Witwatersrand University Press.

————. 1989a. Southern Africa's place in the archaeology of human understanding. *South African Journal of Science* 85: 47–52.

————. 1989b. Theory and data: A brief critique of A. Marshack's research methods and position on Upper Palaeolithic shamanism. *Rock Art Research* 6: 38–53.

————. 1990a. *Discovering southern African rock art.* Cape Town: David Philip.

————. 1990b. Documentation, analysis and interpretation: Dilemmas in rock art research. Review of "Rock paintings of the Upper Brandberg. Part I: Amis Gorge." *South African Archaeological Bulletin* 45: 126–36.

————. 1990c. On Palaeolithic art and the neuropsychological model. *Current Anthropology* 31: 407–8.

————. 1991a. Upper Palaeolithic art in the 1990s: A southern African perspective. *South African Journal of Science* 87: 422–29.

————. 1991b. Wrestling with analogy: A methodological dilemma in Upper Palaeolithic art research. *Proceedings of the Prehistoric Society* 57 (1): 149–62.

————. 1992. Ethnographic evidence relating to "trance" and "shamans" among northern and southern Bushmen. *South African Archaeological Bulletin* 47: 56–60.

————. 1993. Southern African archaeology in the 1990s. *South African Archaeological Bulletin* 48: 45–50.

————. 1994. Rock art and ritual: Southern Africa and beyond. *Complutum* 5: 277–89.

————. 1995a. Modelling the production and consumption of rock art. *South African Archaeological Bulletin* 50: 143–54.

————. 1995b. Perspectives and traditions in southern African rock art research. In *Perceiving rock art: Social and political perspectives*, ed. K. Helskog and O. Bjøner. Oslo: Novus.

————. 1995c. Seeing and construing: The making and "meaning" of a southern African rock art motif. *Cambridge Archaeological Journal* 5: 3–23.

————. 1995d. Some aspects of rock art research in the politics of present-day South Africa. In *Perceiving rock art: Social and political perspectives*, ed. K. Helskog and B. Olsen. Oslo, Norway: Novus Forlag.

————. 1996. "A visit to the Lion's house": The structure, metaphors and sociopolitical significance of 19th century Bushman myths. In *Voices from the past: /Xam Bushmen and the Bleek and Lloyd collection*, ed. J. Deacon and T. A. Dowson, 122–41. Johannesburg: Witwatersrand University Press.

————. 1997a. The Mantis, the Eland and the Meerkats: Conflict and mediation in a nineteenth-century San myth. In *Culture and the commonplace: Anthropological essays in honor of David Hammond-Tooke*, ed. P. McAllister, 195–216. Johannesburg: Witwatersrand University Press. *African Studies* Special Issue 56 (2).

————. 1997b. Prise en compte du relief naturel des surfaces rocheuses dans l'art pariétal Sud Africain et Paléolithique Ouest Européen: etude culturelle et temporelle croisée de la crayance religeuse. *L'Anthropologie* 101: 220–37.

————. 2000. *Stories that float from afar: Ancestral folklore of the San of southern Africa*. Cape Town: David Philip.

————. 2001. Brainstorming images: neuropsychology and rock art research. In *Handbook of rock art research*, ed. D. S. Whitley, 332–57. New York: AltaMira Press.

————. 2002. *The mind in the cave*. London: Thames and Hudson.

Lewis-Williams, J. D., and M. Biesele. 1978. Eland hunting rituals among northern and southern San groups: Striking similarities. *Africa* 48: 117–34.

Lewis-Williams, J. D., and G. Blundell. 1997. New light on finger-dots in southern African rock art: Synesthesia, transformation and technique. *South African Journal of Science* 93: 51–54.

Lewis-Williams, J. D., and T. A. Dowson. 1988. The signs of all times: Entoptic phenomena in Upper Palaeolithic art. *Current Anthropology* 29: 201–45.

————. 1989a. *Images of power: Understanding Bushman rock art*. Johannesburg: Southern.

————. 1989b. Theory and data: A brief critique of A. Marshack's research methods and position on Upper Palaeolithic shamanism. *Rock Art Research* 6: 38–53.

————. 1990. Through the veil: San rock paintings and the rock face. *South African Archaeological Bulletin* 45: 5–16.

————. 1992. Art rupestre San et Paléolithique supérieur: Le lien analogique. *L'Anthropologie* 96: 769–90.

————. 1993. On vision and power in the Neolithic: Evidence from the decorated monuments. *Current Anthropology* 34: 55–65.

————. 1994. Aspects of rock art research. In *Contested images: Diversity in southern African rock art research*, ed. T. A. Dowson and J. D. Lewis-Williams, 201–21. Johannesburg: Witwatersrand University Press.

————, eds. 1994. *Contested images: Diversity in southern African rock art research.* Johannesburg: University of the Witwatersrand.

Lewis-Williams, J. D., and J. H. N. Loubser. 1986. Deceptive appearances: A critique of southern African rock art studies. In *Advances in world archaeology*, vol. 5, ed. F. Wendorf and A. E. Close, 253–89. New York: Academic Press.

Lewis-Williams, J. D., J. F. Butler-Adam, M. O. Sutcliffe. 1979. Some conceptual and statistical difficulties in the interpretation of southern San rock art. *South African Journal of Science* 75: 211–214.

Lewis-Williams, J. D., T. A. Dowson, and J. Deacon. 1993. Rock art and changing perceptions of southern Africa's past: Ezeljagdspoort reviewed. *Antiquity* 67: 273–91.

Lewis-Williams, J. D., G. Blundell, W. Challis, and J. Hampson. 2000. Threads of light: Re-examining a motif in southern African rock art. *South African Archaeological Bulletin* 55: 123–36.

Lommel, A. 1967a. *Shamanism: The beginnings of art.* New York: McGraw-Hill.

————. 1967b. *The world of early hunters.* London: Evelyn, Adams & Mackay.

Lorblanchet, M. 1977. From naturalism to abstraction in European prehistoric rock art. In *Form in indigenous art: Schematisation in the art of Aboriginal Australia and prehistoric Europe*, ed. P. J. Ucko, 44–56. Canberra: Australian Institute of Aboriginal Studies.

————. 1984a. Grotte de Cougnac. In *L'Art des cavernes: Atlas des grottes ornées Paléolithiques Françaises*, 483–87. Paris: Ministère de la Culture.

————. 1984b. Grotte du Pech-Merle. In *L'Art des cavernes: Atlas des grottes ornées Paléolithiques Françaises*, 467–74. Paris: Ministère de la Culture.

Lorblanchet, M., M. Labeau, J. L. Vernet, P. Fitte, H. Valladas, H. Cachier, and M. Arnold. 1990. Palaeolithic pigments in the Quercy, France. *Rock Art Research* 7: 4–20.

Loubser, J., and G. Laurens. 1994. Depictions of domestic ungulates and shields: Hunter/gatherers and agropastoralists in the Caledon River Valley area. In *Contested images: Diversity in southern African rock art research*, ed. T. A. Dowson and J. D. Lewis-Williams, 83–118. Johannesburg: Witwatersrand University Press.

Maggs, T. M. O'C. 1967. A quantitative analysis of the rock art from a sample area in the western Cape. *South African Journal of Science* 63: 100–104.

Maggs, T. M. O'C., and J. Sealy. 1983. Elephants in boxes. *South African Archaeological Society, Goodwin Series* 4: 44–48.

Malmer, M. P. 1993. A poet's ambiguity. *Cambridge Archaeological Journal* 3 (1): 113–18.

Manhire, A. H., J. Parkington, and R. Yates. 1985. Nets and fully recurved bows: Rock paintings and hunting methods in the western Cape, South Africa. *World Archaeology* 17: 161–74.

Manhire, A. H., J. E. Parkington, A. D. Mazel, and T. M. O'C. Maggs. 1986. Cattle, sheep and horses: A review of domestic animals in the rock art of southern Africa. *South African Archaeological Society, Goodwin Series* 5: 22–30.

Marshack, A. 1969. Polesini: A reexamination of the engraved Upper Palaeolithic mobiliary materials of Italy by a new methodology. *Revisa di Scienze Preistoriche* 24: 219–81.

———. 1972. *The roots of civilization.* London: Weidenfeld & Nicolson.

———. 1976. Some implications of the Palaeolithic symbolic evidence for the origin of language. *Current Anthropology* 17: 274–82.

———. 1977. The meander as a system: The analysis and recognition of iconographic units in Upper Palaeolithic compositions. In *Form in indigenous art: Schematisation in the art of Aboriginal Australia and prehistoric Europe,* ed. P. J. Ucko, 285–317. Canberra: Australian Institute of Aboriginal Studies.

———. 1979. Upper Palaeolithic symbol systems of the Russian Plain: Cognitive and comparative analysis. *Current Anthropology* 20: 271–311.

———. 1985. Theoretical concepts that lead to new analytic methods, modes of inquiry, and classes of data. *Rock Art Research* 2: 95–111.

———. 1986. Reply to comments. *Rock Art Research* 3: 67–82.

Marshall, L. 1959. Marriage among the !Kung Bushmen. *Africa* 29: 335–65.

———. 1960. !Kung Bushman bands. *Africa* 30: 325–55.

———. 1961. Sharing, talking, and giving: Relief of social tensions among the !Kung Bushmen. *Africa* 31: 231–249.

———. 1962. !Kung Bushman religious beliefs. *Africa* 32: 221–51.

———. 1965. The !Kung Bushmen of the Kalahari Desert. In *Peoples of Africa,* ed. J. L. Gibbs. New York: Holt, Rinehart & Winston.

———. 1969. The medicine dance of the !Kung Bushmen. *Africa* 39: 347–81.

———. 1976. *The !Kung of Nyae Nyae.* Cambridge, Mass.: Harvard University Press.

Mason, R. J. 1957. The Transvaal Middle Stone Age and statistical analysis. *South African Archaeological Bulletin* 12: 119–43.

———. 1962. *The prehistory of the Transvaal.* Johannesburg: Witwatersrand University Press.

Mazel, A. D. 1989a. People making history: The last ten thousand years of hunter-gatherer communities in the Thukela Basin. *Natal Museum Journal of Humanities* 1: 1–168.

———. 1989b. The Stone Age peoples of Natal. In *Natal and Zululand from earliest times to 1910, a new history,* ed. A. Duminy and B. Guest, 1–27. Pietermaritzburg: University of Natal Press and Shuter & Shooter.

McCall, D. F. 1970. *Wolf courts girl: The Equivalence of hunting and mating in Bushman thought.* Ohio University Papers in International Studies, Africa Series, no. 7. Athens: Ohio University, Center for International Studies.

McLuhan, M. 1967. *The mechanical bride.* London: Routledge.

Méroc, L., and J. Mazet. 1977. *Cougnac.* Gourdon: Edition des Grottes de Cougnac.

Miller, D. 1987. *Material culture and mass consumption.* Oxford: Blackwell.

Miller, W., comp. 1972. *Newe Natekwinappeh: Shoshoni stories and dictionary.* University of Utah Anthropological Papers 94.

Ministäre de la Culture. 1984. *L'Art des cavernes (Atlas des Grottes Ornées Paléolithiques françaises).* Paris: Author.

Munn, H. 1973. The mushrooms of language. In *Hallucinogens and shamanism*, ed. M. J. Harner, 86–122. New York: Oxford University Press.

Needham, R. 1967. Percussion and transition. *Man* 2: 606–14.

Neihardt, J. G. 1979. Black Elk. In *Shamanic voices: A survey of visionary narratives*, ed. J. Halifax, 95–102. Harmondsworth: Penguin.

Nettleton, A. 1984. San rock art: Image, function, and meaning (A reply to A. R. Willcox). *South African Archaeological Bulletin* 39: 67–68.

Noll, R. 1985. Mental imagery cultivation as a cultural phenomenon: The role of visions in shamanism. *Current Anthropology* 26: 443–61.

Omnès, J. 1982. *La grotte ornée de Labastide (Hautes-Pyrenees)*. Lourdes: J. Omnés.

Orpen, J. M. 1876. A glimpse into the mythology of the Maluti Bushmen. *Cape Monthly Magazine*, n.s., 9 (49): 1–13.

Oster, G. 1970. Phosphenes. *Scientific American* 222 (2): 83–87.

Pager, H. 1971. *Ndedema*. Graz: Akademische Druck Verlagsanstalt.

———. 1973. Rock paintings in southern Africa showing bees and honey hunting. *Bee World* 54: 61–68.

———. 1975a. The antelope cult of the prehistoric hunters of South Africa. In *Les religions de la préhistoire*, ed. E. Anati, 401–11. Capo di Ponte: Centro Camuno di Studi Preistorici.

———. 1975b. *Stone Age myth and magic*. Graz: Akademische Druck Verlagsanstalt.

———. 1976a. Quantitative analyses elucidate the motives of the South African rock painters. *Almagoren* 5: 219–26.

———. 1976b. The rating of superimposed rock paintings. *Almogaren* 5: 205–18.

Parkington, J. 1969. Symbolism in Palaeolithic cave art. *South African Archaeological Bulletin* 24: 3–13.

———. 1989. Interpreting paintings without a commentary. *Antiquity* 63: 13–26.

Parkington, J., R. Yates, A. Manhire, and D. Halkett. 1986. The social impact of pastoralism in the southwestern Cape. *Journal of Anthropological Archaeology* 5: 313–29.

Pfeifer, L. 1970. A subjective report of tactile hallucinations in schizophrenia. *Journal of Clinical Psychology* 26: 57–60.

Pfeiffer, J. E. 1982. *The creative explosion: An enquiry into the origins of art and religion*. New York: Harper & Row.

Potgieter, E. F. 1955. *The disappearing Bushmen of Lake Chrissie*. Pretoria: Van Schaik.

Prins, F. E. 1990. Southern Bushman descendents in the Transkei—rock art and rain making. *South African Journal of Ethnology* 13: 110–16.

———. 1994. Living in two worlds: The manipulation of power relations, identity and ideology by the last San rock artist of the Transkei, South Africa. *Natal Museum Journal of Humanities* 6: 179–93.

Prins, F. E., and H. Lewis. 1992. Bushmen as mediators in Nguni cosmology. *Ethnology* 31: 133–47.

Propp, V. 1968. *Morphology of the folktale*. Austin: University of Texas Press.

Radcliffe-Brown, A. R. 1952. *Structure and function in primitive society*. London: Cohen & West.

Rasmussen, K. 1929. Intellectual culture of the Iglulik Eskimos. Report of the fifth Thule Expedition 1921–24, 7 (1). Copenhagen: Glydendalske Boghandel, Nordisk Forlag.

Reichel-Dolmatoff, G. 1969. El contexto cultural de un alucinogeno aborigen, *Banisteriopsis caapi*. *Academia Colombiana de Ciencias Exactas, Físicas y Naturales* 13 (51): 327–45.

———. 1972. The cultural context of an aboriginal hallucinogen: *Banisteriopsis caapi*. In *Flesh of the gods: The ritual use of hallucinogens*, ed. P. T. Furst, 84–113. New York: Praeger.

———. 1978a. *Beyond the Milky Way: Hallucinatory imagery of the Tukano Indians.* Los Angeles: UCLA Latin America Center.

———. 1978b. Drug-induced optical sensations and their relationship to applied art among some Colombian Indians. In *Art in Society*, ed. M. Greenhalgh and V. Megaw, 289–304. London: Duckworth.

Reinach, S. 1903. L'art et la magie: À propos des peintures et des gravures de l'Age du Renne. *L'Anthropologie* 14: 257–66.

Renfrew, C. 1982. *Towards an archaeology of mind.* Cambridge: Cambridge University Press.

———. 1993. Cognitive archaeology: Some thoughts on the archaeology of thought. *Cambridge Archaeological Journal* 3 (2): 248–50.

Report 1883. *Report and Proceedings of the Government Commission on Native laws and customs. G.4—1883.* Cape Town: Government Printer.

Richards, W. 1971. The fortification illusions of migraines. *Scientific American* 224: 89–94.

Riches, D. 1994. Shamanism: The key to religion. *Man*, n.s., 29: 381–405.

Riddington, R. 1988. Knowledge, power and the individual in subarctic hunting species. *American Anthropologist* 90: 98–110.

Ritter, D. 1970. Sympathetic magic of the hunt as suggested by petroglyphs of the western United States. In *Actes du Symposium International d'Art Préhistorique*, ed. E. Anati, 397–421. Valcamonica: Centro Camuno di Studi Preistorici.

Ritter, D. W., and E. W. Ritter. 1972a. Medicine men and spirit animals in rock art of western North America. In *Acts of the International Symposium on Rock Art at Hanko*, 97–125.

———. 1972b. Prehistoric pictography in North America of medical significance. In *Medical anthropology*, ed. P. X. Grollig, S. J. Haley, and H. B. Haley, 137–238. The Hague: Mouton.

Rosenfeld, A. 1971. Review of: Notations dans les gravures du Paléolithique superieur, by A. Marshack. *Antiquity* 45: 317–19.

Rosenthal, E., and A. J. H. Goodwin. 1953. *Cave artists of South Africa.* Cape Town: Balkema.

Rudner, J. 1971. Painted burial stones from the Cape. In *Rock paintings of southern Africa*, ed. M. Schoonraad. *South African Journal of Science* Special Issue 2: 54–61.

Rudner, J., and I. Rudner. 1970. *The hunter and his Art.* Cape Town: Struik.

Ruspoli, M. 1987. *The cave of Lascaux: The final photographic record.* London: Thames & Hudson.

Sacks, O. W. 1970. *Migraine: The evolution of a common disorder.* London: Faber.

Sales, K. 1992. Ascent to the Sky: A shamanic initiatory engraving from the Burrup Peninsula, northwest Australia. *Archaeology of Oceania* 27: 22–35.

Salmon, M. H. 1982. *Philosophy and archaeology.* New York: Academic Press.

Sarbin, T. R. 1967. The concepts of hallucination. *Journal of Personality* 35: 359–80.

Sassen, K. 1991. Rainbows in the Indian rock art of desert western America. *Applied Optics* 30: 3523–27.

Sauvet, G. 1982. Comment on: The economic and social context of southern San rock art, by J. D. Lewis-Williams. *Current Anthropology* 23: 443–44.

Sauvet, G., and S. Sauvet. 1979. Fonction sémiologique de l'art parietal animalier franco-cantabrique. *Bulletin de la Société Préhsitorique Française* 76: 340–54.

Sauvet, G., S. Sauvet, and A. Wlodarcyyk. 1977. Essai de sémiologie préhistorique. *Bulletin de la Société Préhsitorique Française* 74: 545–58.

Scarre, C. 1989. Painting by resonance. *Nature* 338: 382.

Schaafsma, P. 1980. *Indian rock art of the Southwest.* Albuquerque: University of New Mexico Press.

Schäfer, H. 1974. *Principles of Egyptian art.* Oxford: Clarendon Press.

Schapera, I. 1930. *The Khoisan peoples of southern Africa.* London: Routledge.

Schmidt, S. 1973. Die Mantis religiosa in den Glaubensrorstellungen der Khoesan-Volker. *Zeitschrift für Ethnologie* 98: 102–27.

―――. 1979. The rain bull of the South African Bushmen. *African Studies* 38: 201–24.

―――. 1989. *Katalog der Khoisan-Volkserzählungen des südlichen Afrikas.* Hamburg: Helmut Buske Verlag.

―――. 1996. The relevance of the Bleek/Lloyd folktales to the general Khoisan traditions. In *Voices from the past: /Xam Bushmen and the Bleek and Lloyd collection,* ed. J. Deacon and T. A. Dowson, 100–121. Johannesburg: Witwatersrand University Press.

Schultes, R. E. 1976. *Hallucinogenic plants.* New York: Golden Press.

Schweiger, D. M. A. 1912. Bushman caves at Keilands. *Catholic Magazine of South Africa* 23 (253): 103–9; (254): 152–59; (255): 204–8; (256): 251–55; (257): 302–4.

Shanks, M., and C. Tilley. 1987a. *Reconstructing archaeology: Theory and practice.* Cambridge: Cambridge University Press.

―――. 1987b. *Social theory and archaeology.* Cambridge: Polity Press.

Sherratt, A. 1991. Sacred and profane substances: The ritual of narcotics in later Neolithic Europe. In *Sacred and profane,* ed. P. Garwood et al., 50–64. Oxford: Oxford Committee for Archaeology.

Shortridge, G. C. 1934. *The mammals of south west Africa.* London: Heinemann.

Siegel, R. K. 1977. Hallucinations. *Scientific American* 237: 132–40.

―――. 1978. Cocaine hallucinations. *American Journal of Psychiatry* 135: 309–14.

―――. 1984. Hostage hallucinations: Visual imagery induced by isolation and life-threatening stress. *Journal of Nervous and Mental Disease* 172: 264–72.

―――. 1985. LSD hallucinations: From ergot to Electric Kool-Aid. *Journal of Psychoactive Drugs* 17: 247–56.

―――. 1992. *Fire in the brain: Clinical tales of hallucinations.* New York: Dutton.

Siegel, R. K., and M. E. Jarvik. 1975. Drug-induced hallucinations in animals and man. In *Hallucinations: Behaviour, experience, and theory,* ed. R. K. Siegel and L. J. West, 81–161. New York: John Wiley.

Siegel, R. K., and L. J. West, eds. 1975. *Hallucinations: Behaviour, experience, and theory.* New York: John Wiley.

Sieveking, A. 1979. *The cave artists.* London: Thames & Hudson.

Siikala, A. 1985. Comment on: Mental imagery cultivation as a cultural phenomenon: The role of visions in shamanism, by R. Noll. *Current Anthropology* 26: 455–56.

Silberbauer, G. B. 1963. *Bushman survey report.* Gaborones: Bechuanaland Government.

Smith, N. W. 1992. *An analysis of Ice Age art: Its psychology and belief system.* New York: Peter Lang.

Smithers, R. H. N. 1986. *Land mammals of southern Africa: A field guide.* Johannesburg: Macmillan.

Smits, L. G. A. 1971. The rock paintings of Lesotho, their content and characteristics. *South African Journal of Science Special Publication* 2: 14–19.

————. 1973. Rock-painting sites in the upper Senqu Valley, Lesotho. *South African Archaeological Bulletin* 28: 32–8.

Snow, D. R. 1977. Rock art and the power of shamans. *Natural History* 86 (2): 42–49.

Solomon, A. C. 1992. Gender, representation, and power in San ethnography and rock art. *Journal of Anthropological Archaeology* 11: 291–329.

————. 1994. "Mythic women": A study in variability in San rock art and narrative. In *Contested images: Diversity in southern African rock art research,* ed. T. A. Dowson and J. D. Lewis-Williams, 331–71. Johannesburg: Witwatersrand University Press.

Spaarman, A. 1789. *A voyage to the Cape of Good Hope.* London: Lackington.

Stanford, W. E. 1910. Statement of Silayi with reference to his life among Bushmen. *Transactions of the Royal Society of South Africa* 1: 435–40.

Stevens, A. 1975. Animals in Palaeolithic cave art: Leroi-Gourhan's hypothesis. *Antiquity* 49: 54–57.

Stevenson, J. 1995. Man-the-shaman: Is it the whole story? A feminist perspective on the San rock art of southern Africa. Master's thesis, University of the Witwatersrand.

Steyn, H. P. 1971. Aspects of the economic life of some nomadic Nharo Bushman groups. *Annals of the South African Museum* 56 (6) 275–322.

Stow, G. W. 1905. *The native races of South Africa.* London: Swan Sonnenschein.

————. 1930. *Rock-paintings in South Africa.* London: Methuen.

Summers, R., ed. 1959. *Prehistoric rock art of the Federation of Rhodesia and Nyasaland.* Salisbury: Rhodesia and Nyasaland National Publications Trust.

Thackeray, A. I., J. F. Thackeray, P. B. Beaumont, and J. C. Vogel. 1981. Dated rock engravings from Wonderwerk Cave, South Africa. *Science* 214: 64–67.

Thomas, E. M. 1969. *The harmless people.* Harmondsworth: Penguin. Reprint 1988, Cape Town: David Philip.

Thomas, J. 1991. *Rethinking the Neolithic.* Cambridge: Cambridge University Press.

Thomas, N., and C. Humphrey, eds. 1996. *Shamanism, history, and the state.* Ann Arbor: University of Michigan Press.

Tilley, C. 1991. *Material culture and text: The art of ambiguity.* London: Routledge.

Tobias, P. V., ed. 1978. *The Bushmen.* Cape Town: Human & Rousseau.

Trail, A. 1978. The languages of the Bushmen. In *The Bushmen,* ed. P. V. Tobias. Cape Town: Human & Rousseau.

Trezise, P. J. 1971. *Rock art of south-east Cape York.* Canberra: Australian Institute of Aboriginal Studies.

Troiakov, P. A. 1975. Economic and Magical functions of tale-telling among the Khakasy. *Soviet Anthropological Archaeology* 14: 146–47.

Turner, V. W. 1967. *The forest of symbols: Aspects of Ndebu ritual.* Ithaca, N.Y.: Cornell University Press.

Tuzin, D. 1984. Miraculous voices: The auditory experience of numinous objects. *Current Anthropology* 25: 579–96.

Tyler, C. W. 1978. Some new entoptic phenomena. *Vision Research* 18: 1633–39.

Ucko, P. J. 1992. Subjectivity and recording of Palaeolithic cave art. In *The limitations of archaeological knowledge*, ed. T. Shay and J. Clottes, 141–80. Liäge, Belgium: Etudes et Recherches Archéologiques de l'Univesité de Liäge.

Ucko, P. J., and A. Rosenfeld. 1967. *Palaeolithic cave art.* London: Weidenfeld & Nicolson and World University Library.

Vandiver, P. 1983. *Paleolithic pigments and processing.* Master's thesis, Massachusetts Institute of Technology, Cambridge.

Van Reenen, R. J. 1920. *Iets oor die Boesmankultuur.* Bloemfontein: De Nationale Pers.

Van Riet Lowe, C. 1941. *Prehistoric art in South Africa.* (Archaeological Series V.) Pretoria: Bureau of Archaeology.

———. 1952. *The distribution of prehistoric rock engravings and paintings in South Africa.* (Archaeological Series 7.) Pretoria: Archaeological Survey.

Vastokas, J. M., and R. K. Vastokas. 1973. *Sacred art of the Algonkians: A study of the Peterborough petroglyphs.* Peterborough: Mansard.

Vialou, D. 1982. Niaux, une construction symbolique magdalénienne exemplaire. *Ars Praehistorica* I: 19–45.

———. 1986. L'art des grottes en Ariege Magdalénienne. XXIIe Supplement a *Gallia Préhistoire.*

Vinnicombe, P. 1967a. The recording of rock paintings: An interim report. *South Africa Journal of Science* 63: 282–84.

———. 1967b. Rock-painting analysis. *South African Archaeological Bulletin* 88: 129–41.

———. 1971. Review: C. K. Cooke, "Rock art of southern Africa." *South African Archaeological Bulletin* 26: 92–93.

———. 1972a. Motivation in African rock art. *Antiquity* 46: 124–33.

———. 1972b. Myth, motive and selection in southern African rock art. *Africa* 42: 192–204.

———. 1972c. The ritual significance of eland (*Taurotragus oryx*) in the rock art of southern Africa. *Actes du Ier Symposium International sur Les Religions de La Prehistoire.*

———. 1975. The ritual significance of eland (*Taurotragus oryx*) in the rock art of southern Africa. In *Les religions de la préhistoire*, ed. E. Anati, 379–400. Capo di Ponte: Centro Communo di Studi Preistorica.

———. 1976. *People of the eland: Rock paintings of the Drakensberg Bushmen as a reflection of their life and thought.* Pietermaritzburg: Natal University Press.

Vitebsky, P. 1995. *The shaman.* London: Macmillan.

Voegelin, E. W. 1938. Tubatulabal ethnography. *Anthropological Records* 2 (1): 1–90.

von Gernet, A. 1993. The construction of prehistoric ideation: Exploring the universality–idiosyncrasy continuum. *Cambridge Archaeological Journal* 3 (1): 67–81.

Wadley, L. 1987. Later Stone Age hunters and gatherers of the southern Transvaal. *British Archaeological Reports International Series 380*, Oxford.

Wadley, L., ed. 1997. *Our gendered past: Archaeological studies of gender in southern Africa.* Johannesburg: Witwatersrand University Press.

Walker, J. 1981. The amateur scientist: About phosphenes. *Scientific American* 244 (5): 142–52.

Waller, S. J. 1993. Sound and rock art. *Nature* 363: 501.

Weil, A. 1986. *The natural mind: An investigation of drugs and the higher consciousness.* Boston: Houghton Mifflin.

Weitzenfeld, J. S. 1984. Valid reasoning by analogy. *Philosophy of science* 51: 137–49.

Wellmann, K. F. 1978. North American Indian rock art and hallucinogenic drugs. *Journal of the American Medical Association* 239: 1524–27.

———. 1979a. North American rock art: Medical connotations. *New York State Journal of Medicine* 79: 1094–1105.

———. 1979b. *A survey of North American Indian rock art.* Graz: Akademische Druck Verlagsanstalt.

Werner, A. 1908. Bushman paintings. *Journal of the Royal African Society* 7: 387–93.

Westphal, E. O. J. 1971. The click languages of South and east Africa. In *Linguisitics in subsaharan Africa*, ed. J. Berry and J. H. Greenberg, vol. 7 of *Current trends in linguisitics*, ed. T. Sebeok. The Hague: Mouton.

White, R. 1985. Thoughts on social relationships and language in hominid evolution. *Journal of Social and Personal Relationships* 2: 95–115.

Whitley, D. S. 1982. Notes on the Coso petroglyphs, the etiological mythology of the Western Shoshone, and the interpretation of rock art. *Journal of California and Great Basin Anthropology* 4: 262–72.

———. 1987. Socio-religious context and rock art in east-central California. *Journal of Anthropological Archaeology* 6: 159–88.

———. 1988. Comment on J. D. Lewis-Williams and T. A. Dowson "The signs of all times: Entoptic phenomena in Upper Palaeolithic art." *Current Anthropology* 29: 238.

———. 1992. Shamanism and rock art in far western North America. *Cambridge Archaeological Journal* 2 (1): 89–113.

———. 1994a. By the hunter, for the gatherer: Art, subsistence and social relations in the prehistoric Great Basin. *World Archaeology* 25: 356–73.

———. 1994b. Shamanism, natural modeling and the rock art of far western North American hunter-gatherers. In *Shamanism and rock art in North America*, ed. S. A. Turpin, 1–43. San Antonio, Tex.: Rock Art Foundation.

———, ed. 1998. *Reader in archaeological theory.* London: Routledge.

———. *The art of the shaman: Rock art of California.* Salt Lake City: University of Utah Press.

———, ed. *Handbook of rock art research.* New York: AltaMira Press.

———. n.d.a. Context, symbol, and meaning in North American archaeology: A study of southern Sierra Nevada rock art. Ms.

———. n.d.b. Ethnography of communication and rock art study in the active voice. Paper presented at the annual meetings of the Society for American Archaeology, Toronto, Canada.

———. n.d.c. Function and meaning in southern Sierra Nevada rock art. Ms.

Willcox, A. R. 1956. *Rock paintings of the Drakensberg.* London: Parrish.

———. 1960. *Rock Paintings of the Drakensberg.* 2d ed. London: Parrish.

———. 1963. *The rock art of South Africa.* London: Nelson.

———. 1978a. An analysis of the function of rock art. *South African Journal of Science.* 74: 59–64.

———. 1978b. So-called "infibulation" in African rock art: A group research project. *African Studies* 37: 203–26.

————. 1984. Meanings and motives in San rock art: The views of W. D. Hammond-Tooke and J. D. Lewis-Williams considered. *South African Archaeological Bulletin* 39: 53–57.

————. 1987. The cultural context of hunter-gatherer rock art. *Man* 22: 171–72.

Wilman, M. 1968. *The rock engravings of Griqualand West and Bechuanaland, South Africa.* Cape Town: Balkema.

Wilmsen, E. N. 1989. *Land filled with flies.* Chicago: Chicago University Press.

Winkelman, M. 1986. Trance states: A theoretical model and cross-cultural analysis. *Ethos* 14: 174–203.

Winkelman, M., and M. Dobkin de Rios. 1989. Psychoactive properties of !Kung Bushman medicine plants. *Journal of Psychoactive Drugs* 21 (1): 51–59.

Winters, W. D. 1975. The continuum of CNS excitatory states and hallucinosis. In *Hallucinations: Behaviour, experience, and theory,* ed. R. K. Siegel and L. J. West, 53–70. New York: John Wiley.

Woodhouse, H. C. 1968. The Medikane rock-paintings: Sorcerers or hunters? *South African Archaeological Bulletin* 23: 37–39.

————. 1971. A remarkable kneeling posture of many figures in the rock art of South Africa. *South African Archaeological Bulletin* 26: 128–31.

————. 1974. Creatures with both human and animal physical features depicted in the rock paintings of southern Africa. *South African Journal of Science* 70: 13–17.

————. 1979. Rock paintings of horses in the north-eastern Orange Free State. *African Studies* 38: 43–46.

————. 1984. On the social context of southern African rock art. *Current Anthropology* 25: 244–46.

————. 1987. Bees and honey in the prehistoric rock art of southern Africa. *South African Bee Journal* 59 (2): 36–41.

Wright, J. B. 1971. *Bushman raiders of the Drakensberg 1840–1870.* Pietermaritzburg: Natal University Press.

Wylie, A. 1982. An analogy by any other name is just as analogical: A commentary on the Gould-Watson dialogue. *Journal of Anthropological Archaeology* 1: 382–401.

————. 1985. The reaction against analogy. *Advances in Archaeological Method and Theory* 8: 63–111.

————. 1988. "Simple" analogy and the role of relevance assumptions: Implications of archaeological practice. *International Studies in the Philosophy of Science* 2: 134–50.

————. 1989. Archaeological cables and tacking: The implications of practice for Bernstein's "Options beyond objectivism and relativism." *Philosophy of the Social Sciences* 19: 1–18.

Yates, R., and A. Manhire. 1991. Shamanism and rock paintings: Aspects of the use of rock art in the southwest Cape, South Africa. *South African Archaeological Bulletin* 46: 3–11.

Yates, R., J. Golson, and M. Hall. 1985. Trance performance: The rock art of Boontjieskloof and Sevilla. *South African Archaeological Bulletin* 40: 70–80.

Yates, R., A. Manhire, and J. Parkington. 1994. Rock painting and history in the south-western Cape. In *Contested images: Diversity in southern African rock art research,* ed. T. A. Dowson and J. D. Lewis-Williams, 29–60. Johannesburg: Witwatersrand University Press.

Yates, R., J. Parkington, and T. Manhire. 1990. *Pictures from the past: A history of the interpretation of rock paintings and engravings of southern Africa.* Pietermaritzburg: Centaur Publications.

Young, R. S. I., R. E. Cole, M. Gamble, and M. D. Rayner. 1975. Subjective patterns elicited by light flicker. *Vision Research* 15: 1289–90.

Index

Numbers in italics refer to figures.

About the Author

J. David Lewis-Williams is director of the Rock Art Research Institute at the University of Witwatersrand, Johannesburg, South Africa. He has worked and published widely on southern African San (Bushman) and western European Upper Paleolithic rock art. He is an elected fellow of the Royal Society of South Africa and former president of the South African Archaeological Society. In 1995, he received his university's Distinguished Researcher Award. He is currently a member of the International Advisory Committee on the Chauvet Cave, France. In 2000, the president of South Africa invited him to translate the nation's new motto into the now-extinct /Xam San language.